3rd Edition

COMMUNI-CATION

Larry L. Barker

Auburn University

Prentice Hall, Inc., Englewood Cliffs, N.J. 07632

Library of Congress Cataloging in Publication Data

Barker, Larry Lee, 1941–
  Communication.

  Includes index.
  1. Communication.   I. Title
P90.B296   1984   001.51   83-16120
ISBN 0-13-153718-0

Editorial/production supervision: Barbara Kelly Kittle
Interior design: Jayne Conte
Cover design: Jayne Conte
Cover photo: Peter Beck, FPG
Manufacturing buyer: Ron Chapman

Chapter opening photo credits:

CHAPTER 1: Ken Karp	CHAPTER 8: Mark Mangold, U.S. Census Bureau
CHAPTER 2: Carmine L. Galasso	CHAPTER 9: AFL-CIO News
CHAPTER 3: Teri Leigh Stratford	CHAPTER 10: UN Photo, Y. Nagata
CHAPTER 4: Ken Karp	CHAPTER 11: F. Armstrong, The University of Texas
CHAPTER 5: Ken Karp	at Austin News & Information Service
CHAPTER 6: Ken Karp	CHAPTER 12: UPI
CHAPTER 7: Ken Karp	CHAPTER 13: Ken Karp

Printed in the United States of America

10 9 8 7 6 5 4 3 2 1

ISBN 0-13-153718-0

Prentice-Hall International, Inc., *London*
Prentice-Hall of Australia Pty. Limited, *Sydney*
Editora Prentice-Hall do Brasil, Ltda., *Rio de Janiero*
Prentice-Hall Canada Inc., *Toronto*
Prentice-Hall of India Private Limited, *New Delhi*
Prentice-Hall of Japan, Inc., *Tokyo*
Prentice-Hall of Southeast Asia Pte. Ltd., *Singapore*
Whitehall Books Limited, *Wellington, New Zealand*

CONTENTS

PREFACE vii

ACKNOWLEDGMENTS ix

part
ONE Communication Elements

1 A LOOK AT HUMAN COMMUNICATION 2

Exploratory Questions 3   Why Study Communication? 4   Selected
Perspectives on Communication 6   Basic Elements of the Communication
Process 9   Levels of Communication 13   Summary 16   Exercises 17

2 LANGUAGE, MEANING, AND COMMUNICATION 20

Exploratory Questions 21   Functions of Language 22
Language Development 23   Meaning 27
Language and Behavior 34   Summary 37   Exercises 38

3 LISTENING AND FEEDBACK 42

Exploratory Questions 43   The Listening Process 44
Types of Listening 48   Barriers and Aids to Effective Listening 49
Feedback 55   Giving Effective Feedback 59
Summary 60   Exercises 61

4 NONVERBAL COMMUNICATION 64

Exploratory Questions 65   Functions of Nonverbal
Communication 66   Types of Nonverbal
Communication 70   Awareness of Nonverbal
Communication 92   Summary 94   Exercises 95

5 INTRAPERSONAL COMMUNICATION 102

Exploratory Questions 103   The Self 104   Self-Concept 108
The Human Hierarchy of Needs 112   The Process of Intrapersonal
Communication 113   The Effects of Intrapersonal Variables on
Communication 119   Summary 125   Exercises 125

part

TWO Interpersonal, Small Group, and Organizational Communication

6 INTERPERSONAL COMMUNICATION 128

Exploratory Questions 129   The Interpersonal Communication
Model 130   Dyadic versus Small Group
Communication 130   Interpersonal Communication
Effectiveness 132   Context and Timing 136   Clarity 136
Open Listening 136   Feedback and Feedforward 136
Nonverbal Behavior 138   Interpersonal Attraction 139
Development of Dyadic Relationships 141   Analyzing Interpersonal
Communication 145   Interpersonal Communication Situations 152
Summary 159   Exercises 160

7 SMALL GROUP COMMUNICATION 164

Exploratory Questions 165   Definitions 167   Some Small Groups and
their Functions 168   Participaing in Small Groups 170   Role Structure
and Status 173   The Development of a Small Group 176   Leaders and
Leadership 177   Problem-Solving Process 186   Other Factors Affecting
Group Performance 189   Analyzing Small Group Interaction 194
Summary 197   Exercises 198

8 ORGANIZATIONAL COMMUNICATION 206

Exploratory Questions 207   What is an Organization? 208
Characteristics of Organizations 209   Types of Organizations 211
Communication Dimensions in Organizations 212
Networks 216   Communication Structures 220
Communication in Organizations 221   Communication Situations 224
Preparing for a Job Search 229   The Interview 241
After the Interview 244   Summary 245   Exercises 246

part

THREE Public Communication

9 ETHICS, INTENTIONS, AND THE SPEAKER-AUDIENCE RELATIONSHIP 250

Exploratory Questions 251   Ethical Responsibility and the Public
Speaker 253   Purposes of Communicating in the Public
Setting 258   The Speaker and the Audience: Audience Analysis 259
Methods of Investigating Your Audience 268
Other Audience Considerations 270   Summary 278   Exercises 280

10 COMMUNICATION GOALS: INFORMATION EXCHANGE, PERSUASION, ENTERTAINMENT 284

Exploratory Questions 285   Information Exchange 286
Entertainment, Ceremonial, and other Special Occasion
Communication 311   Summary 314   Exercises 315

11 DEVELOPING AND ORGANIZING THE MESSAGE 320

Exploratory Questions 321   Narrowing the Topic 322
Selecting the Topic 323   Gathering Source Materials 324   Parts of the
Speech 326   Arrangement of the Body of the Speech 334   Principles of
Outlining 339   Supporting Material 342   Summary 346   Exercises 347

12 SPEECH DELIVERY 350

Exploratory Questions 351   Communication Apprehension 353
Principles 355   Physical Delivery 359   Vocal Delivery 365
Style 371   Summary 374   Exercises 375

13 COMMUNICATION THROUGH THE MASS MEDIA 378

Exploratory Questions 379   Characteristics of Mass
Communication 381   Mass Communication Media 385   Functions of
Mass Communication 387   Advertising 392   Public Relations 393
Effects of Mass Media 393   Appearing on Radio and Television 399
The Future of Mass Communication 403
Summary 405   Exercises 406

APPENDIX A: Sample Speech: Children's Television Viewing, The Parent's Role 410

APPENDIX B: Sample Outlines 416

GLOSSARY 420

INDEX 430

PREFACE

Personal relationships often fall into habitual patterns that we call "ruts." In many dating or family relationships, one partner often complains that the other is "taking me for granted." Similarly, two nations who share a common border may "take for granted" that citizens of each country will be able to cross the other's border—that is, until some crisis occurs. Taking for granted one's parents, friends, husband, wife, or children happens to most of us at one time or another. Taking things for granted tends to increase in direct proportion to the number of activities and relationships we share.

This text focuses on one aspect of our daily lives that we often take for granted—communication. We often forget that we must work to make communication pleasant and effective. When we ignore important aspects of communication, breakdowns ranging from hurt feelings to wars between nations may occur. Now, before it appears that we are claiming that this text provides the ultimate solution to mend friendships and prevent wars between nations—let us make it clear it does not. However, this book does attempt to increase awareness of communication elements and variables that can improve the quality of our daily lives. The text focuses on the total range of communication behaviors we engage in daily, in formal and informal settings and in our private as well as professional lives.

Communication, third edition, is designed specifically for students in introductory speech and communication courses. It covers a broad range of topics over the entire spectrum of communication behaviors and activities. It also includes some unique emphases that should be noted.

The earlier editions of *Communication* contained several features that appealed to a substantial number of its users. These included (1) a complete "minitext" in public speaking within the larger comprehensive text; (2) an extensive chapter on intrapersonal communication; (3) a major emphasis on nonverbal communication throughout the text accompanied by a fully developed chapter on nonverbal behaviors; (4) emphasis on receiver-oriented communication in the chapter on Listening; and (5) an integrated set of chapters on interpersonal communication. These features have been retained in the third edition and several new ones have been added. These new features include:

1. An extensive revision of Chapter 2, dealing with language development and language use. The expanded chapter integrates new theory and research into the discussion of language development, use, and style.

2. A reorganization of chapters throughout the text, reflecting user comments and suggestions from teachers who taught from past editions. The major reorganization is in the section on Public Communication. Hopefully, the new structure for this section will make the text more teachable and relevant for students.

3. Expanded chapters in this edition on Listening and Feedback (3), Nonverbal Communication (4), Small Group Communication (7), Ethics, Intentions, and the Speaker-Audience Relationship (9), Developing and Organizing the Message (10), and Communication Through the Mass Media (13).

4. An expanded "glossary of terms," coded to bold faced type within each chapter in the text. This glossary was revised to increase student efficiency in using the text. Many terms have been added to the glossary in this edition that were not included in previous versions.

5. A completely revised instructors manual. The new manual contains numerous instructional aids as well as class-tested and item-analyzed examination items to help instructors in preparing tests and quizzes over text material.

In addition to the new materials noted above, the text also features (1) numerous visual examples and illustrations, including photographs, cartoons, and drawings; (2) a new text design for reading ease and increased student interest; (3) exploratory questions at the beginning of chapters to help students identify the most important concepts covered; and (4) complete summaries, activities, and exercises at the end of each chapter.

ACKNOWLEDG-MENTS

I would like to take this opportunity to thank the many people who contributed to the formation and production of this text. Within the Prentice-Hall organization, I would like to extend thanks to those who helped in the development and creation of the book in this and previous editions: Jack Kelly, Susanna Lesan, Ruth Kugleman, Florence Silverman, Toni Goldfarb, Margo Jossem, Sharon Cohen, Marietta Benevento, Cecil Yarborough, Brian Walker, John Busch, Steve Dalphin, Barbara Kittle, Jayne Conte, and Ed Stanford.

The second edition of *Communication* included numerous contributions and editorial aids provided by Kittie Watson. Kittie not only screened and carefully worked with the entire manuscript in the second edition, but wrote original drafts for that edition's chapters titled "A Look at Human Communication," and "Organizational Communication." Her time, energy, and devotion to the project were greatly appreciated.

Deborah Roach served as editorial assistant and contributor to the present edition. She meticulously combed the manuscript to update research, provide relevant examples, and make the text more readable and accurate. Her efforts were outstanding and my special thanks go out to her.

In addition, several of my friends and students (not mutually exclusive categories) helped with the research and development of individual chapters in previous editions. Special thanks to Reneé Edwards, Loretta Malandro, Janice Lumpkin, Frances Sayers, Ginger Tubbs, Debbie Smith, Cheryl Fisher, Karen Harris, and Sondi Feldmaier. Bob Kibler, Wini Vallely, John Stone, and John Garrison also provided encouragement for the project, as did several of my other colleagues (some of them known to me who served as reviewers). Karl Krayer, Kathy Wahlers, and Charles Roberts, who used previous editions of the text, were especially helpful in providing feedback from their classes.

Special thanks goes to Frank E. X. Dance for this special contributions to this text, particularly in the first edition. Frank was inadvertently omitted from the acknowledgments in the first edition, and to add insult to injury, his name was misspelled in the second! Thanks also to my students during the past year who were patient with me while I worked on this revision, and to students over the past eighteen years who helped provide examples and insights.

I personally hope that this third edition of *Communication* will serve your needs. I welcome letters, cards, or calls concerning specific items in the text that you like or dislike as well as suggestions for change in the future.

L.L.B.

Professor
Department of Speech Communication
Auburn University, Al., 36849

Ph (205) - 826-4682

COMMUNICATION

A LOOK AT HUMAN COMMUNICATION

1

Exploratory Questions

1. Why should we consider communication to be a process?
2. What are the differences between verbal and nonverbal, oral and written, formal and informal, intentional and unintentional, and machine and animal communication?
3. What are the seven elements in the communication process and how do they relate?
4. What does it mean when we say that feedback is positive? negative? ambiguous?
5. What are the six levels of human communication and how might we best explain them?

WHY STUDY COMMUNICATION?

Approximately 70 percent of our waking day is spent in one or more types of communication. Talking to others, reading books and newspapers, listening to lectures, watching television—these activities link us to our environment, permit the development of higher mental processes, and help to regulate all human behavior. It may seem obvious to say that communication is important, but, in fact, communication experiences shape the very quality of our lives.

The fact that you are reading this book and are probably enrolled in a speech communication course right now suggests that you are aware, at least to some extent, of your communication behavior. This is an important first step. In this book we've attempted to bring together selected materials on the present state of human communication theory and research, along with basic principles of effective communication useful in a variety of social settings and interactions. The key word that guided us in the writing of this book is *you.* Yes, you, the person reading these words. We have emphasized the aspects of communication that affect you each day. By increasing your knowledge and understanding of these principles of communication, we hope to accomplish our chief aim: to help you become a more effective communicator.

So, before you close this book and go back into the fast-paced, ever-changing world of CB radios, telecommunication satellites, and talking computers, take some time to acquaint yourself with communication and how well you communicate.

Communication Checklist Take a moment to determine how you feel about your own communication. Use the following questions to help provide information about your satisfaction with your communication behavior.

1. In what types of communication settings are you most comfortable (for example, with a date or in the family)?
2. In what communication settings are you usually uncomfortable (for example, before a class or in a church group)?
3. In communication situations where you feel uncomfortable, how do you usually deal with them (for example, cut the communication short or become aggressive)?
4. What areas of your speaking ability do you feel need improvement (for example, use of vocal expression or use of gestures)?
5. With what areas of your speaking ability are you satisfied (for example, eye contact or organizational skills)?

If you are honest with yourself in answering these questions, you can begin to more fully determine how well you communicate. The establishment of specific goals with regard to the communication skills you want to improve is also a good idea at this point. Goals such as "I want to be able to express my feelings to my parents more completely" or "I want to be able to better organize a speech" are examples of specific goals you might identify. The awareness of your own unique communication skills and problems, coupled with your desired goals for improvement, should make your course in speech or communication more effective and enjoyable.

Defining Communication

If you were asked to define communication for E.T. (the Extraterrestrial), where would you begin? You might mention a speaker, a listener, sharing of information, transmission of symbols, or a variety of other descriptive terms. As you try to define communication, you may find problems in choosing the right words to express your ideas. You may also find it difficult to answer E.T.'s questions. You might have a difficult time because defining communication is similar to trying to define love. Intuitively, you feel you understand it, but it's difficult to put into words.

Communication theorists have never completely agreed on a single definition of communication.[1] It all depends on one's perspective. For our purposes we will define **communication** as a process of interrelated elements working together to achieve a desired outcome or goal. Since communication is a process, it is dynamic, ever-changing, and unending. The talk you had with a friend yesterday affects you as a communicator today. The hundreds of bits of information, ideas, and opinions you process, evaluate, and store each day also change you to some extent. By tomorrow you will have changed even more. Fortunately, this process is usually slow and subtle. Otherwise, you might be in a constant state of confusion and frustration.

Experiences do not occur in isolation from one another. One experi-

[1]B. Aubrey Fisher, *Perspectives on Human Communication Research* (New York: Macmillan, 1978), pp. 7–11.

ence affects another, and not always in a simple, direct manner. For example, your girlfriend tells you without warning that she is dating someone else. This may result in your lashing out at your roommate later that day when he gently reminds you that it's your turn to clean the apartment. The next morning both you and your roommate may perform poorly on the big chemistry test because of your preoccupation with the previous day's communication experiences—and the process continues.

SELECTED PERSPECTIVES ON COMMUNICATION

As you can see, communication is more than one person speaking and another person listening. This section will explain some of the complexities of communication by looking at the dimensions of verbal and nonverbal, oral and written, formal and informal, intentional and unintentional, and man-machine and animal communication.[2] (Later we will examine the communication process and levels of communication.)

Verbal and Nonverbal Communication
Usually, when we think of communication, we think of spoken messages. However, communication includes both verbal and nonverbal symbols. *Verbal communication* refers to symbols which have universal meanings for all involved in the process. These spoken or written verbal symbols are known as *language.* (Chapter 2 covers language in detail.) Symbols other than written or spoken words are known as *nonverbal symbols.* These include gestures, body actions, tone of voice, use of space, and touch. (Chapter 4 is devoted to nonverbal communication.)

Nonverbal messages usually complement verbal messages. A service station attendant usually points and uses other gestures while giving directions to a stranger from out of town. At other times nonverbal symbols replace verbal messages completely. Teachers with cold, fixed stares can easily tell students to be quiet without uttering a word. It is important to note that when nonverbal messages contradict what you say verbally, others usually believe the nonverbal message. For example, when a husband tells his wife verbally that he is interested in hearing about what happened at a political rally as he continues to read the newspaper, he communicates disinterest nonverbally.

Oral and Written Communication
You probably already know many of the differences between oral and written communication. *Oral communication* refers to messages that are transmitted "out loud" from one person to another. Most messages are verbal, with complementary nonverbal messages. Each day we participate in oral communication either as speakers or as listeners when we answer the telephone, listen to a lecture, watch television, or turn on a radio.

[2]Larry L. Barker and Robert J. Kibler, eds., *Speech Communication Behavior* (Englewood Cliffs, N.J.: Prentice-Hall, 1971), pp. 3–9.

Written communication is taking place right now as you read this book. **Written communication** is primarily verbal, but nonverbal characteristics can affect written messages. We get a different feeling when we receive a personal handwritten Christmas card than when we receive a mass-produced printed one from an insurance company. Oral and written communications serve different purposes and are used both independently and in combination. Written reports or term papers use a formal style, while oral reports are usually more conversational, with more informal language. Many television commercials use written reinforcement of an oral message when stressing the effectiveness of a new cold capsule, and a typed résumé presents an applicant more professionally than does a handwritten one.

We have all been involved in formal and informal communication situations. In formal communication such as public speaking or mass communication, we pay more attention to both verbal and nonverbal messages. Language use is more precise, with careful attention paid to grammar. People are more concerned with items such as dress, posture, or eye contact. Formal communication is also used with persons of higher perceived status. For example, during an appointment with a university dean, a student would probably avoid the use of slang, sit up straight, dress neatly, and make eye contact. **Formal and Informal Communication**

In informal communication such as interpersonal and small group communication, people are more at ease and can be themselves. Observers would notice more hesitations and slang in verbal messages and less attention to nonverbal messages such as clothing, posture, and eye contact. When going to a party at a friend's house, you probably wouldn't hesitate to sit on the floor, go to the refrigerator for something to eat, or use the telephone. At a party at your boss's house, however, you probably would be hesitant to sit on the floor, go to the kitchen, or use the phone without asking permission.

Most communication that takes place has a purpose, but sometimes we take part in communication without realizing it. **Intentional communication** occurs when messages are sent with specific goals in mind. Comedians such as Steve Martin tell jokes to get laughs and entertain audiences. Radio spots are designed to persuade people to vote for local candidates, buy products, or donate time and money. **Intentional and Unintentional Communication**

Other communication takes place **unintentionally,** without the communicator being aware of it. The greatest number of unintentional messages are nonverbal. Often our nonverbal behaviors speak louder than words. Students or employees who are continually late for class or work might be communicating that they are moonlighting, are irresponsible, or have unreliable alarm clocks.

Sometimes intentional communication is made to appear unintentional. Many lawyers tell their clients how to dress for the courtroom. For example, at her trial Patty Hearst wore conservative old clothing, which included a large, loosely fitted blouse, under the instruction of her attorney, F. Lee Bailey. The old clothing was used to deemphasize the fact that she was wealthy, and the large blouse was used to give the impression of weight loss to arouse sympathy among the jurors.

Man-Machine Communication

There has been an increased use of machine communication in our society. There are person-to-machine, machine-to-person, and machine-to-machine communications. Communication from humans is still necessary to create and maintain these mechanical creations, but who knows what the future may bring? One toy currently on the market helps children learn to spell. The toy says a word and the child is supposed to spell the spoken word. The child (and in some cases an adult) gets two attempts, with the machine giving verbal responses for correct and incorrect spellings.

In addition, there are increasing numbers of people who not only are purchasing electronic video games but who also have at least one (if not more!) home computers for private use. Among the uses of such computers are maintaining the family budget, typing and editing correspondence, and storing and retrieving important personal and professional documents. Although this book focuses primarily on human communication, it is necessary to mention man-machine communication because of its increasing importance in each of our lives.

(AT&T Co. Photo Center)

Many current areas of human communication research were preceded by Animal Communication studies of animal communication. Researchers have found similarities between animals and humans in areas such as territoriality and sex roles. Patterns of interaction have been observed in bee and ant colonies, in porpoise communication, in monkey and ape communication, and among talking birds. Although similarities between animal and human communication form an interesting area of study, caution must be used when associating one with the other. For example, we often associate friendly dogs with open mouths (smile) and consider wagging tails as a friendly gesture; in reality, dogs may wag their tails and show their teeth before attacking or biting another animal or a person.

BASIC ELEMENTS OF THE COMMUNICATION PROCESS

From what we've been saying, you may be getting the impression that communication must be difficult, if not impossible, to study and understand If it is ongoing, how do we stop it? If it has no beginning or end, how does one get hold of it? Although the task is not easy, it is not impossible. The communication process is a system that involves an interrelated, interdependent group of elements working together as a whole to achieve a desired outcome or goal. We can study communication in much the same way we study biological systems within our own bodies. We determine the elements involved (circulatory and digestive systems), analyze how those elements affect one another, and can thus determine the nature of the process as a whole.

Applying this approach to the communication process, we find seven elements: (1) a source/encoder of communication, which sends (2) a message (3) through a channel(s) to (4) a receiver/decoder, who (5) responds via feedback with (6) possibilities of communication breakdowns in each stage of communication. However, none of these elements is meaningful outside of (7) a situation or context in which they may be interpreted. Figure 1–1 gives us a visual representation of the communication process. (Other models are included in Chapters 5 and 6.)

FIGURE 1-1   The Communication Process.

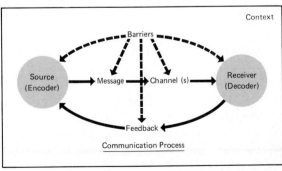

The Source/ Encoder

The *source,* or encoder, makes the decision to communicate. The source also determines what the purpose of the message will be: to inform, persuade, or entertain. You may ask how the message gets from the source to the receiver. First, the source must *encode* or create a message. That is, the information that the source wishes to convey must be put into a form that can be sent to the receiver. The source generates a message through his or her past experiences, perceptions, thoughts, and feelings. Every ounce of your being may tell you that you are in love, but until you code those feelings into a form that can be transmitted to yourself or the person you love, communication cannot take place.

Message

The second element of the communication process is the *message,* or what is being communicated. The source encodes an idea and then determines whether or not he or she wants to inform, persuade, or entertain. After deciding what message will be transmitted, the source uses symbols to get the message across to others. These *symbols* stand for other things. The eagle, the flag, and Uncle Sam are all symbols of the United States, for example. But the most important symbols are words, which can represent objects, ideas, and feelings. These words permit us to share our thoughts with other members of our species. Important as words are to us, they can be tricky. We must remember that words are symbols. They represent things, but are not the things themselves. That lanky, bearded old man we call Uncle Sam represents the United States, but he is *not* the United States—in fact, he doesn't even exist. The letters *a-p-p-l-e p-i-e* represent an all-American pastry, but they are *not* an apple pie.

To increase the likelihood of successful communication, the source must try to encode in a way that the receiver understands, so that the receiver can properly decode (interpret) the message. For example, many American tourists in Paris have discovered that even though their command of French is minimal, it is sometimes easier to communicate in halting French than in English. Some Parisians, despite their fluent knowledge of English, refuse to decode an "inferior" tongue.

Channel

Channels are the means (that is, pathways or devices) by which messages are communicated. Channels may be described and analyzed in two different ways. The first involves the form in which messages are transmitted to receivers. Forms include both verbal and nonverbal channels of communication. We use our five senses to receive messages from others. We may hear a presidential address over a radio, watch an Olympic gymnast perform a routine on television, smell the aroma of Thanksgiving dinner when opening the door to our grandmother's house, taste the flavors in "Baseball Nut" ice cream from Baskin-Robbins, or hug a friend to congratulate her on becoming engaged.

Channels may also be described according to the manner of presentation employed in communication. The source may speak face-to-face with the receiver, use a public address system to talk with a hundred listeners, or talk over radio or television to millions of receivers. Each of these examples would demand different manners of presentation. Depending on the situation, the source would concentrate on verbal and/or nonverbal channels of communication. If the speaker were on radio, physical appearance wouldn't matter, but if performing on television or before a live audience, personal appearance could easily influence the reception of the message. For example, when we go to watch a circus, we expect the clowns to have painted faces and appropriate costumes. If they were dressed in regular street clothes, their performances wouldn't be as effective. Whatever channels of communication are used, the source must learn to adapt the message to make use of the most appropriate channels available for the situation.

The person (or persons) who attends to the source's message is the ***receiver.*** The act of interpreting messages is called **decoding.** Receivers decode messages based on past experiences, perceptions, thoughts, and feelings. We receive messages through all our senses, but most often we decode messages by listening or seeing. We first have a physiological reception of stimuli (a noise hits our eardrum or a movement catches our eye). We then pay attention to both the verbal and nonverbal stimuli (reduce all the stimuli bombarding us to one or two we can cope with more easily). Next, we try to understand the stimuli and interpret them into messages (decide that the noise is a telephone bell or that the movement is a friend waving to us across campus). Finally, we store this information for later use so that next time we will be able to respond to the stimuli more quickly. It is important to remember that receivers make immediate decisions about what they will respond to in a given situation. During a lecture an audience member may decide to take a nap. During an argument with your boyfriend or girlfriend, you may listen only to negative comments. During a crowded party you may watch the nonverbal behaviors (yawns, off in a corner alone, and so on) of your date to decide when it's time to leave. As sources of communication, we need to learn to analyze our prospective receivers to determine which communication messages will be most effective.

Receiver/ Decoder

Of course, all of us are both encoders and decoders; that is, we are capable of both transmitting and receiving messages. When you receive a message, you must interpret it and then encode a response. The response may be silent, noisy, or somewhere in between, depending upon the situation and the existence of any barriers to communication.

Another element in the communication process is **feedback.** Each party in communication continuously sends messages back to the other. This return process is called feedback. Feedback tells the source how the receiver has interpreted each message. For example, if at the airport you ask your departing friend about his itinerary, and he replies that he didn't pack one, you know your message has not been understood. This kind of feed-

Feedback

back, which conveys lack of understanding, is known as **negative feedback. Positive feedback,** on the other hand, indicates that the receiver has understood the source's message. It does not necessarily mean that he or she agrees with the source, just that the message was interpreted accurately. Feedback can also be ambiguous, not clearly positive or negative. "I see" and "mm-hmm" can be examples of **ambiguous feedback.** The good communicator is always sensitive to feedback and constantly modifies his or her messages as a result of the feedback received. After a discreet pause, for example, you might ask your friend not about his "itinerary" but about the cities he plans to visit.

Feedback doesn't have to come from others. We can and do get feedback from our own messages. The fact that we can hear the words we speak and see the sentences we write sometimes lets us correct our own mistakes.

Barriers   The human communication system can be compared with a radio or telephone circuit. Just as in radio transmission, where distortion can occur at any point along the circuit (channel), there can be similar **barriers** in human communication. The source's information may be insufficient or unclear. (A love-struck hero may think he is ill rather than in love.) Or the message can be ineffectively or inaccurately encoded. (Our hero may know he's in love but can't find the proper words to convey his feelings until it's too late. That is, his signals may not be transmitted rapidly or accurately enough.) The wrong channel of communication may be used. (He may sing a love song or send flowers when she doesn't like love songs and is allergic to flowers.) The message may not be decoded the way it was encoded. (The object of our hero's love loves him too—like a brother.) Finally, the receiver may not be equipped to handle the decoded message in such a way as to produce the response (feedback) expected by the source. (Our heroine skips town after receiving our hero's impassioned love letter.) Barriers to communication also occur if the sender and receiver are not on the same "wavelength." This is as true in human communication as it is in radio transmission. On the human level being on the same wavelength involves shared experiences. That is, the source can encode only in terms of the experiences he or she has had. This is why two people from completely different cultures may find it difficult, if not impossible, to communicate. For example, imagine trying to convey the idea of an "I Love Lucy" show to someone who has never even seen a television set. Figure 1–2 shows the necessity for overlapping fields of experience in communication.

Naturally, no two wavelengths can be exactly alike, because each human being's experiences are unique. Communication will be most effective, however, if the circles that represent the fields of experience of the source and the receiver have a large area in common. If there have been no common experiences (that is, if the circles don't meet), communication will be impossible.

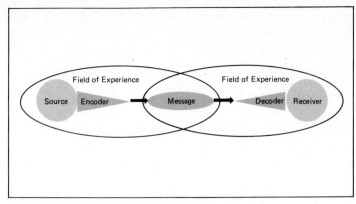

Field of Experience   Field of Experience

Source Encoder → Message → Decoder Receiver

FIGURE 1-2 Interpersonal Communication.[3]

Intricately related to the concept of shared field of experience is the concept of **context,** or situation. This element of communication is, perhaps,
the most important; it affects each of the other elements as well as the
communication process as a whole. Look, for example, at the following
communicative situation: While working in her office one afterno n,
Debbie overhears her office mate Cindy saying to someone in the hall,
"Not only do I not have time to see you now; in a hundred years I
wouldn't find the time." Had Debbie not peered down the hall in amaze-
ment, only to see Cindy smiling and directing this comment to one of the
latter's good friends, she probably would have completely misunderstood
the message she overheard! With the context supplied, an accurate meaning could be assigned to Cindy's comment.

Context or
Situation

LEVELS OF COMMUNICATION

Communicaton is often thought of as an interaction between two people.
However, we participate in several levels of communication each day.
Communication transactions include (1) intrapersonal, (2) interpersonal,
(3) small group, (4) public, (5) organizational, and (6) mass transactions.
Figure 1–3 describes differences between the levels of communication
(Miller, 1978).[4] Generally, distinctions are made between communication
levels by the number of sensory channels available and immediacy of
feedback.

The number of communicators automatically affects the other dimensions of communication transactions. When watching Johnny Carson
on "The Tonight Show," we observe two levels of communication: inter-

---

[3]Model 1–2 is from Wilbur Schramm, "How Communication Works," in *The Process
and Effects of Mass Communication,* ed. Wilbur Schramm and Donald F. Parks (Urbana, Ill: University of Illinois Press, 1971), pp. 4–8.
[4]Adapted from G. R. Miller, "The Current Status of Theory and Research in Interpersonal Communication," *Human Communication Research,* 4, no. 2 (Winter 1978).

CATEGORIES	NUMBER OF COMMUNICATORS	DEGREE OF PHYSICAL PROXIMITY	AVAILABLE SENSORY CHANNELS	IMMEDIACY OF FEEDBACK
Mass communication	Many	Low	Minimal	Most Delayed
Organizational communication				
Public communication				
Small group communication				
Interpersonal communication				
Intrapersonal communication				
	One	High	Maximal	Most Immediate

FIGURE 1-3   Distinguishing Characteristics of the Levels of Human Communication.

personal communication and mass communication. When Johnny interviews one of his guests, he is involved in interpersonal communication. Since they are close to one another, all the sensory channels are available to them. They are face-to-face, free to shake hands and touch each other, able to smell cologne or body odors, and so on. They also get immediate feedback such as laughs, facial expressions, or verbal rebukes.

With mass communication, all the situational categories are altered. Instead of being beside Johnny Carson, you may be in Auburn, Alabama, watching Johnny on television. You become one of millions watching him each evening. Because you are so far from California, where the show originates, there are only two sensory channels available: hearing and sight. Reception from these sensory channels is limited because cameras switch back and forth, commercials interrupt, there may be reception difficulties, or you may be watching black and white instead of color television. Finally, with mass communication, feedback is delayed. Nielson ratings don't come out every month, and you cannot be sure that your personal letter will be read by anyone, much less by Johnny Carson.

As we begin looking at communication, it is important to remember that it is a process. We begin with *intrapersonal communication* and gradually work up the continuum to mass communication. The most basic and important level of communication is intrapersonal communication. This takes place when an individual sends and receives messages internally. Babies first communicate with themselves before they communicate with others by crying to say that they are hungry, wet, or in pain. Later in life we make conscious reminders to pick up the laundry, feed the dog, or water the plants. We also communicate with ourselves at an unconscious level. Usually we don't notice our heart rates, brain activity, or body tension, but they are essential to our survival and tell us about our internal processing (see Chapter 5).

Intrapersonal communication is the foundation on which interpersonal communication is based. Successful communication with others depends first upon effective communication with ourselves. **Interpersonal communication** is usually thought of as occurring between two people. When you call a friend on the phone, go for a job interview, or ask a teacher about your last test grade, you are participating in interpersonal communication. The responsibility for successful interaction is shared between two people. The closeness of the communicators places greater attention on the nonverbal responses from others as we monitor feedback (see Chapter 6).

When you and a friend are talking and another person joins you, the three of you are involved in **small group communication.** Communication is more complicated with a group of three or more persons. Think about how confusing a family dinner can be with everyone talking at once, or about the satisfaction you feel when the combination of individual talents results in an A on a group project. In successful small group communication, each participant has the potential of communicating and adding to the interaction, but this is not true with some levels of communication (see Chapter 7).

With **public communication,** one person addresses a group in a lecture or public speech, and the audience usually does not participate. Try to remember the last time you spoke before a group. It may have been during "show and tell" in the first grade, giving a toast at a friend's wedding rehearsal, or demonstrating the latest food processor to a group of homemakers. With public communication, a speaker is concerned about personal appearance, delivery, the message, and the audience and their response. Speakers learn to adjust their delivery styles to the type of audience they're addressing. A young architect showing some plans to a group of executives is more concerned about clothing, language, and reasoning than he or she would be if demonstrating Amway products to family and friends. The public communicator controls the communication process almost completely (see Chapters 9 to 12).

An area of communication that has recently gained attention is **organizational communication.** School systems, businesses, governmental agencies, and nonprofit groups are all interested in finding ways to analyze and improve managerial styles, work environments, leadership, the flow of information, job satisfaction, and productivity. Organizations usually have a chain of command, with one or several top managers making decisions and controlling communication. More and more organizations are incorporating management training and development programs concerned with communication. Effective communication in organizations ensures efficiency for consumers. For example, the Camaro you order from a local Chevrolet dealer will be made to your specifications, assembled properly, shipped on the appropriate date, and checked for safety and performance before you drive home (see Chapter 8).

The communication level with the most process control is **mass communication.** Types of mass communication include radio, television, newspapers, magazines, CB radios, the recording industry, and so on. Mass communication affects every aspect of our daily lives. We wake up to music on the radio, read a newspaper over coffee, notice signs as we drive to school or work, study from textbooks, listen to traffic reports on our CBs, watch the news and favorite shows on television, and go for futher entertainment to the local movie theater. Mass communication is everywhere, and it is difficult to turn it off even for a few minutes. The characteristics of mass communication include large audiences, message reproduction, rapid distribution and delivery, and low cost to the consumer (see Chapter 13).

Hopefully, after examining the six levels of communication, you will see that communication involves more than just two people interacting with one another. Intrapersonal, interpersonal, small-group, public, organizational, and mass communication each contain a source, messages, channel(s), receiver(s), and feedback. The interaction of these basic elements within the overall context leads to communication.

SUMMARY

Communication is a dynamic, ever-changing, unending process by which people transmit information and feelings to others. Communication plays a major role in all of our lives. Hopefully, by increasing your knowledge and understanding of the principles of communication, you will become a more effective communicator. Seven basic elements of the communication process are (1) source, (2) message, (3) channel, (4) receiver, (5) feedback, (6) barriers, and (7) context, or situation. The source of communication sends a message (made up of signs or symbols) through verbal and nonverbal channels to a receiver. As receivers decode messages, they respond through feedback, which causes them to be the next source of communication. Effective communication can be hindered by barriers interacting with each element in the process.

The process of communication has many dimensions and occurs on many different levels. Four dimensions of human communication are verbal and nonverbal, oral and written, formal and informal, and intentional and unintentional communication.

Man-machine and animal communication also must be considered. The six levels of communication include (1) intrapersonal, (2) interpersonal, (3) small group, (4) public, (5) organizational, and (6) mass communication. On an intrapersonal level both the sending and the receiving of messages take place within one individual. Communication on the interpersonal level is characterized by a give-and-take between senders and receivers of messages.

Interaction among three or more communicators is known as small group communication. Small group communication involves a different set of communication roles and functions than those found in two-person communication, primarily because of the increased number of communicators present. Communication is almost entirely one way in the public communication situation. The public speaker holds a distinct advantage in that he or she controls the communication process almost completely. All levels of communication function in organizations. Differences between small group and organizational communication include a formal structure designed to achieve specific goals through managerial control, leadership, technology, and communication networks. The final level of communication, mass media, has developed communication to its fullest extent, exerting an immensely powerful effect on modern society. Today, more than ever, we are a media society because of audience interest, diversity in messages, rapid distribution, and low cost to the consumer.

The remainder of this book is designed to increase your knowledge and your understanding of communication. Chapter 2 begins by explaining the most basic components of human communication, language, and meaning.

Exercises

GROUP EXPERIENCES

Breakdowns

Description: The human communication system is a complex process in which breakdowns can occur at any point. In this chapter a simple six-part model was presented, consisting of (1) source, (2) message, (3) channel, (4) receiver, (5) feedback, and (6) barriers. The purpose of this activity is to identify the communication breakdowns that can occur at each stage in the communication process.

Procedure: Think of an important communication you want to make to another person. For example, you may want to tell your parents that you plan to quit school for a semester. Whatever your communication, identify the (1) source, (2) message channel(s), (3) receiver, (4) types of feedback, and (5) barriers that could occur at each of these stages.

Discussion: Were you able to identify a potential breakdown for each of the five parts of the model? By identifying various types of breakdowns, you should be able to analyze communication problems that you experience daily. The next time you encounter a communication problem, attempt to determine where the breakdown occurred. This should help you to avoid unnecessary breakdowns.

Walk a Mile in My Shoes

Description: **Successful communication depends to a large extent on the source encoding a message in a way the receiver understands. In any communication transaction both the source and the receiver have a field of experience that in some cases may be shared and in other cases completely separate. When the fields of experience for the source and the receiver are different, special attention must be given to the differences in the transmission of the message. An effective method is "to walk a mile in the other person's shoes." This activity is designed to demonstrate (1) the importance of shared fields of experience between the source and receiver and (2) a method for dealing with the different fields of experience of the two parties.**

Procedure: **There are two stages in this activity. The first stage involves role playing in a situation in which the source and receiver do not share a field of experience. Although a sample situation is provided, you may wish to write your own. A three- to five-minute dialogue should take place between the following characters. Each character should be played as a person who not only does not share a field of experience with the other person, but who also has no understanding of the way in which the other person views the world.**

Source	*Receiver*
A college freshman who wants his parents to sign a permission slip to allow him to live in off-campus housing instead of in a dormitory.	A parent who never went to college and who considers the purpose of college to be "education," not "socialization."

Stage two of this activity requires that the two role players switch roles. In other words, the college freshman should play the parent in an attempt to see the world through the eyes of the parent, and the parent should now be playing the college freshman. In this reversed role playing, each person should attempt to understand the other's position based on his or her life experiences.

Discussion: **In the first stage of the role-playing situation, the characters had different fields of experience. Communication under these conditions is very difficult, if not impossible. In the role-reversal situation, each character tried to bridge the gap by seeing the world through the eyes of the other person. If you face a similar situation, try to step back and understand how the other person experiences the world.**

Responding

Description: **Feedback is an important element in the communication process. The three types of feedback include (1) negative feedback, con-**

veying a lack of understanding; (2) positive feedback, indicating that the receiver has understood the source's message; and (3) ambiguous feedback, which is not clearly positive or negative. This activity will help you to identify the different types of feedback.

Procedure: After reviewing the following example, write a negative, positive, and ambiguous feedback response to each of the three statements listed below.

Example

Statement: I would like to go to a private college. I have heard that you can get a better education there.

Positive Feedback: You might check into a private school and see how you feel about its educational program.

Negative Feedback: Private schools have poor athletic programs—why would you want to go there?

Ambiguous Feedback: I see.

Statement 1: I think people from the North weigh more than people from the South—probably because of the climatic differences.

Statement 2: If I had my choice, I'd never work for anyone but myself.

Statement 3: I hate taking basic course requirements. It seems to me that since I'm paying for my education, I ought to be able to decide what courses to take.

Discussion: A good communicator is always sensitive to feedback and constantly modifies his or her messages as a result of the feedback received. Feedback can be conveyed through both verbal and nonverbal channels.

PERSONAL EXPERIENCES

1. Is it true that it is impossible **not** to communicate? Gather evidence based on logic or personal experience that proves or disproves this statement.
2. Select a person with whom you spend a great deal of time. Observe the type of feedback this person gives you. Is it mostly positive, negative, or ambiguous? Do you tend to like people who give you positive feedback?
3. Are you a good communicator? Take a day and find out. Determine your awareness of the various elements of communication by observing yourself. Do you attend and respond to both verbal and nonverbal messages?

DISCUSSION QUESTIONS

1. What is communication? Identify the basic elements of communication.
2. How does communication today affect communication tomorrow? Discuss the possible effects on the communication process or on you as a communicator.
3. How does a communication message get from the source to its destination?
4. Identify three different ways in which communication breakdowns occur.
5. How does feedback (negative, positive, and ambiguous) affect the communication process?

LANGUAGE, MEANING, AND COMMUNICATION

Exploratory Questions

1. What are three functions of language? Can you give some examples?
2. What are two theories of the acquisition of language skills?
3. What process is involved in language development?
4. What is the meaning of semantics?
5. What is the difference between concrete and abstract language?
6. What is the difference between denotation and connotation?
7. Can you describe the concept of communicator style, including the ten variables which affect others' perceptions of our style?
8. What are four major communicator styles?

> Take care of the sense and the sounds will take care of themselves.
>
> Lewis Carroll

The importance of language is almost too obvious. After all, if language did not exist, there would be no written symbols, and, of course, no books like this one to read. Nevertheless, it is necessary to reemphasize a well-known fact: Language *is* important. Language has, however, become one of those facts of life we take so completely for granted that we rarely recognize its essential nature until a situation arises when language cannot be used.

Most of us have experienced situations when speaking was impossible. Laryngitis, for example, can be one of the most frustrating illnesses, for somehow we always think of so many things to say when we cannot speak.

Of course, inability to speak does not prevent the use of written language. Although it is much more time consuming, you can write down your thoughts. But take this situation one step further: You are playing charades and can neither speak nor write. Trying to communicate your ideas in this situation may be bothersome indeed. You may even find yourself inadvertently blurting out a word or two. Fortunately, after the game is over you can go back to your talkative ways. But for many people who are handicapped, this frustrating existence is permanent. Such individuals certainly do not take language for granted.

Language is the communication of thoughts and emotions by means of a structured system of symbols. In our language these symbols are known as **words.** The word *book,* for example, is just an arbitrary combination of letters that, over time, has come to be accepted as the **symbol** for the type of object you are now holding in your hands. The ability to use these symbols defines language skill.

FUNCTIONS OF LANGUAGE

Language fulfills three main functions: labeling, interaction, and transmission of information.

Identifying an object, act, or person by name, so that it can be referred to in communication, is known as **labeling.** Once something is named, it takes on all the characteristics and meanings that different people associate with its label. Your meaning of the word *dog,* for example, might include the ferocious Great Dane next door and your aunt's neurotic Chihuahua. The same is true of our own names—they are both badges of our identity and symbols in their own right.

The next function of language, **interaction,** focuses on the sharing and communication of ideas and emotions. Language transmissions can produce sympathy and understanding or anger and confusion. Thus, language serves as the basis for both positive and negative interactions between individuals.

Through language, information can be passed on to other individuals. This function of language often is referred to as **transmission.** Consider all the information you send and receive daily, from the first "good morning" you hear until the last sentence you read before turning off the light at night. Voices, books, television, signs, lectures—there is no end to the ways language can transmit information.

The most important aspect of language, especially in the history of human civilization, is its ability to transmit information across time. Language connects the past, present, and future. It ensures the perpetuation of our culture and traditions. Older generations die, but they are able through language to leave behind their ideas, accomplishments, failures, and plans for the future. Thus, later generations do not have to repeat the trials and errors of their predecessors but can adapt and constantly improve upon the successes of the past. Just think how little of your present knowledge comes from your own experience and how much is based on long-accepted facts. It will certainly be apparent that language has enabled us to advance intellectually, psychologically, and culturally.

LANGUAGE DEVELOPMENT

Newborn babies have only a few ways to communicate—body movements, facial expressions, and sounds that are generalized to many needs. A cry, for example, can mean fear, hunger, pain, or any number of other things. However, as they grow, babies come to discover language and its importance in ensuring their personal well-being.

Babies discover that language is useful for expressing their own feelings and conveying the feelings of others. Their first "Ma-Ma" or "Da-Da" produces immediate smiles and caresses. Their later, more sophisticated expressions, such as "I love you" or "Go away," will continue the process of exchanging emotions through language. This aspect of language is quite important in creating psychological balance and good adjustment.

During their early years children also discover the meaning of "yes" and "no." No longer can they do everything they wish and still please others. Through spoken and, later, written symbols as well, they come to

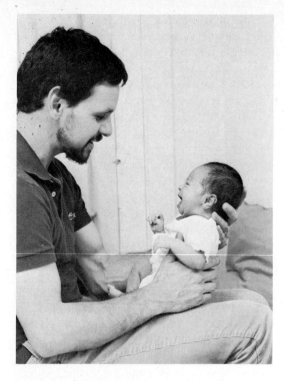

understand their culture and its expectations. Language thus serves as a means of socialization—teaching mores, norms, and accepted behavior.

Theories of Language Development

From childhood to old age we all use language as a means of broadening our knowledge of ourselves and the world about us. When humans first evolved, they were like newborn children, unable to use this valuable tool. Yet once language was developed, the possibilities for mankind's future attainments and cultural growth were increased.

Many linguists believe that evolution is responsible for our ability to produce and use language. They claim that our highly evolved brain provides us with an innate language ability not found in lower organisms. Proponents of this **innateness theory,** most notably Eric Lenneberg, say that our potential for language is inborn but that language itself develops gradually, as a function of the growth of the brain during childhood. Therefore, there are critical biological times for language development— once the growth of the brain is complete (in the early teens), it is much harder to learn language.

There is much evidence to support this theory. More and more schools are discovering that foreign languages are best taught in the lower grades. Young children can often learn several languages simply by being exposed to them, but adults have a much harder time of it.

Although some aspects of language are undeniably innate, language does not develop automatically, in a vacuum. Children who have been isolated from other human beings do not possess language. This demonstrates that interaction with other human beings is necessary for proper language development. Some linguists believe that this interaction is more basic to human language acquisition than any innate capacities. These theorists view language as *imitative, learned behavior.* In other words, children learn language from their parents by imitating them. Parents negatively reinforce inexact imitations and positively reinforce more precise imitations, thus gradually shaping their children's language skills.

There are elements of truth in both the innateness and the learning theories of language development. Currently accepted explanations tend to borrow from each viewpoint. Noam Chomsky, for example, says that we are all born with "language acquisition devices" (LAD for short). This doesn't mean that grammar is somehow innately in our heads but rather that these LAD's help us sort out the language we hear, and understand its grammatical rules. From listening to adults American children learn, for example, that the usual sentence order is subject-verb-object. They will therefore begin to put words into this order. Children from another culture will learn the grammatical rules of their society. Thus, Chomsky's view suggests an interaction between innate (LAD) and learned aspects of language.

Children who for one reason or another have been isolated from speaking humans during the critical periods in which language normally develops find it very difficult, if not impossible, to acquire language abilities. Scientists explain that these children have passed crucial biological times in their neural development, critical periods during which language learning must occur. Once passed, these developmental stages can never be recaptured. Both learning and innate or evolutionary factors are important for proper language development.

"You mene I've bin spending this whol term with a defektiv reeding machin?"

(© 1975 S. Harris)

Even when infants are surrounded by speaking adults, it takes about two years for them to actually learn to speak. In the first month or so, babies make many noises. Contrary to popular ideas, these sounds have no real meaning. This fact has been demonstrated in controlled studies of mothers who listened to their babies from behind screens. The mothers were unable to accurately link particular cries with specific situations, such as a wet diaper or an empty bottle. Investigators thus believe that the sounds newborns make are just reflexive attempts to exercise the vocal cords and related muscles. It is only at the age of two or three months that infants begin to make sounds that have specific meanings. During this **babbling stage,** as it is known, babies can make not only all the sounds of their own language but also those of all the languages in the world. For example, American infants may distinctly make the sounds of a French "r" or German "ü."

After a year most babies begin to observe their parents' speech more and more, and their babbling begins to approximate their parents' sounds. As we mentioned, this imitation is usually reinforced by smiles and praise. From one year on, then, children learn more and more words. By age two they have built up a speaking vocabulary of about three hundred words. Their comprehension vocabulary (words they understand but do not yet use) is even larger.

Until some time after the second year, children's speech is **holophrastic;** that is, they use one word to mean a number of things, or several words run together to signify one thought. For example, the word *hug* may mean "Daddy, I want a hug" or "I am hugging my teddy bear." *Mamagive* becomes a single word symbol that means "Mama give." It is not until the **analytic stage,** after the second year, that the child learns that *Mama give* consists of two separate units, and begins to experiment with their order: "Me give Mama hug," "Mama give me hug."

(Ken Karp)

Semantics is something defined in dictionaries as "the science of the meaning of words"—which would not be a bad definition if people didn't assume that the search for the meaning of words begins and ends with looking them up in a dictionary.

S. I. Hayakawa

By the time children are six years old, they seem to know all the grammatical rules that enable them to speak correctly. However, the learning process never ceases. Your vocabulary can continue to increase as long as you live; every new experience can increase it.

MEANING

Semantics

So far our discussion of language has focused on words. Once you have acquired language, you still must learn to use the words to communicate effectively. Gradually you learn to combine your words in an infinite variety of ways to transmit an infinite number of messages. Still, transmission of messages is not enough. You also want them to be received and understood. Commonality of language between speaker and listener is, obviously, essential for this understanding. What is even more essential is commonality of meaning.

But what is meaning? To take an example, the word *jaram* does not exist in your vocabulary. It should have no significance for you whatsoever. It *means* nothing. Let's say, though, that you are now shown an object called a "jaram." Hereafter, the word *jaram* will bring to mind a picture of that object. Now the word has meaning for you. The use of words such as *jaram* as symbols representing objects and concepts is known as the **symbolic process.** The study of the relationship between these word symbols and their meanings is called **semantics.**

Semantics is quite a complicated endeavor, since there are many symbols and many dimensions of meaning. Words have three dimensions of meaning. The **symbol** refers to objects in the real world, and the **sense** to subjective feelings we have about the symbol. The **referent** is the actual object as it exists in reality. Thus, your meaning of the word *football* is a function of the symbol (the word *football*), the sense (pleasant feelings brought on by the thought of last year's winning season), and the referent (an actual football). Of course, this analysis applies only to the linguistic level of meaning. We cannot forget that there are philosophical, psychological, and logical levels of meaning as well.

Abstraction and Concreteness

Determining meanings is further complicated when the words in question are not concrete. **Concrete** words symbolize objects or events that can be pointed to, touched, experienced, or felt. **Abstract** words, on the other hand, represent things we can't sense directly. How do we define abstract terms such as *freedom, honesty, religion,* or *politics*?

No matter how difficult it may be to define abstractions, they are very important to the communication process. With abstract words we are able to extend the level of our thoughts and speech beyond the concrete, everyday world. We can talk about the complicated areas of right and wrong, discuss things that we can't see, and consider the future as if it existed today.

Ambiguity and Vagueness

Two other language variables that affect understanding are ambiguity and vagueness. **Ambiguity** arises for the simple reason that human language customarily assigns one symbol to several things or categories. Consider the word *heavy.* One can have heavy luggage, a heavy yield of grain, a room heavy with moisture, a heavy odor, heavy gunfire, heavy food, heavy features, a heavy date, and a heavy book, both in weight and in profundity.

Vagueness presents more problems. Meaning is relative; if you are told to look for the tall man at the train station entrance, the speaker's meaning of *tall* is the important issue. Vagueness leads to trivial arguments—such as "I say it's green," "Well, I say it's blue"; but also to more serious ones, such as "Where does truth end and falsehood begin?" and "What is the meaning of meaning?"

Denotation and Connotation

Meaning is also affected by the denotation and connotation of particular words. **Denotation** is the objective reference of a word; that is, its factual, concrete meaning. Dictionary definitions present denotations. Some words are primarily denotative, but most words also possess less definable connotations. **Connotation** refers to meanings beyond the objective reference. The word *automobile,* for example, denotes a four-wheeled motor vehicle. Yet it may connote little or nothing to one person, anger to someone who has just been fired from an automobile factory, and pleasure to someone who has just bought a new sports car. Very specific words—*chair, desk, book,* and so forth—are usually without connotation for most people. Other words, such as *obsolete* and *respectable,* can fall either way, depending on context, while words such as *fantastic* and *horrible* are almost totally connotative in nature.

We acquire our connotations from social and personal experiences. The word *farm* means something different to a city dweller than to a country person. The more two people have in common—the more similar their backgrounds, past experiences, attitudes, and outlooks—the better chance they have of attaching the same meaning to a word or concept.

Consider the following situation. Greg is talking with his parents, and all is going well. They are communicating for a change. Then the conversation turns to the subject of drugs. Communication comes quickly to an end. Greg and his parents stop communicating because they have different connotations for the word *drug.* But the word is only a small part of a larger problem. Greg, his mother, and his father have different attitudes about many things, and this difference in attitudes influences the connotations they attach to many words. The end result of these differing connotations is often only too similar to this example—breakdown of communication.

Another factor that influences meaning is **style,** or how we choose, organize, and use those features of the language that are open to individual selection.

Style

The rules of our language dictate the arrangement of words in sentences (subject, verb, object) and frequently determine which forms of words must be used (present or past tense, singular or plural verb). These are not matters of style, but of grammar. Style, on the other hand, refers to an individual's characteristic tendencies to choose particular kinds of words (simple versus multisyllabic, factual versus descriptive), particular sentence constructions (short versus long, complete versus fragmentary), or even particular phrases ("you know," "I mean," "right on").

Style is influenced by variables in the speaker as well as in the listener. Have you ever wondered why it seems difficult to talk with some people and easy with others? Think for a minute about blind dates you've had, parties you've attended, or plane trips you've taken. Pleasant interactions are usually associated with people you hit it off with immediately. Even though you may have found commonalities, successful communication was probably based on more than similar professions or common interests.

Personality differences do exist between communicators, and we tend to make positive and negative judgments based on specific communication styles. We often base first impressions more on how a person says something than on what is said: "She turned me off with her sarcastic comments." "The salesman sounded so sincere that I wanted to buy from him." "She really had a way of making people feel right at home." In fact, the first few minutes of interpersonal interaction often determine whether or not we will continue interaction. These minutes are also often the key to business achievement, social success, family harmony, and sexual satisfaction. Hemming and hawing, overusing profanity, and cutting off another person who is speaking all indicate the influence of personality on communicator style.

Although up to this point we have been discussing the concept of style in general, two specific groups of researchers have been interested in "communicator style," specifically. Robert Norton, for example, has defined communicator style as "the way one verbally and preverbally interacts to signal how literal meaning should be taken, interpreted, filtered, or understood."[1] As a result of his perceptions, he likewise has discriminated

[1]Barbara M. Montgomery and Robert W. Norton, "Sex Differences and Similarities in Communicator Style," *Communication Monographs* 48, no. 2 (1981), pp. 121–132.

ten variables, or components, which seemingly contribute to an individual's communicator style. These include

1. Dominance, or tendency to take control in social interactions;
2. Contentiousness, or argumentativeness and aggressiveness;
3. Preciseness, or degree of concern with accuracy, documentation, and proof in informative interactions;
4. Attentiveness, or sensitivity to others;
5. Friendliness, or willingness to establish interpersonal relationships;
6. Openness, or willingness to reveal personal information or to express feelings and emotions openly;
7. Degree of anxiety or nervousness when interacting with others;
8. Animation, or amount of expressiveness and interest when conversing with others;
9. Dramatic behaviors, or degree to which he or she dramatizes events, creating closeness among interactants; and
10. The overall impression or image which a person presents when she or he interacts with others.[2]

Norton, however, is not the only researcher who is interested in communicator style. Another program of research which has resulted in several communication training programs emphasizing the importance of understanding communicator styles is that of Wilson Learning Corporation, entitled "Managing Interpersonal Relations," or simply, MIR.[3]

Unlike the work of Norton, but not unrelated, Wilson Learning researchers have focused on four basic styles of communication, based on different combinations of assertiveness and responsiveness. Assertiveness is viewed as the amount of control one tries to exert over another, while responsiveness is the amount of control one has over one's own feelings and emotions. Figure 2–1 helps to explain the relationship between assertiveness and responsiveness. The program helps participants to determine whether they have a driver, expressive, amiable, or analytic communicator style. Characteristics of these communicator styles include:

1. Drivers are task oriented and assert themselves while controlling displays of emotion. Drivers tend to be cold and abrupt. They get to the point and expect others to do the same.
2. Expressives are social individuals high in both assertiveness and responsiveness. They feel a need to control conversation, so they are very impulsive but relationship oriented.
3. Amiables are supportive specialists. They do not assert themselves but are very responsive. They are more concerned with relationships than with the task.
4. Analytics are task oriented and are usually unassertive and unresponsive. They are systematic, organized, and information centered. They need order, and often work from an agenda.

[2]Montgomery and Norton.
[3]Wilson Learning Corporation, *Managing Interpersonal Relations* (Eden Prairie, Minn.: Wilson Learning Corporation, 1975).

NON-RESPONSIVE

Reserved, unreponsive
Poker face
Actions cautions or careful
Wants facts and details
Eye contact infrequent while
  listening
Eyes harsh, severe, or serious
Limited use of hands, clenched
  tightly, folded, or pointed
Limited personal feelings, story
  telling, or small talk
Preoccupied or vigilant

NON-ASSERTIVE

Few uses of voice to
  emphasize ideas
Expressions and posture are
  are quiet and submissive
Deliberate, studied, or
  slow in speech
Indifferent handshake
Asks questions more often
  than makes statements
Vague, unclear about what
  is wanted
Tends to lean backwards

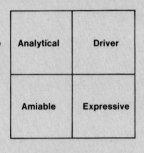

ASSERTIVE

Emphasizes ideas by
  tone change
Expressions are aggressive
  or dominant
Quick, clear, or fast paced
Firm handshake
Makes statements more often
  than asks question
Lets one know what
  is wanted
Tends to lean forward to
  make a point

RESPONSIVE

Animated, uses facial
  expressions
Smiles, nods, frowns
Actions open or eager
Little effort to push for facts
Eye contact frequent while
  listening
Friendly gaze
Hands free, palms up, open
Friendly gestures
Shares personal feelings
Attentive, responsive, enjoys
  the relationship

Recognition is most accurate by observing one dimension at a time

FIGURE 2-1 *Guideline for Recognition.*

Although each of us has a dominant communicator style, according to these researchers, we display characteristics of all styles. Communicating with someone of our own style is usually easy; however, problems occur when communicators are on two different wavelengths. Can you remember situations in which you wished a friend would hurry and get to the point, or instead, elaborate and give all the details? Often we need to be more sensitive to other communicator styles.

We need to be aware of our own style so that we can communicate more effectively: When we understand our own style, we can adapt to the styles of others. This adaptation is known as ***role shifting***.[4] Figure 2–2 presents ways for different communicators to adapt. When role shifting, you try to analyze the listener's style and interact accordingly. Role shifting is especially important when two people communicate using opposite styles. For example, expressive executives could easily frustrate analytic executives by interjecting jokes and anecdotes during business meetings. The analytic executives would want only the bare facts without all the "fooling around."

We frequently "tailor" our language to the particular purpose of our communication. MIR is designed to help people adapt to various situations through systematic training. Knowing your communicator style can benefit you whether you want to persuade or to inform others. A nuclear physicist uses scientific jargon with colleagues, but not with those outside the field. Physicians often have a habit of talking to their patients as if the latter were up on the latest medical terminology. As a result, patients sometimes feel alienated, especially when Latin terminology seems to change their simple complaint into what sounds like a fatal illness. A considerate doctor uses terms easily understood by the patient.

	DRIVER	EXPRESSIVE	AMIABLE	ANALYTICAL
BACK UP STYLE	Autocratic	Attacker	Acquiescer	Avoider
MEASURES PERSONAL VALUE BY	Results	Applause	Attention	Activity
FOR GROWTH NEEDS TO	Listen	Check	Reach	Decide
LET THEM SAVE	Time	Efforts	Relationships	Face
NEEDS CLIMATE THAT	Allows to build own structure	Inspires to their goals	Provides details	Suggests
TAKE TIME TO BE	Efficient	Stimulating	Agreeable	Accurate
SUPPORT THEIR	Conclusions and actions	Dreams intuitions	Relationships and feelings	Principles and thinking
GIVE BENEFITS THAT ANSWER	What	Who	Why	How
FOR DECISIONS GIVE THEM	Options and probabilities	Testimony and incentives	Guarantees and assurances	Evidence and service
SPECIALTY	Control	Social	Supportive	Technical

FIGURE 2–2 Social Style Summary.

[4]John Bledsoe, "Your Four Communicating Styles," *Training Magazine* (March 1976), pp. 18–20.

WORDS IN WONDERLAND

Lewis Carroll was an English mathematician and logician whose real name was Charles Lutwidge Dodgson. He is remembered not for his contributions to mathematics or logic but as the author of **Alice's Adventures in Wonderland** and **Through the Looking-Glass**. These great works are sometimes called "nonsense" literature, but from the excerpts that follow we can see that even in wonderland Carroll was concerned with the logic of words and how they represent reality.

"Come, we shall have some fun now!" thought Alice. "I'm glad they've begun asking riddles—I believe I can guess that," she added aloud.

"Do you mean that you think you can find out the answer to it?" said the March Hare.

"Exactly so," said Alice.

"Then you should say what you mean," the March Hare went on.

"I do," Alice hastily replied: "at least—at least I mean what I say—that's the same thing, you know."

"Not the same thing a bit!" said the Hatter. "Why, you might just as well say that 'I see what I eat' is same thing as 'I eat what I see!'"

"You might just as well say," added the March Hare, "that 'I like what I get' is the same thing as 'I get what I like!'"

"You might just as well say," added the Dormouse, which seemed to be talking in its sleep, "that 'I breathe when I sleep' is the same thing as 'I sleep when I breathe!'"

"It **is** the same thing with you," said the Hatter, and here the conversation dropped. . . .

Alice's Adventures in Wonderland

"I don't know what you mean by 'glory,'" Alice said.

Humpty Dumpty smiled contemptuously. "Of course you don't—till I tell you. I meant 'there's a nice knock-down argument for you!'"

"But 'glory' doesn't mean 'a nice knock-down argument,'" Alice objected.

"When I use a word," Humpty Dumpty said, in rather a scornful tone, "it means just what I choose it to mean—neither more nor less."

"The question is," said Alice, "whether you **can** make words mean so many different things."

"The question is," said Humpty Dumpty, "which is to be master—that's all."

Through the Looking-Glass

As we have seen in the previous discussions, language is a highly complex, yet powerful, phenomenon. However, we can all strive to become more aware of the subtle but powerful influence of words in our lives. Alfred Korzybski, a pioneer in the area of General Semantics—the study of the structure and function of speech and resultant behavior—observed that people often falsely identify with words. We sometimes respond to words as if the words themselves were the referent objects they symbolize. In fact, many individuals are tyrannized by words. For example, just hearing the word *spider* may cause someone with a fear of spiders to shiver. The spider itself does not have to be in sight; the symbol, not the referent, causes the response.

Korzybski's Laws

This observation led to Korzybski's law of **non-identity,** which says, simply, that a word is **not** the thing it represents. The word *cat* and the animal itself are not one and the same thing. (See Figure 2–3.)

Korzybski's second law, that of **non-allness,** reminds us that a word cannot symbolize *all* of a thing. *Cat* may bring to mind your own pet and the expensive show animal you saw on TV last night. However, *cat* may symbolize something quite different for an African who has experienced cats of a larger and more ferocious variety than the string of "Fluffys"

FIGURE 2-3 Korzybski's Three Laws.

you have owned and loved. Neither you nor the African, though, might think of an Egyptian god or a Canadian lynx. Clearly, language never conveys *everything* about *anything.*

Korzybski's third law concerns **self-reflexiveness.** It explains that a word can refer not only to something in the real world but also to itself. Not only does the word *cat* refer to a kind of four-legged animal in the real world, but it also refers to the word formed in English by the letters *c-a-t,* or the word formed in Italian by the letters *g-a-t-t-o.*

LANGUAGE AND BEHAVIOR

Our discussion of connotation and style showed the effects of environmental and personal variables on an individual's language usage. It is also important to recognize that language variables affect our attitudes and behavior.

We know, for example, that people who share a given speaking style often share a similar culture and beliefs. In fact, linguists have found that speech style not only contributes to a group's identity and cohesion,[5] but it often serves a useful purpose in effective communication. In many areas of Europe, for instance, people of adjoining villages regard politeness to be a function of the use of one's own community's speech dialect, particularly in interactions between members of two or more different communities.[6] Likewise, results of a study conducted by John Gumperz in 1971 have shown the importance of dialect maintenance among different caste groups in northern Indian villages. As he notes in the following description of one specific village,

> The most deviant minority dialect was that of the sweepers, who earn their livelihood by working as servants and cleaners in the homes of majority dialect speakers. In this village, where peasant women are unable to leave their homes except on special occasions, sweepers serve as the main carriers of gossip. In fact, they spend most of their waking hours either listening to or talking to speakers of the majority dialects. Yet they would no more imitate the speech of their employers than adopt their clothing. To do so would be to risk inter-group conflict.[7]

Although speech styles have a useful function, as we have seen, they may also serve their users in a negative way. This situation usually arises when nonusers of a major style or dialect come into contact with people who are unaware of their function and importance, or who tend to see things and people categorically. Perceptions regarding the Amish people of the Pennsylvania Dutch area illustrate this point. Although the people of this region may share both similar culture and beliefs, it is not necessarily true that everyone who speaks with a Pennsylvania Dutch accent will prefer old-fashioned clothes and horse-drawn wagons. Assuming such automatic relationships between particular linguistic styles and particular personal traits is known as *semantic,* or *linguistic, stereotyping.* For example, many people unfairly underestimate the intellectual ability of people who speak slow and halting English. Conversely, linguistic stereotyping may also produce a perception of intellectual superiority for a speaker with a crisp Oxford accent.

Linguistic Stereotyping

As you may have guessed by now, most semantic stereotypes are negative. They are particularly harmful for individuals who share easily recognizable (yet nonstandard) dialects such as Black English or Louisiana creole. Perhaps the greatest damage, however, comes when speakers of the standard or majority dialect of a culture believe that nonspeakers are somehow inferior. In fact, studies have shown that many employers in

[5]Geneva Smitherman, *Talkin and Testifyin: The Language of Black America* (Boston: Houghton Mifflin, 1977).

[6]John Gumperz, "Dialect and Conversational Inference in Urban Communication," *Language in Society* 7 (December 1978), pp. 393–409.

[7]Gumperz, p. 394.

(Forsyth/Monkmeyer Press Photo Services)

American businesses and industries today are guilty of such perceptions, which in turn has affected their hiring (and firing) policies.[8]

The question, then, becomes: What can we do, given this knowledge concerning linguistic stereotypes? For "native" speakers the solution seems to reside in concern and awareness—awareness concerning the information we have presented and a concern for consistency in acting upon it, whether in interpersonal interactions or on the job.

For nonnative speakers the solution is more complex and will involve a weighing of alternatives and their consequences. To disregard the importance of competence in the standard dialect or style may result in diminished opportunities and rewards. At the same time, it is crucial that an individual be aware of the importance of his or her social identity, which is intimately tied to the language in which he or she takes an active part.

Perhaps one answer lies in the individual's ability to achieve some degree of linguistic competence in both communities. Although such an

[8]Edward Anderson, "Language and Success," *College English* 43, no. 8 (December 1981), pp. 807–812.

attempt would be both difficult and frustrating, it could provide a means by which the "bilingual" or "bidialectical" individual may more effectively communicate.

When Clark Gable said "Frankly, my dear, I don't give a damn" in *Gone With the Wind* (1939), millions of people were either shocked or titillated. Times have changed. Four-letter words don't offend as they once did. New words come into the language almost daily, as they always have. As the norms and mores of a society change, so does its language. Both society and language reflect the "liberated" spirit of the twentieth century.

Making
Language
More Effective

Unfortunately, liberated language often means sloppy, imprecise language, too. Although people seem to be communicating *more* these days, they may be understood *less.* As a student of speech and language, you should be aware of the trend. Above all, try to speak as clearly as possible. That is, use words whose meanings can be understood by those listening to you. To do this you must relate to your listeners; the more understanding you have of their beliefs and experiences, the more effective you will be in your choice of words. Try not to be ambiguous. If, for example, we had begun this paragraph by saying "Try to speak clearly," and did not elaborate further, you might have thought we meant "Don't mumble."

Use vocabulary appropriate to yourself, your listeners, the subject, and the occasion. Slang may be understandable to your peers but not necessarily to individuals younger or older than you. Those who do not know your jargon should not be expected to understand it. And even if your slang is familiar to your audience, consider the setting as well. You would be wise to use different terminology in a classroom discussion of a sexually explicit book than you would in a private conversation with the same classmates.

Finally, both the quantity and the quality of what you say are important. We get tired of listening to a person who rambles on and on about the same thing. Although a certain amount of repetition is inherent in oral communication, be careful not to "overkill" your subject.

SUMMARY

Language is our most important tool of communication. It provides us with a means of labeling, or identifying by name, an object, act, or person we wish to refer to. It is the basis of interaction, the sharing of ideas and emotions, and finally, the means by which we transmit information among ourselves and through the ages from one culture and generation to the next.

There are two major theories of language development: innateness theory and imitative theory. Innateness refers to the inborn ability to speak a language. The imitative theory holds that language is a learned behavior. While these are the two basic viewpoints, many other theories draw upon them. Language development occurs for the most part in early childhood.

Meaning is the essential part of any message. Understanding between individuals depends upon similarity of meaning. Semantics is the study of the relationship between our words and their meanings. Abstraction is the ability to give symbolic meaning to those things that cannot be sensed—concepts, ideals, and so forth. Ambiguity and vagueness arise because one word or symbol can have several meanings, and meaning itself is relative.

Words are also denotative and connotative. They may have concrete and factual meanings, or they may represent something beyond the objective reference.

Meaning is also influenced by style. Each individual has his or her own characteristic way of communicating. Style is influenced by our personalities, our purposes, and our communication settings. In short, these variables and the laws of self-reflexiveness, non-identity, and non-allness (and their use) may drastically affect communication outcomes.

The variables of language also affect our attitudes and behavior. We sometimes assume relationships between linguistic styles and personal or cultural traits. This process is known as linguistic stereotyping and usually has a negative effect upon communication. Linguistic stereotyping plays a large part in racism and causes individuals to react to words and symbols as if they were reality itself. In order to overcome linguistic stereotypes, we must be aware of their existence and concerned with their effects. In addition, each of us should strive to make language more effective. Speaking as clearly as possible, using words which can be understood by others, relating to our listeners, and using language which is appropriate to ourselves and others are only a few of the ways in which we may begin to be more concerned and effective communicators.

Exercises

GROUP EXPERIENCES

Meanings Are in People

Description: The fact that a single word is used when referring to many different things (the example *heavy* was used earlier) points to the fact that people attach meaning to symbols: Symbols have no meaning in and of themselves. This activity will focus on the multiple meaning we attach to words.

Procedure: Divide into groups of four to six. Each group should list as many different meanings as possible for the words given below. In listing the meanings, a phrase should be used to make clear the specific meaning of the word. Do as many as you can in five minutes. When the time is up, each group should read its list of meanings for each word. If a particular meaning is challenged, a standard dictionary or dictionary of slang should solve the argument.

Word List

cracked	book
spirit	black
lid	hot
down	fly
high	

Discussion: What types of communication problems do multiple word meanings create? Do word meanings change with each generation of people? How can you use these and similar words in such a way as to make their meaning more explicit?

Do Your Symbols Convey Your Sense?

Description: Alfred Korzybski offers three basic laws, the first of which is the law of non-identity. This law says that the word is not the thing it represents. We often forget how inadequate language is in describing our emotional feelings, for example. This activity will provide you with the opportunity to explore the limitations of language.

Procedure: Divide into groups of four to six. Each group should take the following common phrases and attempt to state them in more precise or explicit language. In other words, you will need to describe what "love" is, for example. After each group has completed the four phrases, they should be read aloud to the rest of the class:

Example	*New Phrase*
I really like him.	have a very positive feeling toward him.
I hate your guts.	
I love you.	
My head aches.	
My stomach is tied in knots.	

Discussion: Do the new phrases sound funny? Are they more explicit than the common phrases? What does the law of non-identity mean to you?

Who's Talking?

Description: How does language affect our behavior? When comparing various languages, English has a distinctive feature. We use the word *I* as a general referent for all the "roles" we play. What "I" do in one situation may not be the same action "I" would take in another situation. Eskimos avoid the direct identification of the term *I* with "self" by using phrases such as "this woman believes" or "this man feels." Eastern philosophy suggests that using phrases such as "I am" or "you are" can be very misleading, for they infer that "you" are the thing, and, moreover, that "you" do not change your basic personality. This activity will provide you with an opportunity to see how often you make use of pronouns such as *I* or *you*.

Procedure: Divide into dyads. You are to have a 10-minute conversation, during which time you cannot use the following words:

I YOU HE   SHE THEY WE

Instead, you should replace these words either with formal statements or with an alternative referent, for example:

> *Normal:* I think that . . . (*I* is unacceptable in this activity.)
> *Formal:* It appears that institutions of education are not receiving the necessary financial support.
> *Alternate:* This woman thinks that institutions of education are not receiving the necessary financial support.
> In asking a question of your partner, you will also have to take special care with the wording, for example:
> *Normal:* What do you think? (The use of the pronoun *you* is unacceptable in this activity.)
> *Formal:* What are some alternative ways of viewing this situation?
> *Alternate:* What does Dick think? (In this case you would the name of your partner to replace the personal pronoun *you*.)

Discussion: Did you experience much difficulty with this conversation? Did the "meaning" in the conversation change with the new referents used? Did you find the conversation more depersonalized when avoiding the use of pronouns? Is it difficult for you to avoid using the word *I*?

PERSONAL EXPERIENCES

1. Sit alone in a quiet room. Very slowly begin saying your name over and over. Do this for 10 minutes and see if your name takes on a different meaning. Then consider whether or not you consider your "name" to be "you." Do you believe that a word in any language is not the thing but rather a symbol for it? Is your name simply a symbol for you?

2. Read the poem "The Jabberwocky" from **Through the Looking-Glass**. Then write your interpretation of this poem. Was Lewis Carroll making a comment on language in general? What do the words mean? Where did you find the meanings of the words (dictionary, context of the poem)?

1. What are the two main schools of thought on language acquisition of children?

2. Discuss the stages of a child's acquisition of language: during the first few months after birth, at one year, at eighteen months, at two years, and at six years.

3. What are the primary advantages and disadvantages of maintaining a nonstandard dialect or style of speaking? In what ways can "standard" users help to increase communication effectiveness between users and nonusers?

LISTENING AND FEEDBACK

Exploratory Questions

1. What are the six stages of the listening process?
2. How do you distinguish between active and passive listening?
3. What four factors affect listening?
4. Can you identify at least five skills that must be developed to improve listening?
5. What are the functions and effects of feedback?
6. How do you increase the effectiveness of feedback?

THE LISTENING PROCESS

We spend nearly half of our daily lives listening, but this does not mean that we are good listeners. Although we hear sounds all around us, it's easy to hear without really listening: "I didn't listen to the exact words, but I did hear them quarreling."

The Hearing-
Listening
Distinction

Hearing, which is only one part of the listening process, refers to the physical act of receiving sounds. It is a passive process that occurs even when we're asleep. Listening, on the other hand, is work. It means not only hearing but paying attention and understanding.

We have probably all had the annoying experience of telling what we thought was a fascinating story, only to discover that our "listener" may have heard our message but did not really listen to it. Several studies of college students showed that they could repeat only 50 percent of a message they had just heard. Effective listening is not a natural ability, but some people do it very well, even establishing reputations as good listeners. "You know, whenever I have a problem, I talk to Jesse. He really listens to what I have to say." There are also trained professionals, such as psychiatrists and social workers, whose jobs are to listen to the thoughts and feelings of their clients. Unfortunately, however, trained listeners and people such as Jesse are in the minority. The majority of us owe it to ourselves and others to improve our listening skills. To achieve that goal, we must seriously study and practice the art of listening.

Six Stages of
the Listening
Process

Our study focuses first on the listening process, which involves six stages: hearing, attention, understanding, remembering, evaluating, and responding (see Figure 3–1). The stages occur in sequence, but they are generally performed with little awareness and often in rapid succession.

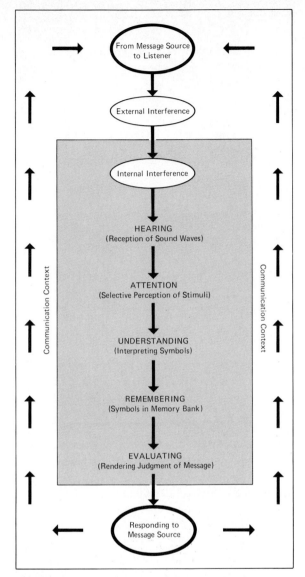

FIGURE 3-1 The Six Stages of the Listening Process.

HEARING   As we mentioned earlier, the term *hearing* is often incorrectly used to mean listening. In fact, hearing is but one stage of the complex process of listening.

Hearing refers to the response caused by sound waves stimulating the sensory receptors of the ear. This is a purely physical response. Therefore, the reception of sound waves, which we know as hearing, does not mean that there is any conscious perception of what is being heard. In

Hearing is only one stage of the listening process. (Marc P. Anderson)

other words, you must hear to listen, but you need not listen to hear. The perception necessary for listening depends on attention.

ATTENTION   Our senses are constantly bombarded by countless stimuli from the world about us. Just as you may feel overwhelmed by the total environment at a circus or a carnival—flashing lights, loud voices, crowds milling about, smells of popcorn, cotton candy, and elephants—so, too, can your mind become overloaded by the barrage of everyday stimuli. However, your brain screens these stimuli and permits only a select few to come into focus. This selective perception is known as **attention,** an important requirement for effective listening.

Strong stimuli such as bright lights, sudden noises, or sharp bumps in the road are sure attention getters. Attention to more commonplace or less striking stimuli requires special effort. For example, you may unconsciously tilt your head to bring your ear closer to the source of a faint noise, or squint your eyes to make out a distant street sign. These **postural adjustments** are aided by physical changes in sensory receptor organs. Such **receptor adjustments** might include tensing of the ear's tympanic muscle for better response to weak sounds, or dilation of the pupils of the eyes to help you see better in a dark room.

UNDERSTANDING   Hearing and perceiving a sound are still not enough for meaningful messages to be received. The next step is **understanding** the symbols we have seen and heard. To do this, we must analyze the meaning of the stimuli we have perceived. It is at this stage of the listening process, for example, that parents begin to tell the difference between a baby's playful babblings and attempts at meaningful speech. Italian and

French, though beautiful and expressive languages, are only collections of pleasant sounds until we learn to understand the meaning of the word symbols.

When we talk about symbolic stimuli, we are talking not only about words but also about other sounds (applause, a fog horn, a siren) and sights (a blue uniform, a skull and crossbones, a flashing red light) which have symbolic meanings as well. The meanings attached to these symbols are a function of our past associations and of the context in which the symbols occur. Thus, we usually associate a siren with an emergency but feel no alarm when the same siren is sounded at midnight on New Year's Eve. For successful interpersonal communication, the listener must understand the intended meaning and the context assumed by the sender.

REMEMBERING   The fourth stage of the listening process, **remembering,** is often omitted by communication analysts, who do not consider it essential to the process. Yet remembering is important to the listening process because it means that an individual has not only received and interpreted a message but has also added it to the mind's storage bank. Of course, anyone listening to the court testimony of eyewitnesses to an auto accident will immediately realize that what is remembered may be quite different from what was originally seen or heard. Just as our attention is selective, so too is our memory.

EVALUATING   A fifth stage in which active listeners participate is the act of **evaluating.** It is at this point that the active listener weighs evidence, sorts fact from opinion, and determines the presence or absence of bias or prejudice in a message. In addition, during this stage the listener renders judgment as a function of these criteria. The effective listener, however, makes sure that he or she doesn't begin this activity too soon. Beginning this stage of the process before a message is completed requires that we no longer hear and attend to the incoming message. As a result, the listening process ceases—and so does our chance to participate as effective listeners.

RESPONDING   The sixth and final stage of the listening process is that of **responding** to a speaker and her message. This stage of the process requires that the receiver complete the process through verbal and/or nonverbal feedback. Because the speaker has no other way to determine if a message has been received (all of your behaviors up to this point have been covert, or elicited intrapersonally), this stage becomes the only overt means by which the sender may determine the degree of success in transmitting her message. The feedback you return may range from silence (if you do not hear a message—or if you are angry), to smiling or frowning, to requesting clarification. By responding to a message in one of these ways, you will have made an active attempt to effectively complete the listening process.

TYPES OF LISTENING

Listening has been classified in a variety of ways by communication scholars. These classifications include the distinction between active and passive listening and, more specifically, distinctions among various types of social versus serious listening situations.

Active listening, as defined by Barbara, differentiates between active and passive listening in the following way:

> In the former, the individual listens with more or less his total self—including his special senses, attitudes, beliefs, feelings and intuitions. In the latter, the listener becomes mainly an organ for the passive reception of sound, with little self-perception, personal involvement, gestalt discrimination, or alive curiosity.[1]

Thus, active listening may be distinguished from passive listening by the degree to which the listener becomes *involved* in a given interaction. However, either form of listening may occur in both serious and social listening situations, which are the next classification elements to be discussed.

Social listening and serious listening are best distinguished by the structure of the communication setting in which they take place. If the situation is more informal and nonstructured than it is formal and structured, social listening will be more appropriate. Conversely, if the situation calls for a more formal and structured format, serious listening may potentially take place.

During informal, social listening the listener's responsibilities are limited to appreciation, conversation, and courtesy. Specifically, appreciative listening (the type of enjoyable, entertaining listening engaged in while attending a concert, playing a record, or attending a poetry reading) requires that the listener respond on a cognitive or affective level. During appreciative listening the listener remains a listener only. Conversational listening, however, implies a constant exchange in the roles of speaker and listener. Courteous listening also involves conversation, but of a more restricted type. For example, if you run into a friend of the family whom you haven't seen in years and never really cared for, you still feel obliged to listen as he fills you in on everything he has done for the last five years.

The most important type of social listening in interpersonal relationships is listening to show affection, caring, and warmth. For example, your best friend has had an argument with her parents and needs to talk to someone. Sometimes you can provide support just by listening.

Some interpersonal listening occurs in formal contexts. One kind of formal, serious listening is critical listening, which involves analysis and evaluation of what is heard. Critical listening requires certain skills, such as the ability to do the following: discern fact from fiction, separate fact

[1]D. Barbara, "On Listening—the Role of the Ear in Psychic Life," *Today's Speech* 5 (1957): 12–15.

from opinion, determine if an argument is based on logic or emotion, maintain an objective attitude toward the source and the message, and clarify ambiguities. For example, as two candidates debate an issue, the critical listener will be concerned with what is said, rather than who said it, and the logic and truth of the arguments.

Discriminative listening is another form of serious listening, the purpose of which is understanding and remembering. In order to understand what you hear, you must be able to tune in to the main ideas, follow the logic of the message, pinpoint important details, and recognize the purpose of the message. Discriminative listening is practiced by the student taking notes on a history lecture or by someone getting instructions from the florist about proper lighting for certain plants.

BARRIERS AND AIDS TO EFFECTIVE LISTENING

Although the six stages of listening are apparent in almost all listening situations, it would be wrong to think that these situations are all alike. The complex process of listening is affected by many variables, which operate differently in different communication interactions. **Environmental setting** is one such variable. (A musical piece is usually more exciting when heard in a concert hall than when played at home on a record player.) Another variable is the **message source** to whom we are listening. (There are some people we love to listen to and others we "tune out.") Of course, the **message** itself is also quite important. (We react quite differently to a mortgage bill and a birthday card.) In addition, the personality and emotional state of the **listener** influence his or her responses. (Sometimes we are eager to listen, and at other times we don't want to bother.) These variables act either as barriers or as aids in the listening process.

If you have ever tried to talk to a friend on a subway train or tried to enjoy a movie when a loud conversation was going on behind you, you know the extent to which noise can affect listening. Environmental noise is both distracting to your attention and detrimental to your ability to hear. Similar interference may be caused by crowding, poor acoustics, or by heat, cold, or precipitation.[2]

Environmental Setting

A physical condition that affects listening behavior in groups and

[2]Robert O. Hirsh, *Listening: A Way to Process Information Aurally* (Dubuque, Iowa: Gorsuch Scarisbrick, 1979), pp. 38–40.

over which the listener may have little control is the seating arrangement of the people involved. A round table aids free-flowing communication and effective listening (see Chapter 4). Other seating arrangements, however, may create barriers.

How near you are to the other participants in the communication is also important. If you are seated at one end of a long table, it is almost impossible for you to listen to a conversation at the other end.

The Message Source

Research has shown that your impression of a person's status determines to a large extent how well you listen to him or her. We all know that we listen closely to people we respect or admire, whereas we often pay little attention to those we feel are our inferiors. Research suggests that females are at a disadvantage when they are a message source. Male speakers are listened to more carefully, and both males and females recall information more accurately from male speakers.[3]

In addition, the speakers themselves determine how easy or difficult the listening situation will be for the listeners. As research suggests, it is much easier for an audience to listen to more fluent speakers (that is, those who use fewer vocal pauses such as "uh" and "um") than to speakers who are less fluent.[4]

The Message

Western Union advertises that mailgrams have more impact than ordinary letters. They are received much less frequently and thus benefit both from novelty and from association with messages of importance. These same factors of novelty and significance apply to all messages. Unusual signs catch your eye on the highway. Thundering brass bands make you stop to see what the parade is all about. In the same way, intense, emotion-filled messages also capture your attention. This explains the great effectiveness of a speaker such as Dr. Martin Luther King, Jr., in his "I Have a Dream" speech.

The Listener

No matter how excellent the acoustics, how prestigious the speaker, or how important the message, communication cannot occur unless a listener is present. The physical state of the listener can affect the listening situation. The deaf or hard-of-hearing listener can obviously be a barrier to communication. If the telephone has ever awakened you from a deep sleep, you know how sleepiness, too, can impair your ability to decipher a speaker's message. Less obvious, however, is the extent to which *psychological* attributes of the listener can also influence the communication process.

LISTENER ATTITUDES AND NEEDS Attitudes can become barriers to effective listening. If you see yourself as superior to others, with nothing to gain from listening to them, you have created a self-imposed barrier to

---

[3]Kenneth J. Gruber and Jacquelyn Gaebelein, "Sex Differences in Listening Comprehension," *Sex Roles* 5 (1979): 299.

[4]Lyman K. Steil, Larry L. Barker, and Kittie W. Watson, *Effective Listening: Key to Your Success* (Reading, Mass.: Addison-Wesley, 1983), p. 66.

communication. Often this causes adults to ignore what children say, just as a senior executive might ignore the suggestions of junior employees. On the other hand, if you feel a speaker is superior, you may be so willing to accept whatever is said that critical listening cannot take place at all.

Even in situations in which the status of the speaker has little effect, listeners are often guilty of prejudging. This point may be illustrated by the many times we find ourselves jumping to conclusions based on our own point of view, as opposed to what the speaker is actually saying. Sometimes we hear only what we expect to hear, no matter what is actually being said. While listening to a political debate, for example, we must be careful not to automatically hear our candidate's opponent make the stupid remarks we anticipate.

Then again, we often hear what we *want* to hear—motive is very important in the listening process. For example, an athlete who has suffered a leg injury consults a doctor for advice. The doctor says to avoid any great physical strain and to engage only in moderate exercise. The athlete goes out and plays an "easy" game of tennis—after all, the doctor said "moderate exercise," didn't she?

Another factor affecting listening is the shared experience, or recognition factor. In a situation in which several conversations are going on at the same time, you will probably tune in to one of them if you hear something to which you can relate. If you are sitting in a crowded coffee shop and hear someone at the next table talking about a movie you have just seen, you will listen more closely than if you had not seen that movie. Suppose that you recognize your name being dropped in a conversation. Aren't you likely to listen very carefully to what is being said?

LISTENING HABITS   Habits have a great deal to do with the way we listen, too. Throughout our lives we develop a series of listening habits, some of which may be undesirable. These habits create a barrier to communication. Early in our school careers, for example, we learn to fake attention in order to please teachers or parents. When these poor listening habits carry over to work situations, problems occur. Deadlines are missed, mistakes are made, and productivity is lowered. For this reason, many major companies now assess listening skills when considering employees for promotion. Faking attention is easily done by looking at a speaker, placing a hand under the chin, or using other gestures that suggest listening.

Another poor listening habit is listening only for facts, a habit that is often encouraged by teachers who test for content but not comprehension. While it is important to be able to separate important ideas and facts from less important ones, the listening process often suffers by a focus only on facts—some meanings and attitudes of the speaker may go unnoticed.

Another bad habit is avoiding the difficult or uninteresting. The lazy listener just "changes channels" when something appears to be too dull or too difficult; or the listener assumes, if he or she doesn't understand an idea the first time it is presented, that it will be repeated later.

Some listening habits. (Marc P. Anderson)

We can miss a great deal of valuable information as a result of such laziness. We are lazy listeners in other ways, too. Did you know that we listen more closely to a message with which we strongly disagree than to a message we feel less strongly about?[5] If you were not aware of this, listen closely the next time you hear a controversial message being presented. You may learn something about the necessity to listen more closely to those to whom you are *less* opposed.

It is not unusual for several barriers to affect any one listening situation. Let us examine the following situation and identify the various barriers that seem to be in operation.

Joan, a college junior, returned to her hometown to attend her high school class reunion. When she arrived at the school, Joan was not sure where the party was being held, but she quickly realized that a lot of noise seemed to be coming from the gymnasium. After mingling with the crowd, Joan spotted a few friends, who waved to her to come over. Just as they started to talk, a rock band began to play, making conversation al-

[5]Virginia Buchli and W. Barnett Pearce, "Listening Behavior in Coorientational States," *Journal of Communication* 24 (1974): 62–70.

ATTENTION FAILURE CAUSES ACCIDENTS

A new technique, the American Diagnostic Method, may be able to identify individuals who are most likely to suffer attention failures, and thus be more accident prone. This technique is a modification of a method developed by a Russian psychologist, A. A. Grunbaum, in 1925. Grunbaum investigated the wandering attention of mental patients by painting numerals on a blackboard in random order and recording the amount of time it took each patient to locate the numbers in their correct order.

The American Diagnostic Method revealed that people involved in the most accidents tended to be either exceptionally fast or unusually slow in locating the numbers. Slow performance indicated momentary attention gaps,

ADM TEST				
26	15	38	28	57
12	24	44	51	23
25	41	17	53	38
52	18	21	31	46

while extremely rapid performance implied the sacrifice of accuracy to speed. The authors of the test claim that the attention-deficient person may excel at athletics, but may also run a greater risk of being involved in an automobile accident.

Adapted from *Psychology Today* 9 (June 1975): 84–85.

most impossible (external interference). After the music the host of the evening, the high school principal, invited everyone to sit down. Since Joan was senior-class secretary, she was invited to sit on the stage at the head table. She found herself at the very end of a long rectangular table, isolated from most of the conversation (seating arrangement). To make matters worse, sitting next to Joan was, of all people, "Big Wally," whose invitation to sit on the stage resulted from his having been elected "class clown." Joan sighed with resignation, deciding she would be eating in silence. Every time Wally tried to speak, Joan cut him off (status and roles; prejudging).

After the meal the former principal addressed the crowd. Seated on the stage, Joan was in a very conspicuous spot. She sat sideways in her chair, focusing in the direction of the speaker, nodding her head every so often as if in agreement, pretending to be listening to every word (faking attention). Knowing she might be asked to comment on the speech some time later in the evening, Joan realized she had better get the main idea of what was said (listening only for main ideas). After several minutes her mind began to wander and she started to think about some of the friends whom she hadn't yet seen (internal interference). After fifteen minutes the principal was still speaking and Joan tuned him out completely (avoiding the uninteresting). Finally, Joan joined in the applause that signaled time for dessert.

Because so many of the factors that affect listening affect it in a negative way, it is very important to work on developing good listening skills.

As mentioned earlier, you listen best if you are motivated to listen; and it helps you to listen if you remind yourself of your motivation be-

Developing
Effective
Listening Skills

> Nothing that man possesses is more precious than his awareness.
>
> Robert Deropp

fore the speaker begins: "If I am ever going to find this gas station, I'd better listen carefully to the directions." It also helps if you make a conscious effort to pay attention. You know when your mind is beginning to wander. If you let it go, you may miss the whole point of the communication; but if you make yourself pay attention at the beginning, it is more likely that you won't wander off in the middle. In addition, it is important to keep an open mind, free of prejudice. The speaker should be judged on what he or she says, not on what you wanted or expected to be said.

RESPONSIBILITIES OF THE LISTENER   As an integral part of the communication process, the listener has specific responsibilities, the most important of which is not only to pay attention, as we've just mentioned, but also to show active signs of attentiveness. A speaker can usually judge the listener's level of attention by the facial expressions, gestures, and nods that express listening activity. A smile or nod can indicate support, while a frown or shake of the head suggests disapproval.

There are specific actions we can take to improve listening attentiveness. During the course of a communication, the active listener might choose to reflect the message back to the speaker by periodically interjecting comments such as, "You're saying that you feel. . . ." Such comments enable you to play an active part in listening as well as to clear up any misunderstanding before it gets out of hand. By just listening passively, you may miss out on part of the communication or misinterpret the message being sent. The listener should also try to recognize the speaker's intent or purpose. You might be inclined to listen more sympathetically to a friend's seemingly endless description of the beach house she has rented for the summer if you suspect an invitation is forthcoming.

You normally have a certain amount of free time during the listening process because of the ***thinking-speaking time differential.*** Since you can think several times faster than someone can talk, you should have enough time to summarize and evaluate what is heard. While evaluating a speaker's message, you should try to figure out the speaker's view of the world and how that influences what he or she is saying. For example, if you know that the politician to whom you are listening believes that national defense is the government's first priority, you can evaluate how this view affects his or her stand on the particular issues being discussed—military spending, foreign aid, the draft, and so forth.

Above all, always attempt to use your powers of concentration to the greatest extent. The most effective way to overcome psychological or environmental barriers to listening is simply by good concentration.

To sum up, you can improve your listening behavior just by being aware of what is happening in a communication situation. Chances are that you already know many ways to be a better listener, but the trick is actually to behave that way during a real listening situation. Some of the most desirable listening behaviors include the following:

1. Concentrate all your physical and mental energies on listening.
2. Avoid interrupting the speaker when possible.
3. Demonstrate interest and alertness.
4. Seek areas of agreement with the speaker.
5. Search for meanings and avoid getting hung up on specific words.
6. Demonstrate patience. Remember, you can listen faster than the speaker can speak.
7. Provide clear and unambiguous feedback to the speaker.
8. Repress the tendency to respond emotionally to what is said.
9. Ask questions when you don't understand something.
10. Withhold evaluation of the message until the speaker is finished and you are sure you understand the message.

FEEDBACK

Communication is a circular process. As a message is transmitted from sender to receiver, a return message, known as *feedback,* is transmitted in the opposite direction. Feedback is a message that indicates the level of understanding or agreement between two or more communicators in response to an original message. Feedback represents a listener's verbal or nonverbal commentary on the message being communicated.

Feedback is an ongoing process that usually begins as a reaction to various aspects of the initial message. For example, a definite response is being fed back to the speaker when we shake our heads affirmatively or look quizzically at him. Feedback plays an essential role in helping us to determine whether or not our message has been understood, whether it is being received positively or negatively, and whether our audience is open or defensive, self-controlled or bored. Feedback can warn us that we must alter our communication to achieve the desired effect. If we are not aware of feedback, or don't pay any attention to it, there is a strong possibility that our efforts at communicating will be completely ineffective.

To emphasize the importance of the feedback mechanism in communication, you need only imagine yourself growing up for the last eighteen years or so, never having received any feedback. No one has praised you as you learned to walk or ride a bike. No one has warned you not to chase a ball into the street or to put your hand on a hot stove. No one has shared your tears or laughter. You probably would not function well at all. How would you appraise your self-concept? What values or morals would you possess? While such an existence is impossible, since a certain amount of feedback comes from you yourself as well as from others in the environment, this example does suggest the various functions and effects of feedback in the communication process.

Types of Feedback

There are two types of feedback: self-feedback and listener feedback (see Figure 3–2).

Self-feedback applies to the words and actions that are fed back into your central nervous system as you perceive your own muscular movements and hear yourself speak. Feeling your tongue twist as you mispronounce a word or, in a library, suddenly realizing that you are speaking too loudly are examples of self-feedback. Another example would be hearing yourself use a word incorrectly, or reversing sounds; for example, asking, "Were you sappy or had?" instead of "happy or sad."

Research indicates that self-feedback is both enjoyable and necessary for normal development. Linguists maintain, for example, that a baby in the *babbling stage* finds pleasure in the actual production of sounds as well as in hearing those sounds. The importance of self-feedback is indicated by findings showing that deaf babies start to babble at the same time hearing babies do, but because they can't hear their babblings, they begin to lose interest, which limits their vocal play.[6] Interestingly enough, visual feedback (through the use of mirrors suspended over deaf babies' cribs) has increased babbling and vocal activity.

The other major type of feedback, *listener feedback,* involves verbal and nonverbal responses. Verbal feedback may take the form of questions or comments. A listener may, for instance, ask a speaker to explain the last point or may give praise for making the story so interesting. Non-

FIGURE 3-2 Self-Feedback and Listener Feedback.

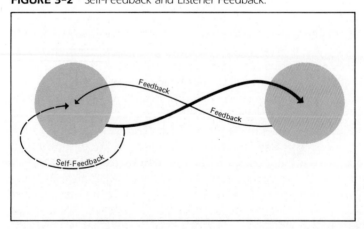

[6]Charles Van Riper, *Speech Correction,* 4th ed. (Englewood Cliffs, N.J.: Prentice-Hall, 1963), p. 79.

verbal feedback may be transmitted by applause or laughter, to indicate approval, or by a blank stare, which might indicate disinterest or confusion. Even silence can act as feedback. If a teacher asks a question and no one answers, the silence may indicate lack of knowledge, misunderstanding, or perhaps dislike of the teacher. If a father asks his son if he has finished his homework and the son doesn't reply, that silence is meaningful.

Feedback serves various functions in the communication process. The first of these functions is to evaluate what is right or wrong about a particular communication. If you give a speech to the class, your teacher will offer criticism and suggestions for improving your delivery. If someone is watching you hang a painting, he or she will give you feedback as you try various positions, to help you find the right place for it. As will be discussed in Chapter 4, nonverbal feedback in the form of nods and hand movements helps to regulate turn taking in conversation.

Feedback can also serve to stimulate change. For example, a popular entertainment magazine, after changing its format by drastically shortening the descriptions of programs in the TV section of the magazine, received so much feedback in the form of angry letters from readers that the publisher not only resumed the program descriptions but elaborated on them as well.

Functions of Feedback

Feedback to stimulate change. (Marc P. Anderson)

A third function of feedback is to reinforce, to give reward or punishment. A father says, "I'm proud of you, son" or "Jim, can't you ever keep quiet!" When used in this way, rewarding feedback encourages certain behaviors, while punishing feedback is intended to discourage certain behaviors. Comedians rely on positive reinforcement from their audience in the form of laughter—and their performance may improve if they sense that the audience feedback is positive.

Effects of Feedback
If you have ever made a phone call and found yourself talking to an answering machine, or prepared and sent a tape to a friend overseas, you may have felt somewhat uncomfortable or even foolish. It is difficult to sound conversational when there is no one on the other end to respond. This example suggests that feedback is an essential part of the communication process. We can see this through the effects of feedback.

Probably the most important effect of feedback on the communication process is in improving the accuracy of understanding. For example, a teacher seeing only blank stares during a complicated lecture might make a conscious effort to repeat and clarify certain points until the audience shows signs of nodding in agreement. As this example indicates, feedback may increase the amount of time necessary for a communication interaction to be completed. Nonetheless, it ensures a more thoroughly and clearly transmitted message.

In terms of intrapersonal and interpersonal communication, the most significant effect of feedback, and one that is often long range, is its impact on self-concept. Surely you know people who have very poor self-images and little feeling of self-worth. It is probable that such individuals have based this self-image on punishing feedback received from family and peers during crucial periods of identity development. On the other hand, an individual who has had considerable rewarding feedback from family and friends is likely to develop a favorable self-concept.

Feedback also affects performance. Sometimes improved performance results from improved self-image. An experiment conducted by music educator Elizabeth Elrod, for example, indicated that elementary education majors could improve their singing ability through the use of positive self-concept building and video feedback. Before the training session, 90 percent of the students claimed they could not sing, but after ten weeks those students who had heard taped replays of their singing were judged by independent observers to be much improved.[7]

Feedback can work in two directions, however. For example, a beginning tennis player who has been praised for being skilled at the sport (rewarding feedback) will probably perceive it to be an easier game than one who performs equally well but has received harsh criticism (punishing feedback). Similarly, a student who fails a test (punishing feedback) may aim for just passing the next one instead of working for an A. Thus, we can see that feedback also affects performance expectations.

[7]"Everybody Sing," *Human Behavior* 4 (August 1975): 63.

Another important effect of feedback on performance concerns task behavior, particularly in small groups. When people find themselves in small group situations in which they don't know the other members of the group, they often suffer from feelings of rejection and hostility. These negative feelings can keep the group from performing any type of cooperative work. Positive reinforcement from group members, as well as from outside observers, will help the group interact better and will ultimately improve performance. For example, a group of quarrelsome young children complimented on how well they are cleaning up their play area may continue the task with renewed enthusiasm.

Feedback can also affect your attitude toward your own messages or toward the messages of others. There is an extensive body of research on this aspect of feedback. Basically, the findings indicate that feedback favorable to a particular message causes the communicator of the message to believe in it more strongly, and causes others to become more favorably disposed to the message than they had been at the start.[8] Punishing feedback, on the other hand, causes negative attitude change in both the speaker and the listener. We have all had experiences which, though less controlled than research studies, help to clarify the findings of these attitude-change experiments. Perhaps you remember a time when you were in a theater, watching a comedy that you and the rest of the audience did not find amusing. No one was laughing. Yet when several members of the audience later began to laugh loudly, your reaction somehow became more favorable. Soon you were laughing, too. This is the reason for using laugh tracks in television situation comedies.

GIVING EFFECTIVE FEEDBACK

Feedback is often so spontaneous that you are unaware of giving or receiving it. Nevertheless, there are ways to consciously make your feedback more effective. One method is to focus on observations rather than inferences. For example, consider the following situation: A young woman passes a friend whom she has dated several times. She says hello, but her friend walks right on by. The next time she sees him, she asks, "Hey, are you mad at me? You ignored me the other day when I saw you downtown." She has assumed a negative motive behind the man's action, although he may simply have been preoccupied. The woman's feedback to her friend would have been more productive if she had relayed the facts, and only the facts, as she understood them: "Hey, I saw you the other day and called to you, but you didn't reply." This would permit the man to make an honest response rather than a defensive one.

Another method for increasing the effectiveness of your feedback is to use description rather than judgment. The captain of a basketball team would be more helpful in coaching her players if she said, "You're not

---

[8]John Gardiner, "A Synthesis of Experimental Studies of Speech Communication Feedback," *Journal of Communication* 21 (March 1971): 23.

running for the ball and you're moving too slowly," as opposed to, "You're really getting lazy."

It is also important to give immediate feedback. We often delay our responses to problems and conflicts and wait for emotions to die down. It is better to deal with anger or hurt when it occurs, when you are in touch with your reactions. Feedback at the time is more specific and accurate than it can be, say, two months later. Yet sometimes extreme emotions make you overreact or respond in ways you regret later on. Again, your feedback should be appropriate to the situation, and controlled to the extent possible.

Limiting feedback is another means of increasing its effectiveness, particularly in a one-to-one situation in which you are the listener. Constantly nodding or interjecting comments in such situations is interfering, at best, and may show superficiality and insincerity, at worst. Thus, it is necessary to guard against overresponding. A smile or nod of agreement to particularly significant statements does more to show that you understand than continuous "uh-huhs."

The act of using conscious feedback techniques may sometimes seem unnatural. However, it is important to remember that effective feedback does improve the communication process. While feedback that is entirely calculated tends to be stilted, awareness of the feedback mechanism and the messages you are transmitting is an asset to communication.

SUMMARY

Despite the importance of listening in the communication process, studies have shown that many of us are poor listeners. We often take listening for granted and place little, if any, importance on developing good listening skills.

The listening process involves six distinct stages: hearing, the physical reception of stimuli; attention, the focused perception of verbal or nonverbal stimuli; understanding, the interpretation of stimuli into messages, which are then cognitively and affectively evaluated; remembering, the storage of these messages; evaluating, weighing evidence, sorting fact from opinion, and, on the basis of these, rendering judgment; and responding, completing the process through verbal and/or nonverbal feedback.

Listening may also be classified along an active-passive continuum, as a function of degree of involvement, as well as along a social-serious continuum, depending on the degree of formality and structure in the context. These classifications, in turn, may be categorized as courteous, appreciative, and conversational listening (on the social end of the continuum) and critical versus discriminative listening (on the serious end of the continuum).

Effective listening can be helped or hindered by factors related to the environmental setting, the source of the message, the type of message, or the personality variables of the listener. Because so many of these factors affect listening in a negative way, it is the listener's responsibility to try to improve his or her listening skills in both social and serious situations.

Perhaps the most important responsibility of the listener is to transmit effective feedback to the speaker. Simply stated, feedback is a reaction to various aspects of a particular message. It may be communicated through verbal comments or nonverbal gestures. While feedback is usually identified with reactions of the listener, there is also a certain amount of self-feedback, which takes place inside the communicator.

Both self-feedback and listener feedback function to regulate performance in communication processes, to stimulate change in listeners, and to reinforce selected behavior patterns. Feedback ensures greater accuracy in interpreting messages. On a psychological level feedback affects our self-concept. Rewarding feedback tends to improve self-image and attitudes, while punishing feedback has the opposite effect. Feedback in groups can help to improve performance of the assigned tasks. Finally, feedback can produce changes in a communicator's attitude toward his or her own messages or toward the messages transmitted by others.

While most feedback is communicated without your full awareness, it is possible to adopt conscious strategies to make your feedback more effective. These strategies focus on observations rather than inferences and on description rather than judgment. In addition, they stress immediate but controlled feedback. Remembering such strategies in everyday feedback situations ensures more effective communication and listening.

Exercises

GROUP EXPERIENCES

Do You Really Understand What I Am Saying?

Description: We use the word *understand* very loosely. Most of the time we mean that we are "hearing" something and translating it into the way we perceive the world—and then we call this phenomenon "understanding." The following experience is an opportunity to see how well you understand another person and how well he or she understands you.

Procedure: Divide into groups of three. Persons A and B should discuss an issue they find controversial. Person C should observe the interaction that takes place and report after the exercise is completed. After each communication between Person A and Person B, the listening partner should attempt to paraphrase the speaker's position until the speaker accepts the paraphrase. An example of this interaction would be as follows:

Person A: I think that war is a waste in general. On the other hand, George Kennan claims that war can clear the path for a new form of government to emerge.

Person B: What I heard you say is that war isn't too bad as long as it serves to clear the way for better forms of government.

Person A: I will not accept your paraphrase.

This process will continue until Person B provides an acceptable paraphrase for Person A. The person doing the paraphrasing should try to use different words than those of the speaker. The interaction should take from 15 to 20 minutes. At the end of that time, Person C should offer an appraisal of what occurred.

Discussion: When you have completed this activity, ask yourself these questions: How long did it take you to provide accurate paraphrases for your partner? How long did it take your partner to provide accurate paraphrases of your position? Was your verbal message clear? What are the implications of this activity? Does it suggest that most of the time we truly do not understand what another person is saying?

Did You See What I Saw?

Description: Our psychological make-up causes us to attend selectively to different stimuli, but we do not necessarily select the same stimuli as another person. We truly see the world through our own set of filters. The following activity demonstrates this idea.

Procedure: Have one person arrange approximately thirty different items on a tray, such as a can opener, lipstick, a pen, a paperclip, and so on. Include (1) items that most people would not know the name of, such as a special tool; (2) items that are typically used by one sex as opposed to the other (pipe, lipstick); and (3) items that are taboo, such as underwear, a sanitary napkin, and so on.

Each individual may take 20 seconds to look at (not touch) the items on the tray. Immediately after you view the tray, try to list everything you saw. (Afterwards you may wish to check your list against a complete list of the items on the tray.)

Discussion: The most obvious finding of this experiment is that people will remember different things. Were the first five items you remembered different from the first five items others remembered? Did you remember the male items? the female items? Did you attempt to describe the items for which you did not have a particular name? By comparison, did you remember more, less, or the same number of items as other people did? Do you selectively attend in listening as well as in seeing?

Silence Is Golden

Description: Most of us are poor listeners. We are usually thinking about what we want to say rather than about what the other person is saying. Try the following experiment, and check out your own listening behavior.

Procedure: Divide into dyads. Person A should begin the conversation by describing a peak experience—a high point in his or her life. Person A should talk in short stretches, no more than 30 seconds at a time.

Person B must then wait 10 seconds before continuing the conversation. Person B should either respond to A or describe a peak experience of his or her own. The same guideline of length applies to Person B.

This process continues with each person waiting 10 seconds before speaking.

Discussion: Does it feel awkward to wait before talking? At which point in listening do you begin to think about what you are going to say? Do you usually try to avoid these "silent spaces"? By the way, are you a good listener?

PERSONAL EXPERIENCES

1. Change the type of feedback you normally give people. For example, listen to a person in a one-to-one interaction without giving any verbal or nonverbal feedback. Make sure that you are not unconsciously nodding your head or shifting your position. Observe the person's reactions to the absence of feedback. After the conversation is over, ask how the person felt—if he or she noticed anything peculiar during the course of the interaction.

2. Take a ride with a friend in a car, on a bus, or on a bicycle. Ride for about 20 minutes and then discuss what each of you observed about your physical surroundings during the ride. Did you notice different things, people, places? Why did you observe different things? Do you tend to associate with people who select the same "stimuli" in the world as you do?

3. Observe yourself during a class of your choice—particularly one in which there is a lecture presentation. Watch the number of times your attention wanders—and for how long.

4. Sit in a public area, such as a library, a town square, or a park, and close your eyes for 10 minutes. Listen to the different sounds around you and try to determine what you are hearing. Would you normally be hearing these sounds if you had your eyes open? How aware are you of different sounds? Do you selectively listen during everyday activities?

DISCUSSION QUESTIONS

1. How do we distinguish **listening** from **hearing**?
2. What qualities does a good listener possess?
3. What effective methods of verbal and nonverbal feedback can you use as a good listener?
4. How does the type of feedback provided by a listener affect the communicator?

NONVERBAL COMMUNICATION

4

Exploratory Questions

1. What are six functions of nonverbal communication?
2. Can you define and illustrate five types of body expressions?
3. What are some examples of nonverbal communication conveyed by facial expressions and eye behavior?
4. What is proxemics and how does physical distance affect communication?
5. How do your clothing and personal appearance affect communication?
6. What five environmental factors influence communication?
7. Why is touch important as a form of nonverbal communication?
8. How do the senses of smell and taste act as communication media?
9. What is paralanguage and what are some of the stereotypes based on paralanguage cues?
10. How can understanding nonverbal communication patterns enable you to relate more effectively to yourself and others?

Much of the time, we communicate through spoken and written language, but our body movements, gestures, and facial expressions are frequently more eloquent than any verbal statement. Even when we try to hide our thoughts and feelings, our nonverbal behavior still sends out messages. We communicate in spite of ourselves.

This chapter is designed to improve your understanding of these often overlooked nonverbal patterns. Perhaps because we acquire nonverbal behavior so early in life, we seldom have reason to think about it afterwards. However, there is a great deal that can be learned from nonverbal expressions—your own and everyone else's.

Before we continue, it is important to emphasize one point: No element of nonverbal behavior—be it a wink, a slouch, a tone of voice, or a gesture—can be interpreted in isolation. Verbal and nonverbal behavior are complementary; neither is really complete without the other. In addition, if we are to fully understand the nature of the nonverbal communication process, we must also consider the context, or the overall situation in which nonverbal behavior occurs, and its relationship to an individual's entire verbal and nonverbal behavior patterns.

FUNCTIONS OF NONVERBAL COMMUNICATION

Nonverbal communication plays an important role in many everyday interchanges. Six basic functions of nonverbal communication are repeating, substituting, complementing, deceiving, regulating, and accenting.

Repeating   "Me?" said José, with wide, innocent eyes, pointing his index finger to his chest. "I'd never do something like that!"

When we communicate with one another, we use words and their nonverbal equivalents at the same time. For example, verbal statements of agreement or disagreement ("Right, right"; "No way"; "Are you kidding?") are often accompanied by a nod or shake of the head to indicate positive or negative feelings. We call these nonverbal gestures *repeating* messages because they convey the same meaning as the verbal message. Of course, either the words or the nods by themselves would be enough—but repeating messages are done almost without thinking. They are a very basic part of language behavior, occurring naturally, without conscious thought or intent.

They were not allowed to say a word, but you knew exactly how they felt by looking at their faces.   **Substituting**

When hearing or speaking is impossible, nonverbal communication often replaces verbal messages. In such instances nonverbal messages are called **substitutes,** because they take the place of words. Thus, someone directing you into a tight parking space might substitute gestures for words when the car's noisy engine prohibits speaking. Another kind of substitution is made when someone with whom you've had an argument attacks you with "looks that could kill."

For nonverbal communication to act as a substitute, it must be recognized and, more importantly, interpreted in the same way by most of the people in a specific group, subculture, or culture. For example, people in the United States interpret the "thumbs down" sign to mean "no." Such well-known substitutes are so universal that they have been recorded in dictionaries of American gestures. Misunderstandings may occur, however, when we try to use our culture's nonverbal substitutes in another culture. Thus, Americans who say "I" by pointing to their chests would not be understood in Japan, where "I" is symbolized by pointing to one's nose.

"You don't believe it hurt, huh? Well, just let me shove you the way that idiot shoved me. You'll see!"   **Complementing**

We also use nonverbal language to complement, complete, or accent explanations of how to do something or in descriptions of specific sizes or shapes. To understand how important these *complementing* actions can be, just try the following, without using nonverbal behavior: Teach a new dance step, explain how to tie a slip knot, or describe the shape of an hourglass.

Complementing behaviors are also used to emphasize emotional feelings or attitudes. The same complementing gesture can accompany quite different emotions, however:

> The five finalists in the essay contest stepped onto the stage. When the fourth runner-up was announced, the remaining contestants applauded loudly. When the winner was finally announced, the first runner-up applauded, but as she congratulated the new winner, tears streamed down her face.

> He that has eyes to see and ears to hear may convince himself
> that no mortal can keep a secret. If his lips are silent, he
> chatters with his fingertips; betrayal oozes out of him at every
> pore.
>
> Sigmund Freud

In this example the complementing gesture of applause was used in each instance—first to express a positive response (relief at still being "in the running") and then to accompany a negative response (disappointment).

Deceiving/ Revealing

"I'll see you and raise you five bucks," Kelly said with his usual poker face.

Sometimes we purposely deceive others or supply them with false information. You may not like a friend's new haircut, for example, but still say, "Your hair looks great!" to avoid hurting his feelings. At the same time that you are saying this and staring convincingly into your friend's eyes, you may be nervously pulling at your coat buttons. If your friend is sensitive to nonverbal behavior, he or she may pick up this contradictory message.

Deception clues (for example, an overly exaggerated smile or a too severe frown) suggest possible falsehood but do not tell what information is being withheld or falsified. *Leakage,* on the other hand, implies "spilling the beans" about the withheld information. For example, biting a fingernail can leak nervousness, or a clenched fist can leak the desire to fight.

Research on deception has demonstrated a relationship between the message-sending ability of a body part and the deception clues and leakage it reveals. Specifically, the face and the eyes are the best senders of messages. Their expressions are easily and quickly disseminated to the observer. Because so much attention is paid to our facial features, however, we all learn to alter these when we want to deceive someone. At the same time, little attention is paid to our hands, legs, and feet. Thus, unconscious movements of these appendages are often dead giveaways of our thoughts. In short, our faces and eyes are the most expressive but tell the most lies, while our hands and feet don't say as much but often tell the truth. Remember this the next time you really want to know what someone is thinking. Listen to the words, look at the facial expressions, but don't forget to look down at the hands and feet. Somewhere in the body's actions, the truth prevails.

Regulating

Lily knew her father wanted to talk. She could feel his steady gaze upon her. As she turned and looked at him, he said, "Lily. . . ."

One of the most common purposes of nonverbal communication is **regulating.** Let's say that you and a friend are discussing a movie you saw the other night. Without regulating messages you might sound something like this:

"Hey, did you catch the movie at the Plaza the other night? O.K., I'm finished talking for the moment. You can speak."
"Thank you. I wanted to answer your question. Yeah. Great. Especially that scene in the woods. . . ."
"Can I talk?"
"You want to talk again? Sure."
"Thanks. I just wanted to say that I let out the biggest scream during that part!"

Fortunately, typical conversations don't require this kind of verbal permission to speak or respond. Instead, nonverbal cues automatically keep the conversation flowing between the turn yielder (the person who has just spoken and is allowing the other to speak) and the turn requester (the person who wishes to speak).

The nonverbal behaviors that mean "I want to talk" and "It's your turn to talk" are rules of interaction that we learn early in life. Nodding and looking at the area around the eyes of the other person are two examples of such nonverbal gestures. Speakers steadily increase the amount of time they spend looking at the listener as their speaking turn nears completion. There is also an increase in the amount of listener nodding as his or her turn to speak approaches. How fast the listener nods and whether or not the nods are accompanied by short verbal statements such as "sure" determine whether or not the listener is requesting time to respond. Slow, silent nods in response to the speaker's request for feedback usually increase the chances that the speaker will continue.

Ed slammed the book shut. "Oh, what's the use! There's no way I'll learn all this by tomorrow!"

Accenting

Another function of nonverbal communication is **accenting,** the use of gestures such as nods, blinks, squints, and shrugs to help emphasize or punctuate spoken words:

Adrienne's cocker spaniel just won first prize in the dog show. As she leads him out of the ring, friends and family congratulate both Adrienne and the dog with warm words, but also with pats on the back.

Accenting can also be achieved by changing the pitch or stress on a word or group of words. In fact, our entire meaning often depends on which words are accented:

I want to dance with him.
I want to dance with *him.*
I want to *dance* with him.

TYPES OF NONVERBAL COMMUNICATION

Many people, because of popularized reading, consider body language to be the only form of nonverbal communication. However, nonverbal communication includes body language and much, much more. Each day we signal our moods, attitudes, and values to others nonverbally. Have you ever dressed up for a job interview, hugged a friend, been late for an appointment, wanted to sit in a certain seat in a class, or used your hands while talking? If so, you were communicating to others nonverbally. Often we are unaware of our nonverbal behaviors. In our attempt to increase sensitivity to different types of our nonverbal behavior, we will examine kinesics and body movement, facial expressions, eye behavior, personal appearance, clothing, proxemics, environmental factors, paralanguage, touch, and taste and smell.

Kinesics and Body Movement The human body is so incredibly versatile that it can send thousands of nonverbal messages. In fact, it is hard to know just how to classify all of these nonverbal communications. Ray Birdwhistell, a pioneer in the field of nonverbal communication, coined the word **kinesics** to describe the study of body movement. Early researchers divided body expressions according to the part of the body involved—facial expression, trunk movements, hand gestures, and so forth.

Birdwhistell viewed body expressions as a language, which, like French or Russian, can be studied, learned, and understood. Recent specialists such as Paul Ekman and Wallace Friesen have focused on the general functions of nonverbal communication discussed previously and have come up with five classes of specific body expressions: emblems, illustrators, regulators, affect displays, and body manipulators.[1]

EMBLEMS **Emblems** are commonly recognized signs (usually gestures) that communicate a message usually unrelated to an ongoing conversation. For example, if you and a co-worker suddenly realized that your animated conversation was disturbing an office mate, you might hold an index finger to your lips. This indication to talk more quietly serves to reduce the volume of your conversation without interrupting its flow. We learn such emblems early through imitation and continue to use them throughout our lives (see Figure 4–1).

FIGURE 4–1   Can You Identify These Emblems?

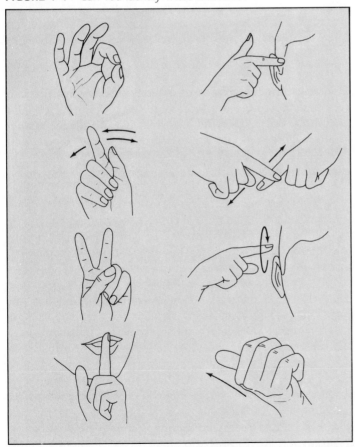

[1]P. Ekman and W. V. Friesen, "The Repertoire of Non-Verbal Behavior: Categories, Origins, Usage, and Coding," *Semiotica* 1, no. 1 (1969): 49–98.

(Ken Karp)

ILLUSTRATORS These body expressions illustrate the verbal language they accompany. *Illustrators* may accent or add emphasis to a phrase; show the direction of thought; point to an object or place; depict spatial relationships, rhythms, or bodily actions; or demonstrate shape. You are using an illustrator when you point to someone across the room while shouting his or her name, or when you use your hands to estimate the length of the fish that got away.

REGULATORS As we explained in the previous section, *regulators* control verbal communication. Regulators such as gazes, nods, and raised eyebrows assist in the exchange of listening and speaking roles among participants in a communication setting. They provide smooth transitions in conversations.

AFFECT DISPLAYS Body changes that convey our internal emotional states are *affect displays.* These emotional displays can involve facial expressions such as angry stares or wide-eyed fear or body movements such as trembling hands or knocking knees. Affect displays are not always strictly tied to what we are saying at the time. For example, a ticket agent may be surprised by the deep sadness that lines the face of a man who has just asked for a ticket on the next plane to Pittsburgh, unaware that the passenger is going home to attend the funeral of a loved one. Because facial affect displays are easily simulated, they often function as deceptors—thus the expression "Smiling on the outside but crying on the inside."

> Beware of the man whose belly does not move when he laughs.
>
> Chinese Proverb

BODY MANIPULATORS ***Body manipulators*** are movements that originally were associated with body functioning—for instance, scratching an itch or rubbing the eyes—but that have come to be used unconsciously and independently of bodily needs. We are all familiar with body manipulators such as rubbing the hands together or pulling an earlobe while talking. Other body manipulators involve the listener (patting someone's hand repeatedly while talking) or handy objects (using a pencil for doodling during a long phone conversation). Body movements such as these, however, are not body manipulators simply because there is contact among body parts.[2] Some may be classified as emblems or illustrators, such as placing the forefinger to the temple as an emblem for thought, or tapping the wrist as an illustrator of the question, "Do you have the correct time?"

BODY MOVEMENT AND POSTURE Body movements fall into one of several different categories of body expressions. How you walk, for instance, is often a strong indicator of how you feel. When you have a problem you may walk very slowly, with your head down and your hands clasped behind your back. You may even pause to kick a rock on the ground. On the other hand, when you feel especially proud and happy, you may walk with your chin raised, your arms swinging freely, and your legs somewhat stiff—with a bounce in your step.

We all know how to "read" such obvious nonverbal cues, but conscious and sustained effort can help you to pick up even more subtle expressions of the nonverbal language. For example, you sometimes use your body parts to show that you are or are not associated with the people near you. Thus, crossing your legs in the same way the person next to you crosses hers may indicate identification with that person. Or, if you are standing and arguing with three other people, you may soon find yourself assuming the body posture of the person with whom you agree—both of you standing with your hands on your hips, for instance, while your two opponents may also assume like postures.

Other movements and gestures show openness and honesty. Holding the hands open while talking indicates sincerity: Hands clenched into fists do the opposite. Similarly, if someone unbuttons or even takes off

---

[2]P. Ekman, "Three Classes of Nonverbal Behavior," in *Aspects of Nonverbal Communication,* ed. W. von Raffler-Engel (Lisse: Swets and Zeitlinger, B.V., 1980), p. 96.

(Ken Karp)

his or her coat in your presence, this conveys openness and friendliness toward you.

In contrast to these gestures of openness are those that indicate defensiveness. The crossed-arm-on-chest position is perhaps the best known defensive gesture. Charles Darwin identified it as a universal trait in all societies, one that can strongly influence the behavior of observers. In fact, communication often comes to a complete halt when someone assumes this position, which says, in effect, "I have now withdrawn from this conversation." Of course, this is not true every time someone crosses his or her arms. However, if it happens during a conversation, you might examine what you have just said or done that would have prompted a withdrawal.

Even the way you sit communicates information. Someone speaking while his or her legs dangle over the arm of a chair might be saying, "I am not feeling cooperative. In fact, I am unconcerned or hostile to your feelings or needs." Similarly, people who sit backwards on chairs or put their feet up on a desk may be signaling their feelings of superiority, saying, "I am the dominant person here."

Such reflections of dominance seem to perpetuate sex role stereotypes. Men, for example, characteristically express dominance by taking up more space in a bed than a woman; crossing their legs at the thighs (which takes up a considerable amount of room); and looking into a woman's eyes while talking to her. Women, on the other hand, often use submissive gestures when they are with men: compressing their bodies into a small space in bed; crossing their legs at the ankles or sitting with uncrossed legs held tightly together (which takes up very little space); and looking down when talking to men. We shall explore such spatial relationships and eye behavior later in the chapter.

The face is perhaps the most obvious vehicle for nonverbal communica- Facial
Expressions
tion. It is a constant source of information to those around us.

When something makes you happy or sad (or produces any other feeling), your nerves immediately send a message to the face, which causes the muscles to contract or relax. The feedback you get from these muscle movements is one of the cues that tells you what emotional feeling you are having. This process is a form of internal self-feedback in intrapersonal communication, which will be discussed in the following chapter.

Think of all the things your face can say about you without your saying a word. Things such as wrinkles, baldness, and coloring comment not only on your age but also on the kind of life you lead—we suspect that people with rich tans spend a considerable amount of time outdoors. The length and style of your hair (and/or beard) and the amount of makeup you wear suggest your economic status, interest in fashion, and sometimes even your politics. All of these things, plus the facial expressions that reveal emotion, can speak for you before you ever open your mouth.

Charles Darwin first argued that many of our facial expressions evolved from the lower animals, and scientists are still debating this issue. On one side of the debate, some research has yielded support for Darwin's theory about universal behaviors.

One study, for example, used photographs of different facial expressions, which were shown to college students in Japan, the United States, Brazil, Chile, and Argentina.[3] Observers from these countries generally agreed on the emotion portrayed by each picture. However, when the identical photographs were shown to Estonian and Kirghiz university students in the Soviet Union—with and without a description of the situation in which the emotional expression might occur—researchers found differences in students' recognition of the emotions when situational cues were supplied, while they found no differences from prior research when situational descriptions were not provided.[4] Results such as these support an alternative theory of facial expressions and their origins: It is the context of the event which supplies the meanings for facial expressions, and thus, it is our culture which is responsible for the ways in which we encode and decode facial expressions. Although the debate concerning the origin of facial expression continues, research has shown that cultures do indeed differ in their *uses* of facial expressions.

Because of dissimilar learning patterns, two cultures may react quite differently to the same stimulus—one, for example, showing disgust at

[3]Paul Ekman, "Face Muscles Talk Every Language," *Psychology Today* 9, no. 4 (September 1975): 36.
[4]T. Niit and J. Valsiner, "Recognition of Facial Expressions: An Experimental Investigation of Ekman's Model," *Tartu Riikliku Ulikooli Toimetised: Trudy po Psikhologii,* 429 (1977): 85–107.

TONGUE DISPLAY

We are all aware of the ways we consciously use our tongues—licking postage stamps and ice-cream cones, expressing disdain, and so forth. A team of researchers at the University of Pennsylvania have now come up with some interesting findings on the use of the tongue on an unconscious level. They discovered that the unconscious display of the tongue is a universal sign of aversion to social encounter. This sign is used not only by all races, both children and adults, but by primates such as orangutans and gorillas as well.

Observing children in a nursery school, Mrs. W. John Smith and Julia Chase noted that the young children tended to show their tongues when they were involved in difficult tasks, such as finger painting, and also when involved in an awkward social situation, such as being scolded. This suggested to the scientists that we display our tongues when we wish to be left alone.

The researchers observed identical behaviors among adults in the general public. Adults too show their tongues when absorbed in tasks requiring intense concentration, such as squeezing into a tight parking space, and when involved in socially threatening situations, for example, being interrupted in conversation.

Even gorillas and orangutans display their tongues in similar circumstances. Although apes show their tongues more prominently than do humans, they do so during complex tasks such as peeling bananas with their toes and in unpleasant situations such as being scolded.

Adapted from "What Your Tongue May Really Be Saying," *Newsweek* (2 April 1973): p. 46.

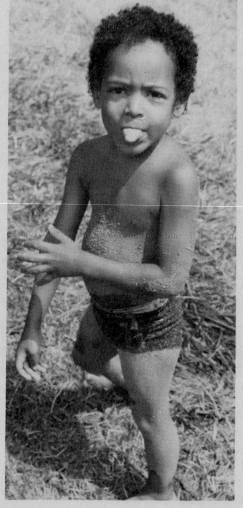

(William E. Frost)

the sight of an insect or snake and the other showing elation because it considers these animals delightfully delicious edibles.

Cultural rules and societal pressures often inhibit spontaneous facial expressions. At early ages children learn which expressions are acceptable and unacceptable by hearing, "If you keep frowning, your face will grow like that" or "A shot is nothing to be afraid of; you've got to act like a big boy now."[5] We also learn how to adapt our facial expressions to meet the

[5]M. L. Hamilton, "Imitative Behavior and Expressive Ability in Facial Expression of Emotion," *Developmental Psychology* 8 (1973): 138.

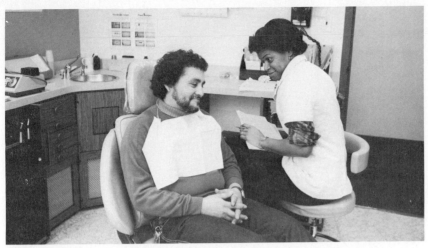
(Ken Karp)

expectations of others. How many times have you smiled politely when receiving an unwanted gift, held back tears after a bitter disappointment, or avoided laughing when watching someone trip over a curb? We all adjust many of our natural facial expressions to those considered to be more appropriate.

For centuries poets and painters have paid tribute to our expressive eyes. Modern-day researchers, too, have been intrigued by the eyes and the many nonverbal messages they convey.

Eye Behavior

Certain eye behaviors are associated with definite moods, reactions, or attitudes. For example, consider the common negative connotation of "small, beady eyes." We also hold stereotypes about eye pupil size. Research indicates that people with dilated pupils are usually rated more attractive and sincere, while those with smaller pupils are often associated with negative characteristics.[6] Similarly, children, with their large-pupiled eyes, seem to project nothing but innocence and sincerity, even when telling lies. Puppies and kittens exert similar eye attraction.

Eye contact is another significant eye behavior variable. Speakers who never look up seem formal or nervous. Speakers who do look at their audience during a speech seem more relaxed and informal. We also tend to feel that their speeches are more genuine. Likewise, a listener who does not look at the speaker detracts from the speaker's image of authority and control. Perhaps this is why angry teachers or parents command, "Look at me when I'm talking to you." Little or no eye contact from a listener may not always anger you, but it does indicate lack of interest in what you are saying.

Our discussion of conversation regulators mentioned some examples of eye behavior. Visual interactions are indeed used to regulate con-

[6]E. H. Hess, "Attitude and Pupil Size," *Scientific American* 212, no. 4 (1965): 54.

(Laimute E. Druskis)

versation. Usually the speaker catches the eye of the listener and thus the listener's attention. Before starting a long speech, however, the speaker will drop his or her eyes. Throughout the speech periodic eye checks ensure that the listener is still there and attentive. Conversely, eye contact is avoided during pauses when the speaker is groping for the right words. When finished, the speaker turns his or her gaze to the listener, signaling that the listener can now have the floor.

Despite this general pattern, there are great individual differences in visual behavior during conversation. Depending on the speaker, gazes directed at the other person can range from about 10 percent to more than 70 percent of the conversation time. It has been suggested that these differences are related to the patterns of dominance and submissiveness we mentioned earlier. Dominant, poised individuals tend to look more at others during conversations than do submissive, socially uneasy individuals.

Proxemics Just as we communicate with words, gestures, or facial expressions, so too can we transmit messages by placing ourselves in certain spatial relations with other persons or objects. The study of these spatial factors—how we react to the space about us, how we use that space, and how our use of space communicates certain information—is known as **proxemics.** For example, the amount of space a person is allowed often communicates the status of that person. Let's say that a household has three sons but only two children's bedrooms. In recognition of the eldest son's status, chances are that he will have a room to himself while the other two children share a room.

SPATIAL ZONES Edward T. Hall, a pioneer in the study of proxemics, specified four spatial zones of interpersonal communication: intimate distance, personal distance, social distance, and public distance.

Intimate distance stretches from actual contact to 18 inches. A parent and child, two intimate friends, or other close pairs would have contact in this zone. Of course, even strangers can be thrown into this intimate zone—on a crowded elevator, for example. However, such forced closeness is usually countered by silence, averted glances, and other nonverbal messages that say, "O.K., this is fine for now, but it's only going to last for a minute, because I don't really know you."

Personal distance, from $1\frac{1}{2}$ to 4 feet, is the zone we use for casual interactions. You would probably assume this distance when talking with a friend at a cocktail party. In contrast, *social distance,* from 4 to 12 feet, is used by people meeting for the first time or by people conducting business. *Public distance,* from 12 to over 25 feet, is most often used in formal address; for example, by a teacher lecturing students or by a politician speaking at a rally.

We also adapt our behavior when forced to interact in a different zone: For example, when even close friends are farther than 12 feet apart (public distance), they often speak in more formal phrases. On the other hand, casual acquaintances placed in an intimate distance usually whisper and use small rather than expansive gestures. Compare the gestures you use when sitting next to a friend to those used to shout a greeting to your neighbor across the street.

Consider also how people who are talking before they get on a crowded elevator usually stop abruptly when the doors close, then con-

(Teri Leigh Stratford)

(Marc Anderson)

tinue their conversation when they step out. It's interesting to note the reactions you get when you do keep a conversation going after entering an elevator. The other people in that confined space can't help hearing the conversation, but they will often turn away or lower their heads and pretend not to listen. It is even more interesting (despite the risk of some strange looks) to watch the response of others when you laugh out loud to yourself in this quiet atmosphere.

It is important to note that these spatial zones, though common for white, middle-class Americans, are by no means universal. Each culture has its own spatial needs. Thus, Arabs stand so close to each other while talking that they can easily touch and perceive body odors and heat—very different from our American "noncontact" culture. We may want to see and hear other people, but by no means do we wish to smell their body odor!

TERRITORIALITY   Scientists have long observed the territorial habits of animals but are only recently beginning to understand that humans exhibit similar territorial needs and controls. In fact, all of us carry our own personal space around with us. This *territoriality*—the need to call space our space—is another facet of proxemics.

Territoriality implies a desire to possess or give up the space or objects around us. For example, different body parts permit us to claim temporary possession of an object. Thus, we often use our hands to reach out and grab an object (as in straightening someone's tie or holding an-

By a man's fingernails, by his coat-sleeve, by his boots, by his trouser-knees, by the callosities of his forefinger and thumb, by his expression, by his shirt cuffs—by each of these things a man's calling is plainly revealed. That all united should fail to enlighten the competent inquirer in any case is almost inconceivable.

Sherlock Holmes

other person's hand). Or, we employ our whole bodies as spatial indicators. Standing with hands on our hips and elbows extended, for instance, claims all of the space around our bodies, saying, "Don't come any closer to me than my elbows, or else!" On the other hand, when we are kissing, we close our eyes, perhaps to break down spatial barriers. "It's okay," we imply. "Your kiss is not infringing on my territory." We also use objects to define our territory. Have you ever used books, paper, pencils, sweaters, and other objects to stake out your space at a library table? Such markers say, "This area is mine."

SEATING ARRANGEMENTS   Did your father always sit at the head of the table in your house? Most often the person who sits at the head of a table will be designated the "leader," whether or not that designation is appropriate. Have you ever avoided taking a chair at the head of a table for this very reason? The two ends of a table and the middle seats on the sides are "hot seats" in which people either do, or at least are expected to, talk more.

These examples illustrate the effects of seating arrangements on interpersonal interactions. Some spatial arrangements, such as a round table, encourage us to face each other and to communicate. Other arrangements—for example, a row of chairs in a theater or classroom—force us to face away from one another. These arrangements naturally produce less interaction.

Thus, different seating arrangements are desirable for different types of interactions. If two people are having a friendly conversation, they might prefer seats at the corner of a table. When working together on a task, they might sit side by side. During competition (playing cards, for example) they would prefer to sit across from one another, thereby making it more difficult to see each other's hand and easier to establish strong eye contact.

Similarly, spatial relationships in the classroom can influence student-teacher interactions. The three most popular ways to arrange classrooms are in rectangular, horseshoe, and modular arrangements (see Fig-

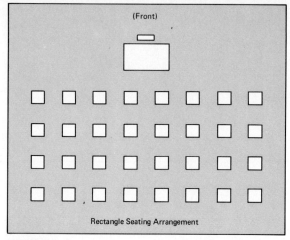

FIGURE 4-2

Rectangle Seating Arrangement

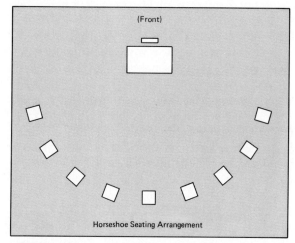

FIGURE 4-3

Horseshoe Seating Arrangement

ures 4–2, 4–3, and 4–4). Most classrooms in America are rectangular, with desks arranged in straight rows. This arrangement is best for information dissemination or straight lectures. Horseshoe and modular arrangements are frequently used with smaller classes. Courses in disciplines such as home economics, architecture, horticulture, and speech communication would be likely to use these arrangements. Both the horseshoe and modular arrangements increase student participation. The grouping of the modular design allows for maximum interaction and is especially effective for teachers who need to work with groups and individual students.[7]

[7]H. Thomas Hurt, Michael D. Scott, and James C. McCroskey, *Communication in the Classroom* (Reading, Mass: Addison-Wesley, 1978), pp. 95–99.

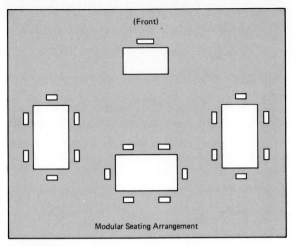

FIGURE 4-4

At this point you may be wondering whether or not students have preferences in seating arrangements. Recent studies indicate that student preferences are determined by the type of course and level of student.[8] A pre-med student, interested only in the facts needed to get an A, would probably prefer the rectangular arrangement. However, a marketing major interested in consumer behavior would probably prefer the horseshoe or modular arrangement so that she could get to know other students better.

Most of us also have preferences about where we sit in classes. Have you ever been disappointed on the first day of class, to find that you couldn't sit in the back row, in front of the teacher, or by the blackboard? A variety of factors such as wanting to sit by the best-looking student, or wanting to be able to see the board, determine seating preferences. Investigations of interactions in classrooms reveal that while seating arrangement, or proximity to the teacher, generally is not strong enough to affect test performance, it is clearly related to student enjoyment, motivation, interest, and feelings of inclusion.[9] Finally, the smaller the class, the higher the students' self-concept, interest in school, and class participation.[10]

Personal Appearance

Each year Americans spend millions of dollars on cosmetics, weight control, and plastic surgery to increase their physical attractiveness. To become beautiful people, we starve ourselves to lose weight, spend count-

[8]James C. McCroskey and Rod W. McVetta, "Classroom Seating Arrangements: Instructional Communication Theory Versus Student Preferences," *Communication Education* 27, no. 2 (March 1978): 99–111.

[9]Richard J. Millard and David V. Stimpson, "Enjoyment and Productivity as a Function of Classroom Seating Location," *Perceptual Motor Skills* 50 (April 1980): 439–444.

[10]Mary L. Smith and Gene V. Glass, "Meta-analysis of Research on Class Size and its Relationship to Attitudes and Instruction," *American Educational Research Journal* 17 (Winter 1980): 419–433.

less hours in front of mirrors styling our hair and applying makeup, use special conditioners to halt thinning hair, and wear clothing to accent a bulge here and minimize a bulge there. We have been told that inner beauty is what counts in relationships, but research analyzing first impressions suggests that physical attractiveness affects interpersonal outcomes. Physical appearance influences job interviews, blind dates, consumer buying behavior, grades in school, and even courtroom decisions.

Although the face usually determines beauty, we are also judged by our body shapes, skin color, and hair. Every time television sets are turned on, advertisers stereotype people according to their physical attributes. Can you remember seeing a fat, unkempt scar-faced doctor recommend a leading aspirin? Advertisers usually hire neat, clean, attractive models to sell their products. Most unattractive individuals are used only in advertisements that feature before-and-after sequences, such as with ways to increase bust size or to achieve younger-looking skin. To look just right, we are encouraged to change our skin color and texture by applying makeup and medications, getting a golden tan, or using special skin softeners. Society also influences our views on hair. Men want to keep their hair because it is masculine to have hairy chests, beards, and mustaches. Women, however, are constantly finding ways to get rid of their hair. By electrolysis, depilation, and shaving, women eliminate unsightly hair under arms, on legs, over lips, and on eyebrows. Certainly, the way we look is important to ourselves and others. We manipulate our physical appearance so that we will be perceived as attractive rather than unattractive.

Clothing It is often said that clothes make a person, but it may be more true to say that clothes *are* the person. Your clothes provide visual clues to your interests, age, personality, and attitudes. Even status information is gained from the clothes' age, condition, and fashion. Some of us are very interested in clothing as a means of keeping up with the latest social changes. Others use clothing as a form of decoration and self-expression. T-shirt designs, for example, are a whole new communication channel between the wearer and the world.

In the popular book *You Are What You Wear: The Key to Business Success,* William Thourlby emphasizes the importance of clothing in the business community.[11] He suggests that clothing determines a person's job success. Thus, dress is an influential variable in the total system of nonverbal communication. It can fulfill functions ranging from protection, sexual attraction, and self-assertion to self-denial, concealment, group identification, and the display of status and role. To take an example, have you ever ignored a traffic signal, perhaps crossing at a "DON'T WALK" sign? If so, it may be because a well-dressed person did the same.

[11]William Thourlby, *You Are What You Wear: The Key to Business Success* (New York: Signet Press, 1978).

One study demonstrated that pedestrians copy others who ignore traffic signals, especially if those others are dressed in a way that represents high status.[12]

ARCHITECTURE AND OBJECTS   Have you ever walked into a room and Environmental Factors immediately felt at home, calm, and relaxed? Or avoided a building that made you feel nervous and insecure? Nonverbal messages from architectural structures and other objects around us can indeed influence our behavior. It is for this reason that dentists have comfortable chairs and pleasant decors in their waiting rooms—all to make us worry a little less. Nightclub, bar, and restaurant owners have also learned that interiors can greatly influence their customers. They realize that dim lighting, a quiet atmosphere, and soft music lead to greater intimacy, which encourages their patrons to stay longer.

These informal observations are supported by scientific studies. One experiment,[13] for example, used three rooms: an "ugly" room, designed like a janitor's storeroom; a "beautiful" room, with carpeting, drapes, and other decorations; and an "average" room, decorated like a professor's office. While located in these different rooms, subjects were asked to rate a series of photographs of faces. Those in the beautiful room gave higher ratings to the faces than did those in the ugly room. While the beautiful room was found to stimulate feelings of pleasure, comfort, enjoyment, and the desire to continue the activity, the ugly room caused fatigue, headaches, discontent, sleepiness, irritability, and hostility. Similar studies of recall and problem solving in these rooms showed better performance in the beautiful surroundings.

COLORS   We all recognize clichés of color and emotion—"tickled pink," "feeling blue," "green with envy," and "seeing red," to name but a few. It is well known that specific colors are associated with particular human moods. As one study demonstrated (see Table 4–1), we tend to describe some moods in terms of a specific color, while other moods are associated with two or more colors.

The difficulty with such research, of course, is knowing whether people pick colors that are truly associated with specific moods, or whether their choices actually reflect learned stereotypes. Do you respond to different colors in different ways? What colors are you wearing at this moment? Do they in any way reflect the mood you were in when you dressed? Answering these questions may give you some interesting insights into your reactions to particular colors. What about color combi-

[12]M. Lefkowite, R. Blake, and J. Mouton, "Status Factors in Pedestrian Violation of Traffic Signals," *Journal of Abnormal Psychology* 51 (1955): 704–6.

[13]A. H. Maslow and N. L. Mintz, "Effects of Esthetic Surroundings: I. Initial Effects of Three Esthetic Conditions upon Perceiving 'Energy' and 'Well-Being' in Faces," *Journal of Psychology* 41 (1956): 247–54.

TABLE 4-1 Association of Moods and Colors

MOOD	COLOR
Exciting, stimulating	Red
Secure, comfortable	Blue
Distressed, disturbed, upset	Orange
Tender, soothing	Blue
Protective, defending	Red, brown, blue, purple, black
Despondent, dejected, unhappy, melancholy	Black, brown
Calm, peaceful, serene	Blue, green
Dignified, stately	Purple
Cheerful, jovial, joyful	Yellow
Defiant, contrary, hostile	Red, orange, black
Powerful, strong, masterful	Black

From L. B. Wexner, "The Degree to Which Colors (Hues) Are Associated with Mood-Tones." *Journal of Applied Psychology* 38 (1954): 432–35. Copyright 1954 by the American Psychological Association. Reprinted by permission.

nations? Are there certain color combinations, say orange and red, that you would *never* wear? Why not? What nonverbal messages do you think you send by wearing such combinations?

TIME   Americans are very preoccupied with time. Just observe the many timepieces around us—clocks in our homes, schools, and work places; church bells chiming every quarter hour; banks lighting up the time, second by second; radio stations announcing the time after every commercial; and almost everyone wearing a wristwatch (some of them even having alarms!). Time is also an important part of our verbal language: "kill time," "use time," "waste time," "it's high time," "time is of the essence," "now's the time. . . ."

Time is significant in nonverbal communication as well. Time is a valued commodity. Time is money—we are paid for the time we spend at work. Time is power—the more time someone gives you, the more important you are. Time is status—we are more punctual for an important business meeting than for a casual get-together. In short, we are compulsive clock-watchers—bound to our watches, time clocks, agendas, and timetables. Time keeps running on . . . running us.

Scientists have discovered that perceptions of time provide important nonverbal cues, cues that vary from culture to culture.[14] Western industrialized cultures, for example, think of time in linear-spatial terms related to past, present, and future. Thus, Americans think of moving "through" time, with the present as the intermediate point between past and future. In contrast, other cultures stress "felt time," the "now" of living for each day and not for the past or future. Greeks, for instance, see

[14]Richard E. Porter, "An Overview of Intercultural Communication," in *Intercultural Communication: A Reader,* 2d ed., ed. Larry A. Samovar and Richard E. Porter (Belmont, Calif: Wadsworth, 1976), p. 318.

"We want it done in tattletale gray."   (George Dole)

themselves as stationary. Time comes up behind them, overtakes them, and then becomes the past. Many American Indians have the same concept. Indeed, the Sioux have no words for "time," "late," or "waiting."

We also make certain assumptions about other people based on their time-consciousness. Those on time for appointments are considered most sociable and composed; those who are early are seen as least dynamic; and latecomers are usually viewed as least sociable, composed, and competent.[15] Bringing it closer to home, consider how someone else's time conceptions affect you. If you discover that your boss or professor is very time-conscious, keeps track of tardiness, absenteeism, and so forth, how might you modify your behavior? How would use of time affect such a boss or instructor?

MUSIC   Have you ever put on soft music to set the mood for a special date or wondered why some restaurants play classical music and others play disco? Maybe you haven't thought about the reasons behind the music selections, but whether you know it or not, music affects us and our interactions with others. Muzak Corporation, the largest producer of music for businesses, corporations, and industries, has provided evidence that music increases production and reduces errors, tension, and absenteeism. In addition, music has been reported to influence concept and skill

[15]L. A. Baxter and J. M. Ward, "An Exploratory Investigation of Diffused Point Arrival Time and Source Credibility" (paper presented at the Western Speech Communication Association Convention, November 1973).

learning, attention span, mental imagery, reading efficiency, and creative abilities.[16]

Music also plays a major role in our society. Americans spend more money on records than they do on textbooks for schools. The power of the music industry can be attributed to its diversity. With more than 8,000 radio stations, we have the freedom to tune into anything from jazz to punk rock. Tastes in music communicate information about others to us. Personality characteristics are often associated with the types of music people listen to. However, to assume that intellectuals listen to classical music, truck drivers enjoy country and western music, and long-haired liberals get into hard rock is to engage in dangerous generalizations. Just as there is diversity in the sounds of music, there is diversity in what people appreciate and like to listen to in music.

Paralanguage The next time you turn on the TV, close your eyes and listen to the actors' voices. What emotions are they portraying? Are the speakers male or female, British or American? How old are they? Try the same experiment while listening to a radio talk show. Is the caller nervous, tired, angry? *Paralanguage*—variations in the voice—is what makes it possible to answer these questions. Paralanguage is "a language alongside of language." It includes vocal characteristics such as pitch, range, resonance, tempo, and quality and various vocal sounds such as grunts, groans, and clearing of the throat.

Although paralanguage is closely tied to verbal expression, it is quite unlike the signs and symbols we know as language. Consider the various voice **pitches.** Some people use a wide range of pitches, talking now in a high voice, now in a low one, while others make few pitch changes, or even talk in a monotone. In addition, we all drop our voices at the end of a statement and raise our voices slightly at the end of a question. Ask, "Where are you going?" and notice how your voice rises on "going." These pitch changes are part of our paralanguage.

Other paralanguage cues relate to **resonance,** the variations from a thin and quiet voice to a loud and booming voice. For example, shyness or embarrassment can affect the voice: Have you ever begun an introduction to a large group of people only to find that nervousness has made your voice fade to a mere whisper?

Some people speak so fast that it is hard to pick up all their words; others speak very slowly. This paralanguage quality is called **tempo.** Good public speakers know that the ability to pause at the proper time and to draw out words for emphasis creates color and interest in what is being said. The nervous orator's short, choppy phrases and monotonous style are a real giveaway to the audience that the speaker is ill at ease and probably inexperienced.

Paralanguage cues are also revealed by voice **quality,** variations of harshness, breathiness, stridency, smoothness of delivery, and similar fac-

[16]Summary in Lawrence Rosenfeld, "Setting the Stage for Learning," *Theory into Practice* 16 (June 1977): 167–73.

tors. Indeed, researchers have found that these paralanguage variables are associated with definite perceptual stereotypes. As we can see from Table 4-2, the interpretation of these paralanguage cues varies with the sex of the speaker.

Paralanguage expressions need not be as subtle as those listed in Table 4-2, however. For example, sounds such as sneezing, coughing, or cry-

TABLE 4-2 Stereotyped Perceptions of Vocal Characteristics

SIMULATED VOCAL CUES*	SPEAKERS	STEREOTYPED PERCEPTIONS
Breathiness	Males	Younger; more artistic
	Females	More feminine; prettier; more petite; more effervescent; more high strung; shallower
Thinness	Males	Did not alter listeners image of the speaker
	Females	Increased social, physical, emotional, and mental immaturity; increased sense of humor and sensitivity
Flatness	Males	More masculine; more sluggish; colder; more withdrawn
	Females	More masculine; more sluggish; colder; more withdrawn
Nasality	Both sexes	A wide array of socially undesirable characteristics
Tenseness	Males	Older; more unyielding; cantankerous
	Females	Younger; more emotional, feminine, high strung; less intelligent
Throatiness	Males	Older; more realistic, mature; sophisticated; well adjusted
	Females	Less intelligent; more masculine; lazier; more boorish, unemotional, ugly, sickly, careless, inartistic, naive, humble, neurotic, quiet, uninteresting, apathetic. In short, "cloddish or oafish" (Addington)
Orotundity	Males	More energetic, healthy, artistic, sophisticated, proud, interesting, enthusiastic. In short, "hardy, and esthetically inclined" (Addington)
	Females	Increased liveliness, gregariousness, "increasingly proud and humorless" (Addington)
Increased rate	Both sexes	More animated and extroverted
Increased Pitch Variety	Males	More dynamic, feminine, esthetically inclined
	Females	More dynamic and extroverted

*For descriptions of these cues, see P. Heinberg, Voice Training for Speaking and Reading Aloud (New York: Ronald Press, 1964), 152-81.

Data from D. W. Addington, "The Relationship of Selected Vocal Characteristics to Personality Perception," Speech Monographs 35 (1968): 498. Table from Mark L. Knapp, Nonverbal Communication and Human Interaction, 2d ed. (New York: Holt, Rinehart and Winston, 1978), p. 332.

ing all serve well-recognized purposes. Similarly, if you walk into a room in which two of your friends are deeply involved in a conversation, rather than standing there until one of them notices you, you might clear your throat. This simple noise communicates your presence, saying, "Hey, look at me. I'm here."

Having seen how paralanguage conveys information about age, sex, emotional states, personality variables, and other common attributes, it should not surprise you to learn that words in themselves account for only 7 percent of the communication of feelings. More important, researchers found, are vocal cues, which account for 38 percent, and facial expressions, which account for 55 percent. To understand how true this finding is, consider a typical conversation. The speakers start out quite friendly but slowly build to a heated argument. As anger increases, voices become louder (intensity), the range of voices increases (pitch), and the speed of the exchange quickens (tempo). Even if you couldn't hear the speakers' angry words, paralanguage factors would immediately tell you that the two people were quarreling.

Touching   Do you often reach out to touch other people? Although ours is not a "contact" culture, touching is, nonetheless, the most basic form of nonverbal communication.

We all use touching at times. To emphasize a point or to interrupt another person, for instance, we may grab the speaker's elbow and interrupt with, "But you don't understand." Touching can be used as a calming gesture, too. We frequently try to comfort someone with a pat on the back and a "there, there." In other situations touching provides reassurance. Not only do we reach out to reassure ourselves of the presence of people we are fond of, but we sometimes do the same with objects—stroking the smooth leather of our gloves, for instance.

These behaviors suggest the importance of touching to human beings. In fact, physical contact with other humans is vital to healthy development. Lack of such contact in childhood may sometimes contribute to physical and psychological problems later in life. To understand this, consider how parents touch their children to communicate their feelings about the children's bodies. By stroking part of a child's body, parents are saying that that part is prized and loved. If certain body parts are ignored or avoided, as is common with anal and genital areas, these areas may seem objectionable to the child and may eventually become a source of shame.

Smell and   Every day we use our senses of smell and taste to receive information
Taste   about the world around us. However, we also use the mediums of smell and taste to send out such information about ourselves. Think, for example, about the last time you were getting ready to go out with a very special person. After getting out of the bathtub, where you showered with deodorant soap and washed your hair with scented shampoo, you proba-

bly put on deodorant or antiperspirant and adorned yourself with after-shave lotion or perfume. You then proceeded to brush your teeth with a fresh-tasting toothpaste and, perhaps, gargled with a "germ killing" mouthwash. Finally, you put on fresh-smelling clothes and odor-free shoes, the former having been washed in a freshly scented detergent and rinsed in a fabric softener, and the latter "freshened" with "odor-eating" talcum powder or foot pads.

It is interesting to note, however, that American perceptions of smells and tastes often differ from the perceptions of members of other cultures. For example, Americans have been conditioned to be ashamed of natural body odors. Have you ever kept your distance from someone for fear that the garlic on your breath would be offensive? Such a feeling of self-consciousness concerning a potential message such as this is only one example of how our culture differs from other cultures. Members of several cultures would feel quite insulted if you deprived them of your breath!

The sense of smell, however, is not the only "silent" sense which sends and receives messages. Likewise, our sense of taste allows us to receive messages of pleasure as well as warning and has the ability both to influence and to reflect our physical needs as well as preferences and attitudes. Do some odors and tastes make you happy, depressed, nostalgic? If you do not quite yet believe in the communicative power of these two senses, be aware of the processes involved the next time you sniff or taste an odor or flavor. You may open yourselves up to an awareness concerning two additional and viable channels of communication.

AWARENESS OF NONVERBAL COMMUNICATION

The previous sections have described some of the meanings attached to specific gestures, body language, expressions, and environmental stimuli. Again, we must assert that these nonverbal messages cannot be viewed in simple black-and-white terms. Like words, nonverbal language has connotations as well as denotations. Just as each of us responds differently to a given word, term, or concept because of our different experiences, attitudes, and beliefs, so too do we respond differently to nonverbal messages.

Awareness of your own nonverbal behavior and that of others can increase your sensitivity in social interactions. Although we are usually attentive to nonverbal stimuli—we purposely wear clothes that evoke a particular response (positive or negative), we reach out and touch a friend who is unhappy to let him or her know that we are there—at other times we overlook or misread nonverbal cues that might enrich our understanding of interpersonal communications. Similarly, just as we may misinterpret the nonverbal behavior of others, they may do the same with us. Thus, you should consider questions such as, "I know what my beard means to me, but what does it mean to my parents?" "Does my being overweight influence her feelings about me?" "I wonder if they think I'm unfriendly because I don't go over and join them."

In the following section we will discuss the factors that affect our interpretation of nonverbal messages.

Context   Context influences our own nonverbal communications as well as our responses to other people's nonverbal messages. For example, when you are at home watching a movie on television, you probably prop your feet up on the coffee table or curl them under you on the sofa. You might noisily dig to the bottom of the potato chip bag, ignoring the crumbs that miss your mouth and fall to your chest. And, if the beer or soda you've been drinking should make you burp—so what? But what if you were watching the same movie in a crowded theater? Your behavior might differ considerably. Even if you wanted to slouch, the stiff theater seats might prevent it. If you insisted on potato chips rather than a less noisy snack, you would probably be more careful not to rattle the bag or scatter the crumbs. And, if the soda had the same effect on you it has at home, you would probably suppress the burp or let nature have its way—discreetly.

We learn appropriate context behaviors by negative reinforcement during childhood. How many times were you told as a child, "Don't put your feet on that table! You're not at home now!" Or, did you ever get stern looks because you talked too loudly in a movie theater or popped your gum in a library? After much scolding and some praise, we learn to vary our nonverbal behaviors according to whom we are with, where we are, and whether or not the situation is defined as formal or informal.

Just as context modifies your own nonverbal behavior, so too does it affect your response to nonverbal messages in your environment. For example, a simple gesture can have several different meanings, depending on the context in which it occurs. Let's say you are driving your car down the road and you spot someone hitchhiking. In a matter of seconds, you must decide whether to stop. What you do is based on contextual variables. First, your mood: Are you feeling helpful, or don't you want to be bothered? Are you in a hurry or on a leisurely drive? Are you afraid of all hitchhikers, never picking them up, or do you usually give them a lift? And what about the environment? Would it make a difference to you if it were daytime or night? On a crowded highway or on a country road? In the summer or during a snowstorm? What about the person himself . . . or herself? Would it matter to you if the hitchhiker were a man or a woman? Or perhaps a man *and* a woman—or a man with his pet German shepherd?

Would the hitchhiker's age and weight influence you? Or clothing, hairstyle, and other gestures? Finally, if and when you do pull over, would you take a few more seconds to change your mind after studying facial expressions, voice, and general demeanor?

As you can see, the same gesture—"Hey, I need a ride. Please pick me up"—can be interpreted in many different ways, depending on the context and, of course, on your stereotypes.

Stereotypes

Like it or not, most of us do have stereotypes about people and the way they act. These stereotypes play a large part in first impressions, for example. Whether or not the stereotypes bear any resemblance to reality, they do exist and must be considered when analyzing interpersonal behavior.

As our hitchhiking example demonstrated, we often make judgments about the personality and behavior of individuals just by observing their physical appearance or superficial actions. In fact, we sometimes make important decisions based on voice alone: "I didn't like the sound of his voice, so I. . . ." "As soon as she started to talk, I knew I could trust her." Researchers have verified this reliance on voice characteristics. In one experiment students listened to two tape recordings of the same speaker. On one recording the speaker used a conversational delivery pattern—that is, a smaller range of inflections, a greater consistency of rate and pitch, less volume, and generally lower pitch than in the second recording, where the speaker used a more dynamic delivery pattern. The students in this study did not realize that they were hearing the same speaker with two different vocal approaches. Instead, they rated the speaker who used the conversational delivery as honest and person-oriented, while the dynamic delivery elicited descriptions of tough-minded, task-oriented, self-assured, and assertive.[17]

Of course, we all have stereotypes about many aspects of behavior other than voice. Do you have certain beliefs about the way people should or shouldn't walk, smile, sit, stand, eat, laugh, sneeze, or cry? Ask yourself why the next time you jump to a conclusion based solely on some aspect of another person's behavior. Chances are your conclusion doesn't reflect the facts of the situation. Herein lies the danger of stereotypes. Too often they turn out to be assumptions completely unrelated to objective facts.

However, the main point of this chapter is awareness: You cannot eliminate your stereotyped response to nonverbal messages, but you cannot disregard those stereotypes either. Thus, if you know, for example, that someone has a negative stereotype about blue jeans, you will either not wear them when you are with that person or will not be surprised or offended by the person's behavior when you do. In short, awareness improves understanding, and understanding improves communication—be it verbal or nonverbal.

SUMMARY

In addition to our spoken and written language, all of us communicate on the nonverbal level of body movements, gestures, facial expressions, tone of voice, and other related signs. Our interpretation of such nonverbal messages is a function both of their context and of their relationship to the communicator's entire verbal and nonverbal behavior pattern.

The six basic functions of nonverbal communication are repeating, substituting, complementing, deceiving, regulating, and ac-

[17]W. Barnett Pearce and Forrest Conklin, "Nonverbal Vocalic Communication and Perceptions of a Speaker," *Speech Monographs* 38 (1971): 235–41.

centing. The body expressions that serve these functions are almost limitless. Specialists have organized these expressions into classes such as kinesics and body movement, proxemics, physical characteristics, environmental factors, touch, and paralanguage. Some classes of body expressions include emblems, illustrators, regulators, affect displays, and body manipulators. These expressions, and the functions they serve, are the subject of the scientific discipline known as kinesics, or body language. This language of facial expressions, eye adjustments, and related body movements is responsible for a significant part of all human communication.

In addition to kinesic messages, we communicate by our relationship to the space about us and our use of that space. Proxemics, the study of these spatial factors, specifies several distinct zones of interpersonal communication, which are affected by our territoriality and by the environmental factors that surround us each day. Thus, your re-sponse to the nonverbal messages sent by others, and your propensity to send nonverbal messages of your own, are affected by a combination of many factors, including the physical characteristics of clothing and personal appearance. Environmental factors such as color, music, time, and architectural stimuli also affect communication. The most basic form of nonverbal communication is touch. The last three areas of nonverbal communication we discussed were the vocal variations known as paralanguage and communication through our senses of taste and smell.

It is important that we become aware of these factors and of the context in which nonverbal messages occur. In addition, we must recognize the perceptual stereotypes that always affect our interpretation of both verbal and nonverbal messages. This heightened awareness can help to assure understanding of others and improved communication on all levels.

Exercises

GROUP EXPERIENCES

How's Your Sign Language?

Description: As children, we used nonverbal communication as our direct statement of what we wanted, while verbal communication was the complement. As we grew older, this process became reversed, so that our nonverbal communication no longer served as a direct statement but as a complement to what we said verbally. Children depend a great deal on sign language (gestures that replace words, numbers, and punctuation). It has been found that children are easily able to transmit and interpret twelve frequently used gestures. Try this activity and see if your sign language is as good as a child's.

Procedure: Divide into groups of four to six members. Each member should try to transmit a short phrase nonverbally. The following list of phrases is offered only as a beginning—these are the phrases mentioned above (that children are able to use quite easily).

Go away	How many
Come here	How big
Yes	Shape (round or square)
No	I don't know
Be quiet	Goodbye
Give me attention	Hi

The first person to accurately guess the message becomes the next transmitter. This process continues until all members have had the opportunity to transmit at least two messages.

Discussion: How well do you transmit and interpret nonverbal messages? Consider this question in light of the activity you have just completed. If you have trouble transmitting messages nonverbally, this may suggest that you need to work on this to improve your communication. On the other hand, if you have trouble interpreting messages, you may be misinterpreting people. Problems with either transmission or interpretation of nonverbal messages may lead to communication breakdowns on an interpersonal or group level.

How Others Stereotype You

Description: Are you aware of how others stereotype you on the basis of your behavior and personal appearance? Not many people are. This activity will provide you with information about how others view you and should also help you to understand your own nonverbal behavior.

Procedure: Divide into groups of four to six members. Each member should make a list of everyone in the group and put his or her name on the top of the list. Across the top of the paper, three categories should be written: books, dogs, and adjectives. Starting with yourself, select one choice from each category that most closely reflects you or the person for whom you are making the choice. When you are selecting, try to determine the specific behaviors that cause you to view a person in a particular stereotyped way.

Category A. Which book would you most likely find ___(insert name)___ reading?

    a How Managers Make Things Happen
    b. How to Read the Stars
    c. The Wild, Wild West
    d. One Hundred Was to Improve Your Golf Swing
    e. The Prophet
    f. How to Eat Better and Spend Less
    g. How to Be Your Own Best Friend

Category B. What type of dog does _____(insert name)_____ remind you of?

a Poodle
b. German shepherd
c. Sheepdog
d. Cocker spaniel
e. Dachshund
f. St. Bernard
g. Chihuahua

Category C. Which group of adjectives most closely describes _____(insert name)_____ ?

a. Open, optimistic, energetic
b. Meticulous, nervous, punctual
c. Soft-hearted, good-natured, loving
d. Competitive, dominant, authoritative
e. Closed, pessimistic, quiet
f. Fun-loving, ambitious, talkative
g. Introspective, spiritual, analytical

Discussion: There are two ways to assess the results of this activity: Either start with a category and discuss each group member in the category or start with a particular group member and discuss him or her in each of the three categories. Whichever method you choose, keep in mind that meanings are in people, not in the words. Therefore, it is very important that you try to provide information on *why* you made a particular selection. Focus on the personal appearance of the person and consider whether you stereotyped hairstyle or clothing in a particular way. If you find that the impressions others have of you are inconsistent with the way you view yourself, then you need to observe your own behavior and personal appearance to understand what you are conveying nonverbally to others. The expansion of nonverbal awareness begins with understanding how you project impressions to others.

It's Not What You Say, It's How You Say It!

Description: This activity can be conducted either in small groups of four to six members or as a demonstration activity in which the majority of the class serves as an audience while four or five individuals play roles in selected situations. Two partners will be needed for each role-playing scene. Two scenes are offered as examples of the type of drama that can be reenacted to illustrate the effects of pitch, rhythm, intonation, intensity, and other vocal qualities. The purpose of this activity is to clearly demonstrate that it's not *what* you say, but *how* you say it!

Procedure: Two partners will be needed for each role-playing activity. Each team can either invent a scene they would like to portray or use one from the following list. In each scene only numbers are to be used—absolutely no words are permitted. For example, practice by reading the following numbers tenderly, angrily, and sadly: 42, 567, 3, 356, 8. Once you get a feel for this, try one of the following scenes. After a team plays a scene, the group should discuss the emotions and feelings that were being conveyed.

Scene 1. Husband and wife. The wife comes home from work and the husband is very irritable after spending the day watching the children and cooking. He displays his irritability the moment she walks through the door. The wife at first tries to be supportive, but then fights openly with her husband.

Scene 2. A couple. In this scene the couple has been dating for a long time. Finally, after waiting for months, he pops the question. The scene is tender and romantic.

Discussion: Are you aware of the subtle nonverbal cues that are transmitted through the voice? Consider how, even if the words are identical, a change in pitch, intensity, or even pause rate can dramatically alter the meaning of a message. After participating in this activity, you should be able to listen to your own vocal characteristics to see how you alter messages. Also consider the extent to which the vocal characteristics of others influence your interpretation of their messages. In other words, is it *what* they say or *how* they say it that counts?

Body Expressions

Description: The body and the face convey many emotional meanings in both speaking and listening. Most of us learn to convey emotions through our facial expressions but have more difficulty conveying emotions with other parts of our bodies. The following activity will provide you with an opportunity to determine how well you transmit and interpret the nonverbal display of emotions through the use of facial expressions and body movement.

Procedure: Write each of the following body areas and emotions on separate cards.

Body Areas	*Emotions*
Whole face	Hate
Whole body	Love

Hands only	Anger
Face only	Surprise
Mouth only	Happiness
Eyes and eyebrows only	Distrust
Feet only	Disgust
Dyad (whole body with another person)	Contentment

Divide into groups of six to eight members (each group needs one set of cards). The first person should select one card from the body area category and one card from the emotion category. The person should then try to portray the selected emotion with *only* the body area designated on the card. The rest of the group has three guesses to determine both the correct body area and the emotion. If the group guesses correctly, the person receives one point. If the group does not guess correctly, the person loses one point. After the first person has finished, the cards should be returned to the appropriate deck. Go around the group until each participant has had three turns. (The number of turns may be modified depending on the number of participants in the group and the amount of time available for the activity.)

Discussion: As a group, identify which emotions were most difficult to convey and which were easiest. Identify which body areas most accurately transmitted the emotional states and which least accurately. Which was more difficult—the transmission of nonverbal messages or the interpretation of them?

Conversation and Space

Description: Particular spatial arrangements may either aid or inhibit interactions. We are constantly readjusting our distance from other people and objects to match the nature of our conversations. The following activity provides you with the opportunity to experience the relationship between conversational topic and distance.

Procedure: Divide into dyads. The members of the dyad should stand directly opposite one another at a distance of 10 feet. Engage in a conversation on any topic you choose, but while you are talking, maintain the distance of 10 feet between you and your partner for 3 minutes. After 3 minutes reduce the distance to 5 feet and continue to talk. You may change topics as many times as you wish. After another 3 minutes reduce the distance to 2 feet, then 12 inches, and finally 6 inches. Each distance should be maintained for a minimum of 3 minutes.

Discussion: **Discuss your reactions to the various conversational distances you maintained with your partner. Did the topic of the conversation or the intensity with which you discussed the topic vary with the different distances? Did certain topics seem inappropriate at particular distances? What types of topics do you consider to be appropriate at the following distances: 10 feet, 5 feet, 2 feet, 1 foot, 6 inches?**

PERSONAL EXPERIENCES

1. Strike up a conversation with a stranger while you are waiting in line, sitting in a bus, or walking on campus. After a couple of minutes, ask if he or she would be willing to participate in an experiment requiring no more than a few minutes. If the person is willing, ask him or her to relate the first impression of you. Stress the need for an honest appraisal of your personal appearance, nonverbal behaviors, and conversational qualities. Is the impression accurate? What was your reaction to the description of you? How aware are you of the nonverbal impression you create?

2. Select a person in one of your classes to observe. Watch your subject over a period of several days and see if you can classify his or her nonverbal behaviors as (a) regulators, (b) illustrators, (c) emblems, (d) affect displays, or (e) adaptors. What does this classification tell you about the person? For example, does the absence of the use of regulating nonverbal behavior suggest that the person may not provide adequate listening response for a speaker?

3. Watch television with a friend, but at separate locations. Have your friend watch the same program you do so that you can compare notes later. However, when you watch the program, turn off the sound completely. Watch the body movements and facial expressions very carefully and try to understand the story line. After the program tell your friend what happened—describe the emotions, the drama, and the interaction between characters in the program. Then listen to your friend's description. What were the major differences in your descriptions? Did the absence of sound produce more information on the nonverbal level while reducing the content of the information, which is obtained through the verbal medium?

4. The next time you have a telephone conversation with someone you have never seen (telephone operator, salesperson), try to determine information about that person on the basis of vocal cues. For example, try to guess age, height, weight, race, sex, and the area of the country he or she is from. After you have made some tentative guesses, check your results by asking your telephone partner to verify the information. Try this several times and see how vocal cues help, hinder, or do not affect the identification of background and personality characteristis of an individual.

5. Observe yourself for a day to determine what relationship you have to time. Record the number of times you look at a clock, ask for the time, or refer to time in any manner. Next, go a step further and determine whether you live in present time, future time, past time, or linear time (no past, present, or future). How well can you relate to people who have a different time orientation than you?

6. Pick a task that takes approximately two hours to complete. Work on the task for one hour in an "ugly" room and one hour in a "beautiful" room. What effect did the difference in environment have on your productivity? Did you experience different physical feelings in each room? Are you sensitive to your environment?

DISCUSSION QUESTIONS

1. What is the difference between nonverbal communication and nonverbal behavior?
2. What are some of the ways (functions) in which we used nonverbal communication?
3. How is the formation of first impressions related to stereotyping?
4. Can you describe your nonverbal behaviors during speaking and listening?
5. What nonverbal behaviors do you use to defend your territory and personal space?
6. To what extent do nonverbal behaviors reflect our attitudes or emotions?
7. Do cultural norms regarding the use of space tell us anything about a given society?
8. How important do you consider paralinguistic cues to be in verbal communication?

INTRAPERSONAL
COMMUNICATION

5

Exploratory Questions

1. What is one example of intrapersonal communication?
2. What are the four communication possibilities of the Johari Window?
3. What three factors shape an individual's self-concept?
4. What are the five levels of Maslow's hierarchy of needs?
5. How do the three levels of stimulus processing operate?
6. How do attitudes, beliefs, and opinions differ?
7. Can you explain and give an example of five defense mechanisms that are used to resolve internal conflicts?

> The easiest person to deceive is one's own self.
>
> Edward Bulwer Lytton

Communication is a two-way process that involves both sending and receiving messages. It would be a mistake, however, to assume that this process requires two participants.

Just recall the last time you were really excited about something and exclaimed aloud, "All right!" Or, you dropped a pencil and found yourself asking aloud, "Where could that pencil have rolled?" These common examples of talking to yourself illustrate basic principles of *intra*personal communication, messages sent and received within the same individual. This is the level on which you communicate with yourself.

Intrapersonal communication takes place whenever you evaluate and react to internal and external stimuli. For example, if you become dehydrated during a hard tennis match, your lips burn and your throat feels uncomfortably dry. Your body's need for water is communicated to you by these outward signs.

Reaction to this kind of discomfort or pain often occurs automatically. When you put your hand on a hot pan, the neurological communication network that receives stimuli transmits and then interprets the sensations of heat. Next, an appropriate neural response is transmitted to your muscles, and you remove your hand. All of this can happen in the fraction of a second it takes you to say "Ouch!"

Intrapersonal communication is more far-reaching than just talking to yourself or crying out in pain, however. As you will read in the following pages, intrapersonal messages reflect your physical self, emotional self, intellectual self, and social self. They also reflect your self-concept and self-related roles and your values and beliefs—in short, your entire personality.

THE SELF

The study of intrapersonal communication begins with knowing yourself. As soon as you begin to examine *the* self, however, you discover that you are, in fact, *many* selves.

Infants do not recognize themselves as beings separate from their environment. This physical recognition usually develops at around eighteen months of age, as children acquire more accurate perceptions of their bodies. Such bodily concepts—better known as body image—are vital for normal mental and emotional development.

The Physical Self

Body image is defined as a person's perception of his or her physical self. While this perception remains fairly constant in a normal individual, it is subject to change at times. If you feel hurt or depressed, you may actually feel smaller, more vulnerable. The reverse is true too—a dieter may have a distorted body image each time he or she gains a pound or two. For the most part, however, a person with a fairly healthy personality will have a fairly healthy body image.

Another self is the emotional self. Emotions are conscious feelings that are accompanied by physiological changes, such as rapid heartbeat, tensed muscles, or raised blood sugar level. Usually we are all too aware of the stimuli that prompt our emotional responses. Barely missing the car that darts out in front of you from a side street can tie your stomach in knots long after the stimulus is gone. At other times, before we realize it, our emotional selves take over. Crying for no reason at all, yelling at your best friend, or laughing out loud while others just smile are all examples of our emotions taking control.

The Emotional Self

The first step toward effective communication with others is successful communication with yourself. (Ken Karp)

The Intellectual Self Your intellectual self, or the self associated with your mental processes, involves mental actions or behaviors such as concept and word formation, use of comparison and contrast, use of logic and reasoning, and the process by which we solve problems and make decisions. At this very moment your intellectual self is functioning as you read this text (that is, if your mind is not wandering to that upcoming weekend). In short, our intellectual self is our mental self—a self which we will learn more about in the following sections.

Habits Each of us possesses **habits,** or repetitive behaviors, that become so automatic that we are hardly aware of them. You may have a habit of biting your nails or stroking your chin while you are thinking, even though you do not consciously choose to do so.

In contrast to these harmless habits, other unconscious behaviors have more serious consequences. Some individuals, for example, always fall in love with the wrong people. Psychologists say this happens not by accident but because there is some conflict within the individual that encourages this type of relationship. Such habitual behavior patterns usually continue as long as they fulfill certain needs within the individual.

Some of these behaviors directly affect our communication. Do you know people who have the knack of always saying the wrong thing at the wrong time, or people who constantly pepper their communication with misused words? TV's Archie Bunker is a perfect example of someone whose misuse of language is a basic part of his character. Archie might accuse a local politician of "invading" (rather than "evading") the issues, while describing his own ideas on the subject as "sensual" (rather than "sensible").

The Unity Principle At this point you may be asking, "If, in fact, I am a product of all of these selves, why am I not more aware of it?" The answer to this question lies first in our need to maintain a unified conceptual system,[1] as evidenced by our inability to process information which is inconsistent with our values, attitudes, and beliefs. Valerie, for example, loves to wake early in the morning, read the *Wall Street Journal,* and have several cups of coffee to start her day. As she rushes her way through a busy week in the office, she also likes to take time to sit, have several more cups of coffee, and talk with her supervisors about both problems and progress in their respective departments. Despite the large amounts of coffee Valerie consumes, what is the probability that a special program on the effects of caffeine on the human system would cause a behavioral change in Valerie's habits? Depending on several factors, there probably would be little or no change. She probably would not even believe the program could apply to herself, and the information would either be lost in memory or would never be processed at all.

---

[1]Seymour Epstein, "The Unity Principle versus the Reality and Pleasure Principles, or the Tale of the Scorpion and the Frog," in *Self Concept: Advances in Theory and Research,* ed. M. D. Lynch, A. A. Norman-Hebeisen, and K. Gergen (Cambridge: Ballinger, 1981).

In addition to the impact that our need for perceptual unity has on our perceptions of the self, several other factors contribute to our illusions of a unified self. These include the use of words such as "I," "me," and "mine," which also reflect unity; our sensations of having one body and one name associated with our bodies (both of which usually remain the same over time, once we reach adulthood); and our observations of the the regularly recurring patterns of behavior which we associate with ourselves. Each of these contributes to the illusion of oneness.

Along with the innate function of our conceptual systems to maintain a unified and happy self, we can also consciously work toward a unified self by increasing our awareness of who we are—our many selves. One such method of increasing awareness is through the use of the Johari Window, a concept which focuses on increasing awareness of the private self and the public self.

The distinction between our private and our public selves is well illustrated by the Johari Window, shown in Figure 5–1. Designed by Joseph Luft and Harrington Ingham,[2] the Johari Window compares aspects of open (public) versus closed (private) communication relationships.

The open section in the diagram represents self-knowledge that you are aware of and willing to share with others. The hidden section represents what you are aware of but not willing to share. The blind section

FIGURE 5-1 The Johari Window.

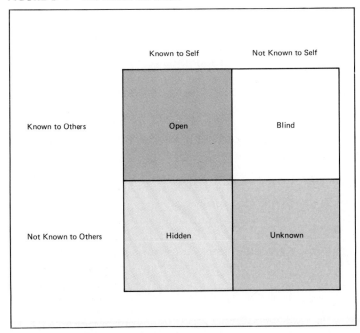

[2]Joseph Luft, *Of Human Interaction* (Palo Alto, Calif.: National Press Books, 1969).

represents information of which you yourself are unaware but which is known to others. The unknown section represents what is unknown both to you and to others.

Although each section of the Johari Window is the same size, different relationships would require different proportions. In a close relationship, for example, the open area might be considerably larger than the hidden area. For communication between casual acquaintances, the hidden area probably would be the largest part of the window.

Let us see how this window applies to a particular communication situation:

> Linda and Tony are reunited after a two-month separation. Linda lets Tony know how much she missed him (open), but does not tell him that she has started to date someone new (hidden). Tony senses that Linda is upset, although she claims that she is fine (blind). The unknown in this situation is a whole range of feelings that are not clear to either of them. For example, both individuals are probably unsure about Linda's feelings toward Tony.

Again, you can use the concept of the Johari Window to increase your self-awareness. This, in turn, should improve your communication with others. As you strive to shrink the blind and unknown segments, you may begin to discover a self you only partially knew before, a self that may or may not resemble the concept you've always had about that person you call "me." The more information you can bring into the open from the hidden, blind, and unknown areas, the better your interpersonal communication will be.

SELF-CONCEPT

Before we begin a discussion concerning the notion of self-concept, take out a piece of paper. On it jot down quickly as many nouns as you can which describe the most important aspects of who you are.[3] The list might look something like this:

> Joanie: woman, athlete, competitor, student, daughter, friend, animal lover
> Jerry: man, student, fiancé, gourmet cook, tennis player, lover, poet

What special descriptive words did you use? How varied was each of the nouns which best describes you?

The first purpose we had in mind when asking you to develop this composite was to illustrate the highly complex and elaborate nature of our self-perceptions. Indeed, one need look no further than the number and variety of the terms to see that our composites reflect a host of ideas which we have of ourselves.

[3]Anthony G. Athos and John J. Gabarro, *Interpersonal Behavior: Communication and Understanding in Relationships* (Englewood Cliffs, N.J.: Prentice Hall, 1978).

Unique among the masses—You! (Mark A. Philbrick)

Second, we wished to demonstrate that this picture we have of ourselves—our **self-concept**—has a strong effect on both intrapersonal and interpersonal communication. For example, Crystal, who thinks of herself as a footloose and fancy-free swinger, would probably enjoy being asked on a cruise by a new man whom she recently met. However, Cindy, whose self-concept includes being a highly religious person, would probably be extremely offended by the same invitation. A good communicator, however, would be one who is sensitive to the self-concepts of others and who would know that their values and attitudes will affect how they respond (the effective communicator would be sensitive and respond quite differently to Cindy and Crystal when inviting the two women on such a cruise).

At this point you may be wondering how our self-concept came to exist? Self-concept is not inborn; rather, it is developed through interaction with people and the environment. Specifically, it develops as a function of three primary sets of variables: our past experiences, the reference groups with which we identify, and the roles which we play in our lives. The interaction between ourselves and these three variables has affected and will continue to affect our self-concepts throughout our lives.

Your past shapes the way you feel about yourself and the way you react **Past** to others. A little boy may stop thinking of himself as Superman after **Experiences** falling down and finding that he is not indestructible. Sometimes past experiences shape your self-concept without your awareness. A child who is constantly criticized at home and made to feel worthless may develop a negative self-concept without realizing the reasons behind it.

Other early experiences can also color your self-concept. A child's school experiences are particularly important. The child who achieves success in the early grades will probably have a better self-concept than a child who has had constant academic failure. In turn, these positive or negative past experiences sometimes create a ***self-fulfilling prophecy.*** Children who see themselves as inferior or dull may perform below their actual abilities. Similarly, children with highly positive self-concepts may prove to be overachievers. Self-fulfilling prophecies can also reinforce self-concept. If a teacher is told that John is a discipline problem, the teacher expects John to misbehave. Sensing this expectation, John may very well cause the trouble that is expected of him. John's self-concept of being "bad" is thus reinforced.

Self-concept is particularly influenced by the socializing and dating experiences of adolescence. The boy who succeeds in getting a date with every girl he asks may come to view himself as a real ladies' man. On the other hand, frequent rejections might cause him to think of himself as a failure. Self-concept is often so shaky during adolescence that many boys ask someone out only when they are sure that the answer will be yes. Girls, too, are frequently unsure of themselves during adolescence, when changing bodies and social expectations can greatly influence self-concept.

Reference Groups   Groups that give you a sense of identity and help you establish your attitudes and values are known as ***reference groups.*** Reference groups contribute to your self-concept. Especially during adolescence, when a person's self-concept is so changeable, groups provide a certain amount of stability.

The adolescent group, like all groups, is characterized by a structure that defines the roles of group members in relation to other members and to those outside the group. The group also provides a set of values or group norms that are common to all the members and distinct from the values they share with outsiders. Thus, group membership enables a member to identify with an established whole. This identification is extremely important because individuals incorporate into their own self-concepts many of the ideas, attitudes, and values of the people with whom they identify.

Roles   Whatever your self-concept, your behavior is strongly affected by the people with whom you interact. Typically, you assume different behavior patterns, or ***roles,*** in different social settings. In fact, the setting often dictates the roles other people are playing and to which you then respond.

ASCRIBED AND ACHIEVED ROLES   Some roles are ***ascribed*** to you and are thus out of your control. They are based primarily on sex, age, kinship, and general place in society. For example, infants are expected to act in a certain way and grandparents in another. In recent years our understanding of ascribed sex roles has undergone striking transformations. Whereas our society once felt that being a female meant being gentle and passive, today many women reject these attributes as artificial and limiting and in no way necessary to being a woman.

Unlike ascribed roles, **_achieved_** roles are earned by individual accomplishment. We all possess different capabilities, and society recognizes these differences. A union steward, an athlete, and a company president all occupy their positions at least to some extent because of their abilities and drive.

SEX ROLES   As we mentioned previously, **_sex roles_** are usually ascribed, defined, and encouraged by each culture. They are a product of the cues children pick up from their surroundings and from same-sex models in the community. In addition, sex-role identity is shaped by children's relations with parents and their relations with one another, the sexual taboos that exist in the culture, and the social class to which the children belong. Obviously, these biologically and socially determined roles are extremely important to the development of self-concept.

SOCIAL ROLES   Each of us also assumes a number of **_social_** roles, defined by our environment. Sometimes an entire structure or organization is based on separate but complementary social roles. In the army, for instance, the roles of the enlisted men, the officers, the cooks, the MPs, the medics, and so on, are clearly defined and join together to form a working unit. Each role has its own duties, skills, and established set of norms. If someone steps out of role, that person is subject to criticism and sometimes to punishment.

It is the combined interaction of your self-concept with these social, sexual, ascribed, and achieved roles that determines your communication behavior in any given situation.

Before special holidays (Christmas, birthdays, and so on) many people make lists of all the things they want. If you were to make a list right now, it might include money, jewelry, clothes, a car, airline tickets, roller skates, or frisbees. These are items some of us want, but what would you include if you had to make a list of your *needs*? Your list would probably look quite different. If you haven't thought recently about what you really need, take a few minutes to do so right now.

Some of our wants and needs are similar because we are driven by common internal motivations. Maslow, a well-known psychologist, examined hundreds of people and discovered five basic human drives. Each of us has physiological, safety, love, esteem, and self-actualization needs. These needs, or drives, are known as the ***hierarchy of human needs.***[4]

1) PHYSIOLOGICAL   Before we attend to other drives, we first have to satisfy desires for things such as food, water, shelter, and sex. If you are hungry after not eating all day, it is difficult to think about studying or playing tennis before you've given yourself some nourishment. If you've pulled two all-nighters in a row, you're probably not interested in going out to have a beer with your friends until you've had some sleep.

2) SAFETY   After we've met all our physiological needs, our next concern is for safety. We like to feel secure, stable, and in control. Many people work hard all their lives and save in every way so that they'll be free from fear and anxiety about money when they retire. All of us think of ways to protect ourselves from danger by doing things such as investing in life insurance, putting locks on doors, or installing smoke detectors.

3) LOVE   Many people would put love as their most important human need, but physiological and safety needs are usually met first or in combination with other needs. Some people feel insecure unless they are dating or married. In this case security and love may be taken care of simultaneously. Love involves another person and is not a one-way street. It is only through giving and receiving affection, care, and concern that we gain approval and acceptance from others. To increase our sense of belonging, many of us get involved in various types of group activities, but generally we satisfy the love need through relationships with family, friends, and lovers.

4) ESTEEM   After we feel loved and accepted, we look for esteem. Usually we must first acquire self-esteem or worth before others will attribute esteem to us. Esteem is a desire for dignity, achievement, competency, and

---

[4]A. H. Maslow, *Motivation and Personality,* 2d ed. (New York: Harper & Row, 1970), pp. 35–46.

(University of Miami, Coral Gables, Florida)

status. Some people get graduate degrees, others master difficult skills in sports, and still others do no more than be themselves to gain admiration and respect from their peers.

5) SELF-ACTUALIZATION   Our last basic human need is for ***self-actualization,*** or striving for all that we are capable of being. Self-actualization includes long-range goals for using our full potential and developing ourselves in all areas. Self-improvement is one form of self-actualization. Throughout our lives we meet small challenges such as winning a marathon (or just completing it), getting an A in physics, writing a novel, or sailing around the world. Our ultimate goal, however, is being and doing all that we are capable of—for personal satisfaction.

THE PROCESS OF INTRAPERSONAL COMMUNICATION

Intrapersonal communication is the foundation upon which interpersonal communication rests. Therefore, it is necessary to understand how you communicate with yourself before you approach the process of communicating with others. Figure 5–2 can help you visualize the intrapersonal communication process. The elements that set the process in motion are called ***stimuli.***

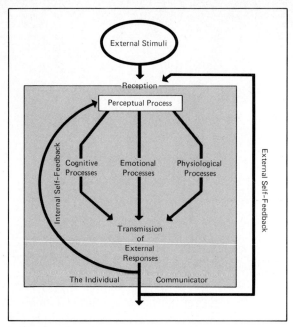

FIGURE 5-2 Intrapersonal Communication.

Internal Stimuli The brain is made aware of the state of the body by nerve impulses, internal stimuli that can prompt you to respond by communicating. Let's say you have the flu. Your muscles ache, your fever is high, and you are depressed. Such a miserable state may prompt you to call a doctor to relieve your physical ills and a friend to relieve your depression. The internal stimuli in this situation have resulted in communication.

External Stimuli External stimuli are, of course, those stimuli that originate in the environment outside of your body. There are two kinds of external stimuli. **Overt stimuli** are received on the conscious level. They are picked up by the sensory organs and then sent to the brain. More than one overt stimulus usually affects a person at any given moment. For example, the pizza being advertised on TV and the sounds and aromas coming from the kitchen can prompt an eager, "What's for dinner?"

  Covert stimuli are external stimuli that are received on the subconscious level. Let's say you are getting dressed for work. One of your favorite songs comes on the radio, so you turn the volume up. The song ends and the news begins, just as you discover a gaping hole in your sock. You find another pair and finish dressing, but you're running late. Is it too cold for your lightweight jacket? You suddenly realize that the weather report has just ended but you have no idea what was said, despite the blaring volume.

> You do not need to leave your room. Remain sitting at your table and listen. Do not even listen, simply wait. Do not even wait, be quite still and solitary. The world will freely offer itself to you to be unmasked, it has no choice, it will roll in ecstasy at your feet.
>
> Franz Kafka

The stimulus of the weather report was received and stored in your brain, but it was below the ***threshold of consciousness.*** Thus, you were not consciously aware of *what* was said, even though you recognized that you were hearing the weather report. Such covert stimuli have been shown to affect behavior and communication. Split-second presentations of the words "Drink Smith's Beer" can indeed make a viewer feel thirsty.

Reception

The process by which the body receives stimuli is called ***reception.*** In intrapersonal communication both external and internal receptors send information to the central nervous system. External receptors for the five senses—sight, sound, smell, taste, and touch—receive stimuli that are changed into nerve impulses and then sent to the brain. These external receptors are located on or near the body's surface and react to physical, chemical, and mechanical stimuli to provide you with information about the environment. Internal receptors such as nerve endings, on the other hand, convey information about your interior state—the dryness of your mouth or the fullness of your stomach, for example.

Although your body receives every stimulus present in a particular communication setting, you could not possibly communicate in response to every one of them. The process that helps you to cope with this jumble of stimuli is called ***selective perception,*** the screening out of a huge number of stimuli present in your environment, which permits attention to just a few. What determines which stimuli we do perceive? The main factor is ***intensity:*** Loud sounds, bright colors, sharp smells, and so forth are often perceived when less intense stimuli are not.

Processing

Processing of internal and external communication occurs at three levels: cognitive, emotional, and physiological. At each level of processing, some stimuli receive more conscious attention than others. This attention is a function of the particular stimulus and of the context in which it is presented. Some stimuli are perceived with full awareness (traffic lights, sirens, TV programs), while others may not be consciously noticed (background noise during a lecture, the hum of fluorescent lights in a room). Stimuli that are perceived consciously, or at least with some awareness, are the first to be processed. Stimuli that are perceived subconsciously are usually "stored" in your memory for later processing.

COGNITIVE PROCESSING **Cognitive processes** include the storage, retrieval, sorting, and assimilation of information. We don't know exactly how such processing occurs; our goal here is simply to describe these processes on both the conscious and subconscious cognitive levels.

MEMORY STORAGE The storage of information that we choose to remember is called **memory storage.** There are three forms of memory storage: (1) sensory storage, in which the information is held for only an instant; (2) short-term memory, in which the information is stored for several seconds; and (3) long-term memory, in which the information is stored indefinitely. **Sensory storage** refers to our ability to hold some information for a fraction of a second after the stimulus disappears. For example, you are not aware of the gaps between frames when you watch a movie because each frame is held in sensory storage until the next appears. The major difference between sensory storage and **short-term memory** is that in the latter, data is analyzed, identified, and simplified so that it can be conveniently stored and handled. Short-term memory is a kind of "holding device" in which you keep information until you are ready to use it or discard it. If such information seems useful, you may transfer it to the permanent storage of **long-term memory** for future reference.

RETRIEVAL Information is stored so that it can be used to help establish the meaning of later incoming stimuli. However, stored information is relatively useless unless it can be retrieved from memory. Such **retrieval** takes the form of either recognition or recall. **Recognition** involves awareness that certain information is familiar, having been experienced previously. **Recall** is more difficult, in that it requires reconstruction of the information that has been stored. For example, while we may recognize a certain word whose meaning we looked up last week, we may be unable to recall its definition.

SORTING Your mind contains countless bits and pieces of information. In any particular processing situation, you must first select or **sort** the most relevant information from your entire storehouse of knowledge. Here again we know very little about the actual workings of our individual selection systems. We do know, however, that such selection processes occur. For example, when we read, we sort the letters until we are able to make words of them.

ASSIMILATION Cognitive processing is not simply the sum of memory storage, retrieval, and sorting functions. Rather, it involves **assimilation,** the process of incorporating some aspect of the environment into the whole set of mental functionings in order to make sense out of what goes on around us. To continue our reading example, your ability to read was first learned, then stored in long-term memory. Whenever you open a book, you retrieve this information, use it to sort the letters on the page into words, and then assimilate the words into sentences and ideas that have meaning for you.

EMOTIONAL PROCESSING The second type of intrapersonal processing is **emotional processing,** which is the nonlogical response of an organism to a stimulus. Later in this chapter we will take a closer look at the different variables that operate in emotional processing. However, it is important to mention here that variables, ranging from attitudes, beliefs, and opinions at the subconscious level to emotions at the conscious level, all interact to determine our response to any particular communication.

PHYSIOLOGICAL PROCESSING The third type of processing occurs at the physiological level. Although ***physiological processing*** is of obvious importance in staying alive, its significance to intrapersonal communication is only beginning to be recognized. Some of the subconscious variables in this process are heart rate, brain activity, muscle tension, blood pressure, and body temperature.

Brain wave activity has been given considerable attention lately as an aid in determining information processing. Have you ever wondered what parts of your brain process certain types of information? Research with an electroencephalograph (EEG) suggests that we alternate between

"*It looks OK to me.*"

(George Dole)

our right and left brain hemispheres to process stimuli. Generally, if you are balancing your checking account, reading a textbook, or writing a term paper, you will be using your left hemisphere. The left hemisphere processes information logically and is concerned with speech and with mathematical and analytical tasks. The right hemisphere, in contrast, processes information abstractly and is involved with imagery, as well as spatial, musical, and **gestalt** tasks. When you listen to your favorite album, imagine how you will look in a new outfit, or sketch a picture, you are using your right brain hemisphere.

Monitoring physiological variables makes it possible to control internal processes. First, we must be aware of what our states are. Awareness is much more developed in some people than in others. For most people conscious physiological awareness is limited to sensations of pleasure, pain, tension, and relaxation. Sometimes **biofeedback,** a form of external self-feedback, is given to help people become more aware of their physiological processing. Subjects are attached to instruments that provide information about physiological levels such as pulse rate, muscle tension, and skin temperature. In some manner this information helps individuals to alter these levels. For example, biofeedback has been used to teach control of bodily functions such as heart rate, blood pressure, epileptic attacks, cardiac stress, and the rate that supplementary blood vessels can be strengthened and activated after paralysis.[5]

Transmission   The process by which messages are sent from a source to a receiver is called **transmission.** In intrapersonal communication the source and the receiver are the same person. Thus, transmission takes place through nerve impulses in the brain rather than through sound waves in the air or words written on a page. The intrapersonal communication cycle is completed when the brain reacts to these nerve impulses by transmitting a message to smooth muscles, which regulate the movements of the body. As we described at the start of this chapter, putting a hot hand on a hot pan causes the individual's touch receptors to send a neural transmission to the brain, saying, "It's hot," which causes the brain to transmit a message to the muscles in the hand, ordering, "Move away from the pan immediately."

Feedback   We usually think of feedback as information from another person. In intrapersonal communication, however, there are two kinds of *self*-feedback—external and internal.

External self-feedback is the part of your message that you hear yourself. This kind of feedback enables you to correct your own mistakes. For example, you would surely backtrack if you heard yourself say something like "external felf-seedback."

[5]Dorelle Markley Heisel, *Biofeedback Strategies for Interpersonal Relationships* (New York: Gordon and Breach, 1981), p. 30.

Internal self-feedback is usually picked up through bone conduction, nerve endings, or muscular movement. For example, you might perceive an awkward facial gesture without actually seeing it—simply by feeling the muscle tension in your face. Again, perceiving this information enables you to correct yourself.

Interference is another important variable in the communication process. *Interference* refers to any factor that negatively affects communication. It can occur at any point along the communication network and at any level of communication. For example, the blast of your neighbor's stereo or a splitting headache might make it impossible for you to read.

A special form of interference occurs intrapersonally when stimuli are processed at one level, although another level is better suited to dealing with them. For example, many people react emotionally to information that should be processed on a cognitive level. Have you ever started crying or gotten angry in response to a bad test score, when if you had remained calm, you might have been able to analyze and profit from the bad news? On the other hand, some individuals insist on processing information on the cognitive level when an emotional response would actually be more helpful. Often a good cry can relieve the pressures of a bad day better than a careful rehash of the day's events.[6]

Interference

THE EFFECTS OF INTRAPERSONAL VARIABLES ON COMMUNICATION

Even though a particular communication may focus on the here and now, your personality and past experience influence your interpretation of it. Thus, it is important to consider the intrapersonal factors that influence the communicators. For example, the experiences of someone who has recently lost a mate will no doubt affect that person's communications on the subject of death.

The way you react to the following situation will be determined by your personal orientation.

Personal Orientation

> Warren and Jerry are interviewing for the job of advertising copywriter in a large advertising agency. Neither of them has had any experience, but both come to the interview prepared to show samples of the kind of work they are capable of producing. Jerry's samples represent many hours of hard work and a little talent, while Warren's show much talent but very little effort—he lifted them almost word for word from a textbook.

How do you feel about Jerry and Warren? Do you respect Jerry for his honesty and hard work, or do you appreciate Warren's craftiness in trying

---

[6]Larry L. Barker and Renee Edwards, *Intrapersonal Communication* (Dubuque, Iowa: Gorsuch Scarisbrick, 1980), pp. 7–8.

to get the kind of job he wants? Your reaction to this situation reflects the values, attitudes, beliefs, and opinions that make up your personal orientation.

VALUES   Each of us maintains a set of **values,** which are moral or ethical judgments of things we consider important. Values can be a source of conflict within an individual as well as a barrier between people of opposing standards. Fearing a malpractice suit, for instance, a doctor who comes upon an accident victim may be reluctant to offer assistance. His or her values will determine what action is taken. Sometimes an individual will voice one set of values and be guided by another. For example, parents may scold their children for dishonesty but think nothing of cheating on their income tax.

ATTITUDES   An **attitude** is a learned tendency to react positively or negatively to an object or situation. It implies a positive or negative evaluation of someone or something. Attitudes operate at three different levels: (1) cognitive, (2) affective, and (3) instrumental. The cognitive level involves a particular belief, the affective level involves a particular feeling, and the instrumental level involves overt behavior or action.

Let's examine a specific situation. Carlotta Ramirez, a member of the state board of higher education, is a strong opponent of free tuition. Her negative attitude can be broken down in this way:

1. Cognitive (belief) = People who value a college education should be willing to pay for it, even if it means going to work to get enough money for tuition.
2. Affective (feeling) = People who try to get something for nothing make me angry.
3. Instrumental (action) = I vote no on the proposal for free tuition at state universities.

(Ken Karp)

BELIEFS, OPINIONS, AND PREJUDICES   We have already used the term *be-lief.* A belief is anything accepted as true. Note that this definition does not imply either a positive or a negative judgment. For example, you may believe that there is life on other planets, yet this belief does not indicate a positive or negative attitude toward that idea. However, if you were to take your belief one step further to say that since you believe there is life on other planets, it would be in our best interests to increase space exploration programs, you would then be voicing an *opinion.* An opinion lies somewhere in between an attitude and a belief. It implies a positive or negative reaction.

Not all our beliefs and opinions are well founded. Sometimes they are based on preconceived ideas and not on our own actual experiences. In this case they are, in fact, prejudices—preformed judgments about a particular person, group, or thing. None of us is free from prejudice, but certain prejudices are more harmful than others. Think for a moment about your own experiences with prejudice, when you were either guilty of prejudice or were its victim. Or consider this example of how foolish our prejudices can be:

> Although it was against her principles, Ruth had agreed to help a good friend out of a tight spot by accepting a blind date with the friend's uncle from Louisiana. Ruth, who had never been south of Philadelphia, just knew that an evening spent with this hick was going to be one of the most boring of her life.
>
> He arrived, and, sure enough, his accent was unlike anything Ruth had ever heard. By evening's end, however, she had changed her mind. Full of New Orleans food and admiration for the most interesting and beautifully mannered man she had ever met, Ruth eagerly awaited their next date.
>
> He never called again. A few weeks later, Ruth learned from her friend that he had returned to New Orleans and, before leaving, had announced: "All Yankee women are alike—hard to please!"

Think about the groups toward which you may be prejudiced. Does this example suggest ways in which you may be oversimplifying to the point of prejudice?

Another way the self affects our communication is through personality variables known as *traits.* Personality traits are those qualities that distinguish one personality from another. As the following examples indicate, some personality traits aid communication, but many are barriers to communication.

Personality Traits

LOCUS OF CONTROL   One important personality variable which affects the communication process is the degree to which we perceive reinforcement either as contingent upon our own behavior (*internal locus of control*) or as a result of forces beyond our control and due to chance, fate, or powerful others.[7] There should be, for example, a difference in communi-

---

[7]Hanna Levenson, "Differentiating Among Internality, Powerful Others, and Chance," in *Research with the Locus of Control Construct (Vol I): Assessment Methods,* ed. Herbert M. Lefcourt (New York: Academic Press, 1981), pp. 15–17.

cation patterns between those who believe that they control events and those who believe that their desired outcomes will accrue as a function of the degree to which they fit in with the beliefs, desires, or attitudes of people who have power over them. The former person, with a more internal locus of control, would be more upfront and direct upon presenting new plans to an upper-level supervisor, while the latter person's communication (the person with an external locus of control) would be more indirect, vague, and ambiguous.

MANIPULATION   Related to the locus of control which a person exhibits is the degree to which he attempts to manipulate others. Generally, people vary with regard to the characteristic of **manipulation,** or the degree to which they attempt to achieve goals by dominating and controlling others. However, research has shown that people who have an external locus of control (that is, who believe that the world is ordered and controlled by others) often desire that control for themselves and tend to exhibit greater manipulative behaviors than people who exhibit an internal locus of control. Given that the latter believe that the world is governed by chance, luck, or fate, they do not generally manifest excessive degrees of manipulation.

DOGMATISM   One of the most difficult personality traits encountered in a communication situation is **dogmatism.** Dogmatic individuals have closed minds and are reluctant to accept new ideas and opinions. Yet they may accept without question the word of certain authorities and expect the same kind of blind acceptance from those they consider their inferiors. Dogmatic individuals often remain steadfast to ideas or opinions in spite of contradictory evidence.

TOLERANCE OF AMBIGUITY   While some people can live with shades of gray, others insist on things being clearly defined and unambiguous. This varying **tolerance of ambiguity** frequently affects the communication process. Consider the following example:

> Phil and Max go to see the movie "Star Wars." After the movie both agree that the film was extremely well done. However, Max is bothered by several inconsistencies that Phil didn't seem to notice. Max points out three areas in the film that he thought were ambiguous. When he asks Phil for clarification, Phil admits that he can't explain the confusing segments of the film.

Phil's tolerance of ambiguity is greater than Max's. Phil was able to ignore the ambiguities, while Max found them troublesome. Perhaps you have experienced a similar situation when reading a complex book or when trying to analyze a particular communication interaction.

SELF-ESTEEM   Communication is also affected by the self-esteem of the sender and the receiver. **Self-esteem,** which is your enduring evaluation of yourself, often determines your confidence in what you are saying and your readiness to accept the view of others. Therefore, in the communication process, it is important to use your perception of another person's self-esteem as a means of evaluating certain messages. For example, individuals with high self-esteem may confidently state an opinion even without sufficient evidence. You might be quicker to question their veracity than that of speakers whose low self-esteem would prevent them from supporting unproven viewpoints.

MATURITY   Of the many personality variables, the one that most strongly affects communication is level of *maturity.* It is difficult to pinpoint the stage at which a person matures psychologically, but we usually judge a person as mature when he or she is able to function independently in a social setting. One measure of such maturity is the individual's ability to satisfy psychological needs for things such as independence, approval, affection, and so forth. What this means in a communication setting is the absence of intrapersonal conflicts that might intrude on objective transmission and interpretation of messages.

We all suffer from varying degrees of anxiety. For most of us anxiety stems from intrapersonal conflicts—conflicts between inner psychological needs and external realities. If severe enough, anxiety can distort your perception of yourself and your environment and thus act as a barrier to communication with others.

Defense Mechanisms

   The self must find various ways to resolve the anxiety produced by such intrapersonal conflict. These methods, known as **defense mechanisms,** help us accept things that might otherwise cause emotional pain. Defense mechanisms, when used in moderation, aid our personal adjustment to the environment. If used too much, however, they can become a crutch that distorts reality.

RATIONALIZATION   Defense mechanisms take many forms. Perhaps the best known is *rationalization,* an attempt to justify our failures or inadequacies. Most of us rationalize from time to time. For example, when Ellen was not hired for a job she wanted very badly, she rationalized her failure by claiming that the man who would have been her boss was threatened by her abilities. Jerry rationalized his rejection by a law school by telling everyone that he really didn't want to go anyway.

PROJECTION   Sometimes we ignore certain traits, motives, or behaviors in ourselves and attribute them to others. This defense mechanism is known as *projection.* Eleanor, who has a weight problem and is constant-

> We introduce ourselves
> To Planets and to Flowers
> But with ourselves
> Have etiquettes
> Embarrassments
> And awes.
>
> Emily Dickinson

ly dieting, goes to lunch with her friend Jan, a perfect size 8. When the women finish eating, Eleanor remarks, "I can tell you're still hungry." Actually, Jan is quite full. It is Eleanor who is still hungry.

INSULATION   One way to resolve conflicts caused by contradictions is to isolate contradictory feelings and/or information. This defense mechanism is known as *insulation.* For example, a member of a radical group who protests police brutality by bombing a precinct headquarters has clearly insulated contradictory behaviors. This person is able to oppose violence on the one hand and participate in violence of a "different" sort on the other.

REACTION FORMATION   Sometimes people deal with "undesirable" urges or behaviors with a defense mechanism known as *reaction formation.* This process involves denial of what you or society consider unacceptable feelings or behaviors, coupled with extreme advocacy of the opposite position. For example, someone who is easily aroused by pictures of nudes may deny this tendency by becoming an outspoken opponent of pornography.

IDENTIFICATION   We have discussed the importance of identification in developing self-concept. The *identification process* can also be used as a defense mechanism against insecurity or inadequacy. Thus, adolescents, who often feel uncertain about themselves, may seek security by identifying themselves with stars of the entertainment or sports worlds. Such identification accounts for much of the popularity of personalities such as Elvis Presley, Linda Carter, Bill Cosby, and the "Fonz."

REPRESSION   Some people deal with unpleasant or unacceptable feelings, desires, or experiences by repressing them. *Repression* is a defense mechanism that keeps certain thoughts and feelings beneath the conscious level. Thus, children brought up in overly strict homes, where outbursts are severely punished, often learn to repress anger.

SUMMARY

The most basic level of communication is intrapersonal, involving the sending and receiving of messages within one individual. This is the level on which you communicate with yourself.

Intrapersonal communication is a function of the physical self, the emotional self, the intellectual self, habits, and private versus public situations. In addition, the need for a unified conceptual system and the picture that you have of yourself—your self-concept—also have a strong influence on these self-communications. Your past experiences, reference groups, and accustomed roles combine in ever-changing relationships to form this self-concept. At the same time, internal and external stimuli affect the cognitive, emotional, and physiological processing of intrapersonal communication.

An individual's intrapersonal communication must be considered in any analysis of interpersonal communication situations. For example, personality variables such as manipulation, locus of control, dogmatism, tolerance of ambiguity, self-esteem, and maturity—and personal orientations, values, attitudes, and beliefs—all intrude on objective transmission and interpretation of interpersonal messages. Communication is further hampered by the many defense mechanisms people use to minimize anxiety.

Exercises

GROUP EXPERIENCES

Who Are You?

Description: Understanding the many selves that exist inside you is not an easy task. In this activity you will repeatedly be asked the question, "Who are you?" At first the answers may come easily, but after several minutes you may be surprised at the increased difficulty you experience in answering the question. The purpose of this activity is to provide you with an opportunity to explore your perceptions of yourself.

Procedure: Divide into dyads. For the first 5 minutes, Person A should ask Person B the question, "Who are you?" Person B should answer this question with very short and concise phrases, such as "I am a student." As soon as Person B supplies an answer, Person A should once again repeat the question, "Who are you?" After 5 minutes the roles should be reversed, and Person B should ask the question.

Discussion: How did your answers illustrate (1) your perceptions of yourself and (2) others' perceptions of you? Do you have "multiple" concepts of your self? What do your answers say about the degree to which your self-concept is negative or positive? Ask your partner what he or she perceives you to be, based on your answers to the question. How does the way you see yourself affect your communication with others?

Cocktail Party

Description: Feedback from other people often plays an important role in the way we feel about ourselves—it may cause us to reevaluate our perceptions of ourselves. This activity provides you with an opportunity to experience the extent to which positive and negative feedback affects your responses to others and your perceptions of yourself.

Procedure: Each participant should receive a self-adhesive label to be worn on the forehead for this activity. Each label will have a short phrase written on it, such as:

> Criticize Me   I'm Boring
> I'm a Clown   Give Me Your Sexiest Look
> Frown at Me   Smile at Me

When you are ready to begin the activity, all participants should have labels placed on their foreheads. *No one is permitted to tell you what your label says.* Participants should move around and talk to people as if they were at a cocktail party. The "cocktail party" should last from 10 to 15 minutes, depending on the size of the group. As you talk with other people, you must respond to their labels (follow the directions on their labels), without actually telling them what their labels say. For example, if players are wearing labels saying "I'm boring," you must act as if everything they say is dull. You can do this by yawning, walking away, closing your eyes, or using your voice to show disinterest.

Discussion: Before you remove your label, try to guess what it says, based on the verbal and nonverbal feedback you have received. Next, classify your label—was it very negative, negative, neutral, positive, or very positive?

Begin the discussion by asking all those people who were wearing negative or very negative labels to share their experiences. Did they have an emotional response to the feedback they received? For example, did they become withdrawn, introverted, or depressed during the cocktail party? Then ask those people who had positive labels if they were talkative, extroverted, smiling, and gregarious. How would consistent positive or negative feedback from significant others (parent, friend) affect your emotions and ultimately your perception of yourself?

PERSONAL EXPERIENCES

1. We all seem to be affected, to varying degrees, by the type of feedback we receive from others. Observe the amount of positive, neutral, and negative feedback you receive during a two-hour period. How do the different types of feedback affect you? How would you react to a large amount of negative feedback?
2. Spend some time alone and consider people or groups with which you identify. Remember that identification is more than just imitation. When you identify with another person or a particular group, you see yourself as an extension of that person or group. What are the problems with identifying with another person or group? Why have you formed identifications with particular people or groups? What do your identifications reflect about your self-concept?
3. Keep a diary for a week. At the end of each day, record the feelings you experienced during the day. For example, you might write that you felt angry for most of the morning, but by the end of the day you felt very calm. At the end of the week, reread your log to determine if (a) you have experienced highly intense feelings that may properly be called emotions and (b) if those feelings were predominantly positive or negative. How does your inner world of feelings affect your communication with others?

DISCUSSION QUESTIONS

1. To what extent can you achieve effective communication with another person without understanding his or her self-concept, attitudes, and beliefs?
2. What effect does a positive or negative self-concept have on your communication with others?
3. What characteristics distinguish achieved roles from ascribed ones?
4. How would you draw the Johari Window for (a) an intimate relationship, (b) a casual relationship, and (c) an initial interaction with another person? Remember that you can change the proportions of any square.
5. How do you use the various defense mechanisms in your daily activites?

INTERPERSONAL COMMUNICATION

6

Exploratory Questions

1. How would you explain the following interpersonal communication skills: timing, clarity, open listening, feedback, and nonverbal behavior?
2. What are the relationships between effective interpersonal communication skills and attraction?
3. How is context important in interpersonal communication?
4. What six skills can be learned and developed to improve self-disclosure abilities?
5. What are some differences among the five phases of relationship development?
6. What are some differences among the five phases of relationship disintegration?
7. What are the four levels of social interaction?
8. What characterizes the three mental outlooks (ego states) of transactional analysis?
9. What are credibility and attraction and how are they related to person perception?
10. What are the seven Katz rules for communication in intimate relationships?
11. What are the guidelines for productive arguments, and what related principles can be used in conflict resolutions?

Will Rogers claimed he never met a man he didn't like. Few of us could honestly make that assertion, but most of us would agree that liking other people and being liked by them is an essential part of our lives. Yet everyone feels isolated and alone at times; everyone feels the need to seek out others, to share feelings and ideas. This sharing—the extension of ourselves to other people and their extensions toward us—is known as **interpersonal communication.**

The previous chapter on intrapersonal communication analyzed messages sent and received within one individual. Of course, the term *communication* is more often identified with transmission between individuals, or interpersonal communication.

THE INTERPERSONAL COMMUNICATION MODEL

Interpersonal communication can occur in any environment, be it formal (the lecture hall) or informal (a check-out line). Most interpersonal messages are informal, however, stemming from everyday, face-to-face encounters. Think of your own communication. From your first "Good morning" to your last "See you tomorrow," your interpersonal communication is usually spontaneous, unplanned, and loosely organized, probably even ungrammatical. With the exception of telephone conversations, most of this communication involves people close enough to see and touch each other. This makes sending and receiving messages much easier and eliminates the need for the kind of formal rules followed in debates, news conferences, or other public speaking situations.

DYADIC VERSUS SMALL GROUP COMMUNICATION

Much interpersonal communication involves a **dyad,** or two people in close contact. The potential for sending, receiving, and evaluating mes-

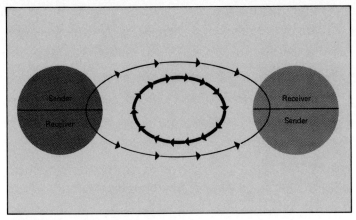

FIGURE 6-1 Dyadic Communication.

sages is divided between the two halves of the dyad (see Figure 6–1). That is, both participants alternate from one role to the other—sometimes originating messages, at other times responding to them. Both roles provide a means for exchanging information, but neither is complete in itself; if one participant only listened, and the other only spoke, communication would soon break down. Thus, communication in a dyad is very much a shared responsibility. This differentiates the dyad from the small group communication situations we will examine in the next chapter. In groups the balance of communication shifts. Because each participant has a different role and status in the group, the potential for receiving and transmitting messages is not evenly divided. Furthermore, group members serve not only as sources or destinations of messages, but they also function as channels to relay the messages of others.

What further differentiates interpersonal and group communication is purpose. Many groups are problem centered; that is, members are working together for a defined purpose, usually decision making or problem solving. In contrast, interpersonal communication in dyads focuses on the *sharing of meaning*. Although interpersonal dyads may also solve problems or make decisions, their messages convey a wider range of feelings and emotions. The information they exchange is not just the dry, factual material common, for example, in a sales meeting. Rather, it consists of meanings derived from personal experiences and observations. These interpersonal messages have a significant psychological impact: The process of translating thoughts into verbal and nonverbal messages increases the communicator's awareness of his or her feelings and self-concept. In turn, the listener's responses confirm or alter these feelings. With effective interpersonal communication, this process becomes reciprocal; both participants strengthen themselves and each other through the sharing of meanings and emotions.

This chapter examines the verbal and nonverbal behaviors and skills that determine our success or failure in such interpersonal communication. Reading about varied interpersonal relationships—husband-wife, parent-child, student-teacher—should provide you with useful insights about your own interpersonal communication.

INTERPERSONAL COMMUNICATION EFFECTIVENESS

Our introductory description of effective, reciprocal interpersonal communication obviously painted an idealized picture. Most of us, unfortunately, are not ideal communicators. The following section explores the principles of self-disclosure, context, timing, clarity, open listening, feedback, feedforward, nonverbal behavior, attraction, and person perception. It is our success or failure in applying these principles that determines how close to the ideal our interpersonal communication will be.

Self-Disclosure **Self-disclosure** lies at the heart of the process of interpersonal communication. It is the vehicle by which others know what is going on inside of you, what you are thinking and feeling, and what you care about. In addition, the degree to which we self-disclose acts as a measuring stick by which others judge us to be lonely or socially skilled.[1]

However, knowing these facts will not always make self-disclosure any easier. Our natural tendency is to hide feelings of incompetence, loneliness, guilt, worries over love and rejection, and conflicts over anger and resentment toward loved ones. Even when the feelings involved are not this intense, self-disclosure may still be difficult because of well-learned habits that help us to avoid emotional hurt. We all learn these evasive strategies as part of our socialization process. They are so rewarding that it becomes difficult to know when to put them away. Often in our society people are accustomed to hiding what they really want, think, or feel. For this reason, self-disclosure becomes a rare and valued gift. Confiding in others and receiving their confidences is, therefore, one of the most effective interpersonal communication tools.

Because of the importance of self-disclosure to the development of interpersonal relationships, communication researchers have explored both the nature and the skills associated with self-disclosing. These include the ability to assert oneself and the development of methods for describing perceptions, interpreting personal understanding, expressing emotions, clarifying intentions, and describing actions. These six skills may be learned, developed, and used to improve self-disclosure.[2]

[1]Gordon Chelune, Faye E. Sultan, and Carolyn L. Williams, "Loneliness, Self-Disclosure, and Interpersonal Effectiveness," *Journal of Counseling Psychology* 20 (March 1981), 140–46.
[2]Sherod Miller, Elam W. Nunnally, and Daniel B. Wackman, *Alive and Aware: Improving Communication in Relationships* (Minneapolis: Interpersonal Communication Programs, 1975), pp. 53–82.

The first and most important of these skills is speaking out for yourself, **Self-Assertion** stating your desires, feelings, and perceptions in a way that identifies them as your own. This **self-assertive** attitude shows that you value yourself. In turn, it leaves room for the listener to assert his or her own feelings and opinions. Saying, "Everyone's going to that new steak house," hides your own feelings behind a mass of general opinion. Better to say, "I want to check out that new steak house." This reveals what *you* want. Similarly a remark such as, "I know you'd like to go to that new steak house," fails to convey your own feelings, and imposes, perhaps incorrectly, an opinion upon someone else.

Another vital skill is the ability to describe your perceptions—the specif- **Sense** ics of what you see, hear, touch, taste, and smell. These messages are elic- **Statements** ited through the use of **sense statements,** or statements which allow others to know how you feel about things that are happening around you. An example of a sense statement might be when Jacqui says to Rich,

(United Nations/Michael Tzovaras)

"You know, when you tap your fingers like that, it makes me feel uncomfortable." Typically, you pay attention to only a small part of the available sense data. This limited awareness often leads you to the wrong conclusions. For example, when a friend arrives at your house two hours late, you might complain, "Oh, you had to rush because you forgot about our date"—that is, until you notice the bruise on her head and the dent in her car's front fender.

Interpretive Statements

It is also important to make precise, ***interpretive statements*** which indicate your personal understanding of a situation. Statements such as these allow one to clarify the situation. "This morning at breakfast when I began talking about buying a new car, I noticed that you got up in a hurry and started clearing the table," is a sense statement that could be followed by the interpretive statement, "I don't think you want to discuss buying a car now."

Feeling Statements

Similar to interpretive statements are ***feeling statements,*** which reveal your emotions to yourself and to those around you. In our breakfast scene effective communication could have continued if the speaker had explained, "I'd like a new car. The old one is falling apart, but I'm really uptight about spending so much money now." In this example feelings were hidden by silence; in other situations the same effect can be achieved by substituting generalizations, opinions, or even accusations for statements of feeling. A shouted, "Men are so insensitive!" may mask

(© 1977. Reprinted by permission of Brenda Burbank)

"Of course you don't understand me, Edwin, because you listen to what I say instead of what I mean."

> The highest compact we can make with our fellow is—"Let there be truth between us two forevermore."
>
> Ralph Waldo Emerson

the more personal and emotional message, "I feel angry when you criticize the way I dress." Similarly, an accusatory, "You spend too much time with your buddies from the softball team," may really mean, "I'm envious of the time you spend with the guys. I miss you and feel that you're rejecting me."

Sometimes you make what sounds like a feeling statement but really do not express your deepest emotions. "I enjoy going out with you," may be a shallow substitute for, "My feelings for you are growing—I love you." This difficulty in expressing deep feelings often reveals your uncertainties about what you really feel. Because you are accustomed to keeping your emotions under tight control, or because you are afraid that exposing your emotions will make you vulnerable to rejection or criticism, you may become unable to reveal these feelings even to yourself. Practice in making statements of feeling can help you resolve these difficulties and improve both self-awareness and interpersonal communication.

Intention Statements

Intention statements let others know the purposes of and motives behind statements or actions. While your intentions may be perfectly clear to you, your friends may fail to recognize them or may misinterpret them: John has spent ten minutes raving about a little-known bluegrass group that's playing at a local bar. Linda doesn't know whether he's just a bluegrass fanatic sharing his excitement about an unexpected find or whether he's angling for a date. An intention statement could clear up her confusion: "I'm telling you about the Charles River Valley Boys because I've been following bluegrass performers for years and they're the best I've ever heard," or "I've been telling you about this group because I'd like you to come with me to hear them Friday night."

Action Statements

Action statements describe what you've done, what you're doing, or what you plan to do. They fill in information the listener might not be aware of and tell him or her what to expect of you. "I tried to reach you all afternoon," or "I'll come over tomorrow at 8:00," are examples of action statements that fulfill these functions. Other types of action statements indicate that you are aware both of your own behavior and of the effect your behavior has on the listener: "Sorry, I feel anxious tonight and haven't been paying attention to what you're saying. I'm not bored with you—I've been worrying about some proposed layoffs at the plant." By describing his behavior, this speaker showed his partner that he cares about her feelings, an important goal in interpersonal communication

CONTEXT AND TIMING

In Chapter 1 we discussed the importance of context. Context refers to the circumstances that surround and give meaning to words or statements. As the context changes, meanings also change. At a funeral, for example, crying expresses grief; yet crying at a wedding is an expression of happiness. Similarly, teasing a co-worker during a friendly lunch about a mistake she has made on the job will probably be taken as a tease. If, however, you tease that person while team-presenting a new project to the boss, your comments may be incorrectly (or correctly!) intepreted as an act of "one-upmanship."

CLARITY

Clarity is the art of saying exactly what you mean, rather than hiding a message that must be decoded by the listener. This is closely related to the skills of self-disclosure we discussed earlier.

After coming home from a party, Barry remarks to his wife, "Jean really knows how to move—I could watch her dance all night." What he really wants to say is, "I like to dance. Why don't you dance with me when we go out?" Barry's wife is likely to misinterpret the spoken message, understanding it as an attempt to inspire jealousy. If Barry had thought and expressed himself clearly and directly, this misunderstanding and the resultant hostility could have been avoided.

OPEN LISTENING

Chapter 3 discussed the difference between hearing and listening. It's easy to hear, letting words float by you without listening, focusing your attention on what is being said, or understanding its meaning fully and completely. *Open listening* takes attention focusing one step further, to the point of forgetting for the moment your own concerns and biases and responding intelligently and sympathetically to what is being said. Consider Marie, who comes home from work exhausted: "I had a tough day at the office. Worked through lunch and then my boss scrapped all my designs for the new showcase." The open listener will resist the temptation to snap back, "You're telling me about tough days! Mine was even worse. . . ." Instead, he or she will hear the speaker out, making responses that indicate attention and concern: "That job has been getting you down a lot lately. Do you think it's time to switch employers?"

FEEDBACK AND FEEDFORWARD

If you have been listening openly to what your partner has said, you will be able to offer positive, constructive feedback. Feedback, a term borrowed from computer technology, originally referred to a self-regulating

(© 1980 by S. Harris)

mechanism that keeps machines running smoothly and efficiently. As we mentioned in Chapter 3, communication feedback keeps interpersonal relationships running smoothly. You provide this feedback by paraphrasing (thus confirming or correcting your understanding of a message), by asking questions (thus demonstrating your interest and your desire for more information), or by responding with feeling statements (showing that you care about your partner). The following dialogue illustrates all three of these forms of feedback:

Andy: My trip to Paris last summer was the most interesting experience of my life.

Mark: You really enjoyed your stay in Paris. What did you like best?

Andy: Well, I lived in a dorm for foreign students and I got to meet people from all over the world.

Mark: I can appreciate your pleasure in meeting people from different backgrounds. Two years ago my family hosted an exchange student from Zambia and I really grew a lot from knowing him.

We often require feedback from others to shape our own behavior. This is especially true in social situations, where we tend to monitor our own actions to conform to the behavior of the group. Social cues are the feedback for this self-monitoring behavior. At a party, for example, self-monitors would model their behavior on that of the other guests, talking quietly when others talk quietly, laughing at jokes that seem to amuse the other guests, drinking only as much or as little as others do. In contrast, nonconformists disregard this situational feedback. They are low self-monitors, following their own inclinations to start dancing while others are engaged in serious conversation, or limiting their own drinking while othes do not.

Concern about social feedback also helps speakers to plan communication strategies. Suppose, for example, that you are nervous about asking a co-worker for a date. From casual conversations during coffee breaks, you know that she likes sports, and you hope she'll agree to meet you at next Saturday night's hockey game. On the other hand, you worry that she might consider Saturday night a "heavy" dating night, inappropriate for a first date. Your reasoning process in anticipating feedback is known as **feedforward.** Feedforward in this situation permits you to set up two possible plans: the evening hockey game and an afternoon gymnastics exhibit. If, when you call your friend, she expresses hesitancy about going to the Saturday game, you can then switch to your contingency plan.

NONVERBAL BEHAVIOR

Nonverbal behavior plays a strong, necessary role in interpersonal relationships. So much can be "said" by a smile, hug, or handclasp that words are often not needed.

As we mentioned in Chapter 4, eye behavior is especially important in interpersonal situations. Studies have shown, for example, that eye contact between close couples is much greater than that between casually dating couples. Besides showing interest and caring, eye contact can also express hostility or the desire for dominance. Indeed, research indicates that competing athletes use staring as an aggressive gesture, similar to the threat displays used by gorillas and other primates. In contrast, the avoided glance often signifies submission.[3]

Touching is another nonverbal factor important in interpersonal relationships. Touching usually communicates intimacy: Couples walk down the street with their arms around each other; a father caresses his baby; a child hugs her dog. Touching can also communicate status and power. Ask yourself, for instance, who would be more likely to use a patronizing pat on the head or an aggressive poke in the chest: a professor or a student; the policeman or the accused; the doctor or the patient; the

[3]Chris L. Kleinke, *First Impressions: The Psychology of Encountering Others* (Englewood Cliffs, N.J.: Prentice-Hall, 1975), p. 26.

boss or the employee. Status differences related to sex also reveal themselves in touching behavior. Who is usually the first to hold the other's hand or to demonstrate physical affection in a male-female relationship? Women have come a long way, but it is still rare for one to make the first move by putting an arm around her date in a darkened movie theater.

INTERPERSONAL ATTRACTION

Self-disclosure, effective timing, clarity, open listening, appropriate feedback, and nonverbal behavior all work together to increase your interpersonal effectiveness. Interestingly enough, this increased effectiveness somehow improves your interpersonal attraction, the "good vibrations," "magnetism," or "invisible force" that somehow draws people together.

What we mean by **attraction** is a positive attitude, movement toward, or liking between two people. What causes this attraction is rarely "love at first sight." Rather, the cause can be found in the complex mix of variables within ourselves and within the other individual. Research indicates that many of the factors that determine attraction relate to interpersonal communication. One example is the factor of propinquity, geographical closeness. Consider railroad commuters, for example. Every day these small groups of people stand together on a platform waiting for their usual train. Before they started commuting, these riders did not know each other. But now because they see each other on a daily basis and share the same territory, they feel a kind of mutual bond. They greet each other with a friendly "Good morning," discuss what TV shows they watched the night before, and moan about the weather. Some of them have lunch together.

(Marc Anderson)

Students' friendships also arise from propinquity. Leah started taking yoga lessons at the YMCA. In the class she met a couple of people who shared many of her other interests, such as Eastern religion, natural foods, and TM. The three students became close friends and continued to see each other after the lessons were over. Sharing a common territory, in this case the YMCA classroom, brought these students together. But so did their similar interests. It is often hard to determine which is more important for interpersonal attraction: Do people form relationships because they share similar interests or common territory, or does the interpersonal attraction come first, making us think that we have common interests? Research supports both viewpoints. On the one hand, individuals who like each other perceive themselves as being more similar than they really are. Studies have shown that friends overestimate how much they share likes and dislikes. On the other hand, much research sustains the belief that people become friends because they share like interests, beliefs, and attitudes. It always feels good to state an opinion or come up with an idea that is readily and willingly accepted by others. Thus, it is not surprising that people feel attracted to, and seek out the company of, other people who agree with and therefore reinforce their own ideas. Receiving this positive reaction about your attitudes gives you faith and confidence in yourself as a human being.

Person Perception As we mentioned earlier, we make first impressions in about fifteen seconds. Later, after we've gotten to know a person better, we make predictions about how he or she will respond in a variety of situations. How many times have you said or heard, "He's always late!" "I never believe anything the paper says," or "We figured you would come around to our way of thinking." Many of our feelings and decisions about others are influenced by their perceived credibility and/or attraction. Thus, our skillfulness in assessing these characteristics accurately affects our ability to maintain interpersonal relationships.

CREDIBILITY   Why is it that when a father tells his quarterback son to try a new play, the son ignores him; but when the boy's coach says the same thing, the son tries it immediately? Or why do we agree with the views and opinions of one politician and reject another candidate with the same views and opinions? Usually our decisions are based on our view of a person's credibility. *Credibility* is whether or not someone is worthy of belief or trust. Generally, our decisions are formed by past experiences, logical reasoning, intuition, and the degree to which we perceive others as similar to ourselves.[4] We go back to the same doctor because she has

[4]Donald Atkinson, Stephen Brady, and J. Manual Casas, "Sexual Preference, Similarity, Attitude Similarity, and Perceived Counselor Credibility and Attractiveness," *Journal of Counseling Psychology* 28 (1981): 504–9.

helped us in the past; we take classes under the same professor because he is an effective and interesting communicator; and we choose friends who like the outdoors as much as we do.

ATTRACTION **Attraction** is similar to credibility in that it is often based on past experience, logical reasoning, and intuition; however, attractiveness is also determined by other factors. Physical appearance is important (see Chapter 4), but much interpersonal attraction is based on human needs. In *The Social Contract,* Robert Ardrey suggests that humans need to feel identity, stimulation, and security in relationships.[5] We make decisions about others after we have evaluated what they can offer to meet our personal needs. Just as we are attracted to others because of what they have to offer us, others are attracted to us because of what we have to offer them. When people are lonely and feel left out of society (identity), they may seek friendships or organizations that encourage participation (such as Parents Without Partners and Weight Watchers). A person who is bored with life may be attracted to people with a broad range of interests and activities for stimulation. A person who has been hurt by a recent romantic involvement may want a platonic relationship with security but without threat.

DEVELOPMENT OF DYADIC RELATIONSHIPS

Thus far we have examined skills that are important in interpersonal relationships, but you may be wondering where these relationships begin. Recent popular reading suggests that individual personalities evolve through a developmental process. Just as personality types evolve through life experiences, acquired knowledge, and environmental factors, relationships evolve in similar ways through time. It may take years to cultivate a friendship made in grade school or only a few seconds with "lovers at first sight."

Think for a moment about the types of relationships you are a part of in your family, school, job, and community. Each relationship has unique qualities that set it apart from others, even though the characteristics may be positive or negative. If we look back to the beginning of each of our relationships, we see that there are a variety of reasons for the involvement. Maybe at one time you needed special care (mother), information (teacher), service (postman), or love (girlfriend/boyfriend). Relationships characteristically follow patterns of development. In his book *Social Inter-course,* Mark Knapp explains interpersonal relationship development and presents phases of relationship development (coming together) and disintegration

Phases of
Relationship
Development

---

[5]Robert Ardrey, *The Social Contract* (New York: Antheneum, 1970), pp. 108–9.

(coming apart).[6] We will discuss five phases of relationship development: initiating, experimenting, intensifying, integrating, and bonding.

INITIATING   During the first stage of relationship development, we make conscious and unconscious judgments about others. Although we are cautious at this stage, within fifteen seconds we have usually sized up the other person. David entered a singles' bar and scanned the room for prospective dancing partners. He stereotyped and classified available women according to personal preferences. After narrowing the field to two women, David determined his approach strategies. Finally, he began a conversation by asking, "Would you like a drink?" "Are you waiting for someone?" "You look like you need company," or "It was nice of you to save me this seat." Sometimes we initiate communication nonverbally. In the same situation the girl at the bar could easily signal for David to leave by looking away, turning her back to him, or moving to another stool.

EXPERIMENTING   After making initial contact we begin experimenting with the unknown. This stage is known as the "do you know" period of interaction. Most relationships do not develop beyond this superficial point. We can all remember situations in which we used small talk to establish a friendly atmosphere. For example, after being introduced to her blind date, Renee attempts to find common interests by asking about Tom's major, family, favorite bars, job, and so on. Renee may not even be interested, but she asks questions to make the situation more comfortable. If initial interaction goes well, each person probes to determine whether pursuing the relationship is worthwhile.

INTENSIFYING   As relationships develop into friendships, participation and awareness are intensified. Gradually, steps are taken to strengthen the bond by asking for and reciprocating favors. The two personalities begin to blend through self-disclosure and trust. Statements such as "I've never told anyone this. . . ." or "There is something you need to know: I was arrested when I was eighteen. . . ." become more common. The verbal relationship usually changes with the couple using nicknames, pet names, and slang. Also more time is spent sharing expectations, assumptions, and experiences. Nonverbal behaviors begin to communicate just as effectively as verbal ones. As a relationship intensifies, you notice mutual winks, nods, touches, and so on.

INTEGRATING   At this point in relationship development, we agree to meet the expectations of the other person. Two people begin to share many commonalities such as interests, attitudes, friends, and property. At this stage the people do not completely lose their identity; however, there is a need to please the other person by giving in to his or her way of life.

[6]Mark Knapp, *Social Intercourse* (Boston: Allyn and Bacon, 1978), pp. 17–27.

Not only do the individuals treat each other differently, but the two are now seen as a unit. In a dating relationship Jim and Candy would tend to dress for each other. Jim is interested in racquetball, so Candy joins a beginning racquetball class. Candy collects antiques, and to help, Jim subscribes to the magazine *Treasures in Your Attic*. When friends have parties, Jim and Candy are invited together rather than individually.

BONDING   In the final stage of relationship development, a formal contract signifies a bonded commitment. In today's society the union may be marriage or a verbal commitment to live together. The **bonding** of any relationship can become a powerful force in making the relationship better or worse. Marriage is the most accepted form of commitment and usually gains social and institutional support. However, the couple also usually has to agree to the rules and regulations of the contract. In many relationships lasting commitment is seen as possible only in marriage. For this reason, many couples end up either splitting or getting married after years of dating. Trial bonding is also used at this stage. After living together secretly for two years, Bill and Amy decided to make their commitment legal by getting married.

As children we are led to believe that relationships last forever, but they don't. Statistics indicate that two out of every three marriages end in divorce. Even the closest of friends go their separate ways over trivial matters, and many job changes are the result of negative interpersonal relationships rather than job dissatisfaction. Just as with relationship development, relationship disintegration can take years—or it can take a few seconds. After their children were married, David and Betty found that they had nothing left in common after thirty-six years of marriage. Identical twin brothers never spoke to each other again after one saw the other with his girlfriend. We have examined patterns of relationship development, and we will now look at patterns of disintegration. The five phases of relationship disintegration are differentiating, circumscribing, stagnating, avoiding, and terminating.

Phases of
Relationship
Disintegration

DIFFERENTIATING   Integration in a relationship signifies a union, and differentiation signifies a separation, or split. Differences occur at every stage of relationship development, but with differentiating there is increased interpersonal distance. At this stage differences become more and more apparent. The people usually begin to want freedom and individuality. Both parties begin to play games that test the relationship and the other person's involvement. After Bob and Kathy had been dating for seven years, friends and relatives expected them to get married. However, during the last few years, the couple began experiencing different lifestyles, and they began to want different things out of life. At one time each knew what the other person wanted, but now they weren't so sure.

CIRCUMSCRIBING   When relationships begin to disintegrate, there is less total communication. Topics of conversation are controlled to reduce conflict and tension. On the surface everything appears to be all right, but underlying difficulties are evident. The presence of others increases interaction and socially the relationship seems unaltered. Sally wondered, after having so much fun at her friend's party, why she and Chip sat in silence all the way home. At this stage of disintegration, there also tends to be less expression of commitment verbally and nonverbally. Affection is given only occasionally, and loving remarks are almost nonexistent.

STAGNATING   During the stagnating stage all efforts to communicate are abandoned. The interpersonal atmosphere is cold. Nonverbal messages are often the only feeling states expressed. As Jane got home from her dance recital, she was met with a cold stare from her husband. We wonder why individuals would continue a relationship that is so unrewarding. Many people stay in relationships because they want to punish the other person, they hope for reconciliation, or they want to avoid the pain of ending the relationship. Sandy was afraid she could not pay the rent on her own, so she continued to live with Lynn, even though it was like having two roommates because Lynn was living with Ron.

AVOIDING   At this stage one or both parties act as though the other person doesn't exist. Each person tries to find ways to avoid interaction. Often meetings are arranged so that there is someone else around or excuses are made for not being able to be with the other person alone. Toward the end of this stage, there is seeking for a permanent state of separation. Linda called John on the phone because they hadn't communicated in two weeks. She said, "John, we need to talk this thing through. Can we get together this weekend? How about Monday? Do you have a test on Tuesday? Okay, then you tell me the next time that you are free and I'll change my plans."

TERMINATING   The termination of a relationship can be immediate or delayed. A friend may die of a heart attack, a marriage may dissolve because of an affair, or your company may transfer you to another city. Termination is dependent upon the type of relationship, perceived status of the relationship, effects of dissociation, and timing factors. As with relationship development, the final stage of relationship disintegration can occur with heated words over a poker game or slowly and unobtrusively by failing to make plans to get together. Methods of termination are usually dependent upon future goals and expectations.

The stages of relationship development and disintegration can occur in order, as we have presented above, or they can start at any phase of development. In a crowded bar a fight might end a relationship that was a minute old. If a person breaks into a movie theater ticket line, you quickly make a judgment and decide that this is a person to avoid.

ANALYZING INTERPERSONAL COMMUNICATION

Our discussion so far has emphasized the processes involved in interpersonal communication. In this section we turn our attention to the people involved and to the interpersonal messages they exchange.

Just as individuals are emotionally healthy and productive, or sick and ineffective, so too are interpersonal relationships. Manipulative involvements are a prime example. In such relationships one or both members try to satisfy psychological needs by smothering the individuality or potential of the other. In manipulative relationships based on dependency, for example, one or both partners may be so "addicted" to the other that he or she drops all outside interests, activities, and friends. Just as the single-minded pursuit of a drug addict destroys his or her life, so can the dependency relationship destroy self-identity, self-respect, and all chances for growth and development. Many marriages suffer from these manipulative tendencies. Conversely, other marriages fail for the opposite reason: lack of involvement. When no effort is made to maintain a marriage, the relationship becomes boring and stale. Such marriages stifle personal growth and self-realization.

> **Types of Relationships**

The ideal marriage, or any interpersonal relationship, is based on growth facilitation. The individuals involved are united but do not lose their identities. Through their shared communication they achieve growth that they would not have reached on their own. In short, the whole exceeds the sum of its parts. The couple becomes not two separate individuals but a pair—more sensitive, loving, and stable than they had been before.

Depending on the type of interpersonal relationship, different forms of communication or social interaction will take place.

> **Levels of Social Interaction**

ALTERNATING MONOLOGUE   The least productive and least fulfilling kind of communication, often seen in manipulative relationships, is the alternating monologue. Each individual knows the other is speaking but does not listen openly to what is being said. Each person is so preoccupied with his or her own concerns that there is no sharing or understanding of ideas. The end of one statement merely signals the beginning of an unrelated reply:

> Bob: You wouldn't believe what I had to do at work today.
> Grace: Oh, yes. Tonight I have to go over to school and take that exam.
> Bob: I almost quit, I was so angry at the boss.
> Grace: I cannot believe how hard I've studied for this test.
> Bob: Maybe I'll quit—get away from it all and have some fun.
> Grace: Hey, now you're talking. Have some fun. That's what I'll do tonight after the exam.

(Ken Karp)

(Ken Karp)

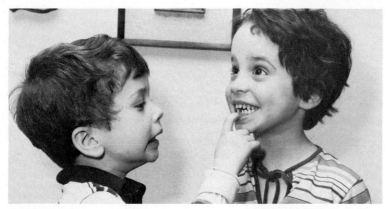

(Ken Karp)

(Ken Karp)

(Teri Lehigh Stratford)

(© 1982 Ed Lettau/Photo Researchers, Inc.)

In interpersonal communication in dyads, participants strengthen themselves and each other through the sharing of meanings and emotions.

(© 1976 Ray Ellis/Photo Researchers, Inc.)

(© 1977 David Barnes/Photo Researchers, Inc.)

STIMULUS-RESPONSE INTERACTION   Stimulus-response communications are no better. In these interactions the speaker proceeds in a set manner, independent of any responses the listener may make. The librarian who requests information to issue a card or the salesman who wants to know what size hiking boots you wear is participating in this type of interaction. They already know what questions to ask, and the responses do not change them.

INTERACTION WITH FEEDBACK   Alternating monologues and stimulus-response interaction are alike in their neglect of feedback. Interactions *with* feedback are more common and more productive. For example, a political canvasser bases his comments on the responses he gets from the voter.

Canvasser:	Excuse me, are you going to vote for Raymond Charles?
Voter:	That socialist? No way would he have my vote!
Canvasser:	Perhaps you received some wrong information about our candidate. Let me tell you a little about him.
Canvasser:	Excuse me, are you going to vote for Raymond Charles?
Voter:	I don't know. But I do know I don't want to be pestered.
Canvasser:	Excuse me. I'll just leave this information with you, so you can read it at your leisure.

Even in these feedback situations, responses may be based as much on habit or learning as on interpersonal factors. Because the canvasser has had many similar experiences in the past, his answers may be automatic, requiring no feedforward or feedback.

INTERACTION WITH EMPATHY   The most productive form of communication is interaction with empathy. Empathy means deep understanding of other people, identifying with their thoughts, feeling their pain, sharing their joy. Such empathy is typical of strong, healthy relationships. Indeed, empathetic communicators know each other so well that they can predict the responses to their messages. For example, Mario says to himself, "I know if I tell May that I'm not crazy about her new dress, she'll be hurt. So instead I'll say, 'May, that dress looks great on you, but I think the green one is even more becoming.' " This illustrates the special feedforward that empathy can produce.

Transactional Analysis   Psychiatrists, social scientists, and communication specialists have developed many complex analyses of interpersonal communication. Although each approach varies, the goal is identical: scientifically proven methodology for improving interpersonal relationships and, thereby, creating healthy, secure individuals who understand and like themselves and can participate in fulfilling, positive interpersonal involvements.

   Transactional analysis (TA) is one approach to this goal of improved interpersonal communication. According to TA theory, everyone possesses three mental outlooks or ego states: Parent, Adult, and Child. The Parent in you acts like a mother or father, nurturing at some times, critical at others, making evaluations and issuing proclamations of wisdom. It is the parent in you who says, "You should brush your teeth twice a day," or "Never do that again!" Your Adult stage processes current information, plans, prioritizes events, and represents logic and reason. In addition, it explores ranges of alternatives, estimates probabilities, and learns from experience, with statements such as, "The next thing to do is. . . ." or "All evidence considered, I think. . . ." Finally, it is the Child in you who elicits the urges, emotions, and patterns of behavior you knew as a youth and uses statements such as "Help me . . . I'm soooo tired," or "Oh no, not again!"[7]

Often each of your three ego states desires something different: The Parent wants one thing, the Adult another, and the Child a third. TA's purpose is to get the three parts of you working together as a functional whole. The best way to achieve this is to be alert to which ego state is in control at any given time. To do this, you must first look at your behavior—both verbal and nonverbal. Where did you learn to point your index finger in that way? Are the words you are using Parent words, such as "cute," "childish," or "immature," or are they Child words, such as "wowee," "No, I won't," and "gee"?

Next, it is important to analyze your interpersonal relationships. What ego state do you bring out in the people you talk with? If your Parent likes to dominate others, it will probably upset the Child in another person. If you act like an Adult, others will probably behave like Adults toward you.

Third, think back to your childhood and remember how you spoke and how your parents spoke to you then. Echoes of your childhood speech indicate that your Child is in control. Similarly, duplicating your parents' speech shows that the Parent in you has the upper hand.

Finally, and most importantly, analyze your own feelings. You should be able to sense which role you are playing at any specific time. But remember that all three states are real and necessary parts of your personality. Trying to banish your Child, for example, would destroy the natural, exuberant, and fun-loving part of you. Similarly, your Parent provides love and support. Rather than suppressing any one of these states, the important thing is to be aware of which state is in control. This awareness will help you to understand yourself better and will alert you to the ego states of people who communicate with you. Thus, you will better understand their behavior toward you as well.

TA describes interpersonal communication in terms of transactions, exchanges of words, and corresponding behaviors. Each statement in a transaction is identified as belonging to the Parent (P), Adult (A), or Child (C).

[7]See Dorella Markley Heisel, *Biofeedback Strategies for Interpersonal Relationships* (New York: Gordon and Breach, 1981), pp. 8–10; and Leonard Campos and Paul McCormick, *Introduce Yourself to Transactional Analysis* (Stockton, Calif.: San Joaquin T. A. Institute, 1974), p. 1.

The diagram in Figure 6–2 represents a simple transaction. The arrows indicate who is saying what to whom. Here interaction is parallel, that is, the communication does not cross into contrasting ego states. The Parent speaks to the Child and the Child speaks to the Parent. Parallel interactions usually proceed smoothly. Where communication breakdowns occur is with crossed patterns—that is, when one ego state of a person is addressed, but another ego state answers. In Figure 6–3 the communicator is speaking as an Adult to the Adult in the listener. However, the listener's Parent responds to the speaker's Child.

Breakdowns in communication also occur in crossed transactions in which statements that seem on the surface to belong to one ego state actually reflect another state on a deeper psychological level. Typically, the surface level is Adult, hiding the Child's true meaning.

For example, in Figure 6–4 Gloria, on the left, seems to be speaking as an Adult, asking advice from Bob's Adult. However, on the psychological level she is turning herself into a Child who has to appeal to an all-knowing Parent to solve a problem. While Bob is willing to assume this role, his efforts are useless. Gloria's Child's ulterior motive was to reject his advice from the start.

Gloria	*Bob*
1. I'd really like to fix up the apartment. Do you have any ideas about what we could do?	**2.** Sure, we could buy a new couch.
3. No, that would be too expensive for us now.	**4.** How about painting the place ourselves? It wouldn't cost much.
5. I thought of that, but we're too tired after work and we like to go away on the weekends.	

FIGURE 6-2 A Parallel Transaction.

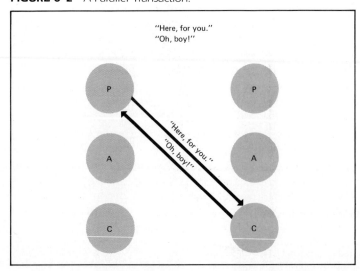

"Here, for you."
"Oh, boy!"

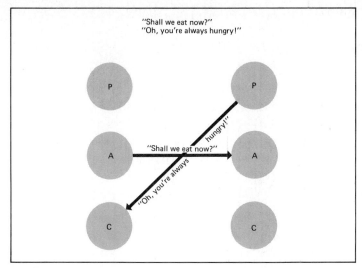

FIGURE 6-3 A Crossed Transaction.

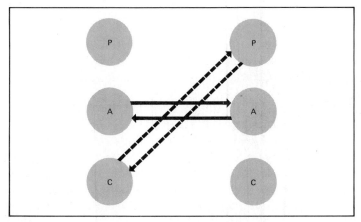

FIGURE 6-4 A Crossed Transaction on Two Levels.

You can probably relate the previous examples to communication experiences in your own life. Remember the principles of TA the next time you feel that your message is simply not getting through to a listener. Is your Parent getting the upper hand, or is your listener's Child just pretending not to hear you? Similarly, as you read the next section on various interpersonal communication situations, try to analyze each interaction in TA terms. Transactional analysis is but one of many communication models. However, it is a useful tool for increasing our understanding of person-to-person message transmission.

INTERPERSONAL COMMUNICATION SITUATIONS

Now that we have investigated the processes and the people involved in interpersonal communication, we will look at several important interpersonal communication situations. As you read through these situations, attempt to apply the concepts which you have learned. Also, attempt to look at each situation from the perspective of the other—whether teacher, parent, or partner in an intimate dyad. At some point in your life, if you are not already doing so, you, too, may take on the roles which are associated with each of these settings. The knowledge which you now have—and a little practice in each situation—may allow you to avoid specific problems in interpersonal relationships.

Student-Teacher Communication

Because students spend so many years in educational settings, it is most important for teachers to promote positive, effective communication. Unfortunately, this does not always happen. Teachers have the same interpersonal difficulties as anyone else. They, like their students, must learn to improve their social interactions.

How then should teachers act to promote better communication? Above all, they must make a strong effort to understand their students' positions and to protect the latter's self-esteem. This means being aware that students, like teachers, have goals, which they should be given the chance to accomplish. For example, if a student says something that disturbs the teacher, the teacher should try to respect the student's opinion and to see beyond the words, to discover the emotions and feelings behind them.

Another approach to good interpersonal communication in the classroom is to encourage students to work together in groups. Such groups make learning more interesting, promote group cohesiveness, and give students good experiences in social interaction. Group discussions that include the teacher can also be used to explore aspects of classroom interaction. This will help the teacher to better understand his or her own behavior and that of the students, both individually and in interactions with one another.

Finally, the teacher must set positive goals. Research has proven that a teacher who expects a student to show little or no intellectual development usually guarantees that result. It is the old concept of the self-fulfilling prophecy at work.

In one study, for example, teachers were told that certain randomly chosen students were academic "spurters" who would show intellectual growth (experimental group). Other students served as controls. The "spurters" not only showed greater intellectual development than the controls, but they were rated by the teachers as having a better chance of future success and as more interesting, curious, and happy. This difference in growth was attributed to the type of interaction that occurred between students and teachers. By facial expressions, body language, and

(United Nations/John Isaac)

verbal messages, the teachers communicated to the experimental students that they expected improved intellectual performance—and the students complied. The obvious lesson is that teachers should raise their classroom expectations.[8]

Just as teachers must improve their communication in the classroom, so too should parents learn to improve communication at home. Many communication breakdowns occur between parents and children because of their differences in goals, outlooks, and experiences. Frequently, parents don't try to understand their children's slang. In turn, the children feel their parents are "out of it."

Family Communication

For example, a father may view his unemployed son as a loafer, a lazy bum. The son, of course, sees it differently. He thinks of his unemployment as a time to relax, get his head together, and figure out what he really wants to do with his life. He does not realize that his unemployment symbolizes something entirely different to his father: a refusal of responsibility, a rejection of the American work ethic. Every time the subject comes up, a fight begins. Nothing is solved, and communication suffers further breakdowns.

What can parents and their children do in situations such as this? Should they continue to bring up the sensitive topic, or perhaps try to bypass it and other subjects that increase family tensions? Again, the solution, although not an easy one, is for each individual to clearly state his or her position, to discuss the differing goals and outlooks, and to try to find some common meeting ground.

[8]Robert Rosenthal and Lenore Jacobson, "Pygmalion in the Classroom: Teacher Expectation and Pupils' Intellectual Development," in *Doing Unto Others,* ed. Zick Rugin (Englewood Cliffs, N.J.: Prentice-Hall, 1975), pp. 41–47.

> It is easier to mend neglect than to quicken love.
>
> St. Jerome

Intimate Communication

When we are children, our most important relationships are with our parents and siblings. As we grow older and go to school, our teachers become important to us; by the time we get into late childhood, relationships with our peers become uppermost. By middle adolescence, though peer relationships remain important, we have begun to develop serious friendships and to date. These serious relationships with another person, which begin at different times for different people, quickly become the most important relationships we have in our lives.

The person you are intimate with is likely to be someone you know well enough to share secrets with. It is someone you can communicate with in a kind of personal shorthand. It is the person who knows best your good points and bad, who knows how you will react to a new experience. It is the person who understands the most about you without your having to say it.

However, intimate relationships, like other interpersonal relationships, are subject to misunderstandings. About two marriages in three end in divorce. *The communication skills that ensure effective message transmission in other relationships are just as important in building a successful intimate relationship.* Just feeling close to another person does not guarantee understanding. Sometimes you may think that you have good communication with another person when you really do not. In fact, your talk may be only an exchange of words, without meaning or feeling. (Spouses can talk past each other as easily as anybody else can.) In an intimate relationship it is important to feel what you are thinking and honestly think of what you are feeling and to communicate both your thoughts *and* your feelings.

The ways to do this are not very different from what we have been talking about throughout this book. First, it is important to understand what you in fact want from the relationship. This is a matter of what you want for yourself and what you want for the other person. To get what you want, you must be open about both your meaning and your feelings. Next, you must empathize with the other person, turning the relationship around to ask what the other person wants. Do you understand the other person's needs, or are you confused about them? Do you have enough information to know the other person's needs? If you do not, you must ask, explaining your confusion and exchanging your feelings. When you are happy, say so; when the other person causes you pain, explain that, and tell openly what you would like to be different.[9]

[9]Mort Katz, *Marriage Survival Kit: A Daily Guide to Happier Marriage* (Rockville Centre, N.Y.: Farnsworth, 1974), p. 33.

Even following these rules cannot guarantee complete confidence in your assessment of intimate relationships. It is often necessary, for example, to clarify the level of your intimacy. How often have you wondered to yourself, "Does this person really care for me?" Fear of rejection usually keeps you from direct questioning of your friends. Nevertheless, verbal and nonverbal cues can give you some answers—and you can use the same cues to let others know your feelings, too.

Murray Davis calls these cues **philemes.** Coming from the Greek word *philia,* meaning an intense, positive relationship, a phileme is "the smallest distinguishable unit of a person's behavior that indicates his level of intimacy with whomever he is interacting."[10] There are as many philemes as there are behaviors that indicate intimacy. Davis therefore also proposes the term **phileme family** for each set of related philemes associated with specific levels of intimacy.

Using this frame of reference, picture two individuals who are each sitting in front of a switchboard. Each row of switches represents a phileme family. When these two people are only acquaintances, all the switches are down. With time, as the intimacy of their relationship grows, more and more switches are turned to the "up" position. Finally, when full intimacy is reached, each phileme switch points up. Of course, this process does not always work smoothly. In many cases, for example, the partners may not move up the same switches at the same time. Thus, they may not always communicate their intimacy level through the same phileme family. In other words, they may not feel equally intimate.

Obviously, most people don't think in terms of philemes in analyzing their everyday relationships. More likely, they convey intimacy through special word choices and forms of address. For example, intimates forego formal titles (Mrs. Smith, Professor Jones) in favor of first names or nicknames. However, these philemes can be switched to indicate suspension of intimacy, either temporarily or permanently. A father, for example, may in anger tell his daughter, "Miss Harvey, I've had enough of your nonsense."

Intimates also use certain terms such as *pal, chum,* and *buddy.* Many of these names relate to the family. *Buddy,* for instance, stems from baby talk for "brother," and *partner* comes from the word for "joint heir." Special friends indicate their feelings of intense intimacy by using pet names or endearments for each other. These endearments fall into groups. The first group, including terms such as *angel* or *divine,* is used to elevate loved ones above human status; the second group lowers the beloved to childlike levels of innocence, with such terms as *baby, pet,* or *honey chile;* the third group compares the beloved to a pleasurable taste, with terms such as *sweetie, sugar,* or *cookie.*

Intimacy is also indicated through choices of language level or vocabulary. Acquaintances rarely use slang with each other. Yet as they be-

[10]Murray Davis, *Intimate Relations* (New York: Free Press, 1973), p. 57.

SHARING SELVES

There are few things that make us feel so warm and satisfied as the beginnings of intimacy with another person. There are also few things that make us feel so cold and alone as when that intimacy dies. James Joyce in this passage describes both the beginning and the end of an intimate relationship, a relationship that is killed by the self-destructive "self-regard" of one of the participants. Those of us who refuse the responsibility of sharing ourselves with other people may find we must go it alone.

He went often to her little cottage outside Dublin; often they spent their evenings alone. Little by little, as their thoughts entangled, they spoke of subjects less remote. Her companionship was like a warm soil about an exotic plant. Many times she allowed the dark to fall upon them, refraining from lighting the lamp. The dark discreet room, their isolation, the music that still vibrated in their ears united them. This union exalted him, wore away the rough edges of his character, emotionalized his mental life. Sometimes he caught himself listening to the sound of his own voice. He thought that in her eyes he would ascend to an angelical stature; and, as he attached the fervent nature of his companion more and more closely to him, he heard the strange impersonal voice which he

recognised as his own, insisting on the soul's incurable loneliness. We cannot give ourselves, it said: we are our own. The end of these discourses was that one night during which she had shown every sign of unusual excitement, Mrs. Sinico caught up his hand passionately and pressed it to her cheek.

Mr. Duffy was very much surprised. Her interpretation of his words disillusioned him. He did not visit her for a week; then he wrote to her asking her to meet him. As he did not wish their last interview to be troubled by the influence of their ruined confessional they met in a little cakeshop near the Parkgate. It was cold autumn weather but in spite of the cold they wandered up and down the roads of the Park for nearly three hours. They agreed to break off their intercourse: every bond, he said, is a bond to sorrow. When they came out of the Park they walked in silence towards the tram; but here she began to tremble so violently that, fearing another collapse on her part, he bade her good-bye quickly and left her. A few days later he received a parcel containing his books and music.

From James Joyce, "A Painful Case," *Dubliners*, pp. 138–39. © 1967 by The Estate of James Joyce. Reprinted by permission of Viking Penguin, Inc., and The Society of Authors.

---

come closer, they increase the amount of slang they use to let each other know that they are part of an elite group that knows the meaning of these words. The intimates now consider themselves set apart from others who do not know the special meanings. Similar efforts to set themselves apart are conveyed in descriptions of their group as "we" or "us," often juxtaposed with "them" of another group. Thus, intimates might say, "We don't like them."

Intimacy also permits you to abbreviate speech forms, in full confidence that your close friends will understand you. Instead of saying, "You know, I think it has started to snow outside," you might nod toward the window and mumble, "snow." Of course, other signs of intimacy are universally understood. The verbal expression, "I love you," and the usual reply, "I love you, too," need no explanation. Similarly, nonverbal gestures such as sitting side by side, sharing long glances, or even spending time together in total silence are all well-known signs of intimacy. Nor must we forget about arguing. A well-established, but dangerously misleading, myth about marriage and close friendship is that happy

couples do not and should not argue. Nothing could be further from the truth. An interpersonal relationship in which anger is ignored and conflict suppressed is not healthy.

People who care about each other will get angry, but their intimacy should ensure healthy, productive conflict and the use of words, not to hurt, but to find out what is bothering each person. Then, bottled-up tensions can be released. **Conflict Resolution**

There is a big difference between this type of arguing and the destructive variety. Whereas healthy conflict stresses the facts, destructive conflict aims for the ego, with statements such as "You're ridiculous," and "Me? You should see yourself." The goal of an argument should be conflict resolution, not character defamation. Better to say, "I hate what you said," than "I hate you because you said it."

Morton Deutsch, an expert on techniques for resolving conflicts, proposes some other principles for settling interpersonal conflicts effectively and efficiently.

1. Concentrate on conflicts over small issues rather than large ones. It is easier to solve small problems first and then move on to the larger, more complicated ones.

2. Recognize the differences in power and ability that exist between participants. People who view themselves as equals tend to stand their ground in an argument; those who recognize the other as an authority figure are more willing to give in.

3. Avoid definitions or solutions that threaten the self-esteem of the participants. When self-esteem is lowered or threatened, people assume a defensive position and are more willing to fight. Increasing self-confidence has the opposite effect.

4. Avoid solutions that ignore important concerns of the participants. If a solution makes us repress some of our concerns, they are bound to erupt later in a variety of unpleasant ways. Repression just makes a situation worse.

5. Sometimes the best way to handle interpersonal conflicts is to avoid them. In most cases, a problem should be approached directly, but a problem so deep and complex that it cannot be resolved—let it rest.[11]

Unfortunately, conflict resolution is not always as easy as these five principles might suggest. Too often it involves much more than verbal aggression. Individuals frequently turn to physical force to settle the situation. Research indicates that such violent conflict resolution is not confined to abnormal, sick families characterized by some pathology such as drugs, alcohol, gambling, or mental disorders. It also takes place in what we consider normal, average families. In 1970 the National Commission on the Causes and Prevention of Crime and Violence found that between one-fourth and one-fifth of the adults questioned felt it was all right for spouses to hit each other. In 1974 an in-depth interview of eighty families revealed that 60 percent of the husbands and wives used physical aggression during marital conflicts.[12]

Because violence as a problem-solving method is learned, these findings cast a shadow on prospects for the socialization of children. Physical force, once it is seen as a successful way of resolving conflicts, is more likely to be used in the next situation. Further, this approach to conflict is passed from one generation to the next. For example, many studies of the family environment of murderers show evidence of extreme parental abuse as well as physical violence between parents. Many homicidal adolescents, furthermore, have a family history of parental brutality and wife beating. Children reared in a family setting with child or spouse abuse are more likely to commit physically violent acts themselves, such as rape, murder, or assault.[13]

[11]Summarized in A. Barbour and A. A. Goldberg, *Interpersonal Communication: Teaching Strategies and Resources* (New York: Speech Communication Services, 1974; ERIC Document Reproduction Service No. ED 085 798).

[12]Suzanne Steinmetz, "The Use of Force for Resolving Family Conflict: The Training Ground for Abuse," *Family Coordinator* 26, no. 1 (January 1977): 20.

[13]Steinmetz, p. 19.

Furthermore, intragenerational patterns of conflict resolution have been observed. Parents who use a certain method such as discussion, verbal aggression, or physical aggression to resolve their marital problems use this same method for the parent-child and sibling conflicts. Also, the children are likely to use the same approach to resolve their problems with their siblings. Finally, these children, when married, often use the same methods in dealing with their own marital conflicts and their disciplinary actions with their own children.

Thus, arguments, and the way they are resolved, can exert a strong influence on many intimate relationships. So, *do* argue, but do it right. Be constructive, not combative. You might even set up a time and place to quarrel; this will give you the opportunity to prepare your defense and a chance to approach the subject calmly and logically. Then, speak clearly, to the point. Avoid "taboo" topics you both know are painful ("If only you had gotten that job you tried for"). Finally, enjoy yourself. Arguing can be fun. Make sure each of you has said all that you wanted to, then end on a high, optimistic note—and do not be afraid to say "I'm sorry."

SUMMARY

Interpersonal communication is the sharing of feelings and ideas with other people. Most interpersonal messages are informal exchanges in dyads—that is, between two people in close contact. The potential for sending, receiving, and evaluating messages is shared between the two members of the dyad. The purpose of their communication usually focuses on the sharing of meaning as well.

Skills related to self-disclosure, context, timing, clarity, open listening, feedback and feedforward, nonverbal behavior, interpersonal attraction, and person perception combine to determine how successfully meaning is conveyed in such dyadic communications. In addition, the people involved bring personality and environmental factors into the interpersonal setting; they too influence the success or failure of the communication process. For example, individuals with manipulative needs often destroy opportunities for communication that might aid personal growth and development of their friends and associates. Similarly, certain types of messages also limit effective social interaction. For example, alternating monologues, in which the speakers seem not to hear each other, and stimulus-response interactions, in which the speakers' set messages are unaffected by their listeners' replies, both hinder effective communication. In contrast, interactions with feedback and with empathy build strong, healthy relationships.

Communication relationships can be shown in many ways. In transactional analysis, for example, our messages are attributed to the Parent, Adult, and Child within each of us. These ego states are characterized by different communication orientations which, ordinarily, are readily interpreted by our listeners. Communication breakdowns occur, however, when you address one ego state of your listener, only to have the listener respond in the characteristic style of another state. Recognizing such problems through systems such as transactional analysis can help you to better understand the problems we all experience in interpersonal communication.

Many communication problems relate to specific communication situations. For example, the specialized interactions between student and teacher, children and parents, husband and wife, and close friends each pose particular hazards and potential conflicts. Communication specialists have formulated specific suggestions for minimizing the hazards in all of these interactions. And, if these suggestions fail, they have also devised techniques for resolving the conflicts that result. Close attention to these methods can assure increased success in all communication situations.

Exercises

GROUP EXPERIENCES

Positive-Negative

Description: One aspect of interpersonal attraction is the extent to which another person shares your attitudes and beliefs. Simply stated, we are more attracted to people who share our attitudes than to those who do not. Consider some of the relationships you have had with others. Those relationships that you remember as good probably were ones in which your ideas were readily and willingly accepted or at least supported. When you have a falling out with another person, you may both have reevaluated each other and may consider the attitudes of the other person to be strange. Since nobody wants to be considered strange, you leave the situation. The purpose of this activity is to magnify the emotional feelings a person has when they are positively and negatively reinforced.

Procedure: Divide into groups of four to six persons. Choose one person as the subject. Select a controversial topic of discussion or a topic that requires planning (such as planning a picnic). During your discussion accept and support all ideas suggested by the subject. Listen carefully to everything he or she has to say. After 5 minutes select another subject. Then, for the next 5 minutes, reject all comments presented by the second subject. Avoid listening to what is said by this subject. Let the subject know that you consider his or her beliefs to be strange, wrong, and worthless. The final part of this activity is a report from the subjects about the emotional states they experienced during the activity. The subjects should indicate how well they liked other group members along with their reasons for liking or disliking them.

Discussion: Most people surround themselves with people who agree with and reinforce their ideas. Let's face it—people who like us can't be all bad! The two subjects most likely had very different feelings about the group. It's hard to create the actual emotional condition in an exercise that you would feel in a real-life situation, because in the back of everyone's head is a little voice saying, "It's just an activity." But the next time you are in a group that evaluates you either positively or negatively, watch your emotional state. Do you tend to like people who like you?

Mr. and Ms. Wonderful

Description: Everyone has varying opinions as to what they regard as attractive. During different periods of time, being pleasantly plump was "in" and looking like Twiggy was definitely "out." In fact, history records periods of time when women were sent to "fattening schools" to prepare for marriage. Today everyone runs to the health farms to lose that extra 10 to 15 pounds. Even within a given period and culture, people simply have different ideas about beauty. This activity will provide you with the opportunity to identify what characteristics of attraction you want in your Mr. or Ms. Wonderful.

Procedure: Now is your chance to become an author and to write a heartrending description of an attractive person at a cocktail party. The scene is set. You, the author, are watching this person from afar. Your attraction is immense, and you watch his or her every move. Write a paragraph describing those physical characteristics that are so magnetic to you. Be adventurous and use the following lines as an example:

I couldn't keep my eyes off his amber-colored hair as it fell feathered from his face. His deep brown eyes were penetrating, and I imagined that they were looking directly at me. I liked the way he moved—with assurance and yet lightness.

The above paragraph is just a beginning. Be creative and write about the physical characteristics you would find attractive in another person. Share your descriptions of Mr. or Ms. Wonderful with others in the class. Read them out loud with the same emotion you used in writing the paragraph.

Discussion: You probably found some of the paragraphs to be funny—maybe even ridiculous; the question is, Would you have been attracted to the same characteristics others wrote about? Discuss the sayings, "Beauty is in the eye of the beholder," and "Love is blind." Are they true? Do you ever see couples that you think are physically mismatched? The final question: What do you really want in a Mr. or Ms. Wonderful?

P.A.C. Responses

Description: Everyone responds out of the Parent, Adult, and Child ego states at different times in different situations. The purpose in understanding these various states is to attempt to bring them together as a functional whole. The first step in achieving this is to understand a Parent, Adult, and Child response when you hear it or say it. This activity will provide you with an opportunity to develop and compare Parent, Adult, and Child ego responses in given situations.

Procedure: Listed below you will find three statements for which you will need to write three responses—one from the Parent ego state, one from the Adult ego state, and one from the Child ego state. Study the example provided and then write your responses to each of the following statements.

Example. "That's the ugliest shirt I've ever seen you wear!"
Child response: "Listen, turkey, I don't care what you have to say!"
Parent response: "You shouldn't say things like that—if you can't say something nice, don't say anything at all!"
Adult response: "Why do you dislike this shirt?"
Statement 1. "I just went to the doctor today and he told me that I'm two months pregnant—I just want to die!"
Statement 2. "I don't think Mark is good enough for Lina—she's got class. What do you think?"
Statement 3. "I want to break up with Mike but I don't know how to tell him. What would you do?"

Compare the responses by acting out the dialogues. Use the intonation you think would be used by someone in the Parent, Adult, and Child ego states.

Discussion: Which ego state do you generally respond with? Do you consider a particular response style to be better than another? What are some of the problems that occur when you have a crossed transaction; for example, between the Parent and the Child ego states?

PERSONAL EXPERIENCES

1. Make a list of three people that you like and three people that you dislike. Consider each person separately and determine how they respond to you. Are they enthusiastic about your ideas? Do they share similar attitudes and beliefs with you? After you have answered these questions, reflect on this one. Do you tend to like people who positively reinforce you, and dislike those who negatively reinforce you?

2. Watch yourself for a two-hour period and record the ego states (Parent, Adult, Child) that you experience. Try to isolate the people or situations that call up the various ego states in you. Do you feel more or less comfortable in the different ego states?

3. Make a list of the suggestions for communicating in intimate relationships that are on pp. 164–65. Look at the list often. Which suggestions do you find easy or difficult to practice? Do they help you to better understand your thoughts and feelings? Do you truly **feel** what you are thinking? Do you honestly **think** of what you are feeling?

DISCUSSION QUESTIONS

1. What role do quarrels or arguments play in an interpersonal relationship?
2. What verbal signals or philemes do you use to indicate feelings of intimacy to another person?
3. What different methods can be used to resolve conflicts?
4. Explain how phases of development and disintegration evolve in interpersonal relationships.
5. How does perceived credibility and/or attraction influence feelings about others?

SMALL GROUP COMMUNICATION

7

Exploratory Questions

1. What are the four characteristics of a group?
2. What are the differences between the two major types of small groups?
3. What examples can you give of group norms?
4. What are the major categories of functional roles and their characteristic behaviors?
5. What five stages can be identified in the development of a small group?
6. How do democratic, authoritarian, and laissez-faire leadership styles differ?
7. What five characteristics typify good leaders?
8. What are some problems involving fact, value, and policy?
9. What seven questions can be used for testing evidence?
10. What are the eight steps on the standard agenda of a problem-solving discussion?
11. What are the differences between quantitative and qualitative methods of evaluating small group interaction?

Think for a moment about all the different groups to which you belong: whether they be social, political, family, academic, religious, vocational, or special interest groups. It is virtually impossible to exist independently of all groups. It has been estimated that the average person is a member of five or six groups at any one time and that the total number of existing small groups may be around 4 billion or 5 billion.

The existence of groups is a basic part of the democratic process. In a society such as ours, the group process plays a significant role in proposing and reviewing the laws that govern our land. The government does much of its work through various committees and subcommittees, which study and propose legislation. In addition, civic groups meet regularly to comment on the actions of government and assure that the voice of the people will be heard. These groups protect the rights of the individual citizen.

The democratic aspect of the group goes beyond politics, however. The family that jointly decides where to go for winter vacation; the union members who meet to discuss contract demands; the student-faculty committee that determines college requirements; and the consumer group that organizes a protest against dangerous toys are all participating in the democratic process on some level.

There are many different types of groups to which you can belong, and there are also many benefits to be gained from participation in groups as well as from observation of group behavior. Participation in certain groups can lead to increased personal rewards, which include change and growth in personality, self-concept, and behavior. Well-known groups such as Weight Watchers, Alcoholics Anonymous, and Smoke Enders are self-help groups that enable people to overcome undesirable habits. As a result of interpersonal interactions, group members derive strength and support from others who are working toward the same goals. Different groups develop as different needs are expressed. Some groups, as in group

> I know of no safe depository of the ultimate powers of society but the people themselves.
>
> Thomas Jefferson

therapy, can contribute to the emotional well-being of the participants. Others may serve social as well as psychological needs.

Participation in groups can also result in professional rewards. A person's ability is often measured by how effectively he or she functions in a small group. A student who participates in student government may be asked to head a campus committee; the parent who functions effectively in a parent-teacher group may be encouraged to run for the school board; or the president of a local chapter of a charity organization may move up to head a regional division.

On a very practical level, the study of the group process can help you function more effectively in the different groups to which you belong. For example, if you are aware of the various factors that can be barriers to decision making, you may be able to help your club, committee, or organization overcome them. In this chapter we will discuss the group process and give explanations and guidelines to help you participate more fully and effectively in small group communication.

DEFINITIONS

The Group

Before discussing the group process, we must decide what we mean by the term *group*. A **group** is any number of people who have a common goal, interact with one another to accomplish their goal, recognize one another's existence, and see themselves as part of a group. To test our definition, let's consider an example—people in line outside a movie theater. Is this a group? Certainly these people have a common goal, since they are all waiting to see a particular film. But these people need not interact with one another to accomplish this goal, although each may be very aware of the presence of the others in line. Now, if someone were to try to sneak in at the front of the line and the people made a unified effort to keep the crasher out, we could say that during that period of time the random collection of people became a group. Looking at our definition, the unified effort to block the line crasher would call for group interaction and awareness of others.

The Small Group

Our main concern in this chapter is the small group. A small group is three or more people interacting face to face, with or without an assigned leader, in such a way that each person influences and is influenced by every other person in the group.

The small group may vary in size, but it is generally agreed that the best size in terms of total interaction and greatest efficiency is somewhere between five and seven members.

There are certain generalizations that can be made about small and large groups. For instance, small groups tend to be more informal and less structured, while larger groups may have to adopt formal rules to keep order. A small group can function effectively without a designated leader, but a large group may need such a person to maintain order and make sure the group performs efficiently. Theoretically, an increase in size increases the group's resource pool, since more people means more information, ideas, and opinions. However, it has been found that the larger the group, the less chance there is for individual participation and the greater the tendency for several dominant or aggressive individuals to monopolize the discussion. This type of behavior causes the shy or less verbal person to withdraw from the interaction and feel a sense of frustration. After the group has functioned for some time, a number of cliques tend to develop, which often hinders the group effort. Therefore, as the group becomes larger, there is greater difficulty in accomplishing a particular task.

SOME SMALL GROUPS AND THEIR FUNCTIONS

The two major types of small groups are primary groups and discussion groups.

The Primary Group The **primary group,** or **psyche group,** functions as a support system for its members. Neighbors who get together daily, friends with whom you go to the movies once or twice a month, and the coffee klatch at work are all groups that usually enjoy conversation as opposed to discussion. Conversation is much more loosely structured than discussion and covers a variety of topics without a particular objective in mind. It is neither unusual nor particularly harmful for one member of a primary group to occasionally dominate the conversation. In a discussion group, however, in which members have a common objective, it is essential that they maintain a balance between speaking and listening activity. Such "rules" are alien to the primary group, which is generally social and tends to be quite informal.

The Discussion Group In addition to the formality of discussion groups as opposed to primary groups, there are certain other characteristics that make discussion groups unique. The **discussion group** is characterized by

1. *Cooperation among its members.* The shared objective of a discussion group is either information sharing or decision making. Group members must recognize their purpose and work toward its end. A discussion group should encourage different ideas and opinions, but group members should remember that there is a shared goal. People whose minds are already made up may be unwilling to cooperate.

2. *Face-to-face interaction.* A discussion cannot take place if group members do not respond, react, and adapt to the communication of other participants. The interaction must be continuous and flow from within the group. If the people merely state preconceived ideas in isolation, apart from the interaction, fruitful discussion cannot take place.

3. *Shared perceptions.* As noted in our definition of any group, participants in a discussion group must see themselves as part of the whole. A person who sees himself or herself as the "entire group" will not consider the contribution of others.

4. *Communication through verbal and nonverbal means.* Obviously, discussion requires verbal interaction, but participants must also be attuned to the nonverbal cues of other group members. For example, an affirmative nod or smile may indicate if a participant is truly in agreement with a particular point or outcome.[1]

Discussion groups can be either private or public. **Private,** or **closed, discussion groups** are those in which there is no audience to listen to or participate in the group discussion. An executive council or a cabinet meeting is an example of a private discussion. The **open** or **public discussion** takes place before an audience. The open discussion may take the form of a **panel,** in which a group of well-informed people exchanges ideas before an audience. A group of doctors, psychologists, and sociologists speaking about the effects of marijuana before a college audience would represent a panel discussion. Similar to the panel is the **symposium,** made up of experts who present their views one at a time. A group of physicians talking about progress in different types of organ transplants to an audience of colleagues is a symposium. If the audience mentioned in these two examples were to actively participate in the discussion, the group would then be called a **forum.**

THE PROBLEM-SOLVING GROUP   One of the most important kinds of discussion groups, the **problem-solving group,** is usually private. The most basic of these groups is the **fact-finding group,** the purpose of which is to gather as much information as possible about a particular issue or problem. Such a task usually requires considerable research. The information collected by the group may then serve as the basis for future policy discussions. One example of a fact-finding group is a committee of university students who volunteered to study the circumstances that led to the closing of their library on weekends and evenings. The university cited lack of funds as the reason for reducing hours. The student group found out how money was distributed throughout the school and where possible sources of relief money might be located. Government officials often appoint fact-finding committees to investigate particular incidents or problems. For example, after a number of schools report a sharp increase in vandalism, a commission might be established to investigate the situation.

[1] John K. Brilhart, *Effective Group Discussion,* 3d ed. (Dubuque, Iowa: W. C. Brown, 1978), p. 5.

(Ken Karp)

A group whose task stems directly from the fact-finding group is the *evaluation group.* This type of group uses the information that has been made available through investigation to determine the scope of a particular problem and the priorities in finding a solution. It will then make recommendations to those who carry out policy. An example of an evaluation group would be a team of efficiency experts who are asked to make suggestions on how a factory's production might be increased while minimizing costs. After an evaluation group offers its recommendations, the *policymaking group* may make particular changes or take certain actions. Sound policymaking must be based on fact finding and evaluation.

We have described the various kinds of problem-solving groups as though they operate in a sequence but separately from one another. This is not always—in fact, not usually—the case. Any task group can perform any or all of these functions. Generally, the group involved in policymaking goes through the fact-finding and evaluation stages as well, to ensure a carefully considered decision.

PARTICIPATING IN SMALL GROUPS

Responsibilities If a small group is going to function successfully, certain attitudes, actions, and behaviors are important. Your first responsibility as a group participant is to keep an open mind toward the issue or problem being discussed as well as toward the other members of the group. You should try to remain objective during the course of the discussion and evaluate information and ideas independently. This means being aware of personal biases to make sure that they do not interfere with a willingness to listen to the ideas of others.

Going one step further, it is important to show a certain sensitivity to the moods and emotional tone of individuals as well as of the group as a whole. Sometimes what people say and what they really believe are two different things—if you are sensitive to other members of the group, you may be able to pick up on this. A different tone of voice, changes in posture and body position, and other nonverbal cues help to either reinforce or contradict what is being said.

Individual members have an obligation to make sure that everyone participates in the group process. For example, a newcomer to the group may feel somewhat intimidated by the other members, particularly if they all know one another well and have worked together for a long time. As a sensitive group member, you should try to make the new person feel at ease and draw him or her into the discussion.

Often participation in a group means preparation or homework of some sort. Sometimes the group may agree to think about a problem or do some research or reading on a particular subject before the next meeting. It is essential to follow through on such assignments. If not, time is wasted and those who have done their work feel frustrated and annoyed. For example, when the social committee of an organization was planning its Christmas party, each member of the committee was supposed to investigate the prices of different restaurants or catering halls where the party could be held. When only three of the seven members came prepared, the group's work was set back at least a week. As part of a group, you have an obligation to other people as well as to yourself.

SPEAKING   Since the group process depends on interaction among members, you must communicate your ideas and opinions as accurately and concisely as you can. Here are some ways to increase the effectiveness of your communication as a group member.   *Communicating*

1. If you find yourself mumbling or rambling on, it may be because you yourself find what you are saying unimportant. If so, don't speak up until you have something you want to contribute.
2. Address your comments to the group as a whole—group involvement is very important in this process.
3. Organize your remarks whenever possible—although the discussion will be based largely on the interaction among different members of the group, and will therefore be spontaneous, certain comments can be prepared for the discussion and used when appropriate.
4. Relate your idea or opinion to what has been said, making the connection clear whenever necessary.
5. Try to state only one point at a time so that the group can digest what has been said. This will also help to keep the discussion on course and let the group respond to individual points.
6. To make sure everyone understands what you are saying, speak concisely and use language that the group members can relate to.

LISTENING AND FEEDBACK   As a group member, you must be both a speaker and a listener. It is just as important to be able to listen effectively as it is to speak effectively. Thomas Scheidel and Laura Crowell, researchers in small group communication, state that there are special listener responsibilities for members of a group.[2] These are listening to understand a speaker's remarks before criticizing or evaluating them; listening to evaluate, or evaluating, a message only after you know what is really being said; and listening to provide support for the speaker (that is, providing cues and encouragement which help the speaker to get his or her ideas across). When these listening skills are ignored, the ineffective listening that results can lead to misunderstandings and delays in the group process.

Sometimes, even though people try to listen carefully, a certain amount of misunderstanding takes place. Sending feedback is one way to help reduce such misunderstanding, and questions can be a valuable form of feedback. Actually, the use of questions can improve communication throughout the group process. At the outset, it helps for members to ask questions relating to the goals and objectives of the group as a whole as well as to the purpose of any particular meeting. Once these goals are established, questions about procedures should be asked. Even when conclusions have been reached, carefully thought out questions can often refine these decisions to a considerable degree.

[2]Thomas Scheidel and Laura Crowell, "The Team Work," in *Discussing and Deciding: A Desk Book for Group Leaders and Members* (New York: Macmillan, 1979), pp. 73–74.

SMALL GROUP COMMUNICATION

BYPASSING   A variety of questions can overcome barriers to communication in small groups. One such barrier is called **bypassing,** a situation in which people are actually talking past each other. In such a situation people argue or reach an impasse when, in fact, they are in agreement.

A major cause of bypassing is ambiguity, or vagueness, on the part of some group members. Questions relating to interpretation or calling for explanation can help bring out the intended meaning. On the other hand, sometimes a person will use stigma words, such as "indecent" or "foaming-at-the-mouth radical," which are emotionally loaded. The person who uses this type of vocabulary is trying to provoke the rest of the group and cause conflict. Without accusing or intimidating the member who uses such language, other members should be quick to ask for clarification.

ROLE STRUCTURE AND STATUS

Over a period of time, all small groups develop a set of norms, rules, and expectations that are unique to that group, based on the interaction among its different members. These norms can determine what is acceptable in speech, dress, and behavior in the group. *Norms*

Sometimes members are unaware that these norms even exist until there is some change in the group. For example, members of a weekly scheduling meeting never realized that they followed a particular seating arrangement until at one session the group was short a chair and the usual pattern was disrupted. Similarly, members of a parent-teachers group were thrown off when a new member addressed them by their first names, which was not their usual practice.

These two examples concern norms which, while influential in terms of interaction among members, are outside the actual group discussion. Other norms actually govern the course of the discussion. For example, it was pointed out to members of an activities committee that during their weekly meetings Richard would always bring the discussion back on course if it seemed to stray, and Elsa would call for periodic summaries of what had been said. Although these behaviors were accepted norms, they were never realized by the group until they were pointed out.

In the previous example, while neither Richard nor Elsa filled the official role of leader, each did, in fact, fill a leadership role. Role structure is one of the most important kinds of norm a group can develop. Sometimes a role is determined by a person's relative status or position. For example, a student representative on the college personnel and planning board might defer to the head of a department because of his or her position relative to the student's own. Yet, while position is influential, role structure develops from within the group, and any and all members of a group can fill a variety of different functional roles. **Functional roles** are those that keep the discussion on course and aid the group in accomplishing its objectives. *Functional Roles*

The functional roles that develop within a group can be divided into two major categories—**task-oriented roles** and **maintenance roles.**

TASK-ORIENTED ROLES These roles are directly related to the group's goal, whether that goal is to gather information, make recommendations, solve a problem, or complete a project. In our example concerning the activities committee, Richard, who kept the discussion on track, and Elsa, who asked for summaries, were both filling task-oriented roles. These are only two of the several task-oriented behaviors of group members. A more complete list of such roles would include

1. *Information or opinion giver:* In this role a group member provides content or well-considered opinions which will help the group move more smoothly toward the best decision. Richard, for example, knows of various fundraising activities which have worked well on other campuses. As an information giver, he would be aware of the salience of this information and would share any ideas which might contribute to his group's needs and set criteria.

2. *Information or opinion seeker:* The group member who takes on this role is usually the person who perceives that the group needs additional data. For example, John might ask, "Have we information which reflects the amount of money which might be raised through each alternative?"

3. *Expediter:* The individual in this role helps the group stick to its agenda and often leads the group back on course when it goes off on a tangent. As the activities committee begins to digress to an irrelevant topic, Elsa might state, "But weren't we in the process of deciding what criteria need to be applied?"

4. *Idea person:* The idea person is an imaginative group member who thinks originally, comes up with several alternatives, and quite often contributes an idea which serves as a basis for the final decision. In order to promote the carnival as the best decision, Jim and Carla might begin a debate on the pros and cons of the carnival as the best alternative.

5. *Analyzer:* This role is played by the individual who is highly skilled in problem solving, who moves the group rapidly to the core of the problem, and who, at times, examines the reasoning behind each contribution to the discussion. The analyzer is recognized by statements such as: "O.K., so far we've managed to narrow our choices to a circus, a car wash, or an auction." "But aren't we overlooking the potential of the raffle that Dave suggested?"[3]

MAINTENANCE ROLES Task-oriented behavior is essential in getting work done, but a group can only be productive if there is interaction among its members. **Maintenance roles** are concerned with the feelings of individual members and the emotional behavior of the group. Maintenance roles include the following:

1. *Active listener:* This role is played by the person who recognizes the contributions of others and who responds with specific verbal or nonverbal reinforcement. A nod of the head, a smile, or a verbal, "Great idea," represent the responses of an active and participating listener.

2. *Game leader:* The game leader is the individual who recognizes when the process is becoming tedious, when fatigue is setting in, or when the discussion

[3]Rudolph F. Verderber, *Communicate,* 3d ed. (Belmont, Calif.: Wadsworth, 1981), pp. 186–87.

A leader—designated or not—is anyone who helps the group toward its goal. (A.T. & T. Co. Photo Center)

is getting out of hand and who has a timely and uncanny ability to create an appropriate joke, digression, or comment to improve the spirits of the group. As tension begins to mount over the decision to be made, Andy might suggest, "Why don't we just quietly break into teams, with each team representing a solution, and let the winners of a pillow fight make the decision?"

3. *Harmonizer:* The harmonizer is the group member who is both perceptive and empathetic and who is able as a function of his or her contributions to reduce or reconcile differences and misunderstandings. When Steve and Karen seem almost ready to come to blows over the choice of a fundraising project, Julia might suggest that the two discover areas of agreement, rather than disagreement, and begin from there.

4. *Gatekeeper:* The role played by the gatekeeper is one of making sure that channels of communication are open and that everyone has a chance to enter the discussion. When Elaine notices that Alison is exceptionally quiet during a committee meeting, she might encourage Alison by asking her opinion.

5. *Compromiser:* During the course of a discussion in which two prominent positions emerge, it is often the compromiser who must act in order to make the decision. In cases such as this, when two decisions may work equally well, the compromiser may be spotted through statements such as: "How can we reconcile these differences so that we all can agree?" or "Rick, Andy, you both have good ideas, but if you look a little closer, you'll see some similarities between the two ideas."

6. *Public relations—the front person:* The front person is the person who possesses skills at interacting with outside groups and individuals and who therefore is skilled in public speaking and interpersonal relations. Because the decision which any group makes will affect those around it, such a person is vital to solution implementation. Once our fundraising committee decides on the best way to raise funds, its public relations person's job only begins.[4]

---

[4]Verderber, pp. 189–90.

SELF-SERVING ROLES Maintenance roles are extremely important in maximizing group efficiency, but sometimes members adopt **self-serving roles** that are counterproductive. These roles have a negative effect on the group's emotional climate as well as on its ability to reach its goals. Self-serving roles include:

1. *Aggressor*—the person who works for his or her own ends by criticizing or blaming others when things get rough.
2. *Blocker*—the person who blocks ideas from group acceptance by going off on tangents or rejecting suggestions on a personal basis.
3. *Competer*—the person who competes with others to gain attention.
4. *Special pleader*—the individual who has his or her own pet ideas and who, regardless of the group, works to integrate those into whatever is done.
5. *Joker*—the member of the group whose behavior includes clowning, mimicking, and generally disrupting the group. While the game leader plays a positive role in the maintenance of the group, the joker is only out for attention.
6. *Withdrawer*—the person who refuses to contribute or to be a part of the group.
7. *Monopolizer*—the group member who feels the need to talk all the time.[5]

The different roles we have been discussing operate in almost all group situations. Awareness of task-oriented and maintenance roles can enable you to overcome self-serving behavior and accomplish the group goal in a positive manner.

THE DEVELOPMENT OF A SMALL GROUP

Although we have discussed the major roles which are a part of small group interactions, we do not want to suggest that effective small group communication takes place either easily or overnight. Every group has to spend both time and energy learning how to communicate and work together. As Giammatteo and Giammatteo (1981) have stated, "It takes time for members, each different, to learn how they can fit into the group and contribute best. Often things seem 'all mixed up,' and group members may quite naturally become disturbed and discouraged—even aggravated at each other."[6] To help people understand these natural "growing pains," these researchers have pinpointed the following descriptive stages in the developmental process of small group interaction:

1. *"Groping":* When the group is first finding out how to plan and work together, they may not all agree. They don't know and understand each other well enough to really trust the others, and they still have to determine each others' skills, knowledge, situation, and attitudes. They often feel uncomfortable and "lost."
2. *"Griping":* The members become discouraged when they can't seem to work

[5]Verderber, pp. 190–91.
[6]M. Giammatteo and D. Giammatteo, *Forces on Leadership* (Reston, Va.: National Association of Secondary School Principals, 1981), p. 28.

together, when there isn't much progress, and when their attempts are frustrated. They say the wrong things, play negative roles, and block group action because they are uncomfortable. This is the place for more "self-other" understanding, for remembering that they are all different but that they all want to do a good job and to be liked by others. Maybe they can learn to understand why others are griping and learn to give themselves time to work things out.

3. *"Grasping":* Ideas and suggestions are beginning to fit. Members begin to agree and can start to see some direction to group activity. Everyone begins to feel more comfortable. Now they are getting somewhere.

4. *"Grouping":* Members are getting to know each other and can understand and enjoy how each person works and fits into the scheme. Group tasks, building roles, and maintenance roles come into play, and a surge of enthusiasm spreads through the group.

5. *"Group Action":* Now the group is in full swing, with members playing constructive roles. Leadership is shared, and everyone is participating. While it was difficult at first, it was worth it to learn to work well together. They have shared in making plans and decisions, have learned together, and feel that this is a good group with which to work. They are busy making their group more democratic.

Now they are ready to tackle other jobs. They will still go through some of these early stages, but each time it will be less disturbing and more effective.[7]

LEADERS AND LEADERSHIP

In the example we have been discussing, we commented that both Richard and Elsa were filling leadership roles when they moved to keep the discussion on course and asked for periodic summaries. These task-oriented roles demonstrated leadership on their part, although neither of them was designated as the leader of the group. In the study of group dynamics, **leadership** is any kind of behavior that helps the group toward its goals, and a **leader** is any person who influences the group in this way. Therefore, according to these definitions, Richard and Elsa not only exhibited leadership, but by doing so became leaders of their group.

Sometimes one or more members of a group become leaders by assuming leadership roles, even if someone else has been assigned or elected to that role. Actually, it is possible for a group to demonstrate effective leadership even when there is no official leader. While it is most desirable for a group to have a designated leader to get things started, it is also good for a group to have shared leadership. For example, it is difficult for the person who assumes several task-oriented roles to assume maintenance roles as well. Sometimes, one or two people will see to it that the social and emotional atmosphere of the group remains conducive to the completion of the goal, while another person will assume responsibility for task-oriented behavior.

[7]Giammatteo and Giammatteo, p. 29.

A CHIEF IS CHOSEN

In William Golding's **Lord of the Flies,** a plane carrying a group of schoolboys goes down on a remote island. The pilot is killed: Only the children survive. Almost immediately they recognize the need for organization and leadership if they are to survive until help arrives.

Jack spoke.

"We've got to decide about being rescued."

There was a buzz. One of the small boys, Henry, said that he wanted to go home.

"Shut up," said Ralph absently. He lifted the conch. "Seems to me we ought to have a chief to decide things."

"A chief! A chief!"

"I ought to be chief," said Jack with simple arrogance, "because I'm chapter chorister and head boy. I can sing C sharp."

Another buzz.

"Well then," said Jack, "I—"

He hesitated. The dark boy, Roger, stirred at last and spoke up.

"Let's have a vote."

"Yes!"

"Vote for chief!"

"Let's vote—"

This toy of voting was almost as pleasing as the conch. Jack started to protest but the clamor changed from the general wish for a chief to an election by acclaim of Ralph himself. None of the boys could have found good reason for this; what intelligence had been shown was traceable to Piggy while the most obvious leader was Jack. But there was a stillness about Ralph as he sat that marked him out: there was his size, and attractive appearance; and most obscurely, yet most powerfully, there was the conch. The being that had blown that, had sat waiting for them on the platform with the delicate thing balanced on his knees, was set apart.

"Him with the shell."

"Ralph! Ralph!"

"Let him be chief with the trumpet-thing."

Ralph raised a hand for silence.

"All right. Who wants Jack for chief?"

With dreary obedience the choir raised their hands.

"Who wants me?"

Every hand outside the choir except Piggy's was raised immediately. Then Piggy, too, raised his hand grudgingly into the air.

Ralph counted.

"I'm chief then."

The circle of boys broke into applause. Even the choir applauded; and the freckles on Jack's face disappeared under a blush of mortification. He started up, then changed his mind and sat down again while the air rang. Ralph looked at him, eager to offer something.

"The choir belongs to you, of course."

"They could be the army—"

"Or hunters—"

"They could be—"

The suffusion drained away from Jack's face. Ralph waved again for silence.

"Jack's in charge of the choir. They can be—what do you want them to be?"

"Hunters."

Jack and Ralph smiled at each other with shy liking. . . .

Reprinted by permission of Faber & Faber Ltd. and Coward, McCann & Geoghegan, Inc. From Lord of the Flies by William Golding. © 1954 by William Golding.

Think for a moment about the groups to which you belong. Is there a designated leader? If so, does that person exhibit leadership in the group? An understanding of the leadership styles and roles we are about to examine can help all members in a group perform more effectively.

Theoretical Approaches

Operating under the assumption that leaders are born, not made, early investigators of leadership looked for traits that distinguish leaders from nonleaders. One such study, conducted in 1948, revealed that leaders score better than others on measures of intelligence, scholarship, dependability, responsibility, social participation, and socioeconomic status. Dissatisfied with this personality-centered approach, later researchers turned their attention to the evaluation of the particular communication behaviors of both leaders and nonleaders. In 1967 Geier found five behavioral characteristics that prevented particular individuals from becoming leaders: being uninformed about the problem under discussion; not participating; being too rigid in opinions and approaches to the problem; being too authoritarian or "bossy"; and being verbally offensive—talking too much or talking in a pompous or overly formal manner. Not surprisingly, still later investigators found that leaders are actually less opinionated and more agreeable than nonleaders.

A second and significantly different approach to the study of leadership focuses not on individual traits but on those behaviors that help the group reach its goals. This functional approach emphasizes the fact that anyone who learns these behaviors can contribute to the group's success. You don't have to be the designated leader of a group to discover that your group is straying from its agenda. Any member of the group who proposes a return to the agenda contributes positively to the group process. Similarly, any member who points out that there is a "hidden agenda" controlling group discussion (a disruptive ego battle or the pushing of special interests) contributes to the group process. Another major leadership behavior is keeping the discussion centered on issues, insisting on the critical evaluation of evidence, and refusing to yield to social pressure. The experienced group member uses the issue-centered approach to rescue discussions that have fallen victim to personality clashes.

Styles of Leadership

There are three basic styles of leadership: democratic, authoritarian, and laissez-faire (see Fig. 7–1). **Democratic** leaders guide rather than direct a group. Receptive to group members' suggestions, these leaders leave most of the actual decision making to the group itself. While this style of leadership is very popular, some less experienced groups feel lost when left on their own to this extent. The effectiveness of this type of leadership, like all others, depends on the power the leader has, the nature of the task at hand, and the interpersonal relationships between the leader and group members. One study has shown that democratically led groups do better than others on measures of creativity and consistency but fall behind in efficiency.

Authoritarian leaders are more directive than democratic leaders. They are strongly goal oriented and have firm opinions on how to achieve these goals. If their competency is respected by group members, the group works well and efficiently; if not, conflict is likely to arise within the group.

The third type, **laissez-faire** leaders, don't direct the group at all. As potential sources of information and feedback on group interaction, they function as observers and recorders, available for advice when the group wants it. This kind of leadership is especially appropriate for groups engaged in creative activity, where more direction would limit or stifle creativity.

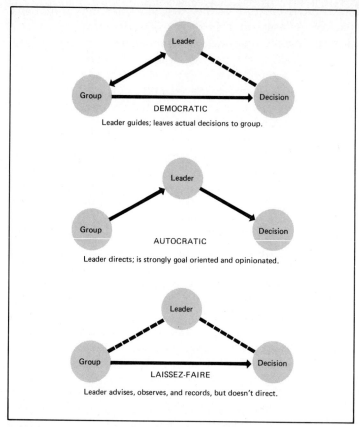

FIGURE 7-1 Three Basic Styles of Leadership.

Whatever the style of leadership chosen, positive evaluations of the group's performance depend on the degree to which each member contributes to the task and maintenance outcomes. In fact, as one study has shown, group members are evaluated more positively by the leader, whatever his or her style, when the latter attributes the group's performance to the group members' efforts.[8] To the extent that leaders believe a performance is controlled by outside forces, such as the leader's direction, group members will be devalued by the leader.

EMERGENCE OF LEADERS   In groups that have no assigned leaders, functioning leaders often emerge through a process of elimination, not through a process of selection. Interviews with group members reveal that during the first phase of the elimination process, members who are uninformed, quiet, or dogmatic are removed from consideration. In the second, longer phase of elimination, over authoritarian or verbally offensive individuals are knocked out of the running. In most cases where a con-

[8]David Kipnis, Stuart Schmidt, Karl Price, and Christopher Stitt, "Why Do I Like Thee: Is It Your Performance or My Orders?" *Journal of Applied Psychology* 66 (1981): p. 328.

> The degree to which I can create relationships which facilitate the growth of others as separate persons is a measure of the growth I have achieved in myself.
>
> Carl Rogers

sensus leader emerges (and this always happens in the most successful groups), a second person—a runner up, so to speak—becomes an auxiliary leader or lieutenant.

SKILLS OF EFFECTIVE LEADERS   As we have stated, earlier periods of research in the area of leadership emphasized the kind of person who would or would not make a good leader—the special traits or characteristics that were a part of effective leadership. More recently leadership has been viewed in light of what effective leaders *do* rather than who they are. As a function of this more recent trend, several authors have attempted to summarize and categorize leadership skills. One such skill description is that of Giammatteo and Giammatteo (1981). They list and briefly describe five of these major skill areas:[9]

1. Skills of personal behavior. The effective leader:
   - Is sensitive to feelings of the group.
   - Identifies self with the needs of the group.
   - Learns to listen attentively.
   - Refrains from criticizing or ridiculing members' suggestions.
   - Helps each member feel important and needed.
   - Should not argue.
2. Skills of communication. The effective leader:
   - Makes sure that everyone understands not only what is needed but why.
   - Makes good communication with the group a routine part of the job.
3. Skills in equality. The effective leader recognizes that:
   - Everyone is important.
   - Leadership is to be shared and is not a monopoly.
   - A leader grows when leadership functions are dispersed.
4. Skills of organization. The effective leader helps the group:
   - Develop long-range and short-range objectives.
   - Break big problems into small ones.
   - Share opportunities and responsibilities.
   - Plan, act, follow up, and evaluate.
5. Skills of Self Examination. The effective leader:
   - Is aware of motivations and motives guiding actions.
   - Is aware of members' levels of hostility and tolerance so that appropriate countermeasures are taken.
   - Is aware of their fact-finding behavior.
   - Helps the group members to be aware of their own forces, attitudes, and values.

[9]Giammatteo and Giammatteo, pp. 3–4.

Now that we have discussed leadership approaches, styles, and skills, we turn to another important area of study in small group communication: the process of group problem solving.

PROBLEM SOLVING
THROUGH GROUP DISCUSSION

We've all experienced the frustration that arises when a group of people can't seem to solve a problem that an individual would solve relatively easily—when, for example, four people spend all night trying to decide which movie to see. Researchers have discovered that the relative effectiveness of group—as opposed to individual—decision making depends on the nature of the problem at hand.

Groups do better than individuals in situations where a pooling of data is necessary, where more knowledge and a greater variety of approaches can contribute to more effective solutions. In policy decisions group participation leads to wider acceptance and better understanding of the solution. The group decision-making process is, however, prone to the problems that arise from any process involving human interaction. For some group members winning an argument may become more important than finding a solution. Other group members may try to dominate the discussion, while others may habitually give in, in order to win group acceptance. The four friends who can't decide which film to see may actually be arguing about social dominance—and not about movies at all.

A decision-making group is simply a group of people who work together to solve a problem by collecting information about the problem, reviewing that information, and then making a decision based on their findings. While we may ordinarily think of decision making as an unexciting or private process, decision-making groups and their decisions actually play a very central—and often very public—role in American life. For example, in August 1974 Americans sat glued to their TVs or radios to hear the House Judiciary Committee argue the pros and cons of impeaching President Nixon. During crucial strike negotiations the media feature dramatic, up-to-the-minute accounts of union-management talks. If you are sensitive to the fact that decision making is a *process,* you can improve your own participation in group discussions and also contribute to the effectiveness of the entire group effort.

Kinds of Topics or Problems | Some topics or problems are better tackled by group discussion than are others. Those that are most appropriate to group discussion fall into three categories: problems of fact, problems of value, and problems of policy. It is important to be able to identify these three quite distinct types of topics; decision-making discussions often break down precisely because the participants don't understand the nature of the problems they're dealing with.

PROBLEMS OF FACT   The first kind of problem or question that may be considered requires that the group investigate the truth or falsity of assertions about actual events or conditions. "Did last week's fatal DC-10 crash result from a defective cargo hatch?" "Do air pollutants from chemical-producing plants pose a health hazard to local residents?" "Is the nation going through a depression?" Sometimes panels of experts are assembled to decide crucial factual issues. Ideally, the beliefs, attitudes, and values of group members don't affect the decision-making process here; instead, members act like detectives, defining their terms ("defective," "health hazard," "depression") and making logical deductions based on evidence. One group goal in discussions of problems of fact is to arrive at a correct and accurate description of the facts.

Interestingly, in this type of decision-making discussion, the fact that everyone agrees is no guarantee that the decision made will be the correct one; everyone may agree and still be wrong. Whether or not a good decision is made by a group considering a problem of fact is determined in large part by how well the members have analyzed and interpreted the information on which their decision is based. It is for this reason that it is so important for all group members to see the "facts" before them in more or less the same light. To avoid misunderstanding, it is necessary for members to ask questions relating to the interpretation of particular words or ideas.

For example, suppose a group were planning a party for a friend. The guest of honor's availability on certain dates would, of course, be one of the important facts to be considered. Also important would be clearing up the confusion created if one friend suggests that the group buy a "substantial" gift as opposed to each person giving something individually. Some friends might think in terms of high price, while others might think that the term referred to the gift itself, meaning something sturdy and practical. Someone has to clear up the confusion and ask for an agreed-upon definition of the word before the problem can be acted upon.

PROBLEMS OF VALUE   Here facts are not the primary issue; instead of using hard evidence, group members base their discussion on attitudes, morals, and values. "Is a citizen ever justified in refusing to fight in a war?" "Should abortion be legalized?" There are no correct or incorrect answers to these questions, but there are acceptable or unacceptable answers. It is the group's goal and responsibility to discover its own bases for acceptability or unacceptability.

Obviously, discussions concerning value will differ greatly from discussions of fact; values are individually held, and they are not always formed (or defended) on the basis of logic. Also, more than one type of problem may, of course, be considered by any particular group. In the example we used above to illustrate problems of fact, questions of value might easily surface and demand attention before consideration of the facts could occur. For instance, questions concerning an appropriate gift might reflect individual values. When one friend suggests that the group buy the guest of honor a fancy cigarette lighter, another friend might question whether the group should contribute to a bad habit. This question would reflect a difference in values.

On the other hand, often during discussions of value, definitions must be agreed on and facts must be determined: Are "undeclared wars" or "policing actions" to be considered in the same category as other wars? At what point is a fetus considered a human being? Problems often arise when groups fail to distinguish value from fact. It is also very important to remember that conclusions reached in discussions concerning values may be agreed to by the participants, but this in no way means that these conclusions have been proved.

PROBLEMS OF POLICY These problems are the most common type of topic for formal decision-making groups, and they are frequently used as topics for class exercises in decision making. Problems of policy are involved in determining courses of action: "How should we allocate our advertising budget this year?" "Should U.S.-Soviet trade agreements be affected by Soviet emigration policies?"

Discussions concerning policy inevitably involve discussions of fact and value. Before deciding on the allocation of their advertising budget, business executives have to identify their target audience, and they also have to know that audience's media habits: How much time do they spend watching TV, listening to the radio, and reading magazines? In order to determine the basis for U.S.-Soviet trade arrangements, policymakers have to deal with a question of value: Does one government have the right to interfere in the internal affairs of another government? Because discussions of policy are liable to raise a great number of subsidiary questions, it is crucial that members of the group recognize when they are and are not addressing the same question. If one congressman, for example, is concerned with the adequacy of current U.S. grain supplies, another congressman is worried about disadvantageous wheat deals of the past, and a third congresswoman is concerned with civil rights in the Soviet Union, their committee's discussion about trade agreements may become disrupted or blocked entirely. If, however, the three concerned members are able to identify these issues separately and agree to discuss them one at a time, they can conduct an effective and productive discussion.

To bring things back to the level of our party-planning group, a question of policy might concern the nature of the party itself. For instance, should the party be a surprise or should it be announced? Should the group send out invitations or just telephone all the guests? These questions all suggest possible actions for the group to consider.

Research for Discussion As the above has indicated, researching facts and evidence is sometimes a crucial part of the decision-making process. John K. Brilhart has divided this preparatory research stage into four distinct phases.[10]

[10]John K. Brilhart, *Effective Group Discussion*, 3d ed. (Dubuque, Iowa: W. C. Brown, 1978), pp. 81–87.

REVIEW YOUR OWN INFORMATION   Whatever your topic for discussion, you will inevitably have some ideas and background information. Now is the time to jot down everything you know about the topic and its causes and effects. Move from a freewheeling kind of thinking to a more organized mode of thought in which you note main issues, subsidiary questions, and supporting details. Make note of information that you don't know now but that would be useful for later discussion.

GATHER NEEDED INFORMATION   This is the active phase of your research: Go out and observe the problem yourself. If your group is trying to come up with ways of reducing the theft of library books, go prowl around the library, watching for security leaks. A second source of information is interviews. Talk to experts; ask the head librarian for an analysis of the theft problem. More information about your topic can come from reading. Check magazines, professional journals, and books for the latest data on your problem. Other informal sources of information are all around you. Ask friends for their ideas about your topic; check TV and radio shows that might give you some useful information; or go to a campus lecture that deals with your topic.

EVALUATE YOUR INFORMATION   Now is the time for you to play the critic, distinguishing facts from opinions. As we noted earlier, statements of fact can be determined to be either true or false on the basis of evidence. Opinions can neither be proved nor disproved; they are not necessarily based on evidence, and they introduce the dangerous element of uncertainty into your discussion. While opinions may become useful in deciding questions of value or policy, it is essential that they be identified correctly. The head librarian's suggestion for installing antitheft devices may be a useful or expert opinion, but it is necessary to recognize it for what it is—an opinion, not a fact.

After you have separated fact from opinion, you must test your evidence for validity. Brilhart suggests the following questions for testing evidence:

1. Are these data related to the question to be discussed?
2. Are they reasonable and consistent with other sources?
3. Is the statement from a direct observer, or a secondary source?
4. Was the source capable of accurate observation?
5. If an opinion, was the source a capable expert in the field?
6. Is the source likely to be biased? If so, for or against his position?
7. In the case of statistics, is the method of collecting data made clear?[11]

Finally, you must test your evidence for accuracy (consistency is a good test here), recency, and completeness. Old or partial information is not useful and may be misleading.

[11]Brilhart, p. 86.

REORGANIZE YOUR INFORMATION AND GATHER MORE, IF NECESSARY
After you have weeded out useless or unreliable information, you can recognize the hard evidence and make a tentative outline of your analysis of the problem as well as suggested steps for its solution. It is important to remember at the close of this stage of the decision-making process that you are engaged in a cooperative effort. Don't regard your research material as weapons stockpiled for battle—view it instead as a collection of accurate and objective information that can be shared with the group to help provide the basis for informed problem solving.

THE PROBLEM-SOLVING PROCESS

Dewey's
Reflective
Thinking
Process
When we are confronted with a problem, we often lose sight of the fact that decision making or problem solving is, in fact, a process. Studies have shown that people tend to respond to problems in an ordered series of steps. John Dewey identified five distinct phases in this pattern of goal-directed or reflective thinking:

1. Recognizing the difficulty.
2. Defining or specifying the difficulty.
3. Raising suggestions for possible solutions and rational exploration of the ideas.
4. Selecting the best solution from among many proposals.
5. Carrying out the solution.[12]

A Standard
Agenda for
Decision
Making
While Dewey's discussion of these five phases of reflective thought originated as a description of the pattern of rational thought, not as a set of rules for decision making, his influence has been so great that later scholars in the field of speech communication have adopted and expanded these steps to form the basis for a standard agenda for decision making.

STEP 1: DEFINING THE PROBLEM   If a group has been given a very specific and clearly defined problem to solve, this step becomes unnecessary. In many—or most—cases, however, a group finds itself in the middle of a difficult situation, and working out a clear definition of the problem becomes an important part of the decision-making process.

Consider the following example: At a certain university eating arrangements have become a problem for a large number of students; many students live off-campus, others have kitchens in their dorms, and still others, commuters, need only a few meals on campus a week. The university meal plan ticket is expensive, the cafeteria food is unappealing, and local grocery stores and restaurants are expensive and aren't open at convenient hours. A group of students concerned with this situation meets to share complaints. The students are aware of the situation, and some have

[12]John Dewey. *How We Think* (Boston: Heath, 1933), pp. 106–15.

Which step of the problem-solving process could this be? (AFL-CIO News)

vague ideas as to possible solutions, but they need to define their problem more clearly. At this stage they have two goals: They want to frame their definition of the problem so as to increase its "solvability," and they want to frame their definition in a way that will promote good discussion and effective interaction. Clearly, posing the question so that it can be answered by a simple "yes" or "no" doesn't help define the problem.

The most effective definitions are problem centered rather than solution centered. "How can we get local supermarkets to lower their prices?" is a solution-centered definition of our sample problem. Hidden in this question is the assumption that there is only one way to solve the problem; this kind of definition effectively short-circuits the entire decision-making process. An alternative definition of the problem—"How can we improve grocery buying and dining facilities?"—centers on the problem and does not limit the range of possible solutions from the beginning.

STEP 2: LIMITING THE TOPIC   After the problem has been defined, limits to the discussion must be set up based on relevance to the group, the importance of specific issues involved in the larger problem, and the amount of time available for discussion. Our hypothetical group, for example, is interested in the high price of groceries, but only in a certain sense. The group is not going to discuss a nationwide boycott of certain supermarket chains; it is interested in the problem of prices only in the immediate area. Similarly, the group has to limit its topic on the basis of the priority of specific issues: Should they focus on the problem of grocery buying, cam-

> The freedom of an individual to act is a factor of his relationship with the other person in a given group.
>
> John Keltner

pus dining facilities, local restaurants—or all three? Obviously, the group's definition of the problem will also depend on the amount of time available—do they have only a few hours, or will they meet over a period of weeks or months, working slowly to find a solution?

STEP 3: ANALYZING THE DATA   At this stage of the decision-making process, the group goes through its evidence, distinguishing relevant from irrelevant material, finding important details, searching for causes of the problem, and working out the dynamics of the situation. Our sample group might at this point evaluate the quality of dining hall food in relation to its price; compare local supermarket prices with supermarket prices in other nearby towns; compile statistics on the number of students who do and do not have meal plan tickets; and collect figures on local restaurant prices.

STEP 4: ESTABLISHING CRITERIA FOR POSSIBLE SOLUTIONS   The group must determine in advance what they expect from their proposed solutions. Our group might decide, for example, that its solution should meet three criteria: It should provide (1) nutritious and (2) tasty food to students (3) at prices they can afford. During this stage of the problem-solving process, group members must keep from judging which of the proposed criteria are acceptable until all suggestions have been heard. The group then selects those criteria that are acceptable to the majority.

STEP 5: SUGGESTING POSSIBLE SOLUTIONS   During this "brainstorming" stage the quantity rather than the quality of proposed solutions is important. Again, the group must not try to come to a decision until all possible solutions have been heard. All possible approaches to the problem should be brought up and discussed: negotiating with the university to change dining hall policies, talking to local supermarket and restaurant owners about student discounts—these ideas and many more may prove worthwhile. Open-mindedness is the rule here. Even seemingly impossible proposals may yield solutions as they are worked over, improved, and modified by the group. An excited, "Hey, let's start our own grocery store!" may just provide the inspiration for the organization of a student cooperative supermarket.

STEP 6: CHECKING THE INDIVIDUAL SOLUTION AGAINST THE ESTABLISHED CRITERIA   Does each solution satisfy the standards the group has already established? Do some of the proposed solutions satisfy the criteria better than others? At this point in the problem-solving process, the group will throw out those solutions that do not meet the established standards, and it will evaluate the remaining solutions in the light of the needs of the problem. In this stage the group must keep its discussion focused on issues, not personalities. Any proposed solution must be judged on its own merits—not on the popularity or loudness of its sponsor.

STEP 7: CARRYING OUT THE SOLUTION   The group must decide how its solution may be carried out within the limitations of its authority, its power, its facilities, and its budget. If our student group has decided to organize an alternative supermarket, should they hire an outside contractor to run the store, or should they run it themselves as a student cooperative? Do they have sufficient manpower, business expertise, and financing to run it themselves? Which plan would result in the lowest food prices? The group must choose the most efficient and effective means of carrying out their solution.

STEP 8: EVALUATING THE EFFECT OF THE SOLUTION   After the solution has been tried, various questions must be asked: Has it accomplished its purpose? Does the new student cooperative market provide better food at more reasonable prices? Has it satisfied the need—do enough students use it to justify its existence? Can improvements be made to increase the effectiveness of the solution? Should students work at the cooperative without wages in return for even lower food prices?

The standard agenda that we have described here is offered as a guide, not as a strait jacket. It is useful only insofar as all group members are aware of it and accept it as a useful and organized way to approach the problem-solving process. Despite the orderliness of the standard agenda, its use does not guarantee effortless solutions. Several other factors affect the operations and outcomes of problem-solving groups.

OTHER FACTORS AFFECTING GROUP PERFORMANCE

One of the most fascinating aspects of group behavior is the uniqueness of each and every group due to the nature of its membership. There are many variables that influence group interaction, but the primary (and ever-present) one is the different personality of each member of the group.

Personality

Each person contributes his or her own experiences, values, attitudes, and personality to the makeup of the group. For example, some people are basically shy and tend to sit back in a group situation, while more aggressive individuals may use the group as an audience for their assertiveness. While some people try to avoid conflict in a group, much

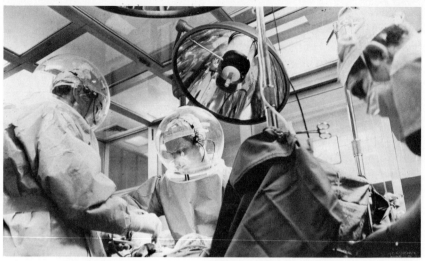

(NASA)

the same as they would in a personal encounter, other people like to provoke conflict and enjoy the combative interaction that often follows. Perhaps you have participated in a group which you felt could have functioned more efficiently if one or two members had been less argumentative or if someone had been more dominant.

Undoubtedly, you have heard the expression "personality conflict" used to describe an irreconcilable clash of personalities. Sometimes such a difference in personality can cause a group to lose sight of its goal and remain unproductive. Yet sometimes differences in personality have a positive effect on group interaction. For example, one person who is particularly task oriented may counterbalance the member who is primarily concerned with the effective behavior of the group. Similarly, a humorous individual can offset someone who is extremely serious or tense. The group is a very complex entity because of the combination of different personalities. The next time you participate in a group or observe one in action, remember that the group is equal to and greater than the sum of the individual personalities of its members.

Cohesion Groups develop personalities all their own. Some groups, for example, always seem to work smoothly and achieve their goals easily, while in other groups interaction is marked by conflict, and progress is achieved slowly, if at all. The American Bicentennial Everest Expedition provides an example of this second type of group. These mountain climbers—who depended on each other for their very survival—didn't socialize, didn't talk to each other much, and expressed a vote of "no confidence" in each other. Adding to these interactional problems was the fact that the team was actually composed of two subgroups whose goals were quite different: There were the climbers, whose goal was to reach the summit as quickly and safely as possible, and there was a TV film crew, whose goal was to capture exciting footage. The group's problems were summed up by one climber: "I just don't get the feeling that this is a team."[13]

A communication expert would diagnose this problem as a lack of group cohesion or solidarity. **Cohesion** is the degree to which group members identify themselves as a team, as a whole, rather than as just a collection of individuals. Cohesion arises from and reinforces shared values, attitudes, and standards of behavior. Cohesion is a crucial factor in a group's success, for highly cohesive groups are more likely to be productive, their members are more likely to feel personally satisfied by the group process, and their interpersonal communication is more effective.

Cohesive groups inspire feelings of loyalty because group members have an emotional investment in the life of the team; they share the same goals and are willing to make personal sacrifices for the good of the group. Interaction in highly cohesive groups has several special characteristics. Because individuals feel secure in these groups, they can tolerate some degree of productive conflict, and they feel free to offer both rewarding and punishing feedback to other group members.

Cohesive groups offer their members greater returns or rewards for their personal investment in the group. In the business world these rewards may take the form of money; for example, a team assembling autos may be paid for the number of cars they produce each week, instead of being paid by the hour. In an academic situation a professor may give the same grade to all students working on a group project regardless of their individual contributions to the project. In both these cases cohesion increases as a result of a shared group goal. Members of the car assembly team will probably work harder to get more pay, and the students will most likely work harder to get a better grade.

Cohesive groups also offer psychological rewards—feelings of belonging and the friendship and respect of other people. In addition, cohesive groups offer their members the reward of prestige, which comes either from the social status of the group or from some group accomplishment. In either case group members share the reflected glory of the group. Finally, and perhaps most importantly, participation in a cohesive group allows each member to experience achievement rewards, the satisfaction that comes from productive work, and the fulfillment that comes from contributing to a valuable and valued cause or goal.

Conflict

The ideal group is highly cohesive, but groups, like most other things in life, are rarely ideal, and conflict, rather than cohesion, often emerges from group interaction. Conflict between groups (**intergroup conflict**) often benefits the groups involved by increasing goal-oriented activity and causing group members to value their work more highly. An extreme case is war, in which conflict strengthens in-group bonds by providing an out-

[13]Jurate Kazickas, "Mt. Everest Climbers Are Bothered by Cameramen, Personality Clashes," (AP), *Tallahassee Democrat,* 19 September 1976, p. 13A.

let for tension and focusing a group's goals. Conflicts usually occur when there are two or more competing or incompatible responses to a single event. Thus, conflict may occur both within the group itself, when individuals experience differing needs or values; or between groups, when the groups have competing interests over the accomplishment of a cooperative goal![14]

In the past it was believed that all **intragroup conflict** (conflict within a group) had the opposite effect—that it had a negative influence, reduced cohesion, decreased productivity, and caused group members to discredit their own achievements. It is now believed that some degree of intragroup conflict is useful and productive. It is possible that when conflict is appropriately channeled, it can contribute to more effective results. Of course, the kind of conflict in mind here is not a pitched battle but an issue-centered form of open discussion and confrontation that uses group problem-solving methods to achieve better solutions.

At times intragroup conflict cannot be avoided; it must be confronted and worked through. The first step in this process is identifying the source of conflict. Lawrence Rosenfeld has identified a number of sources of conflict, both personal and impersonal, that a group may encounter.[15] Problems of time and space, varying levels of energy and understanding among individual members, and a lack of information or method of operation are but a few of the sources of trouble Rosenfeld cited. Often the real source of conflict lies hidden below what people seem to be arguing about. As in the case of the "hidden agenda" mentioned earlier, two participants may seem to be arguing over an issue (Air pollution is increasing in our region—No, it isn't), while what is really at stake is something else (I'm an expert on this subject—No, you aren't). Once the real source of conflict has been identified, the solutions may be directed toward either the individual or the group. The individuals may decide to tolerate the conflict. Our two belligerents, for example, may agree to accept the fact that each feels the other to be an ignoramus. In this case, as in others, further probing into the nature and causes of the hostility may simply increase that hostility (Let me count the ways in which you are an ignoramus).

Group conflicts that continue after the cause has been identified may sometimes be resolved through **bargaining** or **arbitration,** processes that create compromise solutions. Unfortunately, compromise solutions often cause new dissatisfactions (Harriet always gets her way—I never get mine), and the original conflict may flare up again or even escalate.

Continuous conflict may be resolved by **integration,** the proposal of new alternatives and new methods of organization. Integration of the conflicting persons or interests results from a clear analysis of the sources

---

[14]H. Wayland Cummings, Larry Long, and Michael Lewis, *Managing Communication in Organizations* (Dubuque, Iowa: Gorsuch-Scarisbrick, 1983).

[15]Lawrence Rosenfeld, *Human Interaction in the Small Group Setting* (Columbus, Ohio: Chas. E. Merrill, 1973), p. 229.

of conflict, a reevaluation of competing positions in the light of one another's needs, and a reorganization that includes the goals of opposing forces.

Sometimes conflict may be ended by asking a few individuals to leave the group. In deadlock situations in which group members can't resolve the conflict, breaking up the group may be the only way to handle the situation.

Another important variable that influences groups is pressure to conform within the group. In and of itself, **conformity** is not a negative force. Sometimes, however, when consensus inhibits dissent, the pressure to conform, or "groupthink," can cause serious errors in decision making.[16] As discussed previously, many of the norms to which a group conforms are productive for the group, enabling it to function more effectively. Actually, conformity, when it occurs naturally, without force, is quite desirable, since consensus is one of the objectives of the group process.

While pressure to conform is sometimes so subtle that a group member may be totally unaware of it, at other times the pressure can be quite open. Group members may be pressured to conform, even when it means going against their better judgment or even their conscience. This sort of overt pressure can result in dissonance, which can erupt in open conflict or take the form of defiance.

For example, an individual may verbally yield to group pressure but then exhibit contradictory behavior. Examine the following situation: Gil's bike club was going to sponsor a charity drive for an undetermined organization. Gil was anxious to support the local animal shelter, but the group made its final decision to support the nearby children's hospital. Gil reluctantly agreed, and the group believed that it had won him over to its side. Yet when it came to active participation in the collection drive, Gil was nowhere to be found. In this case Gil gave the group what it wanted to hear when it wanted to hear it, but he refused to conform in his actions.

The consequence that may result when group members are pressured to conform will vary depending upon the situation, the force of the pressure, and the people involved. Consider another example: After three weeks of testimony, a jury was asked to determine the guilt or innocence of the accused. From the very outset most of the jurors were convinced that the defendant was guilty. After three days and endless hours of discussion, all but one of the jurors voted to convict the accused. The holdout was subjected to group pressure, both overt and subtle. Everyone was tired and anxious to go home. On the next day the twelfth juror gave in to the group pressure, and the accused was found guilty. This is obviously an instance in which group pressure—whether for good or ill (depending

---

[16]I. L. Janis, *Victims of Groupthink: A Psychological Study of Foreign Policy Decisions and Fiascos* (Boston: Houghton Mifflin, 1982. 2nd ed.).

upon the actual guilt or innocence of the accused)—greatly affected a group's decision.

Some group members are more susceptible to group presssure than are others. The following personality characteristics identify those who are most vulnerable to group pressure:

1. *Level of self-confidence.* The better one's self-concept, the more resistant one will be to group pressure.
2. *Regard for authority.* A closed-minded person, defined as one who relies on the accuracy and correctness of authority, will be more apt to conform to group pressure.
3. *Intelligence.* The greater one's intelligence, the less likely one is to conform.
4. *Need for social approval.* As you might expect, the greater one's need for approval, the more apt one is to conform.

Other variables that influence conformity concern the situation in which the group finds itself. Situational variables include:

1. *The size of the group.* Conformity usually increases as the size of the group increases, but only until there are four members; thereafter, conformity decreases as the group increases.
2. *Group structure.* Group structures that permit a great deal of interaction between members produce more conformity than those that limit interaction.
3. *Difficulty of the task.* Conformity usually increases as the task becomes harder.
4. *Degree of crisis or emergency.* The old adage that there is safety in numbers may account for the increase in conformity during a crisis situation. For example, a group of shipwrecked survivors floating on a raft in the middle of the ocean would probably exhibit a high degree of conformity since deviation from the norm could mean disaster.

Whatever the mechanisms affecting a particular group—personality, cohesion, conformity—it is the responsibility of each and every group member to try to make the most of the positive potential of these forces. By becoming a member of a group, you and the others have elected to pursue certain objectives as a team. When what needs to be accomplished is kept firmly in view, individual differences can often be recognized as the stumbling blocks they are and can be temporarily shelved while the solution is sought in an open-minded way.

ANALYZING SMALL GROUP INTERACTION

Hopefully, the explanations and guidelines presented in this chapter will help you to participate more fully and effectively in small groups. One way to apply these principles is to observe group interaction. We should now be able to recognize characteristics of effective and ineffective small groups by examining group goals, member participation, types of listening and feedback, group roles, and styles of leadership.

Groups are often evaluated on the outcomes and products the mem-

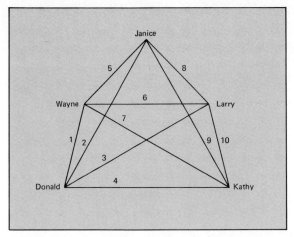

FIGURE 7-2 Channels of Communication in a Five-Member Group.

bers produce. Group membership can be beneficial to some and detrimental to others. Alcoholics Anonymous is successful to a person who attends and never drinks again. The Humane Society may be seen as unsuccessful when animals have to be put to sleep because they are not adopted.

Groups are also evaluated by what actually takes place during a group interaction or meeting. Individuals such as Bales and Lashbrook have even developed quantitative (number and amount of member participation) and qualitative (evaluate member response in terms of benefit to the group) methods to analyze group interaction. Their guidelines will help you evaluate groups that you observe and of which you are a member.[17,18]

Figure 7–2 shows a five-member group with ten possible channels of communication. The lines between the group members represent the ability to respond (verbally and nonverbally) back and forth. Donald can initiate a conversation with Kathy just as easily as he can with Larry, Janice, or Wayne. By examining the number of times a person speaks, you can evaluate factors such as leadership style, member participation, roles, and so on. The small slashes on the lines in Figure 7–3 indicate the number of times each person spoke to another member during a specified period.

If this were a family trying to decide where to go for a vacation, who do you think would have the most to say? Probably the parents. In Figure 7–3 you'll notice that more communication is directed to Donald than to anyone else. We could assume that he is the father and that Janice is the

[17]Edward M. Bodaken, William B. Lashbrook, and Marie Champagne, "Proana 5: A Computerized Technique for the Analysis of Small Group Interaction," *Western Speech* 25 (1971):112–15.
[18]Robert F. Bales, *Interaction Process Analysis: A Method for the Study of Small Groups* (Cambridge, Mass.: Addison-Wesley, 1950).

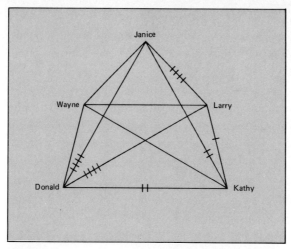

FIGURE 7-3 Number of Times Group Member Spoke.

mother. What would you guess about Kathy, Larry, and Wayne? Maybe Larry is the oldest child, because he interacts more than Kathy and Wayne, or maybe he is more assertive than they are. We might guess that Wayne is a small child or baby since no communication is directed to or from him.

If this were a business meeting, we might assume that Donald was the designated leader or chairman of the board. We could also guess that his leadership style is authoritarian. We would probably be concerned that Wayne did not participate, but he may have another function (for example, recorder, trainee). Much can be assumed from these simple diagrams. However, it is often important to determine the quality as well as the amount of interaction.

Decisions about the quality of communication are based on a number of factors. It is important to know whether the group's purpose serves a social or task function. For example, if the group meets socially to celebrate a member's birthday, then no one would expect organized, purposeful conversation. On the other hand, if a group meets with a specific goal, then the functions of group members are important. A group of surgeons deciding which patient will receive an eye donation would need to get to the point immediately without sharing the tales of their latest golf game or fishing expedition.

When observing a group that is task oriented, we need to be aware of member functions. Does a member tell a joke just to get attention or to release tension? We also need to observe types of listening behavior and feedback. Do members listen to what is being said, or do they go off on a new tangent each time they speak? When a group is involved in brainstorming, are members accepting of others, or do they (verbally and nonverbally) chastise others for "far out" suggestions? Diagrams can be used to determine which members are most productive or meet group goals.

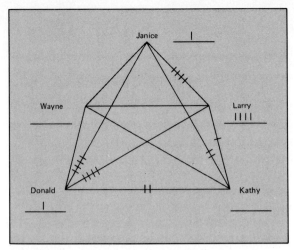

FIGURE 7-4 Diagram to Determine Productive Group Members.

Figure 7–4 includes a space for interactions that are not beneficial to the group. For example, if Larry started talking about a song that he wrote when the group was assigning duties for a dance marathon to fight muscular dystrophy, he would not be adding to the group purpose and would be involved in nonpatterned interaction. A slash would be drawn beside his name and not on the line between members because he didn't add useful information or respond to a comment from another member.

SUMMARY

It is almost impossible to exist independently of all groups. Understanding the group process can help you get more out of your participation in groups. As a participant in a group, you have certain responsibilities. These include keeping an open mind to all ideas, showing sensitivity to other members, communicating ideas, opinions, and information as accurately and honestly as possible, using appropriate questions when necessary, and doing all the homework or preparation required.

It is also helpful to be able to analyze the role structures, norms, and outcomes that function in your group. Attention to the norms that develop will enable you to determine which of these are beneficial to the group and which are counterproductive. To

further increase productivity, you and the other group members should assume various task-oriented roles, including information or opinion giving, information or opinion seeking, expediting, contributing ideas, and analyzing. These kinds of actions keep the discussion on course and aid the group in accomplishing its objectives.

You should also be concerned with the emotional behavior of the group. Concern for the social and emotional climate of the group is shown when members assume maintenance roles, which include active listening, game leading, harmonizing, gatekeeping, compromising, and "fronting" for the group. Indifference to the group and its goals often results in self-serving roles, which can obstruct the group's progress. Although each member in the group has his or her individual role to play, effective group interaction does not take place automatically. The group must go through several stages of development, including groping, griping, grasping, grouping, and group action.

Although some people seem to be good leaders by nature, specific leadership skills can be learned. Good leaders tend to have skills in the areas of personal behavior, communicating, equality, organization, and self-examination.

The three basic types of leadership are democratic, authoritarian, and laissez-faire styles.

When approaching a problem, it is usually best to follow an orderly sequence to arrive at the best possible solution. Problems of fact, value, and policy can all be discussed by groups, but it is extremely important for the group to understand the agenda, which is based on John Dewey's pattern of reflective thinking. These steps are defining the problem, limiting the topic, analyzing the problem, establishing criteria or standards, suggesting possible solutions, checking individual solutions against all the criteria, carrying out the solution, and evaluating the effect of the solution on the problem.

Cohesion can be the key to effective group discussion and action. Groups that are not cohesive often fail to solve problems effectively. Loyalty and allegiance are fostered in cohesive groups. Conflict can destroy cohesion in a group, but at times it may also contribute to more effective results. It is the responsibility of all group members, not just the leader, to deal with conflict in an objective and reasonable manner. Conformity, when it is not forced, is very desirable, since consensus is one of the objectives of the group process.

Exercises

GROUP EXPERIENCES

Group Roles and Behavior

Description: Task-oriented and maintenance roles in groups are related to the roles people play in life. This activity is designed to explore the relationship between behaviors and roles. If you receive a "behavior" that seems contradictory to a role, try it anyway. They may work together better than you think!

Procedure: Divide into groups of six. Write each of the following behaviors and roles on separate index cards:

Task Behaviors	Maintenance Behaviors
Elaborator	Blocker
Encourager	Withdrawer
Gatekeeper	Dominator

Roles

Mr. Garcia: Runs a small grocery store.
Mrs. Garcia: Wife of Mr. Garcia and mother of seven children.

Father Hollen: Priest, and dedicated missionary of his faith.
Dr. Redding: Scientist, winner of several international awards.
Ms. Valentine: Sales manager of Honeywell, Inc.
Elaine Warner: M.D., General Practitioner.

Each group member should select at random a role and a behavior. Take 5 minutes and look up your behavior in the chapter to make sure you understand what it involves. Do not show anyone the cards you selected.

All six members should meet as a group, playing their assigned parts. The problem you face as a group is to decide which two people can leave the island where you are stranded. Only two people may leave, and there is no guarantee that they will be able to send help or that they will reach their destination. For the people who stay on the island, there is plenty of fresh water, but food is scarce. Decide in 15 minutes.

Discussion: Read aloud your role and describe the behavior you were asked to portray. Did you have trouble combining the role and behavior? Did you recognize the roles and behaviors that others were playing? Can you draw any conclusions regarding the relationship between roles and behaviors in groups?

The Power Trip

Description: The distinction between leaders and leadership has been discussed in this chapter. Leadership behavior (any behavior that helps a group clarify and achieve group goals) can be observed on both the verbal and nonverbal levels. This activity explores the relationship between power and influence and, subsequently, power and leadership. During the activity you should pay particular attention to the nonverbal behaviors that communicate influence, power, and dominance.

Procedure: Divide into groups of six to eight members. Each group member should be given an equal amount of money. Although many variations are possible at this point, one method is to distribute ten pennies, one nickel, one dime, and one quarter to each participant.

Stage 1. For the first 5 minutes of the exercise, group members should be instructed that they may give some, all, or none of their money away to other members. However, during this time period they may not physically take money from another member. (A distinction is made between "taking" money and "receiving" money.) This means that they may not take money from any player, but they can accept money that is given to them.

Stage 2. The second stage of this exercise is the "taking" period. During the next 5 minutes, group members are instructed that they may "take" money from any group member, but they may no longer give money away. (This part of the exercise may become very lively, because group members may forcibly try to take money from a resistant member. This is an anticipated part of the exercise.)

Stage 3. At the end of the second 5 minutes, group members are told to stop and count the money they have. The group member who has accumulated the largest amount of money then becomes the group leader. By virtue of being the group leader, all the members of the group must give him or her their money so that the leader then has all the money for the group.

Stage 4. The leaders from each small group now come together to form their own "power" group. Their group members can stand around them and give them advice during the rest of the activity, but their group leader may not respond verbally to the comments.

Stage 5. Stages 1 and 2 (5 minutes of giving, 5 minutes of taking) are repeated for the group leaders.

Stage 6. Each group leader should count the final amount of money collected. Each leader can decide whether to keep the money or to distribute it in some manner to the fellow group members. The decision of each group leader should be verbalized and carried out.

Discussion: Now here is an interesting question: Is the person with the most power likely to be the leader? How are we persuaded to entrust other people with leadership authority? Is the use of money realistic and meaningful as a source of power? Is "power" a characteristic of a leader?

To Lead or Not to Lead

Description: The three types of leadership styles—democratic, authoritarian, and laissez-faire—are explored in this activity. The democratic leader guides rather than directs the group; the authoritarian leader is more directive than the democratic counterpart; the laissez-faire leader does not direct the group at all. In the following activity you will have an opportunity to experience the effects of all three types of leadership.

Procedure: Divide into groups of six to eight members. The group should identify one person to play the democratic leader, one person to play the laissez-faire leader, and one person to play the authoritarian leader. The leadership should rotate every 5 minutes so that all three leaders have an opportunity to direct (or not direct) the group. Each group should select a task, such as planning a hike, a dance, a clean-up project for the city, or a recycling project.

Discussion: After 15 minutes each group should evaluate (1) its task orientation and (2) its social dimension (cohesion) during each type of leadership. Which type of leadership provided a balance between the task orientation and the social dimension? Did any particular type of leadership promote either the task orientation or the social dimension? Which type of leadership do you prefer? Why? Under which conditions would each of the three types of leadership be effective?

Questions As Feedback

Description: Questions can be a valuable source of feedback when they are used appropriately. Questions involve a matter of choice in terms of timing and the nature of the question itself. Sometimes a lack of questions can leave many issues unresolved in the minds of group members. This activity should help to make you aware of the appropriate use of questions of fact, value, and policy.

Procedure: Divide into groups of five to seven members. There are two parts to this activity. The first part is to be done individually. Complete the "situations" given below by providing an example of a question of fact, value, and policy. After each group member has completed the situations, you should engage in a discussion to compare responses. The following situation and responses are offered as a sample.

Sample Situation. A group member's parent has recently passed away. Sandy suggests that a large arrangement of flowers be sent to the funeral home. Richard suggests that the money would be better used if it were sent to the American Cancer Society. Carol, somewhat concerned about the decision, suggests that the decision be postponed until all members are present.

> Question of fact: What is meant by "large" in reference to an arrangement of flowers?
> Question of value: Why the American Cancer Society? Why not another organization that has a broader appeal?
> Question of policy: Should all members be asked to contribute a given amount of money, even if they do not support the final decision?

Situation 1. Michael was named as chairman of his department's picnic committee. Fulfilling his role as an authoritarian leader, Michael decided that the picnic should be held at a nice park that had good athletic facilities. In addition, he stated that it would cost $50, leaving $20 in the fund for the next six months. He pointed out to the committee members that the decision was entirely in the hands of the committee and was not subject to a vote by the student body. What questions of fact, value, and policy should be asked to clarify the issues?

Situation 2. Richard is sitting around with a group of old college friends, trying to plan a five-year reunion. The group is having difficulty locating the addresses of approximately 20 of the 200 classmates. Don suggests that they place an advertisement in the newspaper to attract these people. Carol and Sandy respond that it would be a waste of money and that the reunion should be planned with the 180 people for whom addresses are available. What questions of fact, value, and policy should be asked to clarify the issues?

Discussion: Compare your responses with those of the other members of your group. Do you feel that in some cases a specific type of question is more appropriate? For example, is a question of fact more appropriate than a question of policy in a given situation? What are the repercussions for the group when questions are not asked? Do questions of fact, value, and policy help the group communication process in terms of clarifying its goal?

How Do You See the World?

Description: Decision-making discussions often break down because the participants do not understand the nature of the questions being raised. A breakdown may also occur simply because each member is viewing the problem from a different perspective. A specific example is when one member argues an issue from the basis of factual information, another from a value position, and another from the basis of policy. Although these three perspectives can be integrated in the discussion process, they may often hinder effective discussion when members refuse to acknowledge the existence of another perspective for viewing the problem or issue. This activity will demonstrate how a breakdown of communication can occur and will suggest alternative methods for avoiding and resolving breakdowns of a similar nature.

Procedure: Divide into groups of five. Each participant should be given one of the roles described below. The audience should be informed as to the context of the situation but, if possible, should not be informed of the individual roles. The context of the situation is as follows: The student government has decided to take some type of action relating to off-campus housing. A subcommittee has been given the mandate (1) to determine if unfair and discriminatory practices by landlords against students exist and (2) to suggest a plan of action to bring problems to the attention of the community. The following roles should be assigned to the participants:

> *Person A:* You are a laissez-faire leader for the discussion group. You see your role as primarily one of observing and repeating what is happening and recording notes for the group.

Person B: You are concerned with facts and facts only. Before you commit yourself to resolving this problem, you will need to know if there is a problem. Examples of questions you might ask include, "What are the landlord-tenant regulations?" and "What is meant by 'unfair' or 'discriminatory' practices?" Do not argue issues unless they involve sound facts that you can relate to. Always bring the discussion back to the facts that are either known in this case or need to be determined.

Person C: You are concerned with attitudes, morals, and values. "Are students justified in not paying rent when they feel that they have been treated unfairly?" "Does society have a right to treat students differently from other people who rent apartments?" Treat all issues from the humanistic point of view by raising questions of justice and injustice. Do not allow yourself to be pulled off these grounds during the discussion.

Person D: You are concerned with policy issues. "How much time and energy should be devoted to this problem relative to other pressing issues in student government?" "What authority do we have as a subcommittee to recommend or carry out particular solutions?" "Are there events in landlord-student discrimination that have already set a precedent?" In order to both ask and answer the type of questions you raise, you will need information based on facts and values. Probe the other discussion members to determine which issues are important to them. Find out how you can use their information to answer your questions.

Person E: For the first 5 minutes of this discussion, you should ask questions of clarification, to determine if you understand the other points of view. After that point urge committee members to discuss separately each kind of issue that arises. Try to direct the decision-making process so that all issues are fairly but distinctly considered.

Discussion: Did Persons B, C, and D continue to discuss separate issues of fact, value, and policy? If they did, you probably had an opportunity to see how the decision-making process breaks down. If each participant is discussing the same problem, but from a different perspective, it is unlikely that an acceptable resolution of the problem will be reached. Was Person E effective in convincing committee members to resolve issues of fact, value, and policy separately? If so, did this help the decision-making process? How can a discussion leader avoid the problems that result from trying to argue, simultaneously, issues of fact, value, and policy?

Group Discussion Contest

Description: This activity will provide you with an opportunity to either observe or participate in a group that uses a standard agenda for solving problems in a logical and objective manner. In this activity the group will be given a time limit to move through all stages of discussion. In natural group discussion settings, it is unlikely that you would see a group move through all stages during one meeting, since most groups progress through the stages over longer periods of time. This activity can be considered a "speeded-up" version of a group engaged in a problem-solving task.

Procedure: Divide into groups of five to seven members. Half of the groups should be observers, the other half participants. The following instructions are written for (1) the problem-solving groups and (2) the observation groups.

Instructions for Problem-Solving Groups. You have 40 minutes in which to discuss a problem from Step 1 through Step 8. The eight stages include

> Step 1: Defining the problem
> Step 2: Limiting the topic
> Step 3: Analyzing the problem
> Step 4: Establishing criteria or standards for possible solutions
> Step 5: Suggesting possible solutions
> Step 6: Checking the individual solutions against all established criteria
> Step 7: Carrying out the solution
> Step 8: Evaluating the effect of the solution upon the problem

Prior to the discussion each member should have a thorough understanding of these steps. In addition, a problem area, such as downtown parking, low-income housing, quality of education, or medical services, should be selected by your group. Your 40 minutes officially begin *after* you have selected the problem area. Your primary task is to systematically evaluate the problem, using the stages listed above, in order.

Instructions for Observation Groups. The purpose of your group is to observe how effectively and efficiently the problem-solving group goes through the eight stages of problem resolution. In addition, you should observe leader emergence, group cohesion, and conflict resolution among group members. Focus your observation on the following questions, in addition to other questions that you feel are important:

> 1. Did the group discussion cover all eight stages of problem solving?
> 2. Was any stage either dismissed or given too much time? Why?
> 3. During which stage in the problem-solving task did you observe (a) leader emergence, (b) group conflict, and (c) group consensus?
> 4. What criteria would you use in determining whether the group was effective in its problem-solving task?

Discussion: At the conclusion of the 40 minutes, each problem-solving group and its observation group should meet together for a 15-minute debriefing period. The observation group should have approximately 5 minutes to report its findings. The problem-solving group should then have an equal amount of time to respond to the observations. Finally, both groups should reach a consensus regarding (1) the effectiveness of the group discussion, (2) the identifiable leaders in the group, and (3) the efficiency with which the group proceeded through the eight stages of problem solving.

PERSONAL EXPERIENCES

1. Attend a group meeting for the first time. Keep your participation to a minimum as you observe the task-oriented and maintenance behaviors used by other group members. Pay particular attention to whether members maintain the same role or change roles. Are there any patterns that show up? For example, is one group member consistently a blocker when dealing with another member?

2. Pick a task-oriented or maintenance role that you can play in a group that you have been part of before. Carefully study the behavior you select so that you can consistently display your chosen role. Following the meeting, ask other group members to respond to your behavior in the group. Then explain your experiment to the other group members so that they can understand what you did and why.

3. Select a group to observe for 30 minutes. While you are observing, apply the criteria you think important for an effective group discussion. Then answer the question, To what extent was the group effective during its discussion or problem-solving task? After you have answered this question, reevaluate your criteria and make any revisions you feel would be appropriate.

4. Select a day during which you can observe your personal decision making. As you watch yourself making decisions, ask yourself the following questions: Which problems could be better resolved by a group than by an individual? What types of decisions do I usually seek advice on? When do I feel the need to share my decision making with another person?

5. Watch a television program that involves a lot of decision making (for instance, a detective program). To what extent were the decisions affected by (a) an authoritarian leader, (b) group pressure, or (c) a democratic or laissez-faire leader?

GROUP DISCUSSION

1. How do you distinguish conversation from discussion in your everyday life?

2. How does bypassing affect the group process?

3. What distinguishes someone who exhibits leadership behavior from a leader?

4. In your opinion, to what extent is group pressure to conform in decision making instrumental, as contrasted to group pressure to carefully evaluate the evidence and options? Consider various types of decision-making groups, such as a jury, a senate subcommittee, and social groups.

5. Why is it important to understand the distinction between questions of fact, value, and policy in reference to group discussions?

6. Under what conditions would the three types of leadership (democratic, laissez-faire, and authoritarian) be most effective? Consider various types of groups, such as a shipwrecked crew, a dance committee, and a jury.

7. Why is it important to analyze small group interaction? Consider differences between quantitative and qualitative analysis.

ORGANIZATIONAL COMMUNICATION

8

Exploratory Questions

1. What are the differences between groups and organizations?
2. What are six characteristics typical of organizations?
3. How would you explain the differences among mutual benefit, business, service, and commercial organizations?
4. What are three methods of organizational control?
5. How would you describe the four major functions of communication?
6. What are three types of message distortion?
7. What are four communication networks, and how do they work?
8. How do the five network structures affect communication in organizations?
9. Why is professionalism important?
10. What are four methods of getting an employment interview?
11. What responsibilities does the interviewer have? The interviewee?

During the past few years, you have been making decisions that will affect the rest of your life. Deciding where to go to college, declaring a major, getting married, or going to graduate school are each important decisions—however, one of your most important decisions concerns your first professional position. If you haven't started thinking about where you want to work after graduation, now is a good time to begin. Most, if not all, college graduates accept their first job in some type of organization, whether it be a hospital, school, governmental agency, business, or church. Although you might have an idea about what you'd like to be doing in two, five, or ten years, you may not have a clear perspective on the structure and communication patterns in organizations.

Effective communication is the key to success in your work. In fact, 80 percent of the people who fail at work do so because they don't relate well to others.[1] Any job you take, whether as an attorney, construction worker, manager, salesperson, minister, psychiatrist, teacher, or patrol officer, requires the ability to communicate. This chapter is designed to help you understand communication in organizations and to give you guidelines for securing a professional position most suitable to your needs.

WHAT IS AN ORGANIZATION?

In Chapter 7 you learned that a group consists of three or more persons with a common goal and the potential for interaction between members. You also found that you are a member of five or more groups simultaneously. Now you may be wondering if these groups are also organizations. Not necessarily. *Organizations* are defined as collected groups of individuals constructed and reconstructed to strive for specific goals that could not be met by individuals acting alone. Although there are similar-

---

[1]Robert Bolton, *People Skills* (Englewood Cliffs, N.J.: Prentice-Hall, 1979), p. 7.

ities in our definitions, an examination of five characteristics of organizations should help explain the differences between casual and organized groups.[2]

CHARACTERISTICS OF ORGANIZATIONS

Organizations are characterized first by divisions of labor and responsibility which help to facilitate specific goals. One goal of Delta Airlines, for example, is to provide transportation. By flying, a casual observer can easily identify major departmental divisions, such as reservations, ticketing, baggage, and personnel. The divisions or departments are created to help the organization perform more efficiently. As the size of the organization increases, so does the number of necessary departments.

A second characteristic of organizations is the presence of one or more power centers. Top individuals review and direct organizational procedures and performance. Decisions are made through managerial control and leadership. If the baggage department manager at Delta gets complaints from several passengers about lost luggage, then it is the manager's responsibility to locate the source of the difficulties and make the necessary improvements.

Third, organizations are characterized by substitution of personnel. People who retire, are fired, accept promotions, move to other companies, or take leaves of absence must be replaced so that the organization will continue to function properly. If a passenger is injured because a flight attendant fails to give instructions about the proper use of safety equipment, the attendant may be fired or placed on probation. As a result of this decision, someone else would now be needed to fill this position.

Interdependence among organizational components is a fourth characteristic of organizations. Departments don't act in isolation, and the performance of one department affects the performance of all other departments. You may have a tight schedule in making a connecting flight from Atlanta to Boston, and as you receive your boarding pass, the ticket agent may inform you that the flight will be an hour late. That would make it impossible for you to make your connecting flight to Boston. Although you appreciate the fact that the mechanic found a faulty wing structure before takeoff, this discovery affected you and the decisions of many others in the Delta organization.

Fifth, organizations are characterized by coordination among their components. The coordination is made possible in an organization by different channels of communication, such as word of mouth, phone calls, and letters. To make sure that a flight takes off at the appropriate time, passengers must be ticketed, ground crews have to service and load the aircraft, pilots and navigators must be informed of their destination, me-

[2]John E. Baird, *The Dynamics of Organizational Communication* (New York: Harper & Row, 1977), p. 15.

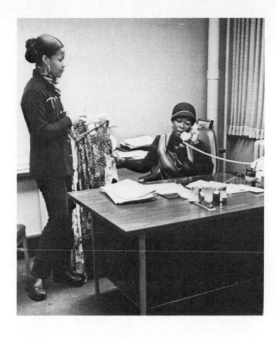

The purposes of an organization underlie any business-related interactions between its employees. (Laimute E. Druskis)

chanical functions of the plane must be in operation, and the control tower must radio that all is clear.

Another important characteristic of organizations is ***repetitive interaction*** between members.[3] Repetitive interaction causes organized groups to have permanence and continuity. When the marketing department at the Coca-Cola Bottling Company meets to discuss the effectiveness of their "Coke Is It" campaign, the members repeat previously established roles, responsibilities, and relationships; a meeting of an unorganized group of people getting together for a beer or dinner will assume different roles and responsibilities based on their moods, whose idea it was to meet, and interpersonal interactions.

Repetitive interaction is more likely to occur in organizations because of their formal structure. Organizations list all personnel with titles, such as President, Secretary, Copy Editor, Cashier, Nurse, Chief Engineer, Professor, or Cook. Organizations also have official names for identification (Sears, Procter and Gamble, RCA, St. Jude's Hospital, Harvard University, and so on).

From this discussion you have probably identified differences between social groups and organized groups, even though social groups often possess one or more characteristics of organizations. In your family, for instance, a childhood responsibility might have been helping with the dinner dishes, mowing the lawn, or washing the family car. Your parents or older brothers and sisters probably shared one or more power centers. Your family may have used substitution of personnel by adopting a child

[3]Richard K. Allen, *Organizational Management Through Communication* (New York: Harper & Row, 1977), p. 8.

or marrying someone, and some family members may have been "fired" through divorce. The differences between groups and organizations lie in the purposes for which organizations are constructed and in repetition of interaction. Now that you have a clearer understanding of organizational characteristics, we will examine the types and functions of organizations.

TYPES OF ORGANIZATIONS

You may already have an idea about what type of organization you would like to work for or with after graduation, but before making a final decision, you should examine organizational goals and power structures. By examining organizational goals, you will be able to determine who benefits most from membership.[4] For instance, in a ***mutual benefit organization*** the members get the most out of participation. Mutual benefit associations include political parties, professional organizations, labor unions, private country clubs, and religious/fraternal organizations.

In a ***business organization*** the owners receive the greatest benefits or profits. Examples of business concerns are banks, motels, retail stores, insurance companies, restaurants, and public utilities. Clients usually receive the most benefits from ***service organizations.*** Civil rights groups, hospitals, schools, social work agencies, reformatories, and mental health centers are classified as service associations. Finally, there are ***commercial,*** or ***commonwealth, organizations,*** which are designed to serve public interests. Commercial associations include law enforcement agencies, post offices, public transportation systems, city recreational departments, the armed services, and educational radio and television stations.

Another way to classify organizations is by examining their means of control. Organizations predominantly fall into coercive, utilitarian, or normative categories.[5] A ***coercive organization*** uses force over its members as a major means of control. Prisons, custodial mental health centers, and governmental dictatorships are examples of this type of organization. The Nazi concentration camps' primary method of control was coercion. A ***utilitarian organization*** controls its members through wages earned, advancement potential, tenure, and reward. Examples of utilitarian organizations are industries, business unions, and farmers' cooperatives. Some organizations also have internal, organized groups (labor unions) which attempt to provide greater rewards and benefits. In states that have right-to-work laws, labor unions provide benefits for all employees, not just those who are members of the union. This is one reason why labor groups are against right-to-work legislation. Finally, a ***normative organization*** controls the actions of its members through compliance with social norms. Members usually think about what ideas should be implemented

[4]Ted Frank and David Ray, *Basic Business and Professional Speech* (Englewood Cliffs, N.J.: Prentice-Hall, 1979), pp. 263–64.
[5]Amitai Etzioni, *A Comparative Analysis of Complex Organizations* (New York: Free Press, 1967), pp. 31–67.

to benefit society as a whole. Religious, political, and voluntary organizations fall into this category. Many religious groups, for example, try to ban X-rated and other controversial movies from theaters because they feel that the effects will be detrimental to society.

It is difficult to classify an organization as having only one goal and power structure. Most organizations have combinations of goals and power centers. For example, the American Red Cross has mutual benefit, service, and commercial goals while having both utilitarian and normative power structures. During university blood drives donors help others and themselves with plasma donations. The Red Cross determines where the blood is sent, at what cost, and when it will be used. Whatever its goal and power structure, it is important for you to understand what type of organization you join and to comprehend communication channels and networks in the organization.

COMMUNICATION DIMENSIONS IN ORGANIZATIONS

Think for a minute about the different organizations and businesses you've come in contact with in the last week. Now try to remember all the different channels of communication you used to get your message across to others. You may have called the power company to have electricity turned on, written a letter to a personnel director to ask about a summer job, told a salesperson nonverbally that you are just looking and don't want any help, or ordered a hamburger and french fries over the intercom at a Wendy's Drive-Thru.

You can probably think of a variety of other situations, but now focus your attention on the internal workings of an organization. How do companies communicate with their employees and customers? Organizations have structured ways of operating efficiently. At a supermarket, for example, a sign over the door reads, "Customer Satisfaction Guaranteed." A customer gets home with a carton of milk and finds that it is sour. The customer returns the opened carton to a cashier, who refunds the money and tells a supervisor, who—in turn—tells the dairy manager, who tells the assistant store manager, who notifies the general store manager about the spoiled product. All organizations have divisions of power to make sure that everything functions smoothly. To help you get a better understanding of communication in organizations, the next section will examine the functions of communication in organizations, formal and informal communication structure, channels of communication, and communication networks.

Functions of Communication in Organizations

Communication in organizations takes various forms. However, whatever its form, communication serves either an (1) informative, (2) regulatory, (3) persuasive, or (4) integrative purpose.[6]

[6]Jerry W. Koehler, Karl W. E. Anatol, and Ronald L. Applbaum, *Organizational Communication: Behavioral Perspectives,* 2d ed. (New York: Holt, Rinehart and Winston, 1981), p. 8.

THE INFORMATIVE FUNCTION   Both employers and employees in an organization need an enormous amount of information in order to function efficiently. Essentially, they need information concerning (1) the job itself, including information focusing on the organization's goals, procedures, and rules; (2) organizational success, such as benefits, profits, and work standards; and (3) the socioemotional state of the organization as a whole.[7]

THE REGULATORY FUNCTION   Communication also acts as a means of control and regulation for the organization. This type of communication usually takes the form of orders, perceived expectations, and company restrictions. Also, this type of communication proceeds from the top of the organization in a downward flow. Its content is usually task related.

THE PERSUASIVE FUNCTION   Closely related to the regulatory function of communication is the persuasive function. This is usually reflected in interpersonal compliance-gaining interactions and is ordinarily in the form of face-to-face requests and personal interactions.

THE INTEGRATIVE FUNCTION   Communication in an organization also acts in an integrative capacity, operating to give the organization both unity and cohesion, identity and uniformity.[8] It includes here the coordination and scheduling of activities; the establishment of provisions for channeling information and authority; and recruitment and training of employees.

Messages that are sent through organizations are formal or informal. The *formal communication structure* functions through company rules, divisions of labor, and power control (or who reports to whom) (see Figure 8–1). For example, at most universities students must petition for grade changes. Students first go to their instructor, the instructor then goes to the department chairman, the department chairman sends a memorandum to the dean of academic affairs, the dean sends notification to the records department, and the records typist finally notifies students about appropriate grade changes. Failure to follow the steps properly results in confusion, no grade change, and, ultimately, no action through the normal channels. Other organizations work similarly, with office workers reporting to supervisors, supervisors reporting to managers, and so on.

    The *informal communication structure* of an organization refers to the interpersonal relationships that develop among employees in addition to the formal communication structure. On-the-job experiences often dictate informal channels of communication. A new salesperson with IBM is trained in marketing strategies, types of territories, and profitable accounts; but it is not until later, after practical experience, that the sales-

Formal and Informal Communication

---

[7]Koehler, Anatol, and Applbaum, p. 8.
[8]Koehler, Anatol, and Applbaum, p. 10.

An informal communication structure. (Irene Springer)

person learns that the best way to get in to see clients is by making friends with the secretary in the front office. Informal conversations often give insights into how to deal effectively with individuals both in other organizations and in your own. The following section will explain how channels are used to disseminate information to others in formal and informal situations.

Communication Channels in Organizations

Organizations are linked together through a series of communication **channels.** The Bell Telephone System would have consumers believe that the telephone is the most effective channel of communication when—in actuality—their organization uses face-to-face interaction, letters, memorandums, and computerized messages to get information to others. Communication channels are often taken for granted, and mostly we use the channel which is most economical and convenient to meet our needs. Currently, because of the gas shortage, many people use the telephone to check on product prices, locations of businesses, and whether or not an establishment stays open on weekends; in the past many people hopped into their cars and actually drove by the businesses in question.

A survey of presidents of the one hundred largest companies in the United States found that the most important messages are sent orally or by combining oral and written methods.[9] Would you be more likely to vote for a candidate who placed a flier on the windshield of your car or one who knocked on your door asking for your vote? Would you be more responsive to a form letter requesting your presence at a court hearing or to a uniformed policeman with a subpoena?

[9]P. Lull, F. Funk, and D. Piersol, *Business and Industrial Communication from the Viewpoint of the Corporate President* (Lafayette, Ind.: Purdue University, Department of Speech, 1954).

Thoughtful consumers and organizations are becoming more aware of how channels affect the reception of messages. The channels we use to transmit messages send cues to receivers about how sources view the receiver and the message.

How the message is sent affects its degree of *immediacy,* or the degree of liking or disliking for a person or task. For example, rather than having to face a boss, an employee might write a letter of resignation. The employee uses a less immediate channel of communication to avoid a personal confrontation. Channels of communication can be ranked in degree from the most to the least immediate.[10]

1. Face-to-face
2. Picture phone
3. Telephone
4. Telegram
5. Letter
6. Direct intermediary
7. Leaked rumor through an intermediary

As mentioned in Chapter 1, the most immediate channel of communication is face-to-face interaction. With face-to-face communication, participants are concerned with verbal as well as nonverbal behaviors and receive direct feedback which allows decisions to be made more quickly than with other channels. A customer who returns a Polaroid camera in person is notified immediately that the camera will be repaired or replaced or that the money will be refunded. The use of picture phones also allows for verbal and nonverbal exchanges, but differences lie in the mechanical nature of the communication and in the power each person has to disrupt the communication process. The president of a textile company may use a picture phone to tell the personnel department that a hundred people must be laid off. Instead of listening to and watching the negative reactions, the president may then quickly sign off.

The next most immediate medium is the telephone. Listeners attend to verbal and vocal cues, but visual messages disappear. With telegrams and letters we are even one more step removed. Nonverbal messages and direct feedback are eliminated with these two message forms. However, since telegrams arrive more quickly than letters, they are considered more immediate. The immediacy of a letter is determined by whether or not it is handwritten, typed by the source, or typed by an intermediary. Job applicants feel more encouraged when a recruiter sends a hand-signed letter of acknowledgment rather than a signature-stamped form letter.

An *intermediary* is a messenger between the source and the receiver. When a direct intermediary is asked to deliver a message, immediacy is decreased because most of the original message is altered by the messen-

[10]Albert Mehrabian, *Silent Messages,* 2d ed. (Belmont, Calif.: Wadsworth, 1981).

ger. The least immediate communication channel is a leaked rumor through an intermediary. The message can be intentional or unintentional. An executive accountant, for example, may tell local freight lines in passing that the Internal Revenue Service will inspect the books of shipping companies in the near future, in hopes that the companies will be prepared. Other information is leaked inadvertently, as when employees overhear news about promotions, new policies, and personnel shortages and tell other employees before official notification is given.

Most communication in organizations occurs in a series. *Serial transmissions* take place through a number of individuals who first act as receivers and then as transmitters of messages to others in the organization. Difficulties arise when intermediaries transmit messages inaccurately. How many times have you had to explain what you actually said when your message was taken out of context by someone else? For example, telling a friend that you don't want to go to a party could be misinterpreted to mean that you don't like the people giving the party. In fact, you might be tired, have an exam, or have other plans. Similar serial transmission problems often occur in organizations.

Research has found that messages are distorted in one of three ways: leveling, sharpening, or assimilation.[11] *Leveling* minimizes or omits information that may be important. For example, employees may say that they take only fifteen-minute breaks, when they actually take twenty- to thirty-minute breaks. *Sharpening* magnifies some details of the message. A secretary who overhears that if production doesn't pick up there could be layoffs might tell other secretaries that they are going to be laid off. The third and most important method of distorting messages is *assimilation.* When people assimilate, they transform messages to fit personal attitudes and expectations. Managers often ask assistant managers to give suggestions to new employees about selling techniques. The new employees could take the message as reinforcement or condemnation depending on their perceptions of the manager's and the assistant manager's motives. A desire for consistency in our attitudes and beliefs makes awareness of assimilation particularly important. Consistency of attitudes will be discussed more completely in Chapter 10.

NETWORKS

Channel selection and organizational network usage affect communication effectiveness. *Networks* are the interconnected channels or lines of communication used in organizations to pass information from one person to another. The flow of communication operates in downward, upward, lateral, and informal networks (Figure 8–1).

Downward networks direct information messages to subordinates. Messages include job instructions, individual evaluation (feedback), orga-

[11]Baird, pp. 258–62.

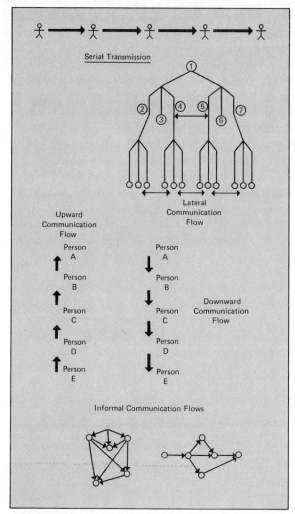

FIGURE 8-1 Networks Showing the Different Flows of Communication

nizational procedures, training, and in-service company-directed propaganda. Downward communication is solicited from employees who want feedback about their job performance, similar to the ways students seek results from tests, papers, and projects. Problems occur when information doesn't filter down to appropriate organizational levels. Because of the serial nature of downward communication, there is distortion and disruption of information before it reaches lower levels. For example, universities write guidelines for all students to follow. In some graduate schools students may not be allowed to enroll as full-time students while working either full-time or forty hours a week. The regulation may be printed in a graduate catalog, but students may not be informed until the administration finds a method of distributing the regulation to the graduate council, department chairpersons, graduate faculty advisors, and, ultimately, the students. Downward communication is sometimes seen as threatening to employees. When a supervisor calls and tells you to come to his or her office, anxiety is usually produced because you are unsure of what issues are involved (job evaluation, promotion, and so on). Top management officials should also be selective in choosing the types of messages sent to subordinates. A personnel director who calls departmental meetings every Monday morning for the same pep talk will eventually be tuned out. Employees get bored with redundant information and are better listeners when meetings are scheduled only when necessary.

Upward communication is another network used in organizations. Managers need to encourage subordinates to send upward communication freely because it is an important indication of how effective downward communication has been. Since managers and superiors control the rewards of their employees through promotion, salary increases, or tenure, upward communication is offered cautiously by subordinates. Just as students refrain from criticism about courses and instructors until after their grades have been posted, employees hesitate to give criticism because they are afraid that what they say may influence their upward mobility. For this reason, some companies have anonymous suggestion boxes. Another problem with upward communication, as mentioned earlier, involves intermediaries. The accuracy of communication can often be im-

A classroom situation can use both upward and downward communication channels.
(Laimute E. Druskis)

proved by skipping some levels and talking with someone at the top. For example, if customers get poor service from waiters, they often get better service by skipping the maitre d' and going to the manager. The most useful way to improve upward communication, however, is by developing trust in your organization. With interpersonal trust at all hierarchical levels, employees feel free to criticize both positively and negatively without fear of reprisal, and this freedom builds cohesiveness in the organization.

Lateral, or *horizontal, communication* takes place between peers at the same hierarchical levels. Communication at the same level coordinates departments and increases emotional and social bonding between peers. Lateral communication often acts as a substitute for upward and downward communication in organizations. Although lateral communication is essential, it becomes dangerous if it replaces other communication networks. For example, employees may complain among themselves about an assembly line inspector who doesn't check safety equipment, when more would be accomplished by skipping this level and using upward communication. The more communication there is between superiors and subordinates, the more likely it is that jobs will be completed on time. Without proper supervision many employees lack the discipline and motivation to continue performing at high levels. It is interesting to note here that subordinates talk more to those above them than to those below them. One reason for this is that people are trying to make a good impression on those at higher levels to ensure promotions and raises in the organization.

Other unstructured, *informal networks* exist in organizations, of which the grapevine is the most popular. The grapevine was once thought to be characterized by disorganized, poorly defined lines of communication, when actually, evidence reveals that grapevines "operate quickly, selectively, and in a well-defined manner, and can possess high accuracy and low distortion."[12] Grapevine communication is one way that cohesion is developed in organizations. In other words, information that is appropriate for grapevines is not something that comes up every day. Notifying co-workers about a surprise party is an example of how many people can be informed just by telling one or two key informants. Problems occur when grapevine communication is used to undermine management. Malignant communication is usually labeled rumor or gossip. One example was the rumor that McDonald's used red worms instead of beef. Many customers began eating at other fast-food restaurants, and eventually McDonald's was forced to air a national publicity campaign disproving the rumor. Within organizations destructive rumors can cause layoffs, poor employee relations, and decreased production. Communication net-

---

[12]Charles Goetzinger and Milton Valentine, "Communication Channels, Media, Directional Flow and Attitudes in an Academic Community," *Journal of Communication* 12 (1962):25.

works serve different functions in organizations, and each is necessary for
the system. Six principles describing the flow of communication in organizations include

1. Communications flow laterally more readily than they flow downward or
   upward.
2. More messages are sent downward than upward.
3. Individuals who are low on the authority ladder are more cautious about
   messages they send upward than are individuals higher on the ladder.
4. People in higher-status positions think they are being heard more accurately than is actually the case.
5. People in lower-status positions distort messages they receive from higher-
   status employees to fit their purposes.
6. Lower-status employees try to move toward higher-status positions and
   away from lower-status positions.[13]

COMMUNICATION STRUCTURES

Communication networks have another characteristic in common—shape.
Network shape affects performance in organizations. Group shapes and
structures were discussed briefly in Chapter 7 without introducing the
concepts of centrality and saturation. *Centrality* refers to the degree to
which a group revolves around one person. The most central position is
the one that interacts with all or most of the organizational members.
Centralized structures or shapes operate more efficiently for simple tasks,
while decentralized shapes work more efficiently for complex ones. Individuals can handle only a certain amount of information at any one time,
and with complex tasks one person would be overloaded, or *saturated,*
with information. Problems occur in organizations when a person exceeds
the saturation point. A switchboard operator working in Sears Roebuck's
catalog department during Christmas might often experience information
overload. Because of the operator's centralized position, people call to ask
about orders or to complain, employees ask about orders for customers
who come to check in person, and supervisors continually give suggestions to increase efficiency.

The most common network structures in organizations are the
wheel, Y, circle, chain, and all-channel formations (see Figure 8–2). The

[13]Allen, pp. 67–68.

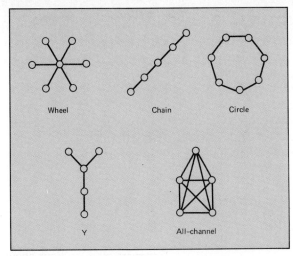

FIGURE 8-2 Common Communication Network Structures.

wheel is a two-way channel of communication. A manager can send messages to employees a, b, c, and d, and they can send messages back to the manager but not to each other. In the **Y network** the central position doesn't communicate with one of the members. The *circle network* permits messages to be sent either to the left or to the right of a position but not to other members. The **chain** is similar to the circle except that the two people at either end of the chain can send and receive messages only from one position. In the ***all-channel network,*** all positions are permitted to send and receive messages from all other positions. The network used determines the type of interaction, and research indicates that individuals who occupy a more central position have higher morale and an increased chance of serving leadership functions.[14]

COMMUNICATION IN ORGANIZATIONS

The first portion of this chapter has examined organizational communication and the function of organizations in society. The next section will consider your role in organizations by looking both at professionalism and at specific communication situations.

What is a professional? A professional may be the punter for the Oakland Raiders, the president of the Exxon Corporation, a detective for the FBI, a CBS newscaster, an editor of a publishing company, a criminal lawyer, or a physical therapist. All professionals, no matter what their line of work, have one common characteristic: commitment to their jobs. Although new employees see themselves as professionals, it is often difficult to maintain a professional attitude. Climbing the ladder of success requires

Professionalism

[14]Dean C. Barnlund, *Interpersonal Communications: Survey and Studies* (Boston: Houghton Mifflin, 1968).

an understanding of how employees' styles, office politics, and personal appearances affect communication and professionalism in organizations.

EMPLOYEE STYLES   Successful managers realize the importance of interpersonal trust and high morale in effective communication systems. Managers at all organizational levels must try to increase subordinates' feelings of individuality and self-esteem. Chapter 2 discussed differences in communicators' styles of language, and this chapter will look at differences in how various people relate to others in the organization. Employees are viewed as manipulators, exploiters, hustlers, managers, or professionals.[15]

Manipulators are individuals who seek to control people and events. Some clever methods they employ to get what they want include using scapegoats (intermediaries accomplish tasks so that if they fail, they—not you—take the rap), passing the buck (saying that someone else should do the work), or using self-effacement (pleading ignorance, sickness, or ineptness so that someone else will do the task). Barbara has worked for *Newsweek* for three years. She tried an advertising campaign that failed, but now she wants to persuade a new employee to try it so that she can receive the glory. If the new employee fails, this time she won't look bad. The goal of *exploiters* is personal gain or profit. They usually live in the future and see everything as their big chance. Exploiters communicate in terms of big lies that might be true. Sometimes exploiters come across as pioneers (seeing opportunities everywhere), record setters (first is best, more permanent, and more successful), or simplifiers (giving exactly what someone wants to gain).

Another communicator style is that of the *hustler.* Hustlers are usually gifted compromisers and win over others through cleverness, wit, and charm. You could imagine a hustler trying something like psyching ("I'm mentioning it to you first, because you're the type we can trust") or documenting evidence ("Look what happened last year; if we don't invest now, we'll lose even more"). Some people communicate with others as *managers.* They lead, conduct, and supervise procedures on behalf of the company or organization. The manager usually asks questions to see how operations are functioning and listens to reports from others while assessing the situation.

TYPE OF EMPLOYEE STYLE   The *professional's* main goal is to help others find themselves and reach their fullest potential. The professional is adept at social exchange and communication. Professionals characteristically trust others because they trust themselves. Also, they give and accept objective appraisals, decentralize authority and responsibility, take risks on people's abilities, believe in constructive work, find pleasure in others' successes, see others as potential leaders, and recognize others' need to be

[15]Frank and Ray, pp. 111–14.

stimulated.[16] Most of us have one or more of these employee communicator styles, and each has its appropriate uses; but for overall communication efficiency, we should strive to act as professionals.

OFFICE POLITICS   We've all heard statements such as: "She got the job because her father is a golfing buddy of the president," "He didn't deserve a promotion, but the top brass were snowed," or "There's no need to work hard, it's all political anyway." Like it or not, office politics do exist, and many bright, highly capable people fail at jobs because of their inability to cope with the situation. Professionals succeed by adapting to office politics. Four common divisions of office politics are cliques, alliances, personality clashes and group revenge, and mentoring.[17]

Cliques are the habitual relationships that develop between employees. This grapevine network often provides useful information; however, as mentioned earlier, cliques can become destructive, especially when employees feel threatened. New employees are seen as threatening because they often perform more efficiently. Can you remember how, when a cute girl moved into town, she was ignored by many females in your school? The local girls were afraid she would be more popular or get their dates. The same fear exists in organizations, where the older or more experienced career employees are afraid the new person will get all the attention. Eventually, relationships will develop for new workers, but before joining or associating with any particular group, all the groups should be considered. It is better to be a rover than to be stereotyped.

Alliances are different from cliques in that an alliance is usually a key helping relationship with someone else. These relationships aren't usually made with authority figures. A new salesperson makes friends with the boss's secretary. Before going out for a business lunch, the secretary warns him or her that the boss doesn't like salespeople to drink on the job, even if the customers want to drink. Allies give helpful hints or cover for their friends when necessary. Another type of office situation to be aware of involves personality clashes and group revenge. Just as there are people who don't play well together in elementary school, there are adults who don't work well together in organizations. Many resignations and firings are due to *personality clashes* rather than job performance or job dissatisfaction. *Group revenge* is a systematic venting of anger or jealousy. When a construction supervisor hired his brother Eddie, a group of construction workers thought their boss was playing favorites, so they tried to make Eddie's life miserable, hoping that he would quit.

Mentoring provides the greatest rewards to a new office worker. A mentor takes a special interest in him or her as a person. A mentor can

[16]Abraham Maslow, *Eupsychian Management: A Journal* (Homewood, Ill.: Richard D. Irwin and Dorsey Press, 1965), pp. 17–33.
[17]John Brady, "The Power of Office Politics," in *The Graduate* (Knoxville, Tenn: 13–30 Corporation, 1979), pp. 37–38, 41.

provide insight into the political games of the department while giving suggestions with the "voice of experience." Mentors act as models for younger, less experienced employees and help to get the latter's feet in the door at higher levels of the organization. Ben worked with Exxon for twenty-eight years. Before he retired, he took a special interest in a new employee, Laura. Ben invited her to business luncheons and introduced her to top petroleum officials. Eventually, when Ben retired, Laura was the logical choice for his position.

Understanding office politics is essential for job satisfaction, and by following a few simple guidelines, you can screen potential positions to select the one which suits you best. First, talk with your faculty and friends who are familiar with a firm's reputation. Second, try to talk with people in the department where you'd be working. Next, develop company profiles from the information you've received, categorizing potential employers. Fourth, try to set up other meetings with people you'd be working with in the company. Finally, try to talk with recent graduates working with the company. By following these instructions, you should be able to select an organization that will best meet your needs.

PERSONAL APPEARANCE   Personal appearance has already been discussed in Chapter 4, yet its importance cannot be overestimated. First impressions made by professionals serve a public relations function for organizations because your appearance sends signals to others about your attitudes, feelings, and personality. For many years IBM salespeople were required to wear dark suits or dresses, which stereotyped them as conservatives. Most companies no longer have stringent dress requirements for their employees, but clothing remains an important aspect of an organization's image. Thus, appropriate appearance is necessary for upward mobility within an organization. Observation of people in higher management positions gives indications of what is appropriate for you to wear. When considering what to wear to your first job interview, it would be a good idea to find out how others who work in the position you are applying for dress. Regardless of your size or sex, clothing should be coordinated in terms of color, line, texture, and style.

COMMUNICATION SITUATIONS

As a professional, you need to be aware of the various communication situations in organizations. From what you have read thus far, you may think that succeeding in an organization involves little more than getting along with others and understanding office politics. While interpersonal relationships are important, the most important form of communication for upward mobility is the formal, structured communication in an organization. The three most common structured communication situations are the interview, the business conference, and the formal presentation.[18]

[18]Robert A. Vogel and William D. Brooks, *Business Communication* (Menlo Park, Calif.: Cummings, 1977), pp. 4–5.

If you have answered survey questions for a public opinion firm, tried to get information from a local politician about foreign policy, answered questions when applying for a job, or given job preferences to a career planning counselor, you have participated in an interview. **Interviews** are the most common form of planned communication and are often defined as "a process of dyadic communication with a predetermined and serious purpose designed to interchange behavior and involving the asking and answering of questions."[19] Although interviews take place for a variety of purposes and in a variety of situations, we are most concerned with interviews in organizations.

TYPES OF INTERVIEWS   There are several different types of interviews, each requiring its own skills and offering its own benefits. During an **employment interview** the employer tries to gain as much pertinent information about the applicant as possible. This kind of interview is usually broad in scope, dealing with all areas of the interviewee's background and personality. The interviewer wants to find out about the applicant's work history, work habits, ability to relate to others, health, and other areas not covered extensively in the résumé or application form. Interviewees, however, do not become merely answer-producing machines. They have their own interests in mind and ask about things such as the working situation, benefits, salary, and opportunities. Thus, information is given and sought by both participants.

In most companies employees are given **appraisal interviews** on a regular basis. In such an interview the worker's past performance and future potential are discussed. The discussion may cover a variety of topics, such as salary, job improvement, outside schooling, or physical health. The objective is clear—to let employees know how they are doing, where they need to improve job performance, and where they are headed. If conducted properly, appraisal interviews also let employees know that their employer cares about their work and their well-being. Walter Mahler suggests six guidelines for conducting effective appraisal or performance interviews.[20] They are

1. Coach on results. That is, stress performance; don't attack.
2. Get down to cases. Be specific about your thoughts.
3. Determine causes. Decide what specific things are leading to actions.
4. Make it a two-way process. Both participants must give and take.
5. Set up an action plan. Decide what future behavior is desired.
6. Provide motivation. Give a reason for changing future behavior.

When employees plan to leave their jobs, they are often given an **exit interview,** which is designed to find out how they feel about the

[19]Charles J. Stewart and William B. Cash, *Interviewing: Principles and Practices,* 3rd ed. (Dubuque, Iowa: Wm. C. Brown, 1983), p. 5.
[20]Walter Mahler, *How Effective Executives Interview* (Homewood, Ill.: Dow Jones and Richard D. Irwin, 1976), p. 112.

company, the working environment, and other job conditions. With this information the company can assess itself and make changes where necessary.

APPROACHES TO INTERVIEWING   Be it an employment, appraisal, or exit interview, the participants can adopt one of two possible communication strategies: directive or nondirective. As interviewer in a **directive interview,** you must have not only a general plan of what you wish to accomplish but also a step-by-step outline to follow. Although this type of interview has the advantage of being thorough, it may be so abrupt and impersonal that the interviewee is uncomfortable. As the following dialogue illustrates, when you are a directive interviewer, you use frank, matter-of-fact questions, which gives you complete control over the discussion:

Interviewer:	(Manager of men's store with opening for salesperson) By looking at your résumé, I can see you already have experience in the retail business. What exactly did your job entail at the department store?
Interviewee:	At first I was at the register, but later I waited on the customers and wrote out sales slips.
Interviewer:	What did you enjoy most about the job?
Interviewee:	I like people and especially helping them out. So, I really enjoyed giving them some help with their purchases and answering any questions they had.
Interviewer:	Is there any particular reason for your leaving the job?
Interviewee:	Since the store was so large, it was sort of impersonal. I want to work in a smaller place where I can deal more with the customers. The department store is often self-service.
Interviewer:	Do you have any plans beyond salesperson?
Interviewee:	Yes, I hope to advance to store manager some day.

In a **nondirective interview,** although you have a plan and purpose in mind, you give interviewees a great deal of leeway in their responses. This kind of interview is not entirely unstructured, however. If an interviewee strays from the subject, he or she is redirected back to the topic. The conversation may run freely, but the major points are developed by the interviewer. The disadvantage of this approach is that you may not obtain all the needed information. The advantage, however, is that an informal atmosphere relaxes the interviewee, encouraging him or her to speak freely. Here is an example of a nondirective exit interview:

Interviewer:	John, I'm sorry to see you leave, but I hear you have a good job offer.
Interviewee:	Yes, B&G Steel Company is looking for a foreman.
Interviewer:	So, tell me all about it.
Interviewee:	Well, I'll be managing about fifty people and getting a lot more money. This will help the problems with the family.

Interviewer:	Problems?
Interviewee:	Yea, you know how it is with two teenage kids . . . dentist, braces, sports and school supplies. I liked this job and I really don't want to leave, but I didn't see any chance of promotion. And I couldn't wait any longer. Oh, and the new place is located pretty close to home, so I don't have such a long drive. The car is getting pretty rundown, and just last week I thought it was a goner—couldn't start it up for several hours!
Interviewer:	You said you liked your job here. Why?
Interviewee:	Well, the fellows in the shop are friendly, and the shop foreman is a good guy.

This sample shows both the strengths and weaknesses of the nondirective interview. Although the interviewee certainly feels relaxed, the interviewer has learned a lot about his personal problems but relatively little about working conditions at the shop. The ability to communicate effectively can obviously pay off in an interview situation. Other aspects of interviewing will be covered in greater detail later in this chapter when we discuss steps in securing your first professional position.

The Business Conference

After you join the work force of an organization, the business conference will be your most frequent formal communication interaction. The ***business conference*** or small group discussion usually involves five to ten people who interact about organizational concerns. Meetings are usually

A business conference.
(© 1980 Catherine Ursillo/Photo Researchers, Inc.)

designed to disseminate information or to develop solutions to current organizational problems. A union spokesperson may explain to a small group of unionized automotive employee leaders the latest features of their negotiated contract, while automotive management personnel get together to discuss methods of dealing with union demands. The business conference is essential to every organization, and the principles presented in Chapter 7 concerning small group communication should provide information to help you participate more effectively both as a group member and as a group leader.

The Formal Presentation

The most structured form of organizational communication is the **formal presentation.** The responsibility is placed on one person to create interest and to motivate the audience to listen. The speaker transmits a message orally with the aid of visual and audio-visual materials. A young architect showing a proposal for a new community sports arena to more established architects in the firm will carefully plan a verbal presentation explaining benefits, square footage, energy conservation features, space usage, costs, and so on, including visual aids to ensure clarity and receptivity of the message during the presentation.

As an employee, you may be asked to explain new organizational policies, teach other employees about the proper use of technical equipment through demonstration, attempt to persuade employees to accept new ideas, and try to motivate employees to greater productivity. Individuals in organizations are unique, and you must understand them before preparing a message to meet their needs. Chapter 9 explains methods of audience analysis which should make your job easier. For a formal presentation you will also be concerned about your delivery, types of com-

Video teleconferencing is becoming widely used as a method of formal communication for nationwide and multi-national corporations.
(A.T. & T. Co. Photo Center)

ORGANIZATIONAL COMMUNICATION

Visual aids can be an important part of a formal presentation.
(A.T. & T. Co. Photo Center)

munication purposes, organization of messages, and how to secure the information to be included in your presentation. Careful consideration of the principles in Chapters 10, 11, and 12 should improve your formal presentation ability.

PREPARING FOR A JOB SEARCH

Anyone who has looked for a job knows that the interview is the most important step in the job-hunting process. If you do not perform well in a job interview, chances are you won't get the position, no matter how well qualified you are. Likewise, if you as the job interviewer do not know the correct skills, you may discourage qualified applicants or simply choose the wrong person for the job. Yet few executives and supervisors make an effort to learn specialized interviewing skills; they underestimate the importance of these interactions. Instead, they handle interviews with little advance planning, relying only on experience and improvisation. An understanding of interviewer responsibilities should give you insights into how to prepare for your first interview.

Even though you may never be a personnel recruiter, there will be times when you will be responsible for conducting interviews. There are formal rules for interview situations. James Black, for example, offers a checklist of principles on sound interviewing practices.[21] First, Black suggests that

Responsibilities of the Interviewer

[21]Jim Black, *How to Get Results from Interviewing* (New York: McGraw-Hill, 1970), p. 1.

as an interviewer, you prepare yourself for the task of gathering a lot of information in a limited period of time. Because the interview is so short, you must decide in advance how much time you wish to devote to each area of discussion. Preparation also includes studying the data already received about the interviewee so that no time is wasted in asking unnecessary questions.

Second, you must define your objectives and follow an organized plan to achieve them. A directionless interview is inefficient and will probably annoy the interviewee, giving him or her a poor impression of the company. Thus, the reason for the interview and the information to be obtained from it must be clear in the minds of both you and the person being interviewed.

Third, the environment of the interview must be considered. Positive communication often depends on comfortable surroundings. The room should be well lit and quiet. To ensure good eye contact and attentiveness, the two participants should always sit facing each other. The accommodations should be relaxed, pleasant, and above all, private. Taking telephone calls in the middle of an interview is rude and wastes valuable time.

Fourth, as the interview opens, it is up to you as the interviewer to break the ice—to make the other person feel at ease. Perhaps a question about an outside interest or about the person's family can serve this function. When interviewing, you should use words and phrases that the interviewee can understand. Trying to impress someone with your high-powered vocabulary will only block communication. Since you would like a productive interview, you must be able to develop a friendly relationship quickly, and, even more importantly, you must create a feeling of trust and confidence. The only way to do this is to be genuinely open and receptive rather than distant, authoritative, or condescending. These positive attitudes show the interviewee that you are sincerely interested in what he or she has to say.

Fifth, as the interviewer, you should decide the nature of the questions that will give you the necessary information. These questions should evoke more than a simple "yes" or "no," which would force you to do all of the talking. Also, the conversation must be free and open, and not become a cat-and-mouse game in which you try to trap the person with trick questions. In this situation you will lose the trust of the person you are interviewing, who will then reveal as little information as possible.

Sixth, you must listen attentively and intelligently. If your eyes wander or if you are constantly glancing at papers on the desk when you interview, the people you interview will feel uneasy. They will either speed up their answers or break off before they finish all that they have to say. On the other hand, if you show interest and attention, they will speak openly and freely and may even give more information than expected. Empathy is also important when listening. You should try to put yourself in the place of the person being interviewed and understand the real meaning behind the spoken words.

Seventh, interviewees should not be rushed into careless answers at the end because you must hurry them out. The interview should end gracefully and naturally. The interviewee will know it is coming to an end by the type of questions being asked and by the way you use your voice.

Eighth, at the end of the interview, interviewees must be told what to expect in the future: when they will find out whether they got the job, or what action will be taken to handle the matters that were discussed.

Finally, when the interviewee leaves, the interviewer's work must be completed. While the interview is fresh in your mind, you should make notes and evaluate the information you received. This evaluation should be as objective as possible. As the interviewer, you must put aside your own prejudices and must not distort the facts. Therefore, you must possess sound judgment, emotional stability, and the ability to make objective decisions.

Now that you are familiar with some of the tasks facing the interviewer, it's time to look at your responsibilities as an interviewee. You may think that all you'll need to do is to answer a few questions, but these questions will probably be the most difficult you've ever encountered, especially if you haven't prepared for the interview in advance. Job hunting is hard work, and sometimes even your preparation might seem difficult. The next few sections provide guidelines and principles to follow while preparing for your first interview.

Responsibilities of the Interviewee

SELF EVALUATION   Do you know who you are? We all think we know ourselves pretty well, but during the next few minutes you may begin discovering parts of yourself that you never knew existed. The first step in preparing for your job search is to conduct a personal inventory. Most interviewees think they know the type of job they're looking for, where they'd like to work, the type of people they would enjoy working with, and so on, but campus recruiters find that students often fail to evaluate their personal and professional goals. Figures 8–3 and 8–4 give guidelines for you to follow when conducting personal and job inventories.

Before you find a satisfactory position, you will need to evaluate your qualifications, preferences, knowledge, training, and experience. Don't just look at your strengths; also look at areas where you need improvement. A favorite question that recruiters ask applicants is, "Now that we have talked about some of your strong points, tell me some areas you feel weak in, and tell me what you are doing to overcome these weaknesses." That's a tough question, and unless you've prepared before the interview, you may have difficulty answering it effectively.

John, an English major, wants to work in a consulting firm developing written communication training programs for business and industry. After John makes a list of his skills and training, he realizes that he's nev-

	(Poor)		(Average)		(Excellent)
	1	2	3	4	5
1. Honest	( )	( )	( )	( )	( )
2. Dependable	( )	( )	( )	( )	( )
3. Motivated	( )	( )	( )	( )	( )
4. Assertive	( )	( )	( )	( )	( )
5. Outgoing	( )	( )	( )	( )	( )
6. Persistent	( )	( )	( )	( )	( )
7. Conscientious	( )	( )	( )	( )	( )
8. Ambitious	( )	( )	( )	( )	( )
9. Punctual	( )	( )	( )	( )	( )
10. Creative	( )	( )	( )	( )	( )
11. Intelligent	( )	( )	( )	( )	( )
12. Mature	( )	( )	( )	( )	( )
13. Emotionally stable	( )	( )	( )	( )	( )
14. Enthusiastic	( )	( )	( )	( )	( )
15. Flexible	( )	( )	( )	( )	( )
16. Realistic	( )	( )	( )	( )	( )
17. Responsible	( )	( )	( )	( )	( )
18. Serious	( )	( )	( )	( )	( )
19. Pleasant	( )	( )	( )	( )	( )
20. Sincere	( )	( )	( )	( )	( )
21. Analytical	( )	( )	( )	( )	( )
22. Organized	( )	( )	( )	( )	( )
23. Appearance	( )	( )	( )	( )	( )
24. Able to get along with co-workers	( )	( )	( )	( )	( )
25. Able to get along with supervisors	( )	( )	( )	( )	( )
26. Oral communication skills	( )	( )	( )	( )	( )
27. Written communication skills	( )	( )	( )	( )	( )
28. References	( )	( )	( )	( )	( )
29. School attendance	( )	( )	( )	( )	( )
30. Job attendance	( )	( )	( )	( )	( )
31. Willing to work long hours	( )	( )	( )	( )	( )
32. Willing to work evenings and weekends	( )	( )	( )	( )	( )
33. Willing to relocate	( )	( )	( )	( )	( )
34. Willing to travel	( )	( )	( )	( )	( )
35. Willing to commute a long distance	( )	( )	( )	( )	( )
36. Willing to start at the bottom and advance according to own merit	( )	( )	( )	( )	( )
37. Able to accept criticism	( )	( )	( )	( )	( )
38. Able to motivate others	( )	( )	( )	( )	( )
39. Able to follow through on something until it is done	( )	( )	( )	( )	( )
40. Able to make good use of time	( )	( )	( )	( )	( )
41. Goal- (or achievement-) oriented	( )	( )	( )	( )	( )
42. Show initiative	( )	( )	( )	( )	( )
43. Healthy	( )	( )	( )	( )	( )
44. Able to follow directions	( )	( )	( )	( )	( )
45. Detail-oriented	( )	( )	( )	( )	( )
46. Able to learn quickly	( )	( )	( )	( )	( )
47. Desire to work hard	( )	( )	( )	( )	( )
48. Moral standards	( )	( )	( )	( )	( )
49. Poised	( )	( )	( )	( )	( )
50. Growth potential	( )	( )	( )	( )	( )
51. Others	( )	( )	( )	( )	( )

FIGURE 8-3 *Analyzing Your Personality Strengths**
Listed above are fifty characteristics that many employers consider positive and important. They are qualities which anyone **could** have, but not everyone **does** have. Rate yourself from "1" to "5" on each factor. Note that this list is not comprehensive; include other traits under number 51.

*Beside any characteristic that you have rated as 4 or 5, describe an instance from your experience when you exhibited this quality. For example, I showed dependability last summer when I . . .

1—not important	2—average importance	3—very important	1	2	3

	1	2	3
1. Challenge	( )	( )	( )
2. Responsibility	( )	( )	( )
3. Stability of company	( )	( )	( )
4. Security of job within company	( )	( )	( )
5. Size of company	( )	( )	( )
6. Training program	( )	( )	( )
7. Initial job duties	( )	( )	( )
8. Advancement opportunities	( )	( )	( )
9. Amount of contact with co-workers	( )	( )	( )
10. Amount of contact with the public	( )	( )	( )
11. Starting salary	( )	( )	( )
12. Financial rewards "down the road"	( )	( )	( )
13. Degree of independence	( )	( )	( )
14. Opportunity to show initiative	( )	( )	( )
15. Degree of employee involvement in decision making	( )	( )	( )
16. Opportunity to be creative	( )	( )	( )
17. Type of industry	( )	( )	( )
18. Company's reputation in the industry	( )	( )	( )
19. Prestige of job within the company	( )	( )	( )
20. Degree of results seen from job	( )	( )	( )
21. Variety of duties	( )	( )	( )
22. What the boss is like	( )	( )	( )
23. What the co-workers are like	( )	( )	( )

FIGURE 8-4   Analyzing Factors of Importance to You in Jobs and Companies.**
Listed above are factors that many people value in jobs and organizations. Rank the factors from "1" to "3" in terms of their importance to you. Put an asterisk beside the five most important factors.

**From Interviewing . . . A Job in Itself. Copyright Lois Einhorn and The Career Center, Bloomington, Ind., 1977, pp. 3–6.

er taken business courses. John can overcome this potential job-hunting weakness by taking appropriate business courses and/or by getting a part-time job in business.

The evaluation form in Figure 8–5 is excerpted from *Jobs '77* by William N. Yeomans. It is designed to help you evaluate your job marketability. By now you should have thought about who you are, what you have done, and what talents, skills, and interests you possess. With all this firmly in mind, complete this questionnaire. The scoring has not been tested scientifically, but it does view applicants in the same way organizations evaluate potential employees.

Results:

35–42 Outstanding! You should be able to pick and choose a suitable position. However, people rarely score this high, so evaluate yourself again to be sure.

20–34 Excellent prospect. You should have several job possibilities without much trouble.

8–19 Average candidate. Job opportunities will depend on the economy and labor market. Need to try to develop some different areas to increase your chances.

SCHOLASTIC STANDING	SCORE
Phi Beta Kappa; top 10% of class	6
Top 25% of class	4
Top 50% of class	2
Lower 50% of class	0

ACADEMIC RATING OF YOUR COLLEGE

Very high; Ivy League caliber	6
Good, well-respected academically	4
Not known for academic excellence	1
Barely accredited or not accredited	0

WORK EXPERIENCE

Full-time work in your major field	6
Summer or part-time work in your major	4
Work in unrelated field	2
No work experience	0

COLLEGE EXPENSES EARNED YOURSELF

75–100%	6
50–75%	4
25–50%	1
Under 25%	0

CAMPUS ACTIVITIES

Major elected offices; many activities	4
Minor elected offices; some activities	2
No elected offices but some activities	1
No elected offices and no activities	0

APPEARANCE

All-American handsome or beautiful	4
Good-looking	3
Nice, but forgettable	1
Weird-looking	0

PERSONALITY

Popularity plus. Well-liked; meet people easily	4
Pretty well-liked; meet people easily most of the time	3
Some friends; not too great at meeting people	1
Zero personality	0

HEIGHT (IF WEIGHT IS PROPORTIONATE)

5'10" to 6'4" for men	3
5' to 6' for women	3
4'1" or under; 6' or over, or overweight, for women	0
Under 5'10", over 6'4", of overweight, for men	0

BEARING (VOICE, POSTURE, EYE CONTACT)

Commanding, immediately impressive	3
Mostly impressive	2
Not too impressive	0
A laugh	0

Total Score _____

FIGURE 8–5 Job Marketability Evaluation Form.

0–7   Not so good. You will probably have difficulty in getting a desirable job. Need to think of ways to improve your score, or you may have evaluated yourself too severely.

You may already know the types of positions for which you'd like to apply, but you may not know what's available to someone with your major, background, and skills. You may have chosen a major because the prospects for earnings looked good, the courses were easy, your parents suggested it, or it was something you'd always wanted to do. After getting your degree, and maybe after getting a job, you realize that you won't be challenged or happy working in this area for an extended period of time. Some people, for example, major in elementary education, get a job, and realize that children drive them crazy. Others get pre-professional degrees and yet are not accepted into medical school, law school, or graduate school. What then? An inventory of your job preferences can help you look for positions to meet your needs. For additional help go to your campus career planning office or to professional personnel agencies, study self-help manuals, or take a course on career planning. Laird Durham's book *100 Careers: How to Pick the One that's Best for You* is very useful. Hopefully, the exercises and examples in this section have given you greater insight into what your strengths, weaknesses, training, preferences, and other qualifications are so that you'll know what you have to offer during a job search.

WRITTEN PREPARATION   You have now evaluated your assets and liabilities and know what you can expect from an organization. With your job objectives clearly in mind, you need to find a way to get an interview. The most widely used method of introducing yourself to an organization is through a letter of introduction and a **résumé**. Although cover letters and résumés are the most commonly used method of getting an interview, many have the opposite or no effect. Abbott P. Smith, a professional recruiting and placement specialist, gives twelve basic guidelines to help you ensure that your next résumé is not your obituary.[22]

1. Do some soul searching before you begin (conduct a personal and job inventory).
2. Write your objective (what do you want to do?).
3. Sell yourself (tell what you have done and what you can do).
4. Be brief and nonrepetitive (aim for a one-page résumé).
5. Write it yourself (steer away from professional résumé-writing services).
6. List the jobs you have held (include job titles and dates).
7. Forget the references (applicants list references that will give positive comments).
8. List personal information first (name, address, phone number, etc.).

[22]Abbott P. Smith, "How to Make Sure Your Next Resume Isn't an Obituary," *Training* (May 1977):63–66.

TABLE 8-1   205 Personnel Managers' Ratings of Importance of Items in Résumé

RANK	IMPORTANT ITEMS	RANK	UNIMPORTANT ITEMS
1	Current address	26	Class standing
2	Past work experience	27	Sources for financing
3	Major in college		college studies
4	Job objectives and goals	28	References
5	Date of availability for	29	Percent of money earned
	employment		for college
6	Career objectives	30	Computer programming skills
7	Permanent address	31	Birthday and birthplace
8	Tenure on previous job	32	Membership in honorary
9	Colleges and universities		societies
	attended	33	Membership in college
10	Specific physical limitations		social organizations
11	Job location requirements	34	Offices held in social
12	Overall health status		organizations
13	Salary requirements	35	Student body offices
14	Travel limitations		held
15	Minor in college	36	Hobbies
16	Grades in college major	37	Foreign language skills
17	Military experience	38	Marital status
18	Years in which degrees	39	Complete college
	were awarded		transcript
19	Overall grade point average	40	Height and weight
20	Membership in professional	41	Number of children
	organizations	42	Typing skills
21	Awards and scholarships	43	Spouse's occupation
	received	44	Spouse's educational level
22	Grades in college minor	45	Sex
23	Offices held in professional	46	Photograph
	organizations	47	Complete high school
24	Statistical or mathematical		transcript
	skills	48	Personal data on parents
25	Spouse's willingness to	49	Race
	relocate	50	Religious preference

Reprinted by permission of American Personnel and Guidance Association.

9. Don't elaborate on personal information (keep it brief).
10. Make it neat (this may be the time to invest in a professional typist).
11. Write a neat, short, personal cover letter (give reason for writing and what you know about the organization).
12. Put yourself into your résumé (find a way to stand out from the other candidates).

Résumé formats and what is included in résumés differ considerably. (Table 8–1 lists résumé terms in order of importance.)[23] Figure 8–6 provides an example of a résumé. Many of you will be able to apply for several types of positions. If you do, you may need to write different résumés directing the content of each to a particular position. Applicants looking for a position in education usually use an academic vita, which

[23]Hubert S. Field and William H. Holley, "Resume Preparation: An Empirical Study of Personnel Managers' Perceptions," *The Vocational Guidance Quarterly* (March 1976): p. 234.

CLARK PAGER

Permanent Address
134 Maytime Drive
Jericho, New York
Telephone: (516) 822-8239

Temporary Address
2417 Broadway Street
New Orleans, Louisiana 70125
Telephone: (504) 861-0041

Job Objective

Full-time summer position working with law firm concerned with athletic arbitration.

Education

1977 to present B.A., 1981, Tulane University, New Orleans, Louisiana 70118
Advisor: Dr. Guy Peters
Major: Public Policy
Minor: Business
G.P.A. 3.2 out of 4.0

1973 to 1977 Jericho High School, Jericho, New York 11753.
Major: College Preparatory

Work Experience

summer 1979 to present Banquet waiter at the New Orleans Hotel to cover
living expenses.

summer 1978 Courrier and office clerk for Blau and Kramer Corporate Law Firm.
Responsible for personal delivery of documents to the Security
and Exchange Commission in Washington, D.C. Also responsible for
updating lawbooks.

summer 1977 Counselor and tennis instructor at Brant Lake Camp, Brant Lake,
New York. Responsible for organizing, assisting, and instructing
camp activities.

summer 1976 Courrier and office clerk for Blau Kramer Corporate Law Firm.

Extracurricular Activities

Responsible for organizing and running intramural sports for the College of
Arts and Sciences.

Sports reporter for WTUL-FM, student-run radio station. Assemble and report
the latest news concerning local, state, national, and world sports on a
weekly basis.

special interests: Sports, theatre arts, and travel.

References

Letters of recommendation and official transcripts will be furnished upon request.

FIGURE 8–6

has a different format. Some valuable source books to help with your preparation include *What Color Is Your Parachute?* by Richard Bolles; *Where Do I Go From Here With My Life?* by John Crystal and Richard Bolles; and *How to Find a Job,* by Darold Larson. Just as the résumé is important, so too is your cover letter. Field and Holley found that personnel managers consider five items important in a cover letter.[24]

1. The position the applicant is seeking
2. The applicant's job objective
3. The applicant's career objectives
4. The applicant's reason for seeking employment
5. The indication that the applicant knows something about the organization

Because you are trying to get an interview with the personnel director, it is also advisable to request an interview in the cover letter and to refer to your enclosed résumé.

FINDING JOB POSSIBILITIES   The interview is the most important step in the hiring process. Some of you may have a job waiting for you, but most of you must find a way to get an employment interview. In *Job Hunting Secrets and Tactics,* Kirby W. Stanat explains four major methods of securing a job interview: (1) answering want ads, (2) taking advantage of college placement centers, (3) employment agencies, and (4) cold calls.[25]

Want ads are the least popular form of organizational recruiting because they often expose employers to militants (EEOC), cost a lot of money, and release competitive information to other companies. Some companies use blind newspaper ads with only box numbers to give themselves greater flexibility. Because of the anonymous nature of a blind ad, the employer is not forced to answer inquiries, leak information to competitors, or conform to governmental equal employment opportunity guidelines. Although blind ads have advantages, they get fewer responses than labeled ads.

When reading want ads, you must learn to understand advertising tactics. Recruiters advertise for the maximum qualifications they can get, with inflated requirements that are not absolute. Of course, some positions will require special expertise. A nurse shouldn't apply for a doctor's position, and a brick mason shouldn't apply for an electrician's position. When answering an ad, you will either be offered the job, rejected, or offered a position not listed in the advertisement.

Newspaper ads usually ask you to send a résumé. If possible, you should avoid using the mail or telephone and try to answer the ad in person. We discussed immediacy earlier in this chapter and explained the importance of face-to-face communication when trying to get positive ac-

---

[24]Field and Holley, pp. 229–237.
[25]Kirby W. Stanat, with Patrick Reardon, *Job Hunting Secrets and Tactics* (Milwaukee, Wis.: Westwind Press, 1977).

(Irene Springer)

tion. It's a lot easier for recruiters to throw a résumé in the trash if they've never met you personally.

The simplest way to get an interview is through your campus placement center. All you have to do is sign up; yet even with this easy procedure, many students fail to take advantage of placement center opportunities. Some think that their grade point average is too low, that only small companies recruit on college campuses, that companies look only for business majors, or that a lot of extracurricular activities are required. Students need to reevaluate the placement center interviewing option because it offers opportunities to students with a variety of backgrounds, experiences, and education.

It may help to familiarize yourself with how the placement center works. Placement offices usually have orientation meetings at the beginning of each quarter or semester, giving essential procedural information. The placement center provides forms and starts personal files for interested students (including alumni). Files include standard data sheets, résumés, letters of recommendation, and interviewing histories. Some centers also provide interview workshops, career counseling, career libraries, and employer information. Centers use open sign-up systems (first come, first served), staff sign-up systems (counselors place students), or card systems (batches of high- and low-priority cards are given for company preferences). No matter which system is used on your campus, you should go through your placement center to get valuable interviewing experience.

You may now be wondering what happens after you've signed up for an interview. When your day arrives, company recruiters are given placement center data sheets and a list of interviewee names with time slots. Your interview begins before you meet the recruiter, as he or she examines your placement file. Next, the recruiter enters the lobby or waiting area and calls your name. Introductions are made, handshakes are exchanged, and then you are led into a small room or partitioned area. The interview area usually consists of two chairs, with one placed behind a desk for the interviewer. Most campus interviews last from fifteen to twenty minutes. At the end of the interview, recruiters usually tell you when you should be hearing from the company. Finally, after you leave, the recruiter quickly jots down impressions before moving on to the next interviewee. This can be a grueling process for both the recruiter and you; but again, you should get as much interviewing experience as possible.

A third method of getting an interview is through an employment agency. Employment agencies vary in size, style, cost, and purpose. Some agencies may have only one or two people placing applicants, while others have divisions for sales, management, engineering, professional, or technical positions. Agencies may treat you very professionally, with preinterview testing and counseling, or they may send you to an interview without preparation. Employment agencies stay in business through the fees they collect from either or both the employer and the interviewee. You may pay 10 to 20 percent of your first year's salary, or the company may pay all fees. As often as possible it is best to interview with fee-paid organizations. Some professional search agencies charge 20 percent and higher but guarantee job satisfaction, testing and training, and résumé-writing services. The purposes of employment agencies also differ. Agencies fill temporary vacancies, place technical or specialty personnel, find executives, or say they can place anyone.

Advantages of using employment agencies include their efficiency, saving time by having others do the searching for you, and confidentiality. One of the best methods of selecting an employment agency is to look at the classified section of your Sunday newspaper to see which agencies do the most advertising. Then, scout several agencies and select two or three that seem most suited to your needs. Tell the agencies that you have registered with other agencies to let them know they have competition. As an interviewee, you must be prepared for critical analysis from agency counselors. They want to increase your job marketability and will sometimes get tough to help you perform more effectively during appointment interviews.

The final way to get an interview is by making cold calls. You can either send a résumé, or phone, or go in person. As mentioned earlier, it is best to go in person, yet this is probably the most difficult and ego-deflating situation of all. Having a job places you in a better bargaining position, but whether you have a job or not, you have to be persistent and make use of special cold-call tactics.

The best time to show up is about 10 A.M. or 3 P.M., because these are the least hectic times in organizations. When making plans, also try to go on Tuesday, Wednesday, or Thursday rather than Monday or Friday. The beginning of the week is busy, and at the end of the week you'll find that the important people may be away. It is best to apply before November 15 and after January 1 because of holidays and fiscal years. If you want to make one friend before seeing a personnel director, it should be the company receptionist. Receptionists have the power to help or hurt your chances of getting an interview. However, even though you want to make friends with receptionists, don't give them your résumé. After you turn over your résumé, you lose bargaining power and may never get a chance to talk to the people who make hiring decisions. You'll learn tricks of the trade with experience. Just remember not to give up until you get the interviews you want.

RESEARCHING THE COMPANY   Before the actual interview it is essential for you to find out about the company. Just as you feel good when someone you meet knows something about you, recruiters are also flattered when you know something about what is important to them: their company. Know everything possible. The knowledge will increase your confidence and ease during the interview. However, remember too that timing is important. Don't interject some obscure company fact at inappropriate times.

The best place to begin is at your placement office. It usually has company literature, annual reports, brochures, and fliers. If not, write or phone the organization and ask them to send you the information. Next, try to talk with people who work in the organization. They'll give you greater insights than any written material could provide. Finally, local libraries usually have information in business periodicals, newspapers, stock market reports, and so on. The questions you will want to answer depend on the type of organization you are investigating. In applying for a teaching position, you'd want to know the number of schools in the district; for a manufacturing firm, you'd be interested in plant locations and competition; and for a bank, you'd probably like to know if it was nationally or state chartered and how many branches it had. Remember, the answers to the questions are intended to help you. Now that you have examined the responsibilities of interviewers and interviewees, you should be ready to think about your first interview. Your confidence should be high because you have evaluated yourself, completed a formal résumé, found job openings, researched the company, and gotten an interview.

THE INTERVIEW

When you are being interviewed, your chief responsibility is to yourself. During an employment interview you owe it to yourself to obtain as much information as you can, so that should you be offered the job, you can make an intelligent decision. Make sure you understand the requirements of the job (just what it is you will be expected to do). If you don't understand something, ask questions until you do. State your qualifications in a positive way, and don't be afraid to mention potential weaknesses in your background (but try to balance them with strengths). The most important thing to do during any kind of interview is to communicate—listen, speak, question, respond, and understand.

The employment interview incorporates everything we've discussed about communication, and more. After your first interview you will know additional areas that you'll need to prepare for the next time. One area that needs no further preparation is that of honesty. There is a misconception that you should say anything to get the job. However, this doesn't pay off. One young man decided to alter his grade point average on his résumé. Instead of putting down his cumulative average, he listed the average in his major course work, which was considerably higher. He interviewed with his placement center and was offered a job in a major duplicating corporation. After he accepted the position and had started training, the company sent for his college transcripts. The personnel director noticed the discrepancy between the grade point averages and called him in to ask him about it. After he told the director what he had done, he was fired for dishonesty.

Lying may not get you fired, but it could cause even more serious problems. New interviewees often fall into the trap of trying to please the interviewer with all their answers. If they are asked if they'd mind traveling, some say no even if they do; or they may say they enjoy working with people, when in actuality they would rather work by themselves or with machines. You may get a job, but your dishonesty will only hurt you. Too many people are miserable in positions they should never have accepted or applied for. When you see that you would be dissatisfied in a position you're applying for, acknowledge it to the recruiter. There may be another position that you'd be better suited for, or the recruiter can keep you in mind if something does become available.

We have already mentioned a few questions that are used during employment interviews. The following list of frequently asked questions should help prepare you further for your first interview. Questions are designed to serve as indicators of your personal background; human relations skills; work background; accident, safety, and health histories; education and training; and personal objectives.

1. What do you see yourself doing in 5, 10, 15 years?
2. How have childhood experiences influenced you?
3. How would your closest friend describe you?
4. Why did you decide to go to your college or university?
5. If you could change anything about your education, what would it be?
6. Do you work well under pressure? (give some examples)
7. Would you rather be a leader or a follower?

8. What motivates you to give the most effort?
9. Are your grades a good indicator of your academic achievement? (explain)
10. Do you have plans for continued study? (explain)
11. How do you evaluate success?
12. Who is the person you admire most? (why?)
13. If you could have an ideal job, what would it be like?
14. Why should I hire you over other candidates?
15. Do you work better alone or with supervision? (explain)
16. Why are you interested in working for our company?
17. What have you learned from your mistakes?
18. What are you looking for in a job?
19. Are you a leader? (explain)
20. What qualities should an effective manager have?
21. How do you accept criticism? (explain)
22. Tell me about yourself.
23. What work experience helps qualify you for this position?
24. How do you spend your free time?
25. What qualities do you think I should be looking for in this position?

The ability to answer these and other questions should give you a good edge over unprepared candidates. Questions you will be asked are important, but you should also be giving some consideration to questions you should ask the interviewer. Toward the end of an employment interview, the interviewer usually asks if you have any questions. A few sample questions follow.

1. What type of training program do you have, and how long will it last?
2. What is the advancement potential in your organization?
3. Does your company help pay for employees to continue their education?
4. Will I have to relocate?
5. How are your employees evaluated?
6. What opportunities do you see for a person with my background?
7. What have been your most rewarding experiences with the company?
8. What is the employee turnover rate?
9. Does the company pay for moving expenses?
10. What weaknesses do you see that I should try to improve?

Job interviews do not consist solely of questions and answers. Several factors work together to make your interview a success or failure. The following list of dos and don'ts should serve as a useful reminder before your interview. Making sure that you do all the dos will not necessarily land you a job, but doing one don't could cause you not to be hired.

Do	Don't
Act natural	Criticize yourself
Be prompt, neat, courteous	Be late
Prepare self and job analysis inventories	Present an extreme appearance
Ask relevant questions	Become impatient
Allow the employer to express him/herself	Become emotional
Make yourself understood	Oversell your case
Listen to the other person	Draw out the interview
Present informative credentials	Make elaborate promises
Think of your potential service to the employer	Come unprepared
Act positively	Try to be funny
	Linger over what the company will do for you (e.g., benefits, salary, promotion)
	Unduly emphasize starting salary

In this section we have covered the three Ps of interviewing: preparation, presentation, and postanalysis. The preparation phase involves four steps: (1) self-inventory; (2) occupation inquiry; (3) preparation of letter of introduction and résumé; (4) putting it all together. The interview presentation itself has four stages: introduction, background, matching, and closing. The postanalysis calls for follow-up and reevaluation of your performance. The important thing to remember about this process is that no two interview situations will be exactly the same. The most you can do is understand the overall process, prepare for that process, and go in with a positive and professional attitude, thinking, "I have something to offer you."

AFTER THE INTERVIEW

Before breathing a sigh of relief, remember that your job search is not over yet. It is not complete until you've secured the position that you've applied for. After each interview applicants can follow three simple steps to increase their chances of getting hired.

Immediately after leaving the interview, write down your recruiter's name, title, and address. Forgetting your interviewer's name could be detrimental to you later, when a secretary calls to set up a second interview and asks if you were interviewed by Mr. Barton, Ms. Kendall, or Mr. Barfield. The recruiter is now a personal contact within the organization, and all additional correspondence should be directed to him or her. You may be asked to send in letters of recommendation, transcripts, or job applications at later times, so be prepared.

After making sure that you remember your interviewer's name, find time to evaluate your interview participation by reconstructing the inter-

*Reprinted from *Planning Your Future* by permission of the College Placement Council, the copyright holder. In Robert A. Vogel and William D. Brooks, *Business Communication* (Menlo Park, Calif.: Cummings, 1977), pp. 42–43.

view situation. Do you think the outcome will be positive or negative? What impressions did you make? Why? After self-analysis you may remember biting your fingernails, interrupting the recruiter, looking at your watch, answering the wrong question, or using profanity. There is a tendency for us to focus on our mistakes rather than to look at the total process. Try to force yourself to remember areas of outstanding performance as well as areas that need improvement, so that your next interview will be more successful.

One last way to leave a favorable impression with a recruiter is to write a letter of appreciation. These letters usually thank the recruiter for his or her time and for the opportunity to meet, and express interest in the organization. You want the recruiter to remember you; even if a company doesn't have a position at the present time, it will be more likely to think of you in the future if you keep in touch. By following these three postinterview guidelines, you should increase your chances of success.

SUMMARY

Organizations are collected groups of individuals constructed and reconstructed to strive for specific goals that could not be met by individuals alone. Organizations differ from groups in their division of labor, presence of one or more power centers, substitution of personnel, interdependence and coordination among organizational components. Organizations are also characterized by repetitive interaction.

Although organizations have characteristics in common, they differ in goals. The Exxon Corporation is a business organization with the goal of making money, while a service organization such as the Humane Society helps animals, without a concern for profit. Another difference is in an organization's method of control. Reformatories use force to keep order, while businesses use wages and benefits to control employees.

Related to the types of organizations and to the form of communication that they stress are the functions of communication. Essentially, communication serves four major purposes in any organization: information exchange, regulation, persuasion, and integration.

Goals and power controls are transmitted to group members through formal and informal structures. The formal structures function through organizational rules and regulations, while the informal structures function through interpersonal relationships among employees. The importance of a message within the organizational structure determines the immediacy of the channel used, with important messages using oral channels alone or in combination with written channels.

Networks refer to the channels or lines used to transmit messages from one person to another. Communication networks operate in downward, upward, lateral, or informal networks. Because of the serial nature of communication in organizations, information is often distorted by leveling, sharpening, or assimilation. The networks in organizations form structures which have shape. The most common network shapes are the wheel, circle, chain, Y, and all-channel structures. The shape of the network influences the effectiveness of communication.

After familiarizing yourself with an organization's communication patterns and structures, it is important for you to understand your position within the organization. Professionalism increases job satisfaction and productivity. Understanding the effects of employees' styles, office politics, and personal appearance should improve communication in organizations. Employees communicate with others as manipulators, exploiters, hustlers, or professionals. Knowledge of office politics should help remind you to select group affiliations carefully. The competitive nature of organizations often causes cliques, personality clashes, and group revenge. However, interactions such as alliances or mentoring should be very satisfying.

Office politics are usually found in the informal communication structures, but for upward mobility, the formal, structured situations are most important. The most common formal communication situations are interviews, business conferences, and formal presentations. Knowing what to expect and which guidelines to follow should help you perform effectively.

Since your first professional position will be in some organization, it is essential for you to understand the methods of starting a job search. Interviewees should start their preparation with self- and job evaluations. With job objectives clearly in mind, interviewees should prepare written communication materials such as a résumé and cover letter, which should help get interviews. Four methods of getting interviews are by answering want ads, using college placement centers, applying to employment agencies, or making cold calls. After interviews have been secured, applicants should research the company and prepare themselves for the actual interview. Finally, the applicant should follow up the interview by writing a letter of appreciation and by evaluating his or her performance. The information in this chapter should help you understand your communication roles in organizations and prepare you to start a job search.

Exercises

GROUP EXPERIENCES

Organizational Networks

Description: Organizations use a variety of networks to communicate with employees. Supervisors use downward communications to give instructions. Subordinates send upward communications to complain about working conditions. Peers communicate laterally to establish interpersonal bonds, and at times everyone communicates at once in haphazard informal networks. For interdepartmental coordination networks are essential, but networks are often used inappropriately. This exercise is designed to provide experience in dealing with communication networks within organizations.

Procedure: Divide into groups of five to seven persons. Within the groups come up with a topic that could be used in the four communication networks. For example, each network is used in training programs in which new employees are instructed on the proper use of copying equipment, regulations, and so on. After the groups decide on topics, get group members to line up in rows (like a train). Exchange topics between the groups. With downward communication person one in the row should pass detailed instructions through channels until they reach their proper destination: person seven. (No feedback should be given, and all communication must move downward.) Next, divide the row into groups of two to three persons and discuss the message laterally; but again, remember that no interactions should take place with others in the chain. After a few minutes form the rows again and send upward communication concerning the initial interaction. Finally, let members discuss the topic with whomever they wish.

Discussion: Which communication network was the most satisfactory? You probably found that each situation contained unique problems. What problems were encountered with the networks? When would the use of one network be most effective? How could organizations improve their internal communication? What organizational network would you like to work in when you graduate?

Who Hires Whom?

Description: Interviews are one of the most difficult interpersonal interactions. You may have taken part in an interview before, but you probably haven't made actual hiring decisions. The next activity is designed to let you observe and participate in all phases of hiring.

Procedure: Select four persons to be interviewees and divide the rest of the class into four groups. As a class, decide for what type of position (with requirements) the interviewees will be applying (for example, college professor, accountant, corporate recruiter, hospital administrator). The groups should get together for 15 minutes and decide the types of questions that need to be asked to get the most information from the applicants without having the benefit of a résumé. The questions asked will determine what information the candidate will give. While the groups are planning their interviewing strategy, the four interviewees will select one person who is underqualified, one who is overqualified, and two who have equally satisfactory qualifications. The interviewees will decide on their qualifications, and many will have similar backgrounds and experiences; but two applicants will have more suitable experiences, training, and education than the others. After 15 minutes, each group will interview each applicant for about 5 minutes; interviewees will rotate between groups. The interviewees should give only the information that they are asked to give. After all applicants are interviewed, the groups will get together and rank the candidates in terms of hiring preferences. Group decisions should be recorded.

Discussion: Did each group hire the best candidate? If not, why? What types of questions were asked? Did they elicit the best information? Why or why not? Did interpersonal decisions affect hiring, or were the decisions based on facts? Answering these questions should help give you an idea of some of the problems facing recruiters and interviewees. Although interviewers usually have the benefit of letters of recommendation and résumés, there are still factors that may not be taken into account; and in many cases two or more applicants are suitable for a position.

Conference Compatibility

Description: One of the most important formal communication situations within an organization is the conference. Interaction patterns during conferences are affected by the purpose of the meeting, the methods of control during the meeting, and group membership. This exercise shows how people participating in conferences affect conference outcomes.

Procedure: Divide the class into male and female groups of five to seven people. Select a controversial topic that encourages active discussion (such as sexual freedom, the Equal Rights Amendment, or homosexuality). Each group should discuss the topic for 5 to 10 minutes. Finally, change groups so that there is only one member of the opposite sex per group; again discuss the selected topic. After the second group discussion, have each member choose the group in which he or she felt most comfortable.

Discussion: Share individual group selections with the rest of the class. What differences were there between the first and second group interactions? Why were there differences? How was the atmosphere affected by different-sex participants? How did your responses change with different group members? What does this exercise tell you about organizational conference effectiveness?

PERSONAL EXPERIENCES

1. Find a local organization to observe for one day. Try to analyze the formal and informal communication structures. Determine the purposes and power structure of the organization. How would you fit into this organization? What kinds of office politics would you have to avoid? After you've decided whether or not you would feel comfortable in this organization, make a list of personal criteria that organizations must meet to satisfy your needs.
2. Set up an interview with a person in your profession who recruits employees. Find out what he or she looks for in potential applicants. Compare your qualifications with the recruiter's standards and then work out a strategy to improve your marketability as an applicant.

3. After completing the personal and job evaluations in this chapter, prepare a résumé. Then go to your campus placement office and follow their procedures for getting a job interview. Make an appointment and prepare for the interview by researching the company, asking yourself sample questions, and so on. After the interview, evaluate yourself and make a list of your own dos and don'ts for your next interview.

4. Choose an organization where you would like to work and list all the positions in the organization. Which positions will you be qualified for when you graduate? Select one position and list all the other positions you would come in contact with in the organization (secretary, supervisor, typist, and so on). How would the communication with these individuals affect you?

DISCUSSION QUESTIONS

1. How can organizations improve their formal and informal communication structures?
2. What communication channels exist in organizations, and what role does immediacy play in their effectiveness?
3. How are messages distorted within an organization's structure? Formally? Informally?
4. What guidelines would you suggest when preparing for a first job interview?
5. Why is it important to understand office politics?

ETHICS, INTENTIONS, AND THE SPEAKER-AUDIENCE RELATIONSHIP

9

Exploratory Questions

1. What are four approaches to ethical considerations?
2. Can you describe briefly the three general purposes of a public speech?
3. How do you select a specific purpose in speech preparation?
4. What are five demographic characteristics of audiences?
5. What strategies should be used for favorable, neutral, and unfavorable audience attitudes?
6. What are four methods of investigating an audience?
7. Can you compare and contrast Hollingworth's five audience types?
8. What is the speaker's responsibility in audience analysis?
9. How do environmental factors influence audience behavior?
10. What are three characteristics of groups that go from nonaudience to audience status?

Communication theory is relatively new, but the study of public speaking dates back to ancient Greece, when Aristotle and his contemporaries defined and practiced the principles of rhetoric. While these principles still provide the foundation of public speaking theory, modern styles of public speaking and public speaking situations are much less formal than they were in Aristotle's time. However, even in our own relatively relaxed culture, public speaking situations can intimidate people who are usually very talkative and outgoing. Although public speaking includes many of the same communication skills as other speaking situations, some who are comfortable in small group communication feel nervous and experience stage fright in a public setting.

Perhaps these difficulties arise because **public speaking** differs from other forms of communication in two ways. First, a public speaking situation includes two distinct and separate roles: speaker and audience. Second, in this speaker-audience relationship, the speaker carries more responsibility for the communication interaction than does the audience. In other communication situations speakers and listeners exchange roles and share this responsibility.

A public speaking situation need not be overly formal and imposing; it doesn't necessarily require a stage to separate the speaker from the audience. All of us participate in public speaking when we contribute to a class discussion, when we make a suggestion at a staff meeting, or when we tell a story at a party.

Public communication, like other forms of communication, serves several purposes. When a karate instructor gives a demonstration on self-defense, he or she uses public communication to instruct. When Ralph Nader speaks on the need for better consumer protection laws, he uses public communication to advocate his point of view. The mayor who delivers an annual Fourth of July speech to the townspeople uses the "soapbox" to stir feelings of patriotism. Public communication can also be used to praise and to blame, to accuse and to defend. When a local political candidate speaks to a community group, he or she may use public communication to blame the current officeholder for everything that's wrong with the community, while the preacher who delivers a eulogy at a memorial service uses the same form of communication to praise the deceased. The prosecuting attorney who addresses a jury uses public communication to accuse the defendant of a crime. To accomplish the opposite end, Richard Nixon used his public resignation speech as a means of defending his honesty and his actions.

Since public speaking is such a useful tool in accomplishing a wide range of purposes, it is important to clear up some popular myths about speechmaking. The first is that the ability to make speeches is natural and cannot be learned. While some people do have a talent for it, effective public speaking can be learned through training and practice. Students who take speech courses generally improve their speechmaking ability and increase their self-confidence.

Effective public speaking depends on content and delivery. Contrary to popular opinion, good intentions are not enough when it comes to making a speech—they do not guarantee an effective presentation. Although someone may have something valuable to communicate, the message will be lost if the delivery is poor. Another misconception, however, is that it is not what you say that is important, but how you say it. The most eloquent delivery cannot save a meaningless message. Both content and delivery are important in achieving effective communication.

Finally, effective public speaking requires that the speaker be responsible for the message he or she presents. Although people who "speak their minds" are often praised for their stamina and courage, the effective speaker knows that, by virtue of gaining the opportunity to speak, she or he also acquires the chance to influence others. Reckless, irresponsible, or unethical speakers can cause great harm both to the members of the audience and to subsequent decisions they might make.

We turn now to one of the most important statements concerning public speaking: An effective speaker is one who begins with a sense of responsibility. Once we have considered the nature and implications of this statement, we may return to a discussion of the overall purposes of public speaking—to inform, to persuade, and to entertain.

ETHICAL RESPONSIBILITY AND THE PUBLIC SPEAKER

It would be naive to believe that all speakers possess the morality and good intentions included in Aristotle's concept of ethos. One need only study the persuasive genius of someone like Hitler to be reminded that public communication can be used for evil as well as good. While ethical problems in communication are most often thought of only in a persuasive context, they apply to informative speaking as well. The student of

(United Press International)

communication must consider the ethics involved in all public communication.

Think for a moment about the nature of American politics today. Party candidates clash both between and within their ranks, and independent candidates clash with proponents of both. Although such "openness" is not inherently negative, speakers of one group often hurl insults at members of the opposing groups, and the recipients of these insults often respond in a similar manner. Due to the amount of time spent in such activities, the issues themselves are overlooked in many instances, and disenchanted voters who are genuinely concerned can do nothing but attempt, with little knowledge or trust, to choose the best candidate for a job.

As one researcher has noted, the lack of trust in public officials today has become a serious problem in our society.[1] Should such a trend continue, the very foundations of democracy could be severely weakened. If we do not believe what others say, persuasion is no longer capable of solving problems in our nation or society.

American politics, however, is not the only arena in which ethics are problematic. In everyday life, ethics, morals, and responsibilities are called into question, leaving many to believe that ethical principles should be left to the individual person. However, at least four different approaches regarding the bases of ethical behavior exist in this country today. These include the beliefs that (1) the ends justify the means; (2)

[1]Bert E. Bradley, *Fundamentals of Public Speaking,* 3rd ed. (Dubuque, Iowa: Wm. C. Brown, 1981), p. 25.

(United Press International)

what is of greatest good for a group should determine the means of persuasion; (3) in order for the best choice to be made, each individual situation must be examined; and (4) we are held by our listeners to be responsible for all that we do and say and, therefore, *should be* responsible for our words and our deeds.[2] Before discussing each of these positions, however, we need a definition of *ethics*. *Ethics*, for us, will be defined as questions concerning the meaning of "good" versus "bad," of "right" versus "wrong," and of "moral obligation."[3] Likewise, we must understand the nature of rhetorical (persuasive) principles themselves, or the means by which arguments are developed, understood, and critiqued. These principles alone are "amoral," or can be used for purposes of evil or good. Armed with this understanding, we turn now to the four existing positions concerning the bases of ethics.

ENDS JUSTIFY MEANS APPROACH   When speakers believe that the ends justify the means in attaining their goals, they adopt the position that any available means of persuasion may be used as long as the end result is honorable, just, or desirable.[4] As a result of such a belief, however, speakers who take this position may distort the truth, conceal motives, twist reasoning, or make emotional appeals in order to prevent their listeners

[2]Bradley, pp. 25–31.
[3]Bradley, p. 23.
[4]Bradley, p. 25.

from making their own rational decisions.[5] The major flaw in this approach to ethics is that often the speaker believes that she or he has either the right or the ability to make such decisions. The Guyana Massacre, which resulted in the horrifying deaths of the followers of Jim Jones, is one instance in which the ends did not justify the heinous means. In short, if we condone the use of such an approach to ethics, we also must be able to ensure that the end is in fact a good and justifiable end. Thus, it is imperative that the speaker who takes this approach be certain that the aims are justifiable and that the choice of rhetorical strategies is not based solely on the desire to achieve the aims or goals.

SOCIAL UTILITY APPROACH   When taking a social utility approach to ethics, the speaker determines the programs he or she is advocating, based on his or her perceptions of the needs of a particular group. As Bradley, however, has noted, a problem arises when attempting to determine the boundaries of the group (Are you interested in ethnic groups or groups defined by geographical region? The country as the group, or society as a whole?)[6] Also, the speaker must take into account the effects of his or her decision on other groups. If, for example, the president of a college decides that campus beautification is the most important priority, how will that decision affect the needs of other campus "groups"; for example, as regards faculty raises, stipend increases for graduate teaching and research assistants, or funding for other campuswide groups?

SITUATION ETHICS APPROACH   The approach taken by a proponent of situation ethics is that consideration must be given to the nature of each individual situation before determining the "best" or "most loving" things to do.[7] As a function of such goals, four factors must be taken into account: (1) the desired end; (2) the means which are to be used to achieve that end; (3) the motive behind the act; and (4) the consequences of the action.

Although, on first sight such an approach seems reasonable and rational, it can often lead to diverse decisions concerning particularly complex problems. (If, for example, lives are at stake, should one share top-secret information in order to save them? For some people the answer would be clear cut; for others, it might not be so clear.) In addition, the use of this approach requires both sophistication and objectivity on the part of its user/proponent—a sophistication and objectivity which simply may not exist.

ETHOS-CENTERED APPROACH   The final approach on which we will focus is the ethos-centered approach. In using this approach, the speaker comes to the public communication setting with the objective of demon-

[5]Bradley, p. 27.
[6]Bradley, p. 27.
[7]Bradley, p. 28.

strating, through particular methods, his or her competence and trustworthiness. As a result, the speaker

1. Constructs a rational basis for argument based on a thorough review of all available information;
2. Presents evidence accurately;
3. Uses sound reasoning;
4. Retains objectivity with regard to groups or organizations with which she/he is affiliated;
5. Gives credit to all sources of information;
6. Stands firm on convictions;
7. Acknowledges when information is incomplete;
8. Avoids oversimplification;
9. Avoids the arousal of emotions on irrelevant bases.[8]

Perhaps this approach to public speaking contains the most effective, overall treatment of ethics. However, it is up to the individual speaker to determine his or her own approach to achieving specific goals and objectives—hopefully, *after* addressing the ethical considerations.

As a nation, we have come to expect politicians to make public promises that are all too often forgotten. We have witnessed the Watergate era, in which high-ranking officials were found to have violated the public trust. We have also witnessed countless advertisements making claims for products and services that are misleading or exaggerated. We have seen newspapers, television, and radio select which news to report according to their editorial bias. Each of these examples represents an affront to our integrity and our sense of fairness and decency. Yet most of these affronts occur within the limits of the law. It is difficult to propose legislation that would protect our integrity but not infringe upon our basic rights. For example, how can a law govern campaign promises without infringing upon freedom of speech? How can a law determine on what page a particular news story should be printed? Aside from being impossible in a practical sense, the very idea suggests a violation of freedom of the press.

As students of communication, we must remember that ethics are separate from law and are based on our moral and not our legal system. It is up to every speaker to examine his or her own ethics and those of the speech before it is presented. A code of ethics that is useful for all speakers states that

1. Lying is unethical.
2. Name calling is unethical.
3. Grossly exaggerating or distorting facts is unethical.
4. Damning people or ideas without divulging the source of the damning material is unethical.[9]

[8]Bradley, pp. 29–30.
[9]Rudolph F. Verderber, *The Challenge of Effective Speaking,* 4th ed. (Belmont, Calif.: Wadsworth, 1979), p. 202.

PURPOSES OF COMMUNICATING
IN THE PUBLIC SETTING

General
Purposes

In order to be successful in a public speaking setting, you must have a clear purpose in mind: As speaker, you must know whether you intend to inform, persuade, or entertain the listeners. Although these three goals will be more fully discussed in the following chapter, we now take a brief look at each.

INFORMATION EXCHANGE   The exchange of information is basic to public communication. All of us have participated in this type of communication situation. The **speech to inform** can take place in a variety of locations: on a football field, in a classroom, or in a convention hall. Similarly, the speech to inform can use a number of formats: instructions, reports, lectures, and demonstration talks are but a few examples. The coach explaining the strategy and tactics of a particular play informs the team through instructions. The surgeon informs colleagues about a new kidney transplant technique by delivering a report on the subject. Airline attendants inform passengers how to prepare for a sudden emergency by demonstrating lifesaving equipment. All of these examples represent public speaking situations in which the speaker's main purpose is to inform.

Since the informative speaker's goal is to successfully transmit information, he or she must present the information in a way that holds the attention of the audience. Perhaps you can remember teachers who could put you to sleep even though they were talking about a topic that interested you. Or perhaps you have had the opposite experience, in which a professor brought life to a subject you had previously considered fatally boring.

The success of an informative speech depends on how well the material is understood. Even if the audience is motivated to listen and the speaker is dynamic, the final evaluation of success must be based on what was learned by the audience. A brilliant speech on newly discovered subatomic particles can be a failure if the audience cannot understand it.

Therefore, you must organize your speech to aid audience learning and aim for clarity and accuracy in your presentation.

PERSUASION   The purpose of persuasion is to influence an audience's behavior or way of thinking. The art of persuasion has been a subject of interest throughout history; it is a powerful tool that can be used for both good and evil. In defining persuasion as a means of bringing about behavior change, Aristotle said that a speaker could accomplish his or her end by using logos (logic and reasoning), pathos (an appeal to the emotions), and ethos (proof of the speaker's morality and credibility). For our purposes we will define **persuasion** as a deliberate attempt by one person to modify the attitudes, beliefs, or behavior of another person or group of people by transmitting a message.

ETHICS, INTENTIONS, AND THE SPEAKER-AUDIENCE RELATIONSHIP

ENTERTAINMENT   We can define the **speech to entertain** as one that is intended to bring the audience pleasure. Such a speech is usually humorous, or at least characterized by some degree of humor. A humorous speech may be gently amusing or boisterously funny. The effect depends upon the speaker's personality, delivery, and brand of humor. A speaker can use exaggeration, sarcasm, witticisms, or burlesque humor when presenting a speech to entertain.

Listeners expend much less effort during a speech to entertain than during an informative or persuasive speech. The very nature of the entertainment speech creates speaker-audience rapport. Usually, such a speech is considerably more informal than other forms of public speaking.

THE SPEAKER AND THE AUDIENCE: AUDIENCE ANALYSIS

Once you have determined your general purpose, it's time to take a look at the audience to whom you are going to speak. To drum up antiwar support during the Vietnam War, Jane Fonda spoke at many colleges and universities. Most of her speeches were very well received and often convinced the members of her audience to support the crusade. Once, while speaking on a Southern university campus, all was going as usual. The audience appeared to be responding favorably to Fonda's persuasions. About halfway through her talk, however, the actress began moving from the injustices of the war into what she considered other wrongs—ROTC on campus and discrimination against homosexuals. The audience's reaction abruptly changed and whatever support Fonda had gained at the beginning of the speech was lost.

Jane Fonda did not know her audience well enough, and she made a naive generalization about the college students to whom she was speaking. She assumed that if they were against the war, they would automatically support other liberal causes such as gay liberation.

As we have mentioned many times, the communication process involves both listener and speaker. A speaker's ideas, speaking style, and nonverbal behavior are only part of successful delivery: The listener is just as important. Without the proper reception and understanding of the message, communication doesn't take place. Therefore, a speaker must always be aware of the audience and its reaction to what is being said. The best way to attain this awareness is through detailed audience analysis.

Audience analysis, or the act of acquainting yourself with your listeners before giving a speech, is very helpful, if not an absolute necessity. Of course, it is impossible to know everything about the members of your audience, but you can aim for a realistic assessment of the overall situation. First, try to learn about those aspects of the audience that will have the greatest effect on its listening behavior. Then, if time and circumstances permit, acquaint yourself with other factors. Let's say that you are going to give a speech on current unemployment problems. It would be more important to learn about the socioeconomic and occupational backgrounds of your audience than about its religious affiliations.

Keep in mind that your own attitudes and stereotypes can influence the way you relate to your listeners. You should overcome your biases so that they will not limit your ability to judge how others think and feel.

Remember too that people always change with time, and so will your audiences. An analysis made several weeks before you speak may not alter drastically by the time you are heard, but some minor changes will naturally occur. Even if you have done a careful job of audience analysis before you walk to the podium, your listeners may change their attitudes *while* you are talking. Prior analysis is only the beginning of understanding and relating to your listeners. While speaking, you must continue your examination, looking for audience reaction to the ideas you are presenting. What clues are your listeners giving you? What are their facial expressions? Are their eyes on you? Are they squirming in their seats, laughing, whispering, applauding? A successful speaker knows how to pick up on such cues, accept them, and then adapt the speech accordingly.

Demographic Analysis What are the ages of the members of the audience? What is their average salary? Is one sex more represented than the other? What kinds of jobs do the people hold? What is their level of education or religious background? These are some of the questions asked when analyzing the demographic characteristics of an audience. **Demography** is the statistical study of populations. In the demographic approach to audience analysis, specific factual information is recorded upon which probable audience reaction is based.

AGE Consider the ages of your audience members when planning your speech. People of different ages like different clothes, listen to different music, and have many different attitudes and beliefs. It is hardly surprising, then, that young, middle-aged, and older people react differently as audience members.

Winston Price, a writer of popular songs for all age groups, was often called on to talk about his career and music in general. His speeches usually resulted in a strong, positive reaction from the audience. One of

What are some of the demographic characteristics of these audiences?
(Ken Karp)

the reasons for his success was his ability to alter the approach and content of his speech depending on the average age of his audience. When speaking to teenagers, he dealt primarily with "top ten" hits and popular rock groups, but these were quickly put aside when he spoke to senior citizens and were replaced by entertainers such as Frank Sinatra, Lawrence Welk, and Guy Lombardo. If Price spoke to an audience composed of all ages, he approached the subject in more general terms giving examples that appealed to all members instead of a select few.

EDUCATIONAL LEVEL Before giving a speech, try to estimate your audience's educational level. This will help you to know what vocabulary, sentence structure, and abstract ideas will be appropriate. Also, it will let you know how many examples and definitions you will have to give in order to be understood. If you speak below your listeners' educational level, they will more than likely not only be bored but will also be angry when they discover they are being patronized. Likewise, if the audience is not as educated as yourself, keep the vocabulary and structure of your speech at the audience's level. Too many speakers throw in technical, difficult terms to show how much they know. Your purpose as a speaker is to communicate, not to boost your ego.

Remember, there is not necessarily a correlation between the amount of education your audience members have and their degree of understanding and knowledge on a specific subject. Besides knowing your audience's educational level, you should, if possible, determine the amount of information it already has on the subject you will discuss. Before giving your speech, try to find out whether or not your listeners have done any reading on the subject, observed it, or perhaps even participated in it. You might want to talk about hang gliding because you went once or twice, but there could be members of the audience who are real pros and could speak more knowledgeably about the sport. Through analysis of your audience's knowledge, you will be able to take advantage of what your listeners already know and give them the added information they need.

SOCIOECONOMIC STATUS Many of your listeners' values and attitudes are based on their economic background, so this aspect should also be taken into consideration when planning your speech. If, for example, you are asked to discuss the school budget for the coming year, a subject that influences tax level, you should be aware of the economic status of your listeners and the weight of their current tax burden.

Audience members are also influenced by their social background and experiences and by the attitudes and values they have developed. No one can totally escape his or her past. Social background, in fact, is often considered to have the strongest effect on listeners, being more important than religion, age, or sex.

OCCUPATION People's occupations often give clues to their educational level as well as to their information on and interest in certain subjects. Although both car mechanics and accountants may be interested in future modes of transportation, the former group would probably be more interested in a new engine part.

(Bill Fitz-Patrick, The White House)

ETHICS, INTENTIONS, AND THE SPEAKER-AUDIENCE RELATIONSHIP

Different occupational groups may be concerned about different aspects of a topic. For example, postal clerks might want to know how a postal law will affect their present salaries, while publishers may be interested in how the law will influence their mailing costs. Similarly, newspaper editors may be interested in learning the facts about a new superhighway; urban planners about the ways it will change the city's environment; and construction workers about the possibility of new job openings.

SEX   In the past men and women were often thought to be interested in entirely different things. With the advent of women's liberation and the entrance of women into every field of endeavor, this "obvious" generalization about men and women is no longer appropriate. Some women are not only interested in automobiles, but they race them as well. Some men are not only appreciative of needlework, but they produce it, too. Therefore, it is harder to differentiate audience interests on the basis of sex than it was in the past.

Nonetheless, the sensitive speaker may still be able to discern meaningful, if sometimes subtle, differences between audiences of men and of women.[10] Obviously, biological differences between men and women can influence interest and attitudes about specific topics. A demonstration of the techniques used in self-examination for breast cancer would certainly be more appropriate for an audience composed mostly of women than for one composed mostly of men. Furthermore, their potential for childbearing frequently disposes women to be more interested in topics that relate to maternity and childrearing, although the interest of men in such topics might equal or exceed the interest of a particular group of women. If you are careful, generalizations about sex can be useful in the preparation and delivery of your speech. However, you must keep in mind that generalizations are just that, and there are always countless exceptions.

GROUP MEMBERSHIP   If you are asked to speak to a specific group or organization, such as the Young Republicans or the American Medical Association, you are one step ahead of the analysis game. The groups people belong to give you many clues to their other demographic characteristics. Most clubs or associations have certain guidelines they wish all members to follow—religious groups follow certain moral codes, political associations advocate certain partisan positions, and so on.

Sometimes referring to your audience's association in your speech can create a closer speaker-listener bond. Let's say you are trying to persuade a group of women faculty members at the local community college to support with financial assistance and volunteer service a newly established women's health center. You might draw a parallel between their fierce battle against the college administration for more equitable salaries

[10]Barbara W. Eakins and R. Gene Eakins, *Sex Differences in Human Communication* (Boston: Houghton Mifflin, 1978), pp. 57–77.

(Ken Karp)

for male and female faculty members and your own group's attempt to provide good, low-cost health services, despite the opposition of the community's medical hierarchy, composed mostly of men. If you are able to identify the group memberships of audience members, you may gain many insights into their attitudes and determine in advance what their reactions will be to your speech.

Psychological Variables   BELIEFS AND VALUES   ***Beliefs*** are those ideas we consider true because of firsthand experience, religious training, or information received from figures of authority. You believe in God because your religion taught you to do so. You believe it will rain tomorrow because the meteorologist has said so. ***Values*** are forms of beliefs that are considered good and desirable by groups of people. Truth, equality, and freedom are considered prized values of a democratic society.[11]

Many of your beliefs and values are acquired early in childhood and, although somewhat altered by new experiences, remain the basis of many of your thoughts and actions. You must therefore pay close attention to these elements when analyzing your audiences. As we mentioned earlier, as an effective speaker, you can appeal to an audience's values to persuade them of your point of view; but in order to achieve this end, you must be sensitive both to your own value structures and to those of your audience. You must seek out the common ground that will give clues to their value structure. Let's suppose that you are going to talk to the Veterans of Foreign Wars about capital punishment, but you do not know

[11]Raymond S. Ross, *Essentials of Speech Communication* (Englewood Cliffs, N.J.: Prentice-Hall, 1979), p. 166.

their basic convictions. Before delivering your speech, you could read recent newspaper and magazine articles about the VFW's reaction to present-day political issues. From these you would be able to infer some of their basic beliefs and adapt the approach of your speech accordingly. Remember, however, that group associations do not always present the whole picture. The views of Democrats and Republicans, for example, often overlap on specific issues; not all Democrats feel one way and all Republicans another.

AUDIENCE ATTITUDES: TOWARD THE SPEAKER   No matter how well you Attitudes know your subject and how capable you are in delivering it, you will not be effective if the audience dislikes you or strongly disagrees with your ideas. An audience's attitudes about the speaker often determine his or her success or failure in communicating the desired message.

What criteria influence an audience's decisions about a speaker? Studies show that audiences base their attitudes on a variety of things. Some are meaningful, such as the person's experience, and others petty, such as the speaker's physical appearance. Research also indicates that physical attractiveness is often more important for females than for males in determining one's attitude toward the speaker.[12] In most cases, however, a speaker's success depends on the listeners' confidence or faith in him or her and what they feel is the speaker's worth or competence. As was pointed out earlier, this is usually referred to as speaker **credibility,** or ethos.

As difficult as it may be to "see ourselves as others see us," it is extremely important for you as a speaker to try to estimate what the audience will think of you. Whether this information is uncovered through informal conversation or through direct questioning of prospective audience members, you should seek out both the positive and the negative expectations of the audience. With this information you can make a deliberate effort to structure the message in such a way as to reinforce the positive expectations and diminish the negative ones.

TOWARD THE SUBJECT   If your audience's attitude toward the subject of your speech is favorable, your task is easier. All you have to do is give the subject a fresh approach and reinforce your ideas. But what do you do if your audience is neutral? People who have no opinions on a particular topic will probably listen to both sides of the issue and keep their minds open to all persuasions and information; but at the same time they may be critical toward everything they hear. Neutrality toward a subject does not mean indifference to it. Neutral listeners are concerned about the subject but have not yet made any final decisions about it. As politicians have discovered, these open-minded audience members may be very important to the outcome of a persuasive speech: They can still be moved to

[12]Robin N. Widgery, "Sex of Receiver and Physical Attractiveness of Source as Determinants of Initial Credibility Perception," *Western Speech* 38, no. 1 (Winter 1974): 13–17.

either side of an issue. This movement is possible, however, only if the speaker presents good, sound evidence to support his or her ideas, relates to the audience by sharing experiences, and answers all questions from the floor.

If you feel that your audience is indifferent to your topic, the only thing to do is to make your speech as interesting as possible. You can do this by finding an appealing, exciting way to cover the topic, by using attention-getting devices, and by playing upon other interests the members of your audience may have that are related to your subject area. The yacht club members might not be concerned with world politics but could be interested in the political implications of maritime law. Mathematics might be exciting to elementary students when related to their everyday adventures or to magic tricks.

If you know that your audience is negatively disposed toward your subject, what do you do? Studies show that communicators try different approaches in order to alter their audiences' perception of the subject and adapt their speeches to the different listening groups. Michael D. Hazen and Sara B. Kiesler reviewed the ways in which speakers react to audience opposition. Their assumption was that the "audience's initial opposition to the communicator's position will be an important factor in determining his strategy."[13] Based on their audiences' initial behavior, speakers sometimes adjust their messages in different ways, such as omitting key discrepant statements; making the message less specific, taking a less extreme position, or using weaker language; and spending more time on issues and problems rather than solutions.

Another way to approach a negative audience is to find some common ground between your differing opinions.

> It was Career Day at George Washington High, a ghetto school. Rose Carlos, a dance instructor, had been asked to talk about the career of a professional dancer to an assembly of high school juniors. Long before she approached the podium, she knew she was going to face an uninterested, if not antagonistic, audience. But Rose was prepared.
>
> "You know, many football players, such as Robert Brooks, learn ballet in order to limber up and play a better game. Those who have tried ballet have found that it has made them more agile and has enabled them to run faster and kick farther. But football players aren't the only athletes who learn ballet; it is practiced by many gymnasts, track stars, and swimmers as well."

By approaching her speech in this way, Rose was able to accomplish several things: (1) She lessened the opposition to her topic; (2) she gave the students someone to identify with; and (3) she dispelled some of the negative stereotypes connected with her subject area.

The most important thing to remember when confronting a negative audience is to remain as calm as possible. If you hope to persuade your

---

[13]Michael D. Hazen and Sara B. Kiesler, "Communication Strategies Affected by Audience Opposition, Feedback and Persuasibility," *Speech Monographs* 42, no. 1 (March 1975): 57.

listeners, be careful not to show anger or impatience with their differing viewpoints. It is quite possible for you and your audience to disagree without losing respect for one another's opinions. If you present yourself and your speech in a fair and reasonable way, you may not only be able to get people to listen to your different ideas, but you may gain some converts as well.

TOWARD YOUR PURPOSE   Every speech you make should have a definite purpose. Without the focus a well-defined purpose provides, your speech may be nothing but a collection of statements with no overall meaning. You will recall that the purpose of any speech is to inform, persuade, or entertain.

Speeches can, of course, have aspects of all three purposes, but there should be only one specific, unifying goal. If you give a speech in support of the liberalization of marijuana laws, you may inform your audience of the history of the drug's use, and perhaps relate some interesting anecdotes, but these are only means to help you accomplish your primary goal of persuasion.

The purpose of your speech will often directly depend on the audience's attitude toward the topic. Let's say that your listeners are already in favor of decriminalizing marijuana. Your purpose then is not to per-

(AFL-CIO News)

suade but rather to reinforce their beliefs and inform them of the appropriate actions they can take in support of their beliefs. However, if your listeners are rigidly opposed to your topic, it might be best not to try to persuade them but simply to inform them of the facts and hope that as a result, your audience will have obtained a more well-rounded impression of the topic. If your audience is neutral or only partially opposed, persuasion would probably be the best approach, while the interest and attention of a totally indifferent audience can often be focused on a particular issue by an entertaining delivery.

A good speaker will try to base the purpose of his or her speech on the desires and expectations of the audience. Listeners are more apt to pay attention to a speech they are prepared for and consider appropriate to their beliefs and the situation. The chances of a speech's success are greater if both the speaker and the listeners have the same purpose in mind.

Nothing angers an audience more than believing that a speaker's purpose is one thing and finding out that it is something entirely different.

> The presentation of a well-known black poet was eagerly awaited by an audience composed mostly of admirers of his works and would-be writers. Their disappointment was tinged with anger when instead of discussing his poetry, he delivered a powerful attack on white middle-class attitudes toward black Americans.
>
> Charles Marsden, a fashion designer, was asked by a woman's club to speak on the history of clothing. The members felt resentful when the lecture turned out to be a sales pitch for Marsden's latest line of women's fashions.

The irritation of the audience members in both cases did the speakers much harm. Had the poet and the designer given the expected information in a pleasing manner, they would have related well to their listeners and greatly furthered their personal causes.

If, prior to your speech, you can discover your audience's purpose and demands, you will know how to adapt your speech to increase the likelihood of a successful outcome.

METHODS OF INVESTIGATING YOUR AUDIENCE

When preparing a speech for one of your college classes, you already know the age, sex, relative economic status, and race of the class members. You can also make accurate guesses about their opinions on issues such as reinstitution of the draft, job opportunities, and higher education. Difficulties occur when you are asked to speak to groups of people that you know relatively little about (in terms of their demographic characteristics, values, beliefs, and attitudes).

According to B. E. Bradley, it is most difficult to obtain data about a specific audience when (1) the geographical area is large and (2) the speaker is unfamiliar with the specific area where the speech is to be given.[14] If this is the case, then speakers must use all the available resources at their disposal.

The most obvious place to begin seeking information is from the people who invited you to speak. Immediately, questions will come to mind, such as: How many people will attend? Are there any specific time limitations or expectations? What does the audience know about the subject? Will they be required to attend? What are their ages? At first, being startled by the invitation, you may not ask all the necessary questions. If this is the case, don't hesitate to call for additional information about your prospective audience.

Invitation Committee

Other valuable audience information comes from reading community newspapers and magazines, listening to local radio stations, and watching local television programs. Sometimes it may even be a good idea to subscribe to various publications for a few weeks before you speak, to get an idea of important issues in the geographical area. Through the mass media you'll find the concerns that are uppermost in the listeners' minds, such as police or teachers' strikes, sports playoffs, or human interest issues such as the activities of the local humane society. Even if your topic is not one of general community interest, being informed about local concerns can aid you in preparing examples and illustrations relative to your audience.

Mass Media Sources

Over the years we have seen the importance of polls in predicting election results. Politicans are extremely concerned about how their platforms are accepted and how popular they are in particular areas. The information received from polls and surveys helps the candidates determine the best method of presenting their arguments and themselves. Beginning speakers can also gain insight from similar information without going to the expense of conducting actual surveys. References such as the *Gallup Opinion Index, Public Opinion Polls,* and *Public Opinion Quarterly* provide useful data on a variety of topics for different geographical regions of the country.

Public Opinion Polls and Surveys

If you live nearby, much can be learned about your prospective audience by talking with local people. Interviews with local leaders and citizens can give you a clearer picture about who is being affected on issues such as waste water facilities, local parks and recreation departments, and health

Personal Interviews

---

[14]B. E. Bradley, *Fundamentals of Speech Communication: The Credibility of Ideas,* 3d ed. (Dubuque, Iowa: Wm. C. Brown, 1981), p. 87.

> A comedian can only last till he either takes himself serious or his audience takes him serious.
>
> *Will Rogers*

facilities. Even if you don't live nearby, after arriving in a particular area, you can talk to people you come in contact with (for example, taxi drivers or hotel managers) to find out the latest issues of concern and even language styles that might be appropriate for your particular speech.

OTHER AUDIENCE CONSIDERATIONS

Audience Types
In 1935 H. L. Hollingworth developed a classification system that described audiences on the basis of their organization and orientation toward the situation in which the speech is given.[15] Speaking before each of these audience types entails unique problems and responsibilities.

CASUAL AUDIENCES Frequently, in large cities, people walking down the street will stop and listen to a soapbox orator preaching religion or some other cause, or watch an entertainer such as a magician or musician. Hollingworth calls such pedestrian audiences **casual.** These so-called audiences show very little, if any, homogeneity and, in fact, are barely audiences at all. They are just small groups of people who have gathered for a short time at the same place.

Soapbox orators or street entertainers who address casual audiences must first get the attention of the pedestrians passing by. This means that they have to spend a lot of time on their speech preparation and delivery. Each street orator attempts to develop his or her own unique speaking style—a specific way to hook the attention of the pedestrians. But, more importantly, these speakers have to *keep* the casual audience there. This means getting the listeners involved. The orator will perhaps fire questions into the crowd, and the entertainer may ask listeners to participate, emotionally or physically.

PASSIVE AUDIENCES The second type of audience is **passive,** or **partially orientated,** and is usually composed of captive listeners. The people who make up this kind of audience have no choice but to listen to the speaker. A church congregation listening to a sermon or club members listening to the after-luncheon speaker are examples of passive audiences.

[15]H. L. Hollingworth, *The Psychology of the Audience* (New York: American Book, 1935), pp. 19–32.

ETHICS, INTENTIONS, AND THE SPEAKER-AUDIENCE RELATIONSHIP

Speakers who confront passive audiences must gain the attention of the listeners and arouse their interest in the subject matter. In order to accomplish this, they can appeal to one or more of the interests that almost all audiences have in common. All people share basic primary interests or needs. Financial security, for instance, is one of the most basic needs of all persons. Almost everyone wants to hear about ways of earning or saving money. If you are trying to get the attention of your audience members, use some examples that are close to home and especially, close to their wallets.

There are other common interests that appeal to audiences although they are not vital to personal welfare. Sports and hobbies are examples of such secondary interests. Suppose you are making a speech about an area of land you think should be converted into a state park. You might draw upon the secondary interests of your audience to advance your argument. If you have ascertained beforehand that audience members are outdoors enthusiasts, you could talk about the hiking trails, camping sites, and observation points which could be made available by such a state park. Or, if they are animal lovers, you might list the types of animals that would be protected in the park. Which secondary interests you draw on will depend on your specific audience and the results of your analysis.

Momentary interests are things that concern us for only a short time and are then replaced by other issues. A new television show or news event may be on everyone's lips for a couple of days. A speaker's reference to such a topic can be used to arouse the attention of the audience. An awareness of the momentary interests of an audience can be a great asset to the speaker.

A casual audience.
(Ken Karp)

ONLY AS GOOD AS THE AUDIENCE

The importance of the speaker-audience relationship is evidenced by an anecdote from the early days of radio.

It was a period of learning by doing. Ed Wynn, called the funniest man in the world, brought his broadway hit "The Perfect Fool" to the WJZ studio one night. Spinning his best joke into the mike, he discovered that it neither applauded nor laughed. In agony, he finally turned to the announcer, saying, "I can't go on."

The show-wise announcer raced into the hall and collected an audience of scrubwomen, telephone girls, and visitors and hastily shoved them into the studio. Excited and delighted, they listened to Wynn's jokes and their roars ripped the roof hangings. Ed came alive as if before a first-night audience and the performance was a triumph. Later, when Texaco hired him as its Fire Chief, his contract guaranteed a studio audience, as indeed it should have—he was its inventor.

From Curtis Mitchell, **Cavalcade of Broadcasting** (Chicago: Follett, 1970), pp. 78–79.

Culver Pictures, Inc.

SELECTED AUDIENCES   Audiences who have collected for a specific purpose are referred to as *selected* audiences. These listeners normally attend a speech because they have some previous interest in the subject. Examples of such selected audiences are environmentalists who come to hear a lecture on the ozone layer, students of the occult attending a talk on witchcraft, and members of the Farmers of America learning about a new irrigation technique.

While "interest catchers" are helpful with passive audiences, what are your responsibilities toward selected audiences that have met for a specific purpose? First, you need not try to attract attention; you already have it. Instead, you should strive to make a strong impression on your listeners so that they remember what you have said after your speech is over. A group of parents who wish to impress upon their fellow PTA members the seriousness of conditions existing in the school might invite an engineer first to inspect the buildings and then to come to the next meeting to discuss the leaking roof, unsafe staircases, and broken windows.

CONCERTED AUDIENCES   The high-level management of Manchester Corporation meets once a month for a round-table discussion of the past

(Stan Wakefield)

four weeks' events. These managers make up a ***concerted*** audience, one that has an active purpose and mutual intersts but no set separation of labor or strict organization of authority. Furthermore, the concerted audience has a high degree of orientation toward the speaker and his or her purpose. An Alcoholics Anonymous meeting is another example of this kind of audience.

Concerted audiences are already impressed and are ready to be led to action. The speaker must therefore enforce the audience's convictions—persuading members and directing their action. Audiences may have very strong attitudes, but having such attitudes and acting on them are two different things. For example, many women who attend National Organization of Women (NOW) meetings have definite proliberation views. This does not always mean that they are taking action, however. A vibrant speaker may be needed to motivate these women to take legal action in cases of discrimination, for example.

ORGANIZED AUDIENCES   Finally, there is the ***organized*** audience, in which listeners are directed totally toward the speaker and all labor and authority lines are strictly designated. A Minnesota Vikings coach lecturing his football team on the upcoming game against the Green Bay Packers is speaking to an organized audience.

Organized audiences are ready for action, but they often have no direction. The speaker's responsibility in this case is to give the listeners specific instructions on the action plans. The Minnesota Vikings coach will discuss specific football moves before the big game with the Packers. The labor leader will advise the union members where and when they should picket.

Effects of the Environment Is your speech being given in a large room or in a small one? Are the chairs comfortable? How are they arranged? What kind of lighting is there, and how good are the acoustics? All of these questions deal with the physical setting of your speech, which will greatly influence your audience's behavior.

Take the room itself, for instance. People will act differently if they are sitting in a large auditorium, a small classroom, or in an informal setting in a house. Compare an audience listening to a formal lecture inside a classroom to one that listens to the same speech in a coffee shop or outside under a tree.

The noises or other distractions around you must also be taken into consideration. Is the room quiet, or must you compete with the sounds of traffic outside and distractions such as air conditioning inside? You should learn how to adapt to such situations. You can project your voice over the noises, pause to let an intrusion pass, or incorporate the competing stimuli into the speech. George Wallace once used an interruption in his favor. During a campaign speech in 1972, he was interrupted by a man walking up the aisle pointing his finger in an obscene gesture. Wallace did not ignore the man, since the audience's attention was already on him. Rather, Wallace pointed out that the man had every right to express his views in public without being harassed. Thus, Wallace made use of the competing stimuli and avoided damage to his presentation.

The atmosphere in a large auditorium with hundreds of unrelated people is, of course, very formal. Listeners usually sit in straight chairs, and all face the speaker. Compare this to a small, informal gathering in someone's home, where the listeners and the speaker have a much more intimate relationship. The listeners are more prone to ask questions and offer comments on the speaker's ideas. The speaker, in turn, is probably more at ease and relates better to the audience. He or she can show more concern for the listeners and can come across with more sincerity.

The size of the audience is a physical condition that affects both your audience's behavior and your reactions to it. You will often be more formal with large audiences than with small ones. You will also have to use more pronounced gestures and a louder voice when addressing a large audience so that members in the back rows get the full impact of the message. In a smaller group your facial expressions and small body movements will communicate with much greater effectiveness.

Many social psychologists, rhetoricians, and educators believe that there is a relationship between audience density and suggestibility. Most researchers agree that a packed audience is easier to speak to than a scattered one.[16] Aides of the late Senator Robert Kennedy, for instance, told supporters that it was better to have a full room of one hundred people than the Hollywood Bowl with one hundred empty seats. Winston Churchill asserted that the House of Commons should be kept small so that it would only accommodate two-thirds of the members of Parliament. He too believed that crowding was preferable to empty seats.

There also seems to be some connection between audience density and anxiety levels.[17] Emory A. Griffin tested the hypothesis that high audience density increases situational anxiety, which in turn leads to greater attitude change in the direction proposed by the speaker. Subjects heard a persuasive speech as members of a scattered, full, packed, or jammed audience. The results proved the hypothesis: Anxiety increased as crowding increased, and listeners in full, packed, and jammed conditions showed more immediate attitude change than those in the scattered situation. Most of these differences, however, disappeared after a few weeks.

The Speaker-Audience Interaction

What distinguishes an audience from a random collection of people? There are three things that happen when groups of people progress from a mere gathering to audience status.

POLARIZATION   The first thing that happens is *polarization,* which provides the structure for an unorganized group of people. It is at this point that audience members recognize their role as listeners and accept someone else as a speaker. Two distinct roles, then, come into existence. While the polarized audience is separate from the speaker, it is also connected to him or her by the communication that occurs. Various aspects of the public speaking situation contribute to polarization, such as seating arrangements in which the chairs face the speaker, or the stage or platform from which the speaker delivers the speech.

Polarization is both normal and necessary in public speaking situations. However, polarization can become too extreme when either speaker or audience becomes alienated from the other. Former Vice-President Spiro Agnew's generalization about some of his audiences—calling them "effete snobs"—no doubt polarized speaker and audience to unhealthy extremes.

SOCIAL FACILITATION   The influence that one audience member has on another is called *social facilitation.* If you are watching a TV comedy alone, you may not laugh out loud even though you think the program

---

[16]Emory A. Griffin, "The Effects of Varying Degrees of Audience Density upon Auditor Attitude" (Paper delivered at the 1972 convention of the Speech Communication Association), p. 1.

[17]Griffin, p. 10.

(Culver Pictures, Inc.)

very funny. With friends, however, you may be prompted to laugh long and loud. Social facilitation may not occur immediately. It often takes a formal audience, the kind in an auditorium or theater, some time to warm up. Few people want to be the first to applaud, cheer, clap hands to the music, or stand for an ovation. Audience members look to one another for reinforcement.

Imagine that you are watching the performance of a Russian dance troupe. At the beginning of the performance, the members of the audience may be very quiet. A few people tap their feet or drum their fingers in time to the music, but most are relatively unresponsive. But as the rhythm of the music and the exuberant movements on stage affect more and more of the members of the audience, a drastic change can occur. Before you know it, you, like everyone else, may find yourself stamping your feet, clapping your hands, and cheering. Even listeners who are usually very quiet and reserved can be influenced by the excitement of an audience.

CIRCULAR RESPONSE When the kind of communication that happens between listeners occurs between the audience and the speaker, the phenomenon is called *circular response.* The speaker says something and the audience responds with nods, applause, or frowns. From these responses the speaker knows how best to slant what he or she says next to hold the attention of the listeners. If the response is favorable, the speaker may exert more effort, which in turn leads to more audience responses and so on. This mutual feedback heightens the participation of both speaker and listeners and strengthens the bonds between them.

Audience analysis is an art, nor a science. Just think of all the variations and combinations that can occur in an audience's demographic and attitudinal characteristics. It is plain to see how difficult, if not impossible, it is to set down specific step-by-step rules to cover all the variables of any particular audience. However, you can ask yourself some pertinent questions before giving your speech. Table 9–1 is a checklist of some of the basics of audience analysis that can help you construct an effective speech. Audience Analysis Checklist

1. Before choosing my speech purpose and topic, do I know the demographic characteristics of my audience, including age, education, occupation, personality, and so forth?
2. Have I a fairly clear notion of how much and what kind of knowledge my audience has about my topic? Will the range of knowledge among audience members be broad or narrow?
3. Have I discovered those basic religious, political, social, and moral beliefs, values, and attitudes that could affect this audience's understanding of my speech topic? Are there likely to be beliefs, values, or attitudes that may interfere with the audience accepting my point of view, arguments, evidence, or examples? Have I taken these into account in planning my speech material?
4. Have I made an objective attempt to learn my audience's attitudes toward my intended purpose, my speech topic, and myself?
5. Do I know what type of audience I will be facing? If I know, have I chosen the level and emphasis of speech materials appropriate for a casual, passive, selected, concerted, or organized audience?
6. Did I consider environmental factors that could affect the comprehension and/or acceptance of my ideas? Can I describe and analyze the physical setting and note its good and bad points? Are there any potential competing stimuli for which I can plan adjustments?
7. What is the occasion for which I am to speak? Is this a regular monthly meeting of Athletes in Action or an annual honors banquet? Is it the Fourth of July or Valentine's Day?

The answers to these questions will provide you with the information you need to increase the chances of a successful presentation. (At the end of this chapter, a form is provided for you to use when analyzing your audience for a specific speech.)

TABLE 9-1 Audience Analysis*

Subject and Purpose	
Subject:	Your general subject area.
Purpose:	To entertain, persuade, or inform.
Specific purpose:	What you want your audience to learn; what action or response you want.
Expected purpose:	What your audience thinks the purpose is.

General Characteristics	
Personality:	Open/closed minded, active/passive, tired/alert, calm/angry, other, mixed.
Knowledge of subject:	None–little, moderate, professional.
Knowledge of speaker:	None–little, same background, family member, friend.

Demographics	
Age:	Up to 12, 13–21, 22–40, 65, over, mixed.
Education:	Elementary, high school, college, graduate school, mixed.
Environment:	Rural, town, small/large city, urban, industrialized, suburbs, other, mixed.
Economic:	Poor, lower middle, upper middle, wealthy, mixed.
Occupation:	Unemployed, student, homemaker, mixed, trade, professional, other, mixed
Sex:	Male, female, mixed.
Group membership:	Sports clubs, lodges, occupational clubs, interest clubs, other, mixed.
Classification:	Casual, passive, selected, concerted, organized.

Attitudes, Beliefs, Values	
Political:	Republican/Democrat, liberal/conservative, independent, other, mixed.
Religious:	Catholic, Protestant, Jewish, other, mixed.
Attitude toward speaker:	favorable, opposed, neutral, indifferent.
Attitude toward subject:	favorable, opposed, neutral, indifferent.
Attitude toward purpose:	favorable, opposed, neutral, indifferent.

Environmental Factors	
Physical setting:	Formal/informal, large/small room, indoors/outdoors, other.
Competing stimuli:	Quiet, moderate, noisy.
Size:	Small, moderate-sized, large.
Density:	Scattered, moderate, compact.
Proximity:	Audience close to speaker/far from speaker, seated in front row/back row/sides.

*Adapted from G. Wiseman, and L. Barker. A Workbook for Speech/Interpersonal Communication (San Francisco: Chandler, 1967).

SUMMARY

Public speaking differs from other forms of communication in two essential ways: (1) Public speaking situations require two distinct roles, that of speaker and audience, and (2) in the speaker-audience relationship, the speaker carries more responsibility for the communication interaction than does the audience.

Perhaps the most important consideration to be made before speech preparation is ethical responsibility. There appear to be four approaches to ethics: (1) ends justifies means approach; (2) social utility approach; (3) situation ethics approach; and (4) ethos-centered approach. Whatever approach is chosen, one should remember the basic code of ethics: (1) Lying is unethical, (2) name calling is unethical, (3) gross exaggeration should be avoided, and (4) damning people's ideas without revealing the source of the material is unethical. After dealing with ethical considerations, the speaker should select both general and specific purposes. The selection should be based on the speaker's own knowledge and interests as well as on a thorough audience analysis.

One system of audience analysis is the demographic approach. This involves the gathering of particular and factual information to predict audience reaction. A speech may be planned according to factors such as the age, educational level, and socioeconomic status of the audience. Other useful considerations are the occupations, gender, or group affiliations of audience members. It is important to avoid stereotyping the audience, however. Demography is best used in a factual, impartial, and nonprejudiced manner.

Other variables that the effective communicator should consider are the beliefs, values, and attitudes of the audience. Familiarity with the political or religious character of the audience may provide many clues about listeners' basic beliefs and common values or convictions.

Effective communication is not likely to take place if listeners are alienated by the speaker, the subject, or the speaker's purpose. A good speaker must present the speech in a way that will emphasize the positive attitudes of the audience while minimizing its negative reactions. A message that is geared to the desires and expectations of the audience will be received more readily than one that is not.

Speaking situations vary according to audience type. There are casual, passive, selected, concerted, and organized audiences, and the responsibility of the speaker is different in each case.

The person who speaks to the casual or pedestrian audience must first attract and then hold the attention of the listeners. The select audience is a group that has met for a specific purpose, and the goal of the speaker should be to strongly impress the intended message upon them. The concerted audience is already impressed but has not yet been directed to action. In this case the speaker may try to reinforce established attitudes and motivate the listeners to take action. The final kind of audience is the organized audience. In this situation the listeners have already been persuaded of the necessity for action and are willing to carry out the specific directions of the speaker.

An intelligent public speaker must be aware of the effects of environment upon communication. Audiences react differently in large, small, formal, and informal speaking situations. Audience density is a factor in successful persuasion. Therefore, conflicting noises and distractions should be taken into account and prepared for, in order to make the smoothest possible presentation.

Those who wish to understand how a group of individuals becomes an audience and how audience reaction works should study the speaker-audience relationship. Polarization, the division of roles, establishes the speaker as separate from the listeners and establishes the connection between the two. Social facilitation involves the internal reaction of an audience. Audience members reinforce the reactions of one another. Circular response involves the speaker in the sharing of excitement.

Audience analysis is an art, and like all arts must be practiced and developed by each speaker. Students of audience analysis who keep in mind the characteristics and values of the listeners, the type of audience they are addressing, and the environment in which they are making the speech are on the way to becoming effective communicators.

Exercises

GROUP EXPERIENCES

Ghostwriting

Description: **Many audience variables need to be considered when preparing a speech or presentation for a group. Analyzing the audience is a key element in public presentations. This activity will give you the opportunity to "advise" a speaker on the elements that should be considered for a given audience and topic.**

Procedure: **Divide into groups of four to six members. Write each of the following topics and targets on a separate piece of paper.**

Topics
1. The use of marijuana should be decriminalized.
2. Women should serve their husbands.
3. All families should be limited to two children.
4. Wearing seat belts should be required for all passengers in cars and buses.
5. Helmets should be required for all motorcyclists.

Audiences
1. Veterans group, fifty males, ages 25–50.
2. College students, thirty males and females, ages 18–30.
3. Feminist group, forty females, ages 18–60.
4. Hell's Angels, thirty males, ages 20–35.
5. Daughters of the American Revolution, twenty-five females, ages 30–80.

Each group should select one topic and one target audience and should prepare a list of recommendations for things the speaker should consider. In preparing this list, the following factors should be considered:

Demographic characteristics
Educational level
Socioeconomic status
Personality
Sex
Group membership

Psychological characteristics
Audience beliefs and values
Audience attitude towards the subject and purpose of the speech

Although you have not been given all of the above information, you will have to make inferences about these variables.
Examples of recommendations include:

1. Avoid the use of idiomatic expressions. This is a professional audience who will expect the use of professional language.
2. You will need to loosen the group up so that they will feel comfortable with one another, since they do not know one another.

Each group should identify its topic and target audience. Then the list of recommendations should be read. Finally, the other groups should evaluate each list.

Discussion: Did the group make logical inferences about the given audience? Did the recommendations reflect the appropriate concerns for the given audience? Were any important recommendations omitted? Do you think that the consideration of audience variables is important in writing an effective speech?

Audience Types

Description: Hollingworth developed a classification system that described audiences on the basis of their organization and orientation toward the speech situation. His audience types include casual, passive, selected, concerted, and organized audiences. This activity will give you a chance to use the Hollingworth classification system.

Procedure: Each person should make up an example of two audience types. The examples should be collected and read aloud to the class. As each example is read, you should classify it as casual, passive, selected, concerted, or organized. After everyone has classified each example, the correct answers should be determined by class discussion. Check your score to see how many correct classifications you made.

Discussion: Beyond the classification of audiences, of what value is the Hollingworth system? How could you use it in preparing a speech for a particular group?

Warm Up

Description: One of the most difficult tasks for a speaker to perform is to try to "warm up" a formal audience. Few people want to be the first to yell, clap hands to music, or even stand for an ovation. This activity will give you an opportunity to develop various warm-up techniques for different audiences.

Procedure: This activity can be done either by groups or by individuals. The procedure is the same for both formats. Two descriptions of specific audiences are provided below. You are to write down all possible alternatives for warming up the given group. Your suggestions should be specific. Some examples include:

1. Tell a joke related specifically to the audience.
2. Bring several members of the audience in front of the group to participate in a demonstration.
3. Socialize with the group before your speech in an effort to relax them.

Setting 1. You have been asked to speak before a group of doctors on malpractice insurance. You are an attorney and have been active in lawsuits against doctors. Some members of the group resent the fact that you have been asked to speak to them. These members see you as the enemy.

Setting 2. You work for the Total Woman franchise. Your message to all women is that they should consider their husbands to be first and foremost in their lives. You have been asked to address a group of husbands who are experiencing some marital difficulties.

Discussion: Have you given careful consideration to the techniques you have selected? Do any of your techniques involve nonverbal behavior, such as smiling or standing close to your audience? What are some indications that an audience is warming up to you as a speaker?

PERSONAL EXPERIENCES

1. Observe a speaker in action, but spend most of your time watching for audience response. What cues did you observe that indicated attentiveness, boredom, interest, or anger? Could you tell when (or if) the speaker won or lost the audience?
2. Have you ever considered how much information you have about people based on age alone? Consider each of the following time periods during which people were born: What do you know about people who were born during 1931–1940; 1941–1950; 1951–1960; 1961–1970? Who were their idols? What was the political climate they experienced?
3. Can you remember a speech that was well received by the audience? To what extent did the speaker's adapting to the audience make the speech a success?

ETHICS, INTENTIONS, AND THE SPEAKER-AUDIENCE RELATIONSHIP

DISCUSSION QUESTIONS

1. How does group membership provide you with clues for presenting an effective speech?
2. What audience factors do you consider important in preparing a speech?
3. What environmental effects should be considered in preparing a speech for a selected audience?
4. How can you assess audience attitudes toward (a) the speaker, (b) the subject, and (c) the purpose of the speech?
5. How might an awareness of the concept of social facilitation affect your preparation of a speech for a formal audience?

COMMUNICATION GOALS: INFORMATION EXCHANGE, PERSUASION, ENTERTAINMENT

10

Exploratory Questions

1. What are the three purposes a communicator may have in a public speaking situation?
2. What are three methods of increasing audience learning?
3. What are three differences between informative and persuasive communication?
4. How would you define Aristotle's ethos, pathos, and logos, and what examples can you give?
5. How does source credibility affect persuasiveness?
6. What is the difference between balance and cognitive dissonance theories?
7. What are some examples of three special occasion speeches?

As we saw in the previous chapter, you must not only know who your audience is, but you must also have a clear purpose in mind in order to be successful in a public speaking situation. This chapter will focus on the three major purposes of public speaking: to inform, to persuade, and to entertain. A good understanding of each will be of great benefit in your first attempts at constructing a public speech.

INFORMATION EXCHANGE

Ways to Increase Learning

In order to facilitate audience learning, a major goal of informative speaking, you must organize your speech for clarity and accuracy. However, there are several additional ways in which a speaker can increase audience learning while presenting a speech to inform. Careful attention to these areas not only improves the chances that an audience will remember what is said but can contribute to the ease with which the speaker is able to deliver the message.

MOTIVATION   The most significant factor in increasing learning is motivation. Before you can learn you must listen; and before you listen you must be motivated to do so. The motivation may come from within (intrinsic) or from an outside source (extrinsic). For example: When Maria attended a seminar on crime prevention, she went because she wanted to learn how to protect herself. On the other hand, her roommate Stephanie went because her sociology professor promised to give extra credit to students who wrote reports on the seminar. Maria's motivation to listen and learn was intrinsic; Stephanie's motivation was extrinsic. Although learning theorists disagree as to which form of motivation creates a greater increase in learning, we do know that an individual needs some type of motivation to listen to and then to learn the information being conveyed by a speaker.

Computerized information exchange.
(Ken Karp)

If a speaker gives an audience a reason or reasons for learning the information, ideas, or skills presented, the audience gives more effort to the learning process. For example, when a representative comes to speak from the American Cancer Society and encourages the women in the audience to have a Pap smear and breast examination and then teaches them how to conduct self-examinations, he or she would probably tell them that doing so will increase the chances of early detection of cancer.

ORGANIZATION It is also the speaker's responsibility to organize his or her ideas so that the information presented to the audience is logical and easy to follow. There has been considerable research on how the organization of a speaker's message can affect listener comprehension, speaker credibility, and listener frustration. In general, the findings of these studies support the claim that the organization of a message influences the audience in its interpretation and evaluation of the message. In studies designed to test the effect of organization on listener comprehension, a well-organized speech is altered by rearranging the structure and presentation of ideas. For example, researchers in one study randomly altered the sentence order in what was originally a well-organized speech.[1] In a similar experiment the order of entire paragraphs was changed.[2] In both

[1]E.Thompson, "An Experimental Investigation of the Relative Effectiveness of Organization Structure in Oral Communication," *Southern Speech Journal* 29 (1960): 59–69.
[2]J. A. Kulgren, "The Effects of Organization upon the Comprehension of a Persuasive Type Speech" (M.A. Thesis, Fresno State College, 1960).

studies subjects who listened to the original, well-organized version of the speeches understood the material much better than those who listened to the scrambled versions. You would probably reach a similar conclusion based on personal experience. Undoubtedly, you find it much easier to understand a speaker who presents ideas clearly and logically than one who is disorganized. Most of us have trouble grasping the main idea of speakers who jump ahead of themselves or who backtrack to fill in information they left out.

Since comprehension is only the first step in learning, we should also discuss the effect of organization on the learning process as a whole. In a recent study Christopher Spicer and Ronald E. Bassett took the comparison of an organized versus a disorganized message one step further to test not only for comprehension but for learning as well. In this study subjects who were presented with an organized description of the rules of the game "Risk" achieved significantly higher scores on a subsequent test than subjects hearing the disorganized version of the message.[3] The conclusion was that effective organization increases learning.

EFFECTIVE DEVELOPMENT OF IDEAS Speakers who are presenting new information must develop their ideas effectively to sustain listener attention and motivation and thereby increase learning. There are specific techniques speakers can use to do this. One technique is to mix new and familiar ideas. Although the purpose of the speech may be to present new and useful information, it is important to connect this information with something that the audience already knows. It is always easier for listeners to understand something they have experienced or can relate to. A person discussing the detrimental effects of television violence on small children would include examples of shows the audience has seen to make the information more meaningful.

Another technique a speaker can use to sustain listener attention combines the elements of conflict and suspense. If a speaker can emphasize opposition or competition through an appropriate image, the audience is more likely to note and remember that particular point. For example, an ecologist might refer to the "race" among the industrial nations to exhaust the earth's resources.

A strong image can serve as a focal point for a speech and give the listeners a major concept upon which they can hang other important bits of information. One key phrase can later trigger a listener's recall of important, related information. A historian describing the circumstances that led to the American Civil War could use the image of a fork in the road, one path leading to an urban, industrialized North, the other to a rural, agrarian South.

In recent years educators have talked about the need for relevance.

---

[3]Christopher Spicer and Ronald E. Bassett, "The Effect of Organization on Learning from an Informative Message," *Southern Speech Communication Journal* 41 (1976): 290–99.

You have no doubt sat through many speeches wondering what the information being conveyed had to do with you and your life. A speaker who can take ideas and associate them with the audience's present concerns, will increase listener attention and interest. For example, an anthropologist could add interest to a discussion of primitive tribal rites by comparing them to some of the customs and rituals of various modern cultures and societies.

Another way in which a speaker can develop ideas effectively and increase learning is through the use of concrete, specific images that convey a sense of realism and vividness. A student delivering a speech on the World Trade Center in New York emphasized the enormity of the structure by pointing out that the building had close to 40,000 doorknobs. Although this bit of trivia is not in itself important, it made a more vivid and lasting impression than would have been made if the speaker had just informed the audience of the building's dimensions.

REPETITION   In every informative speech, regardless of subject, some information is more important than the rest, and it is the speaker's responsibility to convey this to the audience. An effective speaker will increase audience learning by emphasizing the most important information through repetition. A speaker can mention a point, underline its importance, mention it again in the middle of the speech, and repeat it at the conclusion. A recording engineer giving a talk to a class of would-be studio technicians might want to emphasize the need for organization during a recording session. He or she may mention it in the introduction simply as a "crucial factor." In the body of the speech, the engineer might quote the current cost of studio time per hour, pointing to the need for an organized use of every single minute. Finally, in the conclusion, organization might once again be stressed as a necessary element of good production.

VISUAL AIDS   In addition to using verbal pictures created through imagery, the speaker may improve a presentation by using a variety of diagrams, graphs, and photographs.

There are several advantages to using visual aids during a speech to inform.

1. By breaking into the verbal flow of the lecture, visual aids can revive interest.
2. They can focus attention on major issues and provide repetition in a concise, stimulating way.
3. By presenting numerical data in graphic form, they can emphasize the significance or bring out the meaning of the data.
4. They can give a measure of concreteness to abstract concepts.[4]

[4]L. S. Powell, *Communication and Learning* (New York: American Elsevier, 1969), p. 58.

(Teri Leigh Stratford)

Visual aids can be of great value in presenting information, but they must be used effectively. The effective use of visual aids includes several important dos and don'ts.

Don't:

1. Talk to the visual aid instead of the audience.
2. Put materials in the hands of listeners until you've finished speaking.
3. Display visual aids until you reach the point in the speech that relates to them.
4. Overdo the use of visual aids during the speech.

Do:

1. Explain the significance of each visual aid and relate it to your speech.
2. Give the audience sufficient time to view and understand the visual aid.
3. Think of all possible hazards before using visual aids.
4. Come prepared with all necessary materials (tape, thumb tacks, projectors, etc.).
5. Prepare visual aids in advance.
6. Use the hand closest to the visual aid as a pointer to avoid turning your back on some audience members.
7. Make sure that the visual aids are clearly visible to all audience members.
8. Be creative to increase interest and variety in the use of visual aids.

A park official may decide to use color slides of various national forests in his presentation. As he talks of the size of the forests, he may show aerial shots to emphasize the number of square miles covered with trees. While describing the wildlife protected in the national parks, he may show slides of various animals and birds. When he wants to make clear the necessity of preventing forest fires, he may follow a series of beautiful images with one of the blackened and smoking ruin of a forest. By means of contrast, and by leaving this last image on the screen for a number of minutes, he will surely give his audience a clear idea of the damage and waste caused by a careless camper.

While most of our discussion of the informative speech has focused on the presentation of information by the speaker, we should mention those situations in which the audience participates in the exchange of information. One popular format in which this occurs is the *platform.*

Audience Participation

A platform format might be used at a public hearing on drainage problems, when citizens report on property damage from recent flooding, and officials relate their efforts to deal with the situation. Similarly, there may be an exchange situation on campus, when the college financial advisor gives an informative speech on how to earn money part time, after which a number of students relate the various ways they have found to earn money for tuition.

The classroom also offers an opportunity for the presentation and exchange of information. Examples would be a home economics class in which students share their special recipes; a crafts class in which students do demonstrations of macramé, needlepoint, and pottery; and a philosophy class in which students explain their orientations to life. In each case, while the primary speaker may be the instructor, the audience also participates in the exchange of information.

PERSUASION

The degree to which an audience is actually persuaded will, of course, vary. A speaker who intends to persuade may (1) convince, (2) stimulate, or (3) move the audience to action. A speaker who attempts to convince intends to get the audience to think, believe, or feel a certain way. A person engaged in a debate, a minister preaching on the evils of materialism, and a business executive who thinks the company should merge with another firm may all use persuasion to convince their audience of a particular belief.

Another type of persuasion comes in the form of stimulation. Generally, a person who wants to stimulate an audience will attempt to reaffirm or strengthen preexisting beliefs or feelings. For example, the union leader who addresses members as they march on a picket line is trying to reinforce their belief in the importance of the strike while strengthening their feelings of solidarity.

The third level of persuasion is the speech that uses persuasion to move members of an audience to action. For example, when coffee prices skyrocketed, different consumer groups addressed communities to gain support for an immediate boycott.

Although we make a distinction between the different degrees of persuasion, keep in mind that these purposes overlap. Obviously, before

> Rhetoric may be defined as the faculty of observing in any given case the available means of persuasion.
>
> Aristotle

you can successfully move an audience to act, you must convince them. Since it is easier to get an audience to believe in something than to get them to act on it, the speaker who wants to activate an audience must use different techniques than the speaker who merely wants to convince.

Informative Vs. Persuasive Communication

The best way to understand persuasive communication is to contrast it with informative communication. Persuasive communication differs from informative communication in three ways:

1. *Climate or environment.* When a speaker delivers an informative message, the relationship between the speaker and the audience is usually neutral. However, when a speaker delivers a persuasive message, there is an emotional atmosphere that may be hostile or inspiring, depending upon the situation.
2. *Response sought.* In general, a persuasive speech will aim for a higher degree of audience involvement or action.
3. *Goals to be achieved.* The goal of an informative speech is to present an audience with new and useful information which they will understand and learn. The goal of a persuasive speech can be either to change an attitude or belief, or to bring a person to act. The goal of an informative speech on what to look for in buying a fur coat is much less controversial than a persuasive speech in which the speaker's goal is to gain support for a boycott of furs of endangered species.

There are several approaches a speaker can use to enhance a persuasive message. Previously we mentioned logos, pathos, and ethos, the three modes of persuasion defined by Aristotle. In the following section we will discuss each of these approaches as well as other methods that can help improve the persuasive speech. The approach or combination of approaches a speaker uses depends on the nature of the subject and the audience involved.

Logos: Reason

Logos refers to a rational approach to persuasion. Based on logic and argumentation, logos is intended to appeal to an individual's sense of reason. For example, a doctor trying to convince his or her colleagues of the value of an experimental surgical technique would be most successful using a rational approach. Citing research studies and including statistics of successes and failures might persuade the listeners to adopt the technique. A member of a consulting firm trying to persuade a business person to adopt an efficiency plan must present hard facts and solid figures to show how the proposed plan will either increase productivity or eliminate waste.

(Michos Tzovaras, Editorial Photocolor Archives)

Aside from facts and figures, logos includes the use of two basic types of reasoning: deductive and inductive. **Deductive reasoning** moves from the general to the specific. The best known form of deductive reasoning is the syllogism. The following is a classic example:

All men are mortal.
Socrates is a man.
Therefore Socrates is mortal.

A syllogism illustrates the deductive process very clearly; the final conclusion follows logically from the first generalization.

Inductive reasoning moves from the specific to the general. If your favorite disc jockey plays two enjoyable selections from a newly released record album, you may induce that the whole album is good and decide to buy it. Sherlock Holmes was known for his ability to draw accurate conclusions about a crime on the basis of specific information or clues.

Of course, both deductive and inductive reasoning can be false. Let us consider an observer at an athletic event who notices that all of the track stars are wearing a particular brand of running shoes. He purchases a pair for his son and is disappointed when the boy fails to finish the marathon race sponsored by a local youth organization. Just because a large number of good runners wear these shoes, it does not follow that any person wearing the same footgear will be a good runner. The deductive process in this case did not prove reliable.

An example of false induction is the case of a woman who hires a small moving company to transport her furniture to her new home in another state. As she unpacks the shipping cases, she discovers that many things have been damaged, and she angrily resolves never to trust a small company again. In reality, many small companies are just as reliable as the larger ones, but she has falsely induced from her particular experience that all small company operations will be equally poor.

When you draw conclusions or make assertions, you must be able to support them by supplying the audience with the basis for your reasoning. In other words, you must convince the audience that your arguments are based on logical thinking.

Reasoning is that process of thinking by which an individual arrives at conclusions. A detective, a scientist, a labor mediator, and a public speaker all use the reasoning process as a tool of their respective trades. The ability to reason or think in a logical way is one of the distinguishing characteristics of the human mind. It is through reason that men and women learn about their surroundings and generalize about their environment. Without this ability we could neither adapt nor function successfully in this world.

As a part of the inductive and deductive reasoning processes we discussed previously, we reason from example, signs, cause, and analogy.

REASONING FROM EXAMPLE   All of us have learned to reason from example. For instance, if you are driving in a state other than your own and the three cars ahead of you make a right turn at a red light, you might reason from their example that such a turn is permitted here, even though it is illegal back home. Using these three specific cases as your example, you conclude or reason that such a move is permissible. In presenting a speech in defense of a state lottery, you might present examples of other states that already have lotteries.

REASONING FROM SIGNS   If you see a line of cars with their headlights on following a hearse, you assume that the cars are part of a funeral procession. If some of the lights in your house begin to flicker and then go out, you probably reason that a fuse has blown. In both examples a conclusion is drawn, based upon a specific sign. This type of reasoning is often used as supporting material for a speech. For example, a speaker discussing foreign policy might use this sort of reasoning when he or she suggests that the withdrawal of an American ambassador from a foreign country is a sign that the United States has broken diplomatic ties with that nation. If the relationship between diplomatic ties and the presence of an ambassador is established, then the conclusion is valid.

REASONING FROM CAUSE   To reason from cause means that you must establish a cause-and-effect relationship between two things. In the 1960s it was found that the drug thalidomide, if taken during pregnancy, caused extreme birth deformities. The link between the drug and the birth defects was well founded. However, it is often difficult to claim that a single cause is responsible for a particular effect. A sociologist may have great

TWO SORTS OF SPEAKERS

Some speakers are more concerned with the style, substance, and ethics of what they are saying than others. Here Plato describes these two kinds of speakers, one careful of content and style, the other concerned only with the effect.

You mean, I said, if I understand you aright, that there is one sort of narrative style which may be employed by a truly good man when he has anything to say, and that another sort will be used by a man of an opposite character and education.

And which are these two sorts? he asked.

Suppose, I answered, that a just and good man in the course of a narration comes on some saying or action of another good man,—I should imagine that he will like to impersonate him, and will not be ashamed of this sort of imitation. . . . But when he comes to a character which is unworthy of him, he will not make a study of that. . . .

Then he will adopt a mode of narration such as we have illustrated out of Homer, that is to say, his style will be both imitative and narrative; but there will be very little of the for-

mer, and a great deal of the latter. Do you agree?

Certainly, he said; that is the model which such a speaker must necessarily take.

But there is another sort of character who will narrate anything, and the worse he is, the more unscrupulous he will be; nothing will be too bad for him: and he will be ready to imitate anything, not as a joke, but in right good earnest, and before a large company. As I was just now saying, he will attempt to represent the roll of thunder, the noise of wind and hail, or the creaking of wheels, and pulleys, and the various sounds of flutes, pipes, trumpets, and all sorts of instruments: he will bark like a dog, bleat like a sheep, or crow like a cock; his entire art will consist in imitation of voice and gesture, and there will be very little narration.

That, he said, will be his mode of speaking. These, then, are the two kinds of style? Yes.

Plato, The Republic, in The Portable Plato, trans. by Benjamin Jowett (New York: Viking, 1948), pp. 381–82.

difficulty proving that an increase in crime is caused by the increased number of crime shows on television. In all probability, there are many causes that contribute to an increase in crime rates.

Therefore, a speaker must use causal reasoning very carefully. For example, in presenting a speech on urban problems, a speaker who contends that inferior education in the city schools is the greatest cause of population movement to the suburbs has to show substantial supporting material.

REASONING FROM ANALOGY   When you reason from analogy, you base a conclusion on a comparison of two situations, events, or ideas. A business executive running for city comptroller may contend that since she was successful in straightening out the finances of a multimillion dollar corporation, she could be equally successful in handling the financial affairs of the city. The comparison between a large corporation and a municipality is the basis of her argument.

The various patterns of reasoning provide only a framework upon which a conclusion can be reached. The validity of any conclusion depends on a logical progression of thoughts and reliable information and evidence

Logical
Fallacies

upon which that conclusion is based. For example, when following a deductive pattern of reasoning, the first general statement must be true in order for the conclusion to hold up. Look at the following syllogism:

All cats have four paws.
Jerome is a cat.
Jerome has four paws.

In this case the conclusion is accurate because a logical progression has been followed and the first generalization is correct. However, suppose the syllogism read:

All cats are gray.
Jerome is a cat.
Jerome is gray.

In this case we have a faulty conclusion, even though the reasoning process was in order.

You must be careful to avoid logical fallacies. Careful analysis of the logic of your position will eliminate the risk of losing credibility due to faulty reasoning. If your audience detects an error in your thinking, it is apt to discount much of what you say throughout the speech. While most logical fallacies are committed unintentionally by the speaker, some speakers use them purposely to confuse or mislead the audience. For example, a speaker might present an argument intended to cloud an issue or distract attention from the main point. Such an argument is called a **red herring.** A speaker who bases a case for legalized gambling on weekly poker and bridge games in the home is trying to obscure the real issues. Such intentional practices are contrary to the ethics of public communication.

However, there are many logical fallacies of which the speaker may be unaware. The most common types include insufficient evidence; unreasonable extrapolation; non sequiturs; and post hoc, ergo propter hoc arguments.

INSUFFICIENT EVIDENCE   The fallacy of insufficient evidence is most common in the inductive pattern of reasoning where a generalization is based on a number of specific cases. Make sure that you present a sufficient number of examples upon which to draw a conclusion.

UNREASONABLE EXTRAPOLATION   Although part of the learning process depends upon generalization, you must not generalize beyond a reasonable point. An extrapolation is an estimate of the future, based upon current trends. In determining the need for a new elementary school, city planners can extrapolate the number of elementary school students there will be in six years when the school is completed. Using present neighborhood population as a basis for prediction, the planning committee could arrive at a reasonably accurate figure. Or, based on current energy reserves, environmentalists can predict when particular forms of fuel will run out. However, sometimes a speaker predicts beyond a reasonable limit. A prediction about the amount of money a newly released film will be making five years from now is an example of unreasonable extrapolation.

NON SEQUITUR Another common logical fallacy is the **non sequitur,** which means "not in sequence." This type of error involves the logical order of thoughts. For example, during an antiabortion speech to a group of young men and women, the speaker concluded: "Once we legalize abortion, the next step is to legalize mercy killing." Although both subjects are moral issues, they are not logically paired. The acceptance of one does not in any way mean that the other will follow. In effect, the speaker is guilty of a non sequitur.

POST HOC, ERGO PROPTER HOC Related to the non sequitur is the **post hoc, ergo propter hoc** argument, which means "after this, therefore because of this." This type of argument suggests a cause-and-effect relationship based on a sequence of events. Although one event may have

The logos, pathos, and ethos of a public speaking situation are not only recognized but controlled by an effective speaker.
(Brigham Young University, photo by Mark A. Philbrick)

followed another in time, the first is not necessarily responsible for the occurrence of the second. When food prices went up shortly after a presidential election, a political opponent claimed that since the increase occurred after the election (after this), the president (because of this) was responsible. The opponent's remarks did not allow for other, more probable explanations, such as a particularly cold winter and a summer drought. Another example is a speaker at an athletic awards dinner who claims that "due to a change in football coaches last year, the team had a better winning record this year." Even though there were new players this year and fewer freshman players, the coach was considered responsible for the recent victories. Although the coach may very well have been responsible for the winning record, cause and effect were not clearly indicated.

The logical invalidity of the post hoc, ergo propter hoc argument can best be shown by the following example: Julie believed that the mirror she broke on Wednesday morning was responsible for her failing a test, getting a traffic ticket, and losing her house keys in the afternoon. In each case Julie herself was responsible for her misfortunes, although she blamed them on bad luck. Since all these events occurred after she broke the mirror, she believed that this event was responsible for her misfortune.

The speaker who is aware of the common logical fallacies will be in a better position to avoid them.

Pathos: Feeling A speaker may decide that **pathos,** an appeal to the emotions, will be more effective than logos, an appeal to reason. The effectiveness of emotional appeals depends on the mood of the audience, attitudes of the audience, and construction of the appeals.[5] Pathos is especially effective in situations in which emotions tend to override logic. Pathos includes reward appeals, fear-arousing appeals, and appeals to needs, desires, and values.

A **reward appeal** promises the listener some personal gain or profit if he or she believes or behaves in the manner suggested by the speaker. The intended reward may be either material or psychological. For example, a high school dropout who hears a speaker at a job placement center may be persuaded to get his diploma in night school if he is made to feel that it will better his chances for obtaining gainful employment. When the same individual attends his first class at the adult education center, he may be even more determined to finish if the instructor speaks about the increased self-confidence and sense of achievement he may expect as a result of his efforts.

The opposite of the reward appeal is the **fear-arousing appeal.** People tend to be more vulnerable to persuasion if they perceive a threat to

---

[5]Ronald L. Applbaum and Karl W. Anatol, *Strategies for Persuasive Communication* (Columbus, Ohio: Chas. E. Merrill, 1974), pp. 102–3.

themselves or their loved ones. An effective speaker can capitalize on a person's fear in order to enhance a persuasive message. Advertisements for home fire alarms and various safety products are examples of this approach.

The effectiveness of a fear appeal was shown in a study conducted by Sidney Kraus and colleagues in which subjects were given several suggestions to follow while watching the solar eclipse. Prior to hearing the recommendations, subjects were warned "to follow these suggestions or you'll burn your eyes out." This fear appeal was so effective that 41 percent of the subjects reported following at least one of the suggestions.[6]

The following is an example of a situation in which the fear appeal was not used and lack of persuasion resulted. In a scenery workshop for the theater department of a university, the instructor presented the ground rules for participation in the class. Along with reminders to show up on time and to clean up before leaving, the students were advised to use the power saws only if supervised, to wear safety goggles and aprons when needed, to remove their jewelry, and to tie their hair back if it was long. The teacher did not really make clear the possibilities for serious harm to his audience, and the students were only too eager to start hammering and sawing. Some weeks later one student lost his footing on a ladder and almost dislocated his arm when the leather thong bracelet he wore about his wrist caught on a protruding nail. In this case a greater fear appeal might have spared someone a badly wrenched shoulder and a puncture wound in the palm of his hand.

While certain fear appeals are justified, others become scare tactics. People are easily persuaded when they are made to feel threatened. Residents of a small middle-class neighborhood in New York City became vehemently opposed to the building of a low-income housing project when community leaders made them fearful that the project would mean an increase in crime and a deterioration of the neighborhood. Although the arguments used were purely emotional, they aroused enough fear and opposition to delay the building for some time. When fear appeals fail to persuade, failure is usually the result of the subject's inability to cope with the danger.[7]

In the previous example the fear appeal was directed at a need for safety and security. Other psychological needs can be targets for the persuasive speaker as well. The need to be loved, the need to be respected, and the need for self-fulfillment can all be used as means of persuading an individual to change attitudes, beliefs, or behavior.

An effective speaker can also use human desires as a means of persuasion. When an attractive actress advertises an automobile, the appeal

[6]S. Kraus, E. El Assal, and M. DeFleur, "Fear-Threat Appeals in Mass Communication: An Apparent Contradiction," *Speech Monographs* 33 (1966): 23–29.

[7]H. Lowenthal, "Findings and Theory in the Study of Fear Communications," in *Advances in Experimental Social Psychology,* vol. 5, ed. L. Berkowitz (New York: Academic Press, 1970), p. 120.

is intended to be sexual. Similarly, promises that a particular soap or cologne will make a man virile or a woman enticing are definitely based on an emotional appeal to desire. Other common targets for the effective persuader are the desire to be powerful, the desire to be unique, and the desire to remain youthful.

Yet another type of emotional appeal aims at our sense of values—the things we consider important. The individual who has two big cars, fancy clothes, and no money in the bank values material possessions over security. The parent who sacrifices a vacation each year to put a child through college values education above leisure. An effective speaker can use a person's sense of values to accomplish his or her end. In a television advertisement a young husband is seen telling his wife that he wants to buy life insurance. Feeling unnerved by the subject, the wife asks that they not discuss it. The husband responds with, "Let's talk about how much I love you, instead." This ad clearly equates love and security and emphasizes the values of the family man.

While each of us has an individual set of values, many of our values are determined by our culture. Various sociologists have come up with a list of values that are characteristically American: Americans tend to

Measure success by economic status
Believe that success is the product of hard work and determination
Believe that competition is essential
Respect common sense
Believe that learning should be practical
Express a desire to be reasonable
Prefer the useful arts
Emphasize the material rather than the aesthetic value of art objects
Admire fairness and justice
Respect the family
Prize the individual above the state
Think equal opportunity should be extended to all minority groups.[8]

While this list is not definitive, it does suggest some of the ideas and values important to most Americans. By appealing to these common values, the speaker will increase the strength of a persuasive message.

A good persuasive speaker will take care not to alienate his or her audience with a badly organized message. One of our primary concerns as listeners is how the organization of a message will affect us on an emotional level. Studies in this area have shown that a well-organized message prevents listeners from feeling frustrated or angry and consequently increases the chance for an appeal to more sympathetic emotions. The im-

[8]Wayne C. Minnick, *The Art of Persuasion*, 2d ed. (Boston: Houghton Mifflin, 1968), pp. 218–20.

(New York Public Library)

portance of this factor is relative to individual listeners, since some people
need greater structure than others to make sense out of a message.[9]

Ethos (source credibility) is the way in which a speaker is perceived by
the audience. According to Aristotle, speakers will be held in high esteem
if they are perceived as intelligent and moral and if they demonstrate
good will toward the audience. Aristotle believed that these qualities
alone were enough to create attitude change. Today we tend to analyze a
speaker's ethos in terms of his or her expertise and trustworthiness. Although a speaker may be judged extremely trustworthy, the speech may
not carry much weight if it concerns a topic about which the speaker
knows little. Similarly, an expert in a particular field may not be persuasive if the audience feels that the person is devious, dishonest, or untrust-
worthy.[10]

Sometimes a speaker's ethos will be established long before a particular speaking situation. For example, a Nobel prize-winning physicist will
probably be highly regarded by an audience due to prior accomplishments. His or her message would probably be more persuasive than that
of a local high school science teacher, even if they presented identical
messages.

**Ethos: Source
Credibility**

[9]A. R. Cohen, E. Stotland, and D. M. Wolfe, "An Experimental Investigation of the
Need for Cognition," *Journal of Abnormal and Social Psychology* 51 (1955): 291–94.
[10]Herbert W. Simons, *Persuasion: Understanding, Practice, and Analysis* (Boston: Addison-
Wesley, 1976).

When speakers lack ethos, it is harder for them to persuade. Let us look at the following situation: A college president, distrusted by the student body because he overreacted and called in the police to deal with a nonviolent protest, called a conference of the student government to persuade students not to discuss the protest incident with the media. The president's ethos at this time was very low, and the students were particularly resistant to his persuasive attempt.

In many situations, however, a speaker is unknown to the audience and approaches the situation without a reputation of any kind. In this case the speaker must *establish* ethos, or credibility, so that the audience will perceive him or her as knowledgeable and trustworthy.

One factor that is influential in establishing ethos is organization. Aside from affecting comprehension, the organization of a speech affects speaker credibility. Studies in this area have shown that a speaker who is well organized in his or her presentation will be regarded as a more credible source than a speaker who is disorganized. In one experiment by Harry Sharp and Thomas McClung, subjects were given pretests to determine their attitude toward a particular speaker. After speeches were presented, subjects were given tests to determine if their attitudes toward the speaker remained the same or shifted in any direction. Using Thompson's version of the organized and disorganized speeches referred to previously, Sharp and McClung found that subjects who were presented with the disorganized version thought "considerably less of the speaker after hearing his talk than before he spoke."[11]

An audience's perception of source credibility can change, as demonstrated by pre- and post-attitude tests. For example, the use of visual aids in organized messages tends to increase source credibility of a speaker as evaluated by attitude tests given before and after the speaker's presentation.

The following is a partial list of variables related to source credibility.

1. Receivers tend to accept conclusions advocated by sources perceived as competent and trustworthy.
2. A high-credibility source can produce more attitude change than a low-credibility source even with highly ego-involved receivers.
3. When a receiver identifies with a source, it may enhance the source's chances of producing attitude change.
4. The receiver's attraction for a source increases as similarity of attitude between the two increases.
5. The status of the speaker can affect his or her persuasiveness.[12]

[11]H. Sharp, Jr., and T. McClung, "Effect of Organization on the Speaker's Ethos," *Speech Monographs* 33 (1966): 182–84.
[12]Applbaum and Anatol, pp. 85–86.

The ability, Phaedrus, to become a finished performer is probably . . . like everything else: If it is in your nature to be a speaker, an eloquent speaker you will be if you also acquire knowledge and practice.

Plato

ONE-SIDED VERSUS TWO-SIDED ARGUMENTS   When presenting a speech to persuade, a speaker must decide whether to present both sides of an issue or argument or only the side he or she is supporting. The effectiveness of either a **one-sided** or a **two-sided presentation** is determined by several factors.

Other Persuasive Techniques

In general, it has been found that a two-sided argument is more effective when the audience is opposed to the speaker's point of view, when it is well educated, and when it will be exposed to opposing arguments in the future.[13] On the other hand, the one-sided argument is more effective, if the audience is predisposed to the speaker's position. For example, the woman who is in favor of abortion does not need to hear a counterargument in order to strengthen her belief. One-sided arguments also tend to be more effective if the audience is less well educated and if it will not be confronted with later attempts at persuasion.

The effective speaker in a two-sided approach can present both sides of an issue and pick apart the opposing argument in order to strengthen his or her own position. For example, a prosecuting attorney can repeat arguments put forth by the defendant and then proceed to show that these arguments are weak, inappropriate, or false.

USE OF EVIDENCE   While you might expect that the use of evidence could only enhance a persuasive message, studies in this area have come up with inconsistent and contradictory findings. While some studies have concluded that the use of evidence is advantageous, others have shown it to be of little significance. In general, the persuasive communicator must assess the subject and audience before relying on evidence to make the speech effective.

For example, an efficiency expert who wants to persuade a group of office managers to use a new type of computer would be wise to include statistical data as evidence. The subject of efficiency is technical and the audience is used to problem solving based on facts and figures. The lis-

[13]G. Hass and D. Linder, "Counterargument Availability and the Effects of Message Structure on Persuasion," *Journal of Personality and Social Psychology* 23 (August 1972):219–33.

teners will be intent on hearing accurate information before allowing themselves to be persuaded.

If speakers have low credibility with their audience, the use of evidence may do little to enhance their position. The audience may "tune out" the facts and figures, thinking them to be as ill founded and unreliable as the speakers themselves. On the other hand, speakers before audiences that perceive them as highly credible need not include evidence in their presentations. The audiences will accept their messages at face value.

When the speaker is perceived by the listener to have authority or economic power over others, the use of evidence will be superfluous. The promise of reward for those who agree and punishment for those who do not will be enough. Similarly, when listeners hold the speaker in a position of respect, they may allow themselves to be persuaded without hearing much hard evidence, in order to win the speaker's approval.

FOREWARNING   Does foreknowledge of a speaker's intent have any effect on the persuasion process? According to a study by C. A. and S. B. Kiesler, prior knowledge of a speaker's intent either reduces the persuasive effect of a message or prevents persuasion from occurring at all.[14]

Of course, it often happens that the speaker's intent is well established long before he or she begins the presentation. For example, when a number of tenants refused to pay a rent increase, the landlord went before the tenant's organization. The landlord's intent was perfectly clear. The audience knew he was there to convince them that they should pay the rent increase and that the increase would mean better service. In a case like this, where the purpose is no secret, effective speakers will reveal their intent in the introduction and give a preview of what they are going to say. It thus appears that they are trying to be straight with the audience instead of trying to manipulate them.

THE CONCLUSION   Conclusions summarize and reinforce the speaker's point of view. Although any speech, regardless of purpose, should have a conclusion, it is particularly important in a speech to persuade. Comparisons between a speech in which the conclusion is left to the audience and one in which it is stated show that an explicit conclusion has a greater persuasive effect. This finding was supported by a 1965 study by Weiss and Steenbock in which two groups of college students were asked to read literature supporting the need for a particular course of study that most of the student body opposed. One group was given a statement with a concluding paragraph. The second was given the identical literature without the conclusion. Student attitudes toward the course were evaluated before and after reading the literature. Measured against a control

---

[14]C. A. Kiesler and S. B. Kiesler, "Role of Forewarning in Persuasive Communications," *Journal of Abnormal and Social Psychology* 68 (1964):547–49.

group that was not given any literature about the course, results showed that the group given the concluding paragraph showed greater attitude change than did the other groups.[15] Therefore, the effective speaker uses the conclusion as a means of enhancing a message.

HUMOR   Another variable that the persuasive speaker should consider is the use of humor. Once again, studies have provided contradictory findings as to whether the use of humor enhances the persuasive attempt or detracts from it. Humor can loosen up a tense atmosphere, emphasize certain key points, and entertain the audience. Yet how much humor to interject, or whether to use it at all, becomes a problem for the persuasive speaker.

Some studies have shown that humor lowers the speaker's credibility. On the other hand, a study conducted by Markiewicz found that humorous sources were considered more trustworthy than serious ones.[16] Perhaps the effect of humor on source credibility and successful persuasion depends on the listener's relation to the speaker. The data are inconclusive. According to some studies, listeners who felt neutral toward or in favor of the speaker's position were equally persuaded by serious or humorous messages. Other studies have shown that humor distracts a negative audience from its preconceived ideas and increases the possibility of attitude change.[17]

Based on the contradictory findings of various studies in this area, we can only advise that the persuasive speaker proceed with caution when using humor. The effective persuader must remember that there are various forms of humor and should evaluate the message and the audience's position before deciding which type and how much humor he or she will use.

PRIMACY AND RECENCY   An important element in organizing your message so that it will have the greatest impact is to determine the placement of various arguments and key points. There are two effects that you should consider in this organization: primacy and recency. In some cases arguments presented first in the speech tend to have the greatest effect in creating attitude change. This is an example of *primacy* organization. Yet sometimes strong arguments presented near the end of a speech seem to be more persuasive. When arguments are presented in this order, a *recency* effect occurs.

To say that one pattern of organization is always more effective than another is incorrect, since existing information is contradictory.

[15]W. Weiss and S. Steenbock, "The Influence on Communication Effectiveness of Explicitly Urging Action and Policy Consequences," *Journal of Experimental Social Psychology* 1 (1965):396–406.

[16]D. Markiewicz, *The Effects of Humor on Persuasion* (Doctoral dissertation, Ohio State University, 1972).

[17]Applbaum and Anatol, p. 104.

However, it is known that certain factors may influence the effectiveness of placing an argument first or last. These variables include the nature of the message, audience position relative to that of the speaker, the interval between arguments, and so forth. The effect of primacy-recency on the organization of arguments within one message and on the order of two opposing messages has been studied.

Although research has not provided any firm rules for the order of presentation of ideas, some general guidelines have emerged. It is important to remember, however, that these are not conclusive or final.

1. With a one-sided persuasive message, building to a climax of strong material at the end of the speech produces a greater effect upon the audience than an anticlimactic arrangement.
2. When presenting a two-sided (pro and con) argument, it is wise to present the first half in a climax order and the second half as an anticlimax. In other words, build to your strongest supporting material and then lead on from strong opposing evidence to weak. The audience, as a result, will evaluate the first half of your presentation more positively than the second.
3. In a one-sided persuasive speech, it is best to underscore weak arguments with strong ones. If a strong argument is followed by several feeble ones, the total impact is lessened.
4. Weak arguments have more effect at the beginning or end of a speech. When contained in the body, they are likely to be overshadowed by the surrounding material.
5. Strong messages presented in a set or in proximity to one another will result in greater audience retention of material. A group of weak arguments (unless they lead up to a more forceful message) will not be particularly effective.
6. In a two-sided presentation, it is best to place the pro, or supporting arguments, before the con, or opposing view.[18]

Theories of Attitude Change

In Chapter 1 we learned that attitudes are the tendency to respond positively or negatively to people, objects, or ideas. When our purpose is to persuade, we want to alter a person's way of thinking or change his or her behavior. Attitude theories help speakers examine methods people use to cope with arguments and ideas that are consistent or inconsistent with their attitudes.

The first of these theories, **balance theory,** originated by Fritz Heider, is based on positive and negative evaluations of all attitude objects, including persons, things, and ideas.[19] The relationship between our positive and negative evaluations determines whether we are in a state of balance or imbalance. A person is in a state of balance if

---

[18]Anthony J. Clark, "An Exploratory Study of Order Effect in Persuasive Communication," *Southern Speech Communication Journal* 39 (1974):322–32.

[19]Fritz Heider, "Attitudes and Cognitive Organization," *Journal of Psychology* 21 (January 1946):107–12.

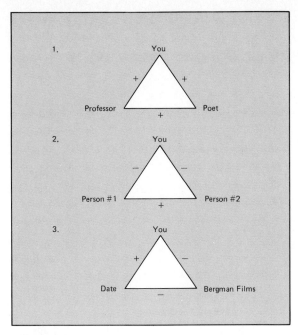

FIGURE 10-1 Balance.

1. Two positively evaluated objects are positively related. For example, if your favorite professor likes your favorite poet, there is a positive connection between two positively related objects (which in this case are the professor and the poet).
2. Two negatively evaluated objects are positively related. For example, you find out that two people whom you dislike are getting married to each other. A balanced state exists here since you are negatively disposed toward both people, who are obviously positively disposed toward one another. You probably will say to yourself, "Good, they deserve each other!"
3. A positively evaluated object dislikes a negatively evaluated object. For example, you find out that the person you are dating dislikes Bergman films as much as you do. In this case, the positively evaluated object, your date, dislikes the negatively evaluated object, the Bergman films.

When the mind is in a state of balance, there is no need for attitude change to occur. However, if a person is in a state of imbalance, he or she may be psychologically uncomfortable and desirous of change.

A state of imbalance may occur in the following situations:

1. When two positively evaluated objects are negatively connected. For example, suppose that favorite professor of yours thought that your beloved poet wrote nothing but drivel. Your respect and admiration for the professor would be in conflict with your respect and admiration for the poet. This situation would tend to make you feel psychologically uncomfortable.
2. When two negatively evaluated objects are negatively related. Suppose the

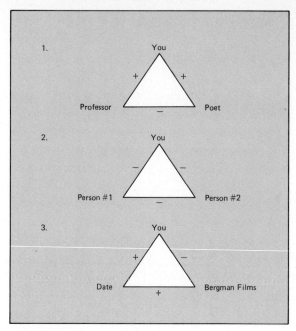

FIGURE 10-2 Imbalance.

two people you disliked so much loathed each other as well. The fact that you shared an opinion with these people would cause imbalance.

3. When a positively evaluated object and a negatively evaluated object are positively related. For example, suppose that your date really enjoyed the Bergman films you disliked so intensely. The state of imbalance would be created by the fact that your date (positively evaluated object) differed with you concerning the Bergman films (negatively evaluated object).

The effective persuader tries to create a state of imbalance in the listener so that persuasion can take place more readily. The imbalance created in the preceding situations might result in the following:

1. It might allow the professor to persuade you that the poet wrote trash.
2. It might lessen or increase your distaste for one of the previously mentioned individuals. You might conclude, "She hates him as much as I do; perhaps she's not so bad after all," or "If he hates her (and heaven knows he's no prize), she must be even worse than I thought."
3. It might allow your date to persuade you to go to the film with him or her.

In public speaking situations speakers can create imbalance by building their own credibility and then speaking in opposition to audience beliefs. Ideally, the audience would then resolve the imbalance by changing its attitudes.

Using Fritz Heider's balance theory as a basis, Leon Festinger proposed a later theory known as ***cognitive dissonance***.[20] According to Festinger, cognitive dissonance is a form of imbalance between pieces of knowledge and/or feelings. Your knowledge, beliefs, and feelings about yourself and your environment may be either in harmony with each other or out of harmony. A person who finds smoking pleasurable must also deal with the information that smoking is dangerous to health. There is an imbalance, or dissonance, between the pleasure felt and the fear-provoking information. To reduce the dissonance, the individual can stop smoking or refuse to believe the information that relates smoking to lung cancer.

No one likes to feel psychologically uncomfortable with his feelings or attitudes. Think about situations in which you have experienced a certain amount of cognitive dissonance. How did you go about resolving the conflict? Cognitive dissonance theory teaches that the public speaker who creates imbalance in audience members risks that they will resolve the inconsistency in ways other than those intended and proposed by the speaker.

For example, a young woman speaking at a health club is trying to persuade her audience to become vegetarians. She cites the youthful appearances of various swamis and the peace of mind of numerous gurus. She extols the healthful qualities of the vegetarian diet and points out the bad effects of eating meat. Finally, she appeals to her listeners on the grounds that it is wrong to kill animals for food. All of her listeners want to be youthful looking and healthy and certainly would enjoy peace of mind. None of them likes to picture the slaughter of animals; however, their food habits and tastes are long established. They may find themselves uneasy and decide, "Oh well, that's all right for her, she's young and healthy anyway. Besides, I'm a working mother. I don't have the time to fool with all the preparation. I just joined this club to get a little exercise." In order to ease the tension created between the argument for a new way of eating and the desire to go on enjoying their steaks and hamburgers, they dismiss her presentation as not applicable to themselves.

Other Persuasive Communication Situations

Persuasive communication is widespread. One of the most obvious settings in which persuasion occurs is in the courtroom. Here the court must decide whether there is enough evidence to warrant a trial, or a jury must decide upon the guilt or innocence of the accused. The prosecuting attorney may use a logical form of persuasion to convince the jury of the defendant's guilt: "The culprit was also described by several witnesses as a middle-aged man wearing unusually large sunglasses and a bright green

[20]Leon Festinger, *A Theory of Cognitive Dissonance* (Stanford, Calif.: Stanford University Press, 1963).

athletic jacket. The defendant was arrested several blocks from the scene of the crime wearing such a jacket. The sunglasses were found in a trash-can in a nearby parking lot. From the color of his jacket and the fact that the sunglasses were found near the scene, it naturally follows that he is the man responsible for the burglary."

A defending attorney may appeal to the emotions of the jury. "The defendant was wearing a green athletic jacket, but he was on his way to his son's Little League game at the local ball park. This is the kind of family man who is more likely to wear an American flag tie pin than a pair of gaudy sunglasses." By associating the defendant with the family, the favorite American sport, and patriotism, the defense counsel attempts to persuade the jury of his client's upright citizenship and innocence.

On a less dramatic but equally effective level, persuasion is also the basis of sales and advertising. The appliance salesman, the encyclopedia salesman, and so forth, all hope to gain access to your home and your pocketbook as they go from door to door. A good salesperson can be so persuasive that many states have adopted legislation that enables a person to cancel an order or void a contract within several days of the initial sale. This type of law protects the consumer who may be "talked into something" by a persuasive salesperson.

Perhaps the most effective sales pitches are the ones that appear on television and radio or in newspapers and magazines. Interestingly enough, the effect of mass media advertising is quite different from the effect of the mass media in general. Studies have shown that while the mass media in general are most effective in reinforcing preexisting attitudes and behaviors, they have little power to change them.[21]

Mass media advertising, however, does have a measurable effect when dealing with less important messages. Otherwise, manufacturers would not invest millions of dollars annually in advertising costs. While sponsors hope to make the audience want to buy their products, they also hope to expose the audience to new ideas and items. Many people go into the food store and buy a product they have just heard about or seen advertised on television. Others are persuaded by their children to buy a new toy that has been bombarding the airwaves. Exposure and the power of suggestion account for the success of mass media advertising.

Not all sales pitches come from manufacturers. In discussing persuasion, we must not overlook the charity drive. We tend to forget this form of selling, since the product we buy is either good will or a tax deduction. The most frequently used approach in a charity drive is the emotional appeal. While certain charity drives occur all year round, they seem to be most prevalent during holiday time, particularly around Christmas. The timing is not accidental, since most people are more vulnerable and charitable at this time of year.

[21]Applbaum and Anatol, pp. 121–22.

ENTERTAINMENT, CEREMONIAL, AND OTHER SPECIAL OCCASION COMMUNICATION

In the beginning of this chapter we divided public communication according to purpose. We have already taken an in-depth look at speeches designed to inform and persuade. We are now ready to focus our attention on the third category, the speech to entertain and the special occasion speech. While these two categories are often thought to be synonymous, it should be pointed out that special occasion speeches include eulogies, farewells, and resignations, which are seldom meant to entertain. However, since many special occasion speeches, such as introductions, acceptances, and after-dinner talks, are often intended to entertain, we will discuss them as separate but related in purpose.

There are many different types of special occasion and ceremonial speeches. Let us take a look at a few of the more familiar ones. A **welcoming speech** may be presented to an individual or an entire group about to join an organization or attending a particular meeting or seminar. The speaker who presents the welcoming speech should mention the group extending the welcome and should make some comment on the occasion. Perhaps you remember the dean of students presenting a welcoming speech at your freshman orientation. Similarly, when you graduate, a fellow student or member of the faculty will welcome the parents and friends of the graduates. A welcoming speech should be brief and to the point. It may be humorous in nature, depending on the situation or occasion.

Kinds of Special Occasion Speeches

Two additional special occasion speeches are the **award presentation** and **acceptance speech.** You are probably familiar with these types of speeches from having seen televised presentations of the Oscar, Tony, and Emmy awards. It is likely that you have participated in some sort of award presentation as a presenter, recipient, or member of the audience. At some time in your life, you may have attended a high school awards assembly, a scouting club breakfast, or a church supper, where awards for superior performance were presented to deserving recipients. Whether an individual presents an award or receives one, he or she should emphasize the significance of the award. While the presentation speech focuses on the many ways in which the recipient qualifies for the award, the acceptance speech is a way of saying thank you.

The **after-dinner speech** is often, but not always, a speech to entertain; certainly, it is intended to make the audience feel relaxed and comfortable. The content of the speech depends on the nature of the banquet. A more formal occasion will warrant a more serious presentation. The after-dinner speech at a hundred-dollar-a-plate political banquet will probably be more serious than the one presented at an annual fraternity ball.

(United Press International)

The after-dinner speech should be relatively brief, since other announcements, introductions, and speeches are usually on the agenda.

In a *farewell speech* the speaker expresses regrets about leaving a particular group or organization and offers thanks to those who are left behind. A person who retires or is joining another company, the valedictorian of the high school graduating class, the employee who has joined the ranks of management, or the man or woman going off the join the military all share a common purpose in saying goodbye and thank you to the people they are leaving.

COMMUNICATION GOALS: INFORMATION EXCHANGE, PERSUASION, ENTERTAINMENT

One particular type of farewell is the **eulogy,** a ceremonial speech which marks someone's death. A eulogy may be presented at the funeral service or at a later date, as a memorial. Numerous memorial services are held on January 15 to mark the birthday of the Reverend Martin Luther King, Jr., renowned civil rights leader. The eulogy is a farewell speech that praises the virtues and accomplishments of the deceased. While a eulogy is often delivered by a member of the clergy, sometimes friends, family, or colleagues make the presentation in addition to or instead of the clergy.

Although there are numerous other special occasion speeches, the last category we will discuss is the **impromptu speech.** "Impromptu" refers to the manner of presentation. An impromptu speech is one that is made on the spot without any sort of preparation. Someone who wins an unexpected award will be expected to give an impromptu acceptance speech. Someone filling in at the last minute for a scheduled speaker may be asked to give an impromptu welcoming or after-dinner speech. The most important thing to remember when delivering an impromptu speech is to stick to the topic and try to present your speech in an organized and interesting manner.

In any special occasion speech or speech to entertain, there are several principles of effectiveness that you should consider. The first of these is **Principles of Effectiveness**

"He tossed aside his prepared speech, but now he can't find his notes for his off-the-cuff remarks."

to use humor appropriately. Remember that not all speeches or occasions should have a humorous approach. If the occasion does call for humor, you must decide if your speech should be really funny or just mildly amusing. Humor should be used as a means of accomplishing your purpose, not of offending or distracting your audience.

Another principle is to have a central theme. This is particularly important in special occasion speeches. The speaker should know his or her purpose and relate the entire speech to that purpose.

Finally, the speaker should avoid belaboring points and should be clear, cogent, and brief. These qualities are particularly desirable in ceremonial or special occasion speeches.

Chances are that, at some time in your life, you will be asked to deliver a special occasion speech or a speech to entertain. It might be at a community affair, at a political banquet, or at a class reunion. If you keep these principles in mind, you will increase your chances of success.

SUMMARY

The major communication goals are information exchange, persuasion, and entertainment. In the first case the speaker must aim for audience learning and comprehension. In the second the speaker tries to modify the attitudes, beliefs, or behavior of the listener. A speaker whose purpose is entertainment must strive to amuse or please the audience.

When presenting an informative speech, the speaker must keep in mind the factors which affect audience learning. The speaker must first try to motivate the audience to listen and learn. The message must be organized, and ideas must be effectively developed. The speaker may emphasize important information by repetition or by the use of visual aids. Information exchange may take the form of audience participation in some cases.

The persuasive speaker has certain tools for changing the attitudes or behavior of the audience. One of these is logos, or logical reasoning. The speaker may employ deductive reasoning, from the general to the specific, or inductive reasoning, from the specific to the general. People also reason by example, signs, cause (and effect), or analogy.

The speaker who wants to persuade by means of logical appeals to reason must keep in mind the possibility of logical fallacy. No matter how well structured the arguments seem, the validity of the conclusion depends on the truth of the original statement, a logical progression of thought, and sound evidence or information.

When appropriate, the persuasive speaker may employ pathos, or an appeal to the emotions of his audience. Pathos includes reward appeals, fear-arousing appeals, and appeals to needs, desires, and values.

Before including pathos in a speech, some knowledge of the audience is necessary. When speaking before a general audience, appeals to the common human values (health, family, integrity, and so on) may be effective. It is important to keep in mind that emotional appeals will have little effect upon the listener who is frustrated and angered by a poorly organized speech.

It is particularly important for the persuasive speaker to establish ethos, or source credibility, with his listeners. People are more easily persuaded if they perceive the speaker as having intelligence, morality, and good will toward the audience. Once again, good organization is very important to the speaker. Credibility is not easily established when the speech is confusing to the listener.

A speaker may increase the persuasive effects of his or her presentation through the use of other techniques. An appropriate use of one- or two-sided arguments, sound and sufficient evidence, or forewarning of purpose may help to change the attitude of the listener. Explicit conclusions and the proper use of humor are also persuasive. Consideration of the primacy-recency effect, the arrangement of ideas and arguments within the speech, may improve the possibility of successful persuasion.

The theories of attitude change available to the speaker may be useful to his or her purpose. If and when a psychological imbalance is created in the listener, the possibility for attitude change is increased. However, there is always the chance that the audience will not resolve such imbalance in the manner the speaker intends.

The final kind of public communication is the speech to entertain, whether for ceremonials, or for other special occasions. The entertaining speech is intended to bring pleasure and amusement to the listener. The special occasion speech may be a way of saying thank you, farewell, or congratulations. It may be an occasion for awarding praise or it may be a eulogy.

All the above share certain elements of effectiveness. Appropriate use of humor, a clear, concise, and well-organized presentation, and a central idea are important in any of these communication situations.

Exercises

GROUP EXPERIENCES

Before and After

Description: Most individuals need some type of motivation to listen to and then learn the information that is conveyed by the speaker. Without even realizing it, most of us continually provide reasons for another person to listen to us in a dyadic conversation. If you are attracted to another person, this may provide extrinsic motivation for you to listen to what he or she has to say. On the other hand, if you have been with a person over time, attraction may no longer serve as an extrinsic motivator. In cases such as these, another form of motivation would have to be developed in order to maintain interest in the conversation. This activity will help you to understand the connection between interest level and motivation.

Procedure: This is a role-playing activity that is most effectively used as a demonstration technique in front of the class. There are two roles, one played by a female and the other played by a male. The team should be asked to play the following three scenes.

Before. This is your first date. You are sitting in a movie theater. You are both extremely attracted to one another and excited about being together. You hang on to every word the other person says because you don't want to miss anything. Show your interest in the other person both verbally and nonverbally.

During. You have been dating for four months. You are at the movie theater again. Your relationship is gradually shifting to where you are more interested in the movie than in each other. You listen to each other on an off-and-on basis.

After. You have been together for a long, long time. You are at the movie theater again. You have heard everything the other person has to say "a million times." Neither one of you listens to what the other person is saying. Carry on an entire conversation where you misinterpret or do not listen to what the other person is saying.

Discussion: This activity demonstrates the existence of extrinsic motivation (attraction to the other person) in the "before" scene. The "during" scene demonstrates the minimal existence of extrinsic motivation, while the "after" scene demonstrates the complete absence of extrinsic motivation for listening to the other person. Logically, it can be assumed that extrinsic motivation can be replaced with intrinsic motivation, which then would increase the listening level. Can you think of a time during which you listened to another person with the absence of extrinsic or intrinsic motivation? Can you provide motivation for others to listen to you on both a physical and a psychological level? In your daily conversations do you provide motivation for the other person (s) to listen?

The 60-Second Commercial

Description: Research suggests that many different variables should be considered when planning a speech for a particular audience. Some of the considerations include extrinsic and intrinsic motivation, organization, effective development of ideas, repetition, and visual presentation. This activity will provide you with the opportunity to use a variety of techniques in an attempt to persuade the audience to remember your product.

Procedure: You are to design a 60-second commercial on a fictitious product or service. You will be paying a high price for 60 seconds of prime time, so the commercial should be designed with extreme care. Your purpose is to motivate your audience to remember the name of your product. Be creative in the design of your commercial.

Discussion: The class period following the presentation of the commercials should be used to test which products were remembered. Take out paper and pencil and list all the products you remember. Next to each product you should identify why you remembered the product. After everyone has completed these lists, check to see which products were remembered the most. Why were some products remembered, while others were not? Consider the repetition, organization, and visual presentation of the message. Do you think it is difficult to develop a "persuasive" message?

How's Your Ethos?

Description: Ethos, or source credibility, refers to the way in which a speaker is perceived by the audience. Some of the findings related to source credibility include:

1. Receivers tend to accept conclusions advocated by sources perceived as competent and trustworthy.
2. A high credibility source can produce more attitude change than a low credibility source, even with highly ego-involved receivers.
3. When a receiver identifies with a source, it may enhance the source's chances of producing attitude change.
4. The receiver's attraction for a source increases as similarity of attitude between the two increases.
5. The status of the speaker can affect his or her persuasiveness.

The following activity provides you with an opportunity to see how these principles work.

Procedure: Which of the above principles of source credibility does this example illustrate?

Sample Situation. In an Arizona state prison, a program was presented on adapting to society after living in prison. Two speakers addressed the group of inmates. The first speaker was Dr. Sharon Stone, a noted psychologist in the area of social adjustment. The second speaker was Ron Harnick, a former inmate who had spent five years in the state prison system. The inmates showed greater interest in listening to Ron Harnick, and, consequently, his speech had a much greater impact than Dr. Stone's.

Two principles can be identified in this example. Principle 3 suggests that when a receiver identifies with a source, it may enhance the source's chances of producing attitude change. In this case it can be observed that the inmates (receivers) identified with Harnick (source) because of the time the latter spent in the prison. Principle 4 suggests that the receiver's attraction for a source increases as attitudinal similarity between the two increases. It may be assumed that the inmates perceived Harnick to have greater attitudinal similarity with them as compared with Dr. Stone.

Now that you have a sample description, divide into dyads and write an example that will serve to illustrate each principle. You may use one example to illustrate two principles. Each dyad should read one example to the rest of the class and ask the other students to explain the applicable principle of source credibility.

Discussion: After writing and listening to various examples, can you identify other principles of source credibility? What are some of the ways in which you can be perceived as more credible? Which methods are most commonly employed by politicians to enhance their credibility?

PERSONAL EXPERIENCES

1. A state of imbalance is said to occur when (a) two positively evaluated objects are negatively connected; (b) two negatively evaluated objects are negatively related; or (c) a positively evaluated object and a negatively evaluated object are positively related. A state of imbalance is psychologically uncomfortable and usually results in an individual's desire for change. Identify a state of imbalance that you have experienced. Which principle does your experience illustrate? Did you do anything to alter the imbalance? What did you do to effect a change?

2. Obtain a copy of a transcript of a speech, or attend a speaking situation in which the speaker is clearly attempting to persuade his or her audience. Was the speaker ethical? List your criteria for a code of ethics in public speaking.

3. A common misconception about public speaking is that the ability to make speeches is instinctive and cannot be learned. Interview one or two people in your community who are considered to be effective speakers. Find out how they began public speaking. Were they ever afraid to speak in front of groups? Did they ever deliver a "bomb"?

DISCUSSION QUESTIONS

1. What are the criteria used to distinguish public communication from private communication?

2. What is an example of a persuasive speech to (a) convince, (b) stimulate, and (c) actuate?

3. Are the qualities of ethos, pathos, and logos inherent in every good speech? Why? Why not?
4. Under what circumstances would a one-sided argument be more effective than a two-sided argument?
5. What forms of motivation would be most effective to use when speaking to a group of college students?
6. In what ways do persuasive messages affect your day-to-day activities?
7. What techniques can a speaker employ to increase audience participation?
8. What are some creative ways you can think of to repeat the same information in different forms?

DEVELOPING
AND ORGANIZING
THE MESSAGE

11

Exploratory Questions

1. What guidelines should you consider when selecting a topic for a speech?
2. What are the functions of an introduction, a body, and a conclusion?
3. What are five standard devices used to achieve an effective introduction and conclusion?
4. How can transitions be used effectively?
5. What are five standard patterns of organization for an informative speech, and how are they used?
6. What are four standard patterns of organization for a persuasive speech, and how are they used?
7. What are five principles of outlining?
8. How would you differentiate between clarification and support?
9. What are four sources of support?

Public speakers, like boy scouts, must be prepared. Speaking in public is a challenge that requires choosing a suitable topic, gathering appropriate information, and organizing the material so that the content can be effectively presented. Taking the time for thorough preparation results in increased self-confidence and improved communication.

This chapter, more than any other in the book, is a kind of handbook of dos and don'ts. It is meant to give you practical advice. It presents suggestions on how to choose your topic, gather source materials, introduce your subject, organize and support the body of your speech, and prepare an effective conclusion. It also shows you the importance of outlining. (See Appendix B, which illustrates how the process works by presenting and annotating an effective speech.)

SELECTING THE TOPIC

Finding a suitable topic is sometimes half the battle. In some instances there is no choice. The topic may already have been decided for the speaker. For example, a union representative may be invited by the membership to discuss pension benefits at the monthly meeting, or a veterinarian who services a rural community may be asked by the local farmers to discuss precautions against cattle diseases.

You and the Topic When you must choose your own topic, however, there are certain guidelines that must be considered. The first concerns you, the speaker—what you know about, what you're interested in, and what you believe in.

KNOW YOUR TOPIC It's always easier for people to discuss subjects they are familiar with than ones about which they know little. An art historian would probably feel quite comfortable discussing Leonardo da Vinci but ill at ease talking about the advantages of solar energy. Although a good speaker researches *any* topic, previous knowledge of a subject can make the selection process easier.

BE INTERESTED IN YOUR TOPIC   It is also very important to select a topic in which you are interested. If you are genuinely interested in the subject you are to speak about, your enthusiasm will be communicated to your audience when you deliver your speech. Interest in your topic also increases motivation to investigate and research it thoroughly.

BELIEVE IN YOUR TOPIC   Consider your personal values and beliefs when selecting a topic. Make sure that your beliefs and the topic you choose are compatible. This is particularly important in persuasive speaking; you could hardly expect your audience to be convinced of the need for tougher environmental laws, for instance, if you yourself were not firmly convinced. A firm belief in your topic will make the presentation more vital to you and to your audience.

NARROWING THE TOPIC

As we saw earlier, once you have selected a topic, you must narrow it down so that it is workable. Don't be like the high school student who decided to deliver his first speech ever on "The French Revolution." How narrow should your topic be? That depends upon your purpose. The thrust of a speech will vary according to whether it is intended to inform, persuade, or entertain. For example, in a well-coordinated effort, several elected city officials addressed their fellow citizens on the financial crisis in their city. The focus of each individual address was different. In a formal televised statement, the mayor, whose purpose was to inform the public of the crisis situation, focused on the current fiscal deficits and the long-range consequences of inaction. At a later press conference, a councilman outlined the kinds of legislation necessary to relieve the crisis situation. A third member of the city council was given the job of persuading the citizens who attended a town hall meeting to write letters or send telegrams to state and federal government officials encouraging them to pass legislation to relieve the financial crisis. Although each speech dealt with the finances of the city, the thrust of each address was determined by the speaker's purpose.

A good speaker should consider personal purposes and goals as well. For example, if you are trying to establish a good reputation with a particular ethnic or occupational group, you should select your topic accordingly.

Another important consideration when defining your topic is to determine your central thought. One of the most glaring faults of beginners and poor speakers is lack of focus. Good speeches are much like other works of art—musical compositions, paintings, plays, or literary works—they consist of separate elements that become unified into a whole by means of a central idea or thought.

GATHERING SOURCE MATERIALS

After selecting your topic and narrowing it down, you can begin to collect the materials you need to build your speech.

Use of Sources It is usually to your advantage to select from a wide variety of sources. The type and number of sources you use will depend on the specific purpose of your speech. When presenting an informative speech on a controversial issue, you should always secure information on at least two opposing views, especially when one source of information is biased. For example, if you were presenting a speech on the gas shortage, you might find that the explanations of the shortage and the consequent increase in prices presented in an oil company publication would be quite different from the facts and arguments put forth in a consumer group pamphlet. In a situation like this, you should consult several sources in order to get the true picture. Of course, when presenting a persuasive speech, you may choose to include only those sources that support your particular point of view. Even then it is important to be aware of the opposition.

Whether you conduct an interview, read a magazine article, or watch a videotape, it is essential to take notes. Your notes should include summaries of the information and direct quotations, particularly if you plan to use them in your speech. Ethical considerations and accuracy necessitate the use of a quotation in the context in which it was found. When direct quotations are not in order, summaries of information are sufficient.

You as Source The most basic and obvious source at your disposal is yourself. Whether you realize it or not, you represent a storehouse of knowledge, experience, and observations. The fact that you remember paying twenty cents for a slice of pizza when you were in junior high school may be trivial. However, if you are going to give an informative speech on inflation and the cost of living, this information could suddenly assume significance. In general, personal anecdotes, examples, experiences, and observations make a speech more meaningful for the speaker and more colorful for the audience.

Interviews You will often find that the best source of materials for a particular subject is another person or group of people. In that case you may want to gather your material by conducting an interview.

PERSONAL INTERVIEW A *personal interview* is conducted on a one-to-one basis with a person who has information or knowledge about the topic of your speech. For example, if you were to present a speech on penal reform, you might want to interview a lawyer, an inmate, a judge, and other individuals connected with the penal system. If you were presenting an informative speech on a particular diet fad, you might find it valuable to interview a doctor, a nutritionist, someone who had success with the diet, and someone who did not. Although a personal interview may provide a sizeable amount of material, information or opinions obtained by this method should not be considered definitive. The impact an interview will have on your audience depends on how that particular audience judges the credibility of your source.

Regardless of the subject, a good interview requires good technique. If you choose to conduct an interview, keep certain things in mind:

1. Remember your purpose and topic and avoid getting sidetracked.
2. As an interviewer, you should try to make the person you interview feel comfortable and willing to talk. Obviously, a cooperative interviewee will make your task much easier.
3. Be prepared for the interview and have definite questions in mind.
4. Since you are trying to find out specific information or opinions, phrase your questions in such a way that they will bring clear responses.

If the topic of your speech lends itself to a personal interview and an appropriate interviewee is available, you will find this method an invaluable source of material.

What type of planning is necessary when the interviewee is unknown to the interviewer?
(Ken Karp)

SURVEY   At times you may need to conduct a survey rather than a personal interview. A *survey* is a detailed gathering of information by questionnaire, observation, interview, and so forth. A survey enables you to gain a cross-section of information and opinions. Suppose you were giving an informative speech on the sexual mores of today's college students. You might wish to conduct a survey of as large a sample of your fellow students as possible in order to obtain some firsthand information. As in the case of the personal interview, the information and opinions obtained through a survey are not meant to be definitive. Although both sources are most useful when used informally, the validity of a survey can be judged in terms of standardization of questions and the selection of participants.

Printed Material   Printed material has long been relied on as the primary source of information for speech content. Such material includes books, magazines, journals, pamphlets, newspapers, diaries, almanacs, encyclopedias, and so on. There are so many different types of printed material that it is essential to know how to locate these different sources and use them properly. Information about some subjects is almost exclusively found in printed material. For example, historical information that cannot be gained through a personal interview may be found in books or in a journal, and reports about current breakthroughs in science or medicine might be located in professional journals or magazines.

Today, thanks to microfilm, printed material can be stored in a minimum amount of space. Libraries are the primary storage houses for printed material, but you may find it necessary or beneficial to search out other sources. If you were doing a speech on alcoholism, you could find printed information in the vertical file of the library, or you might visit a local branch of Alcoholics Anonymous and pick up pamphlets or newsletters regarding their programs and services. Many such special interest groups, consumer organizations, churches, trade unions, and so on, publish their own small newspapers or booklets about their activities.

Electronic Media   Modern technology has provided us with additional sources of material in the form of electronic media. Films, television, cassettes, records, and videotapes are all valuable sources of information that can aid you in the preparation of a speech. For example, the now famous Zabruder film of the Kennedy assassination proved to be a vital source of evidence for those who urged further investigation of the shooting. Also, since the advent of videotape, many events have been captured on film and are available as source material for the speaker.

PARTS OF THE SPEECH

All speeches, regardless of their purpose or length, should be composed of three basic units: the introduction, the body, and the conclusion. Each of

A young historian went to the Ivory Coast to tape legends from an Akan tribal chief.
(Marc & Evelyne Bernheim, Woodfin Camp Associates)

these parts serves at least one function that is essential to the effectiveness of the speech. Although each part of the speech should flow smoothly into the next, each unit should be identifiable upon analysis of the text.

Examine the following two brief speeches, which were prepared for a training seminar for magazine salespeople. Read each presentation carefully and decide which one is more effective.

> There are many different magazines from which a person can choose. For the sports enthusiast, there are magazines like *Sports Illustrated* and *Field and Stream*. The homemaker might want to learn new recipes or tips on decorating from the *Ladies Home Journal* or *Redbook*. Those who enjoy literary magazines may turn to the *Saturday Review* or *The New Yorker*, while others may be interested in general news magazines like *Time* or *Newsweek*. These magazines vary in price and frequency of publication and are available through our subscription service.
>
> * * * * *
>
> Have you ever been stuck in a doctor's office or train station without anything to keep your mind off waiting? Or maybe you were stuck inside with

a cold or waiting for a delivery? Perhaps if you had an interesting magazine to read, the waiting wouldn't seem so long.

There are many different and interesting magazines from which one can choose. For the sports enthusiast, there are magazines such as *Sports Illustrated* and *Field and Stream*. The homemaker might want to learn a new recipe or tips on decorating from a magazine like the *Ladies Home Journal* or *Redbook*. Those who enjoy literary magazines may be interested in reading a copy of the *Saturday Review* or *The New Yorker*, while others might be interested in a general news magazine like *Time* or *Newsweek*. These are just a few of the many magazines which can be readily purchased by subscription.

The number of magazines published is quite large. One can safely say that there is a magazine for every area of interest, whether it be crafts, sports, science, health, automobiles, food, fashion, gardening, or anything else. And what makes it even better is that they are all available through subscription.

Although these two speeches contain basically the same information, the second speech is obviously more effective. It has a carefully developed introduction, body, and conclusion.

The Introduction

The ***introduction*** of a speech must first catch and then focus audience attention as well as preview the body of the speech. Sometimes just getting started is one of the most crucial and difficult tasks in presenting a speech.

Often a speaker has to compete with a noisy or inattentive crowd. In such cases it is even more important to capture the audience's attention with an effective introduction.

There are several standard devices you can use for an effective introduction. These include the use of a startling statement (By the year 2025 the earth will run out of food), a rhetorical question (Did you ever wonder what your life would be like had you been born in another era?), statistics (Only 1,400 out of 2,000 college freshmen will earn their degree), a humorous statement (If all the world's a stage, then a lot of us get bit parts), or a famous quotation (You may fool all the people some of the time; you can even fool some of the people all the time; but you can't fool all of the people all the time). Of course, sometimes one statement produces two or more effects. For example, the statement "One out of every three marriages ends in divorce" uses statistics but may also be somewhat shocking to an audience.

THESIS STATEMENT The introduction of a speech should also include a ***thesis statement*** that presents the specific purpose of the speech. The purpose can sometimes be worked into the opening device for getting attention. For example, a museum sponsor might begin a fundraising speech with:

You don't have to go to a peep show to see some of the most beautiful nudes imaginable. Some of the world's most famous nudes can be found right here in our museum. But, unless we can find a way to raise twenty thousand dollars for maintenance costs, these nudes are going to be left out in the cold!

The opening line of this introductory paragraph begins with an unexpected or startling statement. Chances are, at least a few ears will perk up with the words "peep show." The remainder of the paragraph suggests that the museum is in financial trouble and must raise money to continue its operations. The last sentence suggests the purpose of the speech and gives some insight into what the main text will be about.

Regardless of the technique you use in your opening, be sure that the introduction is appropriate, is in good taste, and says exactly what you want it to say. You should not use a joke or anecdote unless it is appropriate to the occasion and relevant to the subject. You should avoid telling a joke or humorous story unless you feel perfectly comfortable with it. Remember, not everyone is a comedian. You should also omit ir-

A speech in preparation: A portion of President John F. Kennedy's inaugural address.

> ask not
> what your country is going to do
> for you — ask what you can do
> for your country — my fellow
> citizen of the world — ask not
> what America will do for you —
> but rather what you can do
> for freedom   Rather ask of us —
> the same high standard of
> sacrifice and strength of heart
> and will that we need for a

relevant "warm up material" and clichéd beginnings such as, "A funny thing happened to me on the way . . ." Your introduction should be relatively brief and direct.

The Body The effective introduction previews the main text of the speech and leads directly into the body. The *body* is generally the largest part of the speech and is intended to present the main points, elaborate on them, and clarify when necessary. It is also a function of the body to develop clear transitions between different ideas.

In an informative speech the body contains the bulk of the information you wish to present. In a persuasive speech the body contains the ar-

(United Press International)

DEVELOPING AND ORGANIZING THE MESSAGE

guments and evidence that support the speaker's position, as well as a refutation of any counterarguments. For example, if you were trying to persuade your audience to support the abolition of capital punishment, the body of the speech would probably include moral and legal arguments along with appropriate supporting material. You might also include statistics to disprove the standard counterarguments, which contend that capital punishment is a deterrent to crime, or those that attempt to justify capital punishment on the basis of "an eye for an eye."

In a persuasive speech the body should include a discussion of the nature, effects, and causes of the problem, issue, or controversy. A politician trying to change the juvenile justice system because it is too lenient might want to include statistics showing a high percentage of juvenile felonies, case histories of chronic juvenile offenders, and the opinions of sources who have experience in the legal system. The speaker should show why the particular problem is meaningful to the audience. In the above example the politician might try to convince the audience that it is no longer safe to go outside or that children and the elderly increasingly fall prey to juvenile criminals.

The body is the longest and most detailed part of your speech, so the arrangement of its ideas is very important. To help you structure the body of your speech effectively, there are certain patterns of organization you can follow. These patterns of organization include a topical pattern, a chronological pattern, a spatial pattern, and various other patterns. Since the organization of the body is so important to effective speechmaking, we will discuss these structural arrangements in greater depth later in the chapter. Simply stated, however, the body of the speech should be presented in a way that is logical, coherent, and easy to follow.

A speech isn't over until the speaker walks away from the podium. Therefore, the **conclusion** of the speech is as important as the introduction. Although the major portion of the speech is presented in the body, it is the conclusion that can leave a lasting impression.

The Conclusion

In general, the conclusion of an informative speech should offer a restatement of the major ideas and a summary of the overall content. Concluding a speech on what to look for in buying a car, a speaker might restate specific guidelines such as economy, safety, and size as well as summarize the ways in which these guidelines can assist the buyer. Similarly, a demonstration talk on how to make a macramé wall hanging should end with a summary of the necessary materials and specific steps involved.

The conclusion of a speech gives you an opportunity to tie up loose ends and bring the speech to a unified end. Since it is impossible for the audience to listen to and remember everything that is said, the conclusion should emphasize the main points so that the audience knows what was most important.

In a persuasive speech the conclusion may be used to arouse the au-

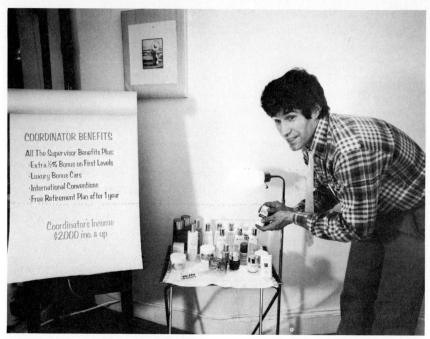

Using visual aids can help summarize key points in the conclusion of a speech.
(Laimute E. Druskis)

dience to action. Let's examine the conclusion to the speech presented by our museum sponsor:

> In conclusion, ladies and gentlemen and patrons of the arts, it is time to assure our magnificent paintings a place inside our museum. For many years you have enjoyed the beauty of these fine paintings. Now it is time to give something in return. Take out your wallet or your checkbook and give what you can to help raise the twenty thousand dollars we need to keep our museum doors open!

This paragraph underscores the purpose of the speech and asks for some action on the part of the audience. A concluding call for action need not always be financial, of course. The president of a parents' group may end an address with a plea to parents to keep their children home from school as a protest against a cutback in school services. Or a union delegate might ask an audience to join a boycott of crops picked by nonunion workers. A political candidate might conclude a rally by asking for volunteers to distribute campaign literature. In each case the call for action would be strongest in the concluding paragraph.

Regardless of purpose, the concluding paragraph should round out the speech and bring it to a satisfying close. The final sentence should signal the end of the speech so that the audience will know that it is over. The speaker may want to close with an emphatic statement or use one of

> Industry in art is a necessity—not a virtue—and any evidence of the same, in the production, is a blemish, not a quality; a proof, not of achievement, but of absolutely insufficient work, for work alone will efface the footsteps of work.
>
> James McNeill Whistler

the devices mentioned in our discussion of the introduction. For example, if you want to leave the audience thinking, you might pose a rhetorical question. Or, depending upon the content of the speech, you might want to conclude with a famous quotation.

Sometimes you might want to coordinate the conclusion with the introduction and use the same type of device or even the same statement. For instance, a community leader who opens with the quote from Abraham Lincoln that we mentioned earlier may close the speech thus: "You cannot fool all of the people all the time; and all of us here tonight know that *now* is the time to demand an end to the irresponsible actions of the City Council." Using the same quotation or same set of statistics not only reinforces a point but also lends your speech a sense of closure and balance.

We should not overlook the use of transitions as an important aspect of speech organization. A ***transition*** is the bridge that allows one idea to flow smoothly into the next.

Transitions

The most important transitions are those between the introduction and the body and between the body and the conclusion. However, they are also necessary between the main ideas within the body. For example, in a speech presented at a block association meeting, a neighborhood detective was discussing an increase in local crimes. One major point was that in recent years there seemed to have been a tremendous increase in auto thefts and robberies. To lead into his next point, the detective added, "But, unfortunately, the problem has not remained in the streets. Latest precinct reports show that household break-ins and burglaries in the area are up 50 percent over last year." The shift from crime on the street to crime indoors was smoothly made by a simple transitional statement.

The complexity of a transitional bridge depends upon how similar the two ideas are that are being connected. Sometimes just a few words or a simple sentence will do. For example, certain phrases, such as "in addition to," "aside from," and "in conclusion," are often used as transitional bridges.

When ideas are not closely related, you may need a more substantial transition, in other words, something that draws a connection between the two ideas or parts. A woman speaking to a group of senior citizens may wish to convince them of the need for an urban renewal project and at the same time assure them of the preservation of their neighborhood. The two points may be related in this way:

> Perhaps you feel that all of these changes I have proposed will destroy the charm of our downtown area. However, along with the plans for change are many plans for the restoration of our historical sites and parks. The kind of rebuilding now proposed will be in keeping with the tastes and needs of our community.

The effective use of transitions is one way to distinguish between a good speech and a mediocre one.

ARRANGEMENT OF THE BODY OF THE SPEECH

Patterns for Informative Speeches We have already mentioned several standard patterns of organization that can help you structure your speech and present your ideas with the greatest effectiveness. The pattern you choose will probably depend on your topic. Certain subjects are best suited to particular patterns of organization. We will now discuss some of the standard patterns most frequently used in the informative speech. It is important to remember that audiences retain more information when speeches are well organized.[1]

TOPICAL PATTERN   One of the most frequently used organizational patterns is the *topical pattern,* in which information is presented according to a specific category or classification. This type of organization is particularly useful when the subject of the speech can be divided into subparts that form a whole. For example, a speaker at a children's concert might introduce the audience to various parts of the orchestra by using a topical approach. He or she could discuss the strings, then the brass, then the woodwinds, and finally, the percussion instruments. Each of the major divisions could then be broken down according to the general characteristics of each group and the specific instruments within each category.

CHRONOLOGICAL PATTERN   A second standard pattern of organization is the *chronological pattern,* which follows a subject in time. The chronological pattern is particularly useful when presenting biographical or historical information or when tracing the development of an idea, institution, or movement. A speech on the development of television could be presented in a chronological pattern, following events from the conception of TV to the present. Or a speech on American fashion in the twentieth century could be divided into decades, mentioning things such as the "Flapper" style of the 1920s and the miniskirt of the 1960s.

[1]C. Spicer and R. E. Bassett, "The Effects of Organization on Learning from an Information Message," *Southern Speech Communication Journal* 41 (1976):298.

A chronological speech may span centuries or days, depending on the scope of the topic. Since it is virtually impossible to do justice in a relatively short speech to a topic that covers an enormous period of time, the speaker must focus on the most important information. You must also make sure that the audience is aware of the time lapse between events, especially when the events or information you are discussing have occurred at uneven intervals. For example, in presenting a biographical sketch, you might connect one event to the next with phrases such as "two years later" or "in a matter of weeks" in order to give the audience some perspective as regards the time that has passed. The use of transitional phrases is particularly important when presenting a speech according to chronology.

Remember, nobody wants to hear innumerable small details. Even in everyday conversation an unnecessarily detailed account of an event or an experience can become very boring. Children are often guilty of this practice. For example, you may ask a child what a certain television program was about, and he or she will repeat an endless sequence of events. Obviously, each step is not an integral part of the story. However, the child has not learned how to decide what information is most important. A speaker must be able to determine the most important information, since he or she cannot include too many ideas, events, or details without causing the speech to become lengthy and tiresome.

SPATIAL PATTERN   Not every subject is suited to every pattern of organization. Topics based on the location of one part in relation to others or on a geographical progression may best be presented in a *spatial* order. A speech that traces the westward expansion of America might be divided according to the extension of different geographic boundaries. (Note that the same speech might possibly be presented using a chronological order as well.) A speech based on Christopher Columbus's discovery of the New World might follow his historical routes.

A spatial organization may be appropriate for certain subjects not related to geography at all. For example, an architect presenting a speech on the pyramids might approach the topic from a spatial order, emphasizing the relationship between one part of the structure and another. A spatial organization enables the audience to visualize the individual parts as they relate to one another in terms of the whole.

PATTERN OF INCREASING DIFFICULTY   Since one of the primary factors in evaluating the success of an informative speech is audience understanding, the speaker must strive to present the speech as clearly and logically as possible. When a topic is relatively complex, the speaker may choose to use a pattern of organization based on *increasing levels of difficulty.* This type of structure is particularly helpful when presenting an informative talk on a subject with which the audience is unfamiliar. When a plant manager explains the changes that will take place within a factory due to automation, he or she may want to present the information in varying degrees of difficulty. Since the comprehension of some ideas is based on understanding other ideas, a pattern of increasing difficulty helps to ease the progression. Audiences feel much more comfortable after they have mastered an idea or understood some particular bit of information. By carefully building one idea upon another, a speaker can present increasingly complex material to an audience whose confidence in its own interpretive and evaluative abilities also increases.

CHAIN-OF-EVENTS PATTERN   As the name implies, this pattern of organization is based on the development of a series of steps, with each step depending on the previous one. For example, a local congresswoman addressing members of the Young Democratic Club in her district might use the chain-of-events method to explain the sequence of events that must occur as a bill goes from the committee stage to its actual enactment as law. Similarly, a weatherman predicting a fifty-fifty chance of a snowstorm might outline the series of weather events that must occur in succession in order for the storm to develop. The *chain-of-events* method is particularly useful when giving a demonstration speech that explains a certain procedure. For example, a salesperson demonstrating the use of a vacuum cleaner would show the customer how to operate the machine according to step-by-step directions.

Patterns for **Persuasive Speeches**

Various patterns of organization are particularly well suited to the persuasive speech. While these methods are not restricted to persuasive speeches, they are often used in them. Remember that the purpose of a persuasive speech is to create attitude change within the listener.

INDUCTIVE PATTERN   The first pattern is the ***inductive pattern.*** This particular pattern of organization is based on the process of inductive reasoning, which we discussed in the previous chapter. In an inductive argument you present the audience with several specific cases that serve as the basis for a generalization. The specific cases must, of course, support the generalization. Therefore, you must avoid examples that are inconsistent with or contradictory to the generalization you wish to make.

The number of specifics necessary to formulate a sound generalization will vary. Although there are mathematical calculations to determine statistical validity, you can usually rely on common sense and intuition to decide upon the minimum number of specific cases that a particular argument demands. For example, a senior citizen who condemns all teenagers as "dope fiends," based on the solitary example of his neighbor's son, lacks a sufficient number of specific examples. Therefore, the generalization is invalid. When the generalization involves a large population, a greater number of specific cases is necessary.

Certain generalizations are easier to support than others. For example, U.S. health officials who sought to end the swine flu inoculation program in 1976–1977 used an inductive argument. Citing several incidents of paralysis as a side effect of the injection, officials provided enough evidence to ban the program. The argument might have followed this pattern:

SPECIFICS: I. Specific cases of paralysis following inoculation.
                     A. Cases of paralysis in Florida.
                     B. Cases of paralysis in Denver.
                     C. Cases of paralysis in New Jersey.
GENERALIZATION: II. The swine flu inoculation can cause paralysis.
CONCLUSION: III. Therefore, the inoculation program is potentially hazardous and should be discontinued.

Based on the occurrence of cases of paralysis following the shots, health officials decided that the inoculation could conceivably have caused paralysis and therefore concluded that the program should be discontinued. The generalization that the inoculation could cause paralysis was evolved through an inductive process based on the occurrence of scattered cases of this side effect. While some experts discounted this argument, emphasizing that the percentage of cases of paralysis was quite small relative to the number of persons receiving the shot, the program was discontinued.

DEDUCTIVE PATTERN   The inverse of the inductive pattern is the **deductive pattern,** in which a speaker applies a generalization to specific cases. The generalization, if accepted by the audience, serves as the basis for an effective argument.

In a deductive pattern of organization, the speaker must draw a conclusion about a specific case based on its applicability to a previously accepted generalization. In Chapter 10 we mentioned the syllogism, which is the most common example of deductive reasoning. An effective argument can be organized in the form of a syllogism. For example, a concerned member of the community may offer the following deductive argument at a public transportation hearing:

GENERALIZATION: We are all agreed that traffic lights reduce accidents.
SPECIFIC: There seem to be a lot of accidents at the intersection of 40th and Vine.
CONCLUSION: Therefore, a light at the intersection of 40th and Vine would reduce the number of accidents.

If the traffic officials agree with the citizen's general statement, they might be quite willing to accept the solution. If the general statement is not accepted by an audience, however, the deductive argument will have little effect. Generalizations based on value judgments are most difficult to validate. Therefore, a speaker must have some insight into the nature of the audience. Let us examine the following deductive argument:

GENERALIZATION: All war is immoral.
     SPECIFIC: Vietnam was a war.
CONCLUSION: Vietnam was immoral.

The effectiveness of this deductive argument depends on the audience's acceptance of the general statement. Undoubtedly, an audience of conscientious objectors would accept this argument. However, the same argument would probably be vehemently rejected if presented before an audience of Veterans of Foreign Wars. Therefore, in preparing a deductive argument, the speaker must be sure that the audience will agree with the general statement.

CAUSE-AND-EFFECT PATTERN   Closely related to the inductive argument is the **cause-and-effect pattern.** In this type of presentation, the speaker establishes a relationship between two events. The speaker attempts to convince the audience that this relationship is one of cause and effect, or that a certain result is the product of a specific event. For example, at a monthly sales meeting, an assistant buyer suggests that the increase in hosiery sales is due to a new line of pantyhose. In this case the argument could be confirmed. According to the record of sales, the new line of pantyhose contributed to an increase of 25 percent of the total volume of hosiery sales. Therefore, the new line of pantyhose (cause) produced an increase in sales (effect). However, not all cause-and-effect arguments can be mathematically determined. For example, how could you substantiate a claim that natural catastrophes such as earthquakes and floods increase as a result of our tampering with the atmosphere? Although it might be argued that these disasters have been more prevalent following milestones in space exploration, it would be impossible to draw a causal relationship between the two events.

Often one effect is the result of several causes. For example, when a heretofore losing team moved into a new stadium and started to win, the cheering fans were convinced that the new stadium brought the team luck. In a case such as this, the exact cause of the team's success would be a combination of things, including perhaps the new stadium, an increase in attendance, errors on the part of the opposition, the return of an important player after an injury, and so forth.

PROBLEM-SOLUTION PATTERN   Another useful pattern of organization for the persuasive speech is the **problem-solution method.** This approach is much the same as the pattern of organization used in group discussions (see Chapter 7). The problem-solving method, first described by John Dewey, includes the following basic steps:

1. What is the nature of the problem?
2. What are the causes?
3. What are the possible solutions?
4. Which is the best solution?
5. How can this solution be put into effect?

Remember our traffic light example earlier? Let's examine this example according to the problem-solution pattern. The nature of the problem concerns the number of accidents at the intersection of 40th and Vine. Causes of the problem include the use of this route as an alternative to the parkway, with a subsequent increase in traffic, and the lack of any traffic signs or personnel. Possible solutions include a traffic light, a police officer to direct traffic, rerouting the traffic, and a four-way stop sign at the intersection. The best solution would be a traffic light, since a police officer would be too costly, a four-way stop sign might prove confusing, and rerouting the traffic would cause congestion on neighboring roads. The solution could best be put into effect by a decision by the Department of Traffic and the installation of the light by the same agency.

The problem-solution pattern is based on a logical, step-by-step analysis of a particular problem. Of course, the analysis of any problem requires considerable research and investigation.

PRINCIPLES OF OUTLINING

Regardless of the organizational pattern you select, an outline helps you in the preparation as well as the delivery of your speech. The outline is a tool that allows the speaker to categorize information and separate main ideas from subordinate ones. For example, in a topical presentation the speaker would classify each aspect of the subject as a main division of the outline. In our previous example of an informative speech on the parts of the orchestra, the strings, brass, woodwinds, and percussion would each be represented as a major category of the outline. Each category would then be subdivided into specific instruments and general characteristics. Part of such an outline would look like this:

Parts of the Orchestra

I. The Strings
  A. Types of String Instruments
    1. Violin
    2. Viola
    3. Cello
    4. Double bass
    5. Harp
  B. Characteristics of the String Instruments
    1. Sounds produced by plucking, bowing, or striking strings
    2. Many are fretted
II. The Brass

A chronological pattern of organization may be used in an outline that divides the topic by specific intervals such as decades, years, or weeks, depending on the scope of the topic. For example, a speech on American automobiles in the twentieth century might be divided into discussions of types of cars at the turn of the century, in the 1920s, in the 1930s, and so forth.

(Ken Karp)

Although the outlines may vary in form, the basic principles remain the same. Some speakers prefer to use Roman numerals for each major part of the speech, using I for the introduction, II for the body, and III for the conclusion. Capital letters are then used for main ideas within the text of the speech. However, regardless of the form, you should remember that details presented in an outline get more specific with each subdivision. Look at the outline in Figure 11-1. Notice how the two major divisions (I and II) relate to the general topic of the outline (Effects of Air Pollution). As you can see, the information gets more specific with each division, and each detail relates directly to the preceding category.

All forms of outlining share certain basic principles. These principles include simplicity, coordination, subordination, progression, and symbolization.[2]

Simplicity   The outline is intended to assist, not confuse, the speaker. Therefore, you should keep the outline simple, so that each line of it represents a single piece of information. You should decide whether to use single words, phrases, or sentences and then be consistent throughout the outline. The outline is a valuable organizational tool if it is not allowed to become too cumbersome.

[2]Glen E. Mills, *Putting a Message Together,* 2d ed. (Minneapolis: Bobbs-Merrill, 1972), pp. 26–29.

✳ Good Outline: ✳

Effects of Air Pollution

I. How Does Air Pollution Affect Health?
  A. What respiratory conditions are related to pollution?
    1. Respiratory condition X
      a. Cases of X
      b. Deaths due to X
    2. Respiratory condition Y
      a. Cases of Y
      b. Deaths due to Y
  B. What allergies are related to pollution?
    1. Allergy Q
    2. Allergy Z
II. How Does Air Pollution Affect Environment?
  A. How does air pollution affect agriculture.
    1. Effect on growth of vegetation
    2. Effect on crop yield
  B. How does air pollution affect the atmosphere?
    1. Increase in carbon dioxide level
    2. Destruction of ozone layer

FIGURE 11-1   A Sample Outline.

The principle of ***coordination*** is basic to the logical arrangement of an Coordination
outline. The speaker must remember that all points within a subdivision
must be related. For example, a speech on Bicentennial sights in the eastern United States might be organized spatially by specific states.

Bicentennial Sights in the Eastern United States
I. Sights in Massachusetts
  A. Concord
  B. Plymouth Rock
  C. Boston Harbor
  D. Liberty Bell

If you know your American history, you will observe that entry D is out
of place, since the Liberty Bell is in Pennsylvania. Incorrect placement of
information is a problem of coordination. Although the above example is
quite obvious, sometimes the speaker may have a difficult time finding an
appropriate spot for certain information. If the information is essential, it
may mean reorganizing the categories to include it.

The principle of ***subordination*** refers to the way a main idea is divided Subordination
into subordinate points, with each specific piece of information relating
directly to the preceding category. In the above example Concord relates
directly to the larger category of Bicentennial sights in Massachusetts,
which in turn relates directly to the overall topic of the speech, Bicentennial sights in the eastern United States.

Progression   It is important to arrange ideas in some sort of logical ***progression.*** For example, in a speech about local government, the speaker might identify the three main categories of the outline as local government in the city, in the county, and in the township. The speaker should then decide upon the order of these main categories, based on either an ascending or a descending order of complexity or size. The speaker should select a logical progression of ideas and remain consistent in the arrangement of major ideas and subordinate points.

Symbolization   The ***symbolization*** of the outline serves as a visual form of the coordination, subordination, and progression of the speech. Therefore, it is important that use of numbers and letters be consistent throughout the outline. To check the coordination of the speech, you may ask yourself, "Do subdivisions A, B, and C all relate to main point I?"

The indentation of subdivisions represents their position as subordinate points. A general rule to follow is that in breaking down a category, there should always be at least two subordinate points. If there is a capital A there should be a capital B. Similarly, if capital A is to be subdivided, there should be numbers 1 and 2. If you find this rule hard to follow, chances are you need to expand particular categories.

Lastly, progression is logically represented through symbolization. If your speech is based on degrees of increasing complexity, you may check that the materials presented in points I and II lead up to and provide the basis for what you will present in division III. (For more detailed outlines, see Appendix B.)

SUPPORTING MATERIAL

One of the advantages of using an outline is that it enables you to see if you have adequate supporting material. Supporting material serves a variety of functions and is essential to all speeches, whether they are to inform, persuade, or entertain.

Clarification   One of the basic functions of supporting material is to clarify an idea, opinion, or argument. Remember that in an informative speech, it is the goal of the speaker to make sure that the audience understands the message. In a persuasive speech you must be sure that the audience has a clear understanding of your position. If you want to entertain or impress an audience with a story of perilous travels in the desert, you may need to make clear the distances between watering places or the hostile nature of the surrounding peoples. Clarification is an important aspect of all speeches.

EXAMPLES   You can clarify an idea, opinion, or concept in many ways. One way is to use an example. The example may be real, hypothetical, or extended. Throughout this text you have been given examples to help you better understand particular concepts. Some of the examples have been real, others hypothetical. A *real example* refers to an event or incident that actually happened. A *hypothetical example* is based on something that could possibly occur but that did not really happen. In the previous section on the organization of persuasive speeches, we offered two examples of inductive reasoning. The swine flu inoculation example was based on real events; the pantyhose example was hypothetical. Yet both examples helped to clarify a description of the inductive pattern that otherwise might have been meaningless to the reader.

An *extended example* is one that is carried out to considerable length in order to clarify or emphasize a very important idea. When singer James Brown talks to young audiences and advises them to stay in school, he offers an example of his own personal experience as a dropout and extends it to what might happen to members of his audience who do the same. In this case his extended example is real. However, a speaker can extend a hypothetical example as well. For instance, a dietician might discuss the future health problems of a hypothetical family indifferent to good nutrition in its members' daily lives.

ILLUSTRATIONS   Another means of clarification is the use of *illustrations.* While examples are verbal illustrations, sometimes the speaker may find a visual aid very helpful in clarifying information. A doctor delivering an informative speech on a new surgical technique for open heart surgery probably would find a series of diagrams useful in his or her presentation. If you have ever attempted to assemble an "easily assembled" piece of furniture or equipment, you may appreciate the value of a visual aid in clarifying otherwise confusing directions.

ANECDOTES   Speakers sometimes use an *anecdote* to clarify a particular idea or point of information. An anecdote is generally a brief story that relates to an important idea in the speech. It is particularly useful as an introductory device when appropriate to the overall topic of the speech. For instance, a young woman who wishes to give a humorous talk about college life may start with an anecdote about finding her mother's old raccoon coat in a trunk in the basement.

An anecdote may be real or imaginary, personal or impersonal. Although an anecdote does not offer any hard evidence, it does help clarify and emphasize your point or position. For example, a fire official delivering a speech to elementary school children on the dangers of false alarms might relate the well-known fable "The Boy Who Cried Wolf" as a way to clarify the message.

DEFINITIONS   After analyzing your topic and audience, you might decide that a definition of terms is necessary to make sure that the audience understands your points. Since language is often ambiguous, it is important that you clarify any misunderstanding relating to definitions of words.

There are several different ways to define a word, idea, or concept. Some ideas can be defined by *description.* For example, in a speech on

> The source of authority may be expert opinion, official pronouncements, religious symbols, the pomp and ceremony of institutional practice, the sayings or doings of the socially elect, or even the printed word or the tone of voice.
>
> Daniel Katz and Richard L. Schanck

the kibbutzim of Israel, a speaker might want to describe this type of communal living in order to clarify audience understanding of the topic.

Sometimes a word, idea, or concept can best be defined by *comparison* or *contrast.* A definition by comparison suggests the similarity of something unknown to something with which the audience is already familiar. Someone discussing musical instruments of the Middle Ages might define a lute by comparing it with a guitar. Similarly, a speaker may define a term through contrast. In the same lecture the speaker might define a clavichord as an early ancestor of the piano, pointing out the essential differences between the two.

Sometimes a speaker has to provide the audience with an *operational* definition, one that is used only for the duration of the speech. For example, the president of a large corporation, addressing stockholders on the success of the company in the previous fiscal year, has to clarify what he or she means by "success." It is possible that the president's definition does not coincide with that of the stockholders.

Support Some material is used to support rather than to clarify. Particularly in persuasive speeches, speakers must carefully provide material that gives substance to their message and enhances their position. Using evidence in a speech supports your position.[3] It also helps sustain attitude change in your listeners.[4]

EXAMPLES Once again, the use of different types of examples can be helpful. You must be sure to use a sufficient number of examples to confirm your ideas or opinions. A journalist reporting on corruption in a city agency should be able to come up with several examples of wrongdoing in order to demonstrate the problem. While one incident might make an important story, many examples would be needed to prove widespread corruption.

You must also give examples that are representative or typical of the position you support. If a psychiatrist advocates a certain kind of therapy for severe depression, he or she might support this position by citing sev-

[3]T. B. Harte, "The Effects of Evidence in Persuasive Communication," *Central States Speech Journal* 27 (1976): 45–46.
[4]J. C. McCroskey, "The Effects of Evidence as an Inhibitor of Counterpersuasion," *Speech Monographs* 37 (1970): 188–94.

eral examples of cases in which this therapy was successful. If the cases described were not cases of severe depression, the examples would be inappropriate and unsupportive.

Examples used to support a position must also be representative of the total picture. When the owner of a nursing home sought to defend himself against media charges of poor conditions, he cited the case of one elderly gentleman who found the home so comfortable that he wrote the owner a thank-you note. On investigation it was found that this example was atypical and certainly not representative of what most of the patients felt. A speaker must be extremely careful when choosing examples.

STATISTICS   Another way to support your presentation is with facts and figures. Statistics can be very valuable if used skillfully. A business executive suggesting a merger with another company could incorporate statistics into the speech to show how the merger would be profitable for the firm. A scientist promoting a particular drug would cite statistical results of different experiments.

It must be stressed that statistics have to be used effectively. In most situations the speaker should round off statistics to the nearest whole number. Remember, the audience is hearing the statistics for the first time, and the numbers must be easily interpreted. Statistics can be intimidating, so avoid overwhelming your audience with too many facts and figures. Fractions and decimals are often confusing and add little to listener understanding. Approximations such as "close to 30 percent" or "over a quarter of a million" give a general picture without burdening the listener with specific numbers. Nonetheless, the speaker must know when it is important to use exact figures. For example, a proponent of a particular bill narrowly defeated by Congress may quote the exact figures when discussing the issue at a press conference to show that there had been considerable support for the legislation.

If you use statistics, you must always make them meaningful for the listener. One way to do this is to present the statistics in the form of comparisons. For example, in a speech on state aid to education, a senator may tell his or her audience of college students that "for every dollar you spend on tuition, the state legislature spends five to educate you." In this case, the relationship between student expense and state expense is made clear by comparison.

The ethical speaker will keep in mind that statistics are often misleading and that certain statistics can be found to "prove" almost anything. The speaker and the audience should be aware that statistics do not always give an accurate representation. For example, an audience was greatly impressed when a golfer reported that he came in third in a recent tournament until they found out that there were only three participants. It is a matter of ethics to avoid such misleading information and half-truths.

Testimony You should not overlook the value of **testimony** as supportive material. A person's testimony can often add validity to an informative or persuasive speech. Of course, the value of testimony depends on the credibility of the source. Basically, testimony can be derived from either a direct witness to an event or from an expert in a particular field. The appropriate use of testimony is determined by the nature of the subject. For example, in discussing the safety hazards in building construction, a speaker might give the testimony of several people who survived the collapse of a recently constructed hotel.

Expert testimony often proves helpful in both persuasive and informative speeches. A speaker supporting the idea of a conspiracy in the Kennedy assassination might cite the testimony of ballistic experts who claimed that more than one gun was fired.

By being careful to provide support and clarification for the ideas in your speech, you can increase the chances that your audience will understand your message and be persuaded by it. Concern for your audience and the integrity of your presentation are key issues in the preparation of a speech. When an audience feels your concern, it is likely to reward you with a positive reaction to your speech and increased credibility.

It should now be evident to you that a well-prepared speech combines many skills and carefully selected elements. Take a look at the sample speech on pp. 410–15. Analysis of any effective speech will reveal the basics with which it was built.

SUMMARY

Careful planning, organization, and preparation are essential when speaking in public. Athletes train for competitive events, musicians rehearse for concerts, and artists sketch before they paint. In the same way, you must prepare yourself to go before your audience.

The success of your delivery will largely depend upon how well you have organized your message.

Begin by selecting a topic that interests you or one that you have some previous knowledge of or familiarity with. Make sure, if your speech is supposed to be persuasive, that your personal convictions are in agreement with your topic.

Good speeches are focused. Decide your purpose in speaking: Will you inform, persuade, or entertain your audience? Your subject should not be too general but should serve as the unifying or central idea of your speech.

As you gather information for your speech, keep your purpose in mind. An objective discussion of a controversial issue requires presentation of opposing views. If your purpose is to persuade, you may rely upon those sources that support your view. There are a wide variety of sources of information. Draw on your own experience, personal interviews, or surveys when appropriate. Take advantage of the wide range of printed materials, films, recordings, and videotapes available.

Consider the functions of the three basic parts of your speech. The introduction serves to catch and focus audience attention. Use the standard introductory devices, statistics, rhetorical questions, famous quotes, and so forth, when appropriate. You present your main purpose and set the tone for your speech in your introduction. The body of your speech will contain the bulk of information and elaboration of your main ideas. These main ideas should be connected by smooth transitions. The conclusion should be used to leave a lasting impression on your audience and to reemphasize your main idea.

As you organize the body of the speech, decide upon a pattern of arrangement. Informative speeches may be topical, chronological, or spatial or follow the patterns of increasing complexity or chain of events. Persuasive speeches may follow inductive or deductive reasoning or develop according to patterns of cause and effect or problems and solutions.

Your outline is a map—be sure to provide yourself with a workable guide for your delivery. Remember the principles of simplicity, coordination, subordination, and progression, and keep your symbolization consistent.

Supporting material is important to clarify and substantiate your ideas. Use real, hypothetical, or extended examples when appropriate. Employ illustrations or anecdotes to clarify your points. Define your terms when necessary by description or by comparison or contrast with terms familiar to the audience. You may reinforce your main ideas with the use of statistics or testimony.

The importance of good preparation cannot be overestimated. Using the methods of organization outlined in this chapter will help you in effective public speaking.

Exercises

GROUP EXPERIENCES

Come On Up and Introduce Yourself!

Description: As outlined in this chapter, the introduction to a speech serves several important functions. One of these functions is to catch and then focus audience attention. If you fail to catch your audience in your introductory comments, it is unlikely that you will get its attention later. This activity will provide you with the opportunity to write several different types of introductions to the same speech.

Procedure: Select a topic for a speech. Then outline the main body of the speech. You will not have to deliver the speech itself, but you will have to deliver "introductions" to the speech. Therefore, it is important that you determine the theme and organizational structure of the speech so that you can preview the body of the speech in your introduction. Now— write three different introductions for the same speech. You may wish to review the various methods suggested in this chapter, such as the use of a startling statement, a rhetorical question, or a humorous statement. Each introduction should be no longer than 60 seconds. After hearing the introduction, your audience should (1) be motivated to listen to your speech, (2) be able to identify your central theme, and (3) have a general idea about what you will cover in the body of your speech.

Each member of the class should be asked to deliver his or her introductions to the rest of the class. The introductions should be done so that no one person will present two or three consecutive introductions. Each introduction should be evaluated by class members, based on the following three scales:

Scale 1. Did the speaker motivate you to listen to the speech? (1) not at all motivated; (2) slightly motivated; (3) motivated; (4) highly motivated.

Scale 2. With what degree of accuracy do you think you can identify the speaker's main theme? (1) not at all accurately; (2) slightly accurately; (3) accurately; (4) highly accurately.

Scale 3. With what degree of accuracy do you think you can describe what the speaker will cover in the body of the speech? (1) not at all accurately; (2) slightly accurately; (3) accurately; (4) highly accurately.

Each speaker should carefully review all the evaluations of his or her introductions. You may wish to add the total number of points possible for each scale and then the number of points actually received on each scale.

Discussion: After reviewing your point totals for each introduction and each scale, can you identify problems with a particular introduction or scale? Do you need to spend more time in preparing introductions? How did your introductions compare with the others presented?

Concluding Remarks

Note: The procedure for this activity is the same as for the activity just described, except that *conclusions* are presented instead of *introductions*.

Patterns

Description: Persuasive speech patterns can easily be identified as inductive, deductive, cause-and-effect, or problem-solution. The purpose of any persuasive speech is to create attitude change in the listener; the various patterns are alternative methods for pursuing that goal. The purpose of this activity is to familiarize you with persuasive speech patterns.

Procedure: Locate three speech transcripts. Analyze each speech to determine the speech pattern used. Keep in mind that a speech may have a combination of patterns. After identifying the patterns in each speech, write a short outline for each. For example, if you have identified a deductive pattern, you should point out the generalization, the specific statement, and the conclusion. Bring your analyses to class.

Divide into groups of four. Compare your analyses of the three speeches. If there are discrepancies among group members as to the patterns used in the speeches, determine the specific conflict. After 45 minutes each group should have reached an agreement on the patterns used in each speech and should report its results to the class.

Discussion: Did you experience any difficulty in analyzing the speeches? Do you believe that organization in a speech is important for producing attitude change? Why? Why not?

PERSONAL EXPERIENCES

1. Start your own collection of jokes, stories, or other types of interesting introductions for speeches. Collect these from books, magazines, television, or public speakers. Your collection can be used for introductions to speeches, stories, or papers.
2. Develop a list of statements made by yourself and others that demonstrate some form of illogical reasoning. Then consider the problems that are created when illogical reasoning is used. How often do you make invalid claims?
3. Identify all the "creative" ways in which you could collect source materials for a speech. Consider, for example, cartoons, fairy tales, and poems. Too often we look only in the standard places (reference books, interviews) for material. Consider the creative use of collections of information parallel to a multimedia presentation.

DISCUSSION QUESTIONS

1. What are some of the principles of outlining you should use in writing a speech?
2. What are the intended purposes of the introduction, body, and conclusion of a speech?
3. Provide an example of the following types of supporting material: illustrations, anecdotes, definitions, and examples.
4. Can a speech effectively use a combination of the spatial, chronological, and topical patterns of organization?
5. What are the factors you should consider when preparing to speak in public? (List the factors in the order in which you believe they should be considered.)

SPEECH DELIVERY

12

Exploratory Questions

1. What six suggestions can you make to control speech anxiety.
2. What are four principles of good delivery?
3. What are the physical elements of delivery?
4. How would you diagram and explain the mechanics of vocalization?
5. How do the four vocal characteristics affect delivery?
6. What are three methods for improving pronunciation?
7. How would you distinguish between formal and informal style in delivery?
8. What are five characteristics of style in delivery?

Public speakers throughout history have been keenly aware of the importance of dynamic delivery. Prophets, poets, philosophers, and storytellers have practiced through the ages to capture the minds and imaginations of their audiences.

As a modern student of communication, you must develop your own manner of presentation. Even the most powerful speech can be ruined by a poor delivery, while a mediocre speech can be improved if delivered in a dynamic way.

The average listener can probably judge the overall effectiveness of a speech, but the public speaker must go further and pay critical attention to the finer, more specific aspects of delivery. For example:

> Jerry Evans, a newcomer running for local office, knew that the success of his campaign would depend on his making himself known and liked by the constituency. Since his platform was basically the same as his opponent's, Jerry felt that the presentation of his speeches would be of even greater importance than the content of his message. Therefore, Jerry was advised to videotape rehearsals of his speech. After the first run-through before his campaign workers, Jerry was quite dissatisfied, although he could not immediately pinpoint the reasons. After analyzing the replay, Jerry noticed that he seldom looked at the audience and nervously jingled the change in his pocket. Although there were bits of humor in the speech, Jerry kept a solemn expression throughout, except once or twice when he laughed very nervously. His gestures seemed awkward and his voice somewhat shaky. Fortunately, he was able to identify his specific delivery problems and overcome them.

We have already discussed body movement, gestures, eye contact, facial expressions, and paralanguage (Chapter 4), but we will now look more closely at these and other important elements of public communication. While this chapter may not help you to win an election, you will be a better public speaker if you follow the principles outlined here.

The importance of delivery goes beyond maintaining audience interest. Research has shown that delivery affects speaker credibility, message comprehension, and persuasiveness.

A speaker's credibility can be established or destroyed during the presentation of a speech. Ethos, the audience's perception of a speaker as trustworthy and sincere, is greatly influenced by delivery. These audience perceptions are changed by nonverbal cues such as the speaker's appearance, facial expression, posture, and gestures.

However, the truly critical audience should always be aware of the difference between perception and reality. While an honest speaker may quite unconsciously project an image of sincerity and trustworthiness, a skillful speaker with the most selfish motives can sometimes create that same impression. For example, the prominent political figure who denies an accusation of wrongdoing can add to his or her credibility by looking directly at the audience, thereby gaining support with nonverbal communication.

Delivery also affects message comprehension. One experiment studied the effect of vocal skills on comprehension. It was found that when speakers demonstrated good vocal skills while delivering difficult or disorganized messages, audiences scored higher on comprehension tests than with less skillful speakers.[1]

In addition to increasing message comprehension and speaker credibility, a good, strong delivery can add to the persuasive impact of a speech. James McCroskey found that good delivery in combination with supportive evidence increased the persuasiveness of a speech,[2] and Albert Mehrabian found that facial expressions and vocal variations were related to a speaker's persuasive ability.[3]

COMMUNICATION APPREHENSION

If you were asked what you fear most, how would you respond? A national polling agency conducted a survey to discover what people fear most. Some of the greatest fears included accidents, death, and heights, but over 40 precent of those polled listed speaking in public as their greatest fear. Maybe you too agree with that 40 percent. But what characteristic of public speaking causes knees to shake, stomachs to turn, voices to tremble, and palms to sweat. (Similar reactions are also associated with other communication situations, such as interviews and blind dates.)

For years stage fright, or speech tension, has been defined as a fear of the situation. However, today most communication scholars believe

---

[1]K. C. Beighley, "An Experimental Study of the Effect of Four Speech Variables on Listener Comprehension," *Speech Monographs* 19 (1952):249–58.

[2]J. C. McCroskey, "Studies of the Effects of Evidence in Persuasive Communication," Speech Communication Research Laboratory Report SCRL 4–67, Department of Speech (East Lansing, Mich.: Michigan State University, 1967), p. 36.

[3]A. Mehrabian and M. Williams, "Nonverbal Concomitants of Perceived and Intended Persuasiveness," *Journal of Personality and Social Psychology* 13 (1969): 37–58.

that these physiological responses are caused by anxiety rather than fear.[4] Fear is a spontaneous response, whereas anxiety involves the anticipation of an event. Fear is usually provoked by an outside stimulus, while anxiety stems from insecurities within a person. Most people don't feel the fear of an automobile accident until after they barely miss a car that failed to stop at a red light. However, before giving a speech, going to a job interview, or meeting a fiancée's parents, many of us feel nervous because we are concerned with and unsure of the outcome. Some of us start to destroy our confidence before speaking assignments are due by telling ourselves, "I can't do this," "I know I'll forget something," "I bore people," or "Nobody is interested in what I have to say." We need to find ways to build our confidence instead of tearing it down.

Before signing up for speech classes, many of us secretly hope that we won't have to get up to speak. Sometimes we can avoid speaking in front of others, but what about the occasions when there is no way out of giving a speech? First, it is important to realize that what you are feeling is a normal response. It is natural to feel nervous before a presentation. In fact, if you don't feel some anxiety, it is likely that your performance will lack the energy needed to keep the speech interesting to an audience. Many coaches check players' palms and energy levels before important games. Because people perform better when there is some tension, coaches select as starting players those who are excited and up for the game. So, if you feel tension before speaking, it is likely that you will perform more effectively than if you feel no tension at all.

Now that we know that speech anxiety is a normal response, you may say, "But everyone can tell I'm nervous, and this bothers me." Well, even if you manifest nervousness, most audience members will not notice it. Research suggests that audiences don't view nervousness as seriously as the speakers do.[5] Audience members don't notice nervousness unless speakers call attention to themselves by saying, "I'm sorry my voice is quivering," "Excuse the paper, but my hands are shaking," or "If I forget something, it's because I'm scared." If you're still not convinced, ask speakers you feel are confident if they were nervous. You'll probably find that they were, even though you didn't notice it.

Sometimes we build our anticipation to such a degree that we have too much energy before a speech. The following suggestions should help both to improve your confidence and to control speech tension.

Practice Research suggests that rehearsing a speech helps to build both confidence and self-concept.[6] If you are not prepared, you will have reason to feel

---

[4]Bert E. Bradley, *Fundamentals of Speech Communication,* 3rd ed. (Dubuque, Iowa: Wm. C. Brown, 1981), p. 426.

[5]Raymond S. Ross, *Essentials of Speech Communication* (Englewood Cliffs, N.J.: Prentice-Hall, 1979), pp. 62–63.

[6]W. D. Brooks and S. M. Platz, "The Effects of Speech Training upon Self-Concept as a Communicator," *Speech Teacher* 17 (1968): 44–49.

tense. It is a good idea to practice to yourself and then to give your speech to friends.

Having set your goals, giving your speech to others helps you learn how audiences will respond and gives you suggestions for improvement.

Physical involvement in your speech helps use excess energy. If your energy has no normal outlet, it will manifest itself in trembling hands, knees, and voice. Using gestures and body movements helps use energy, emphasize points, and maintain audience attention. Like speeches, gestures and movements should be practiced and experimented with before the final presentation. If you feel that you have too much energy before speaking, try taking a few deep breaths, using isometric exercises, or systematic relaxation. — **Use Physical Activity**

When students try to memorize, they put themselves at a disadvantage. Speakers begin to worry about forgetting something—and usually do. If a speaker does forget, there are usually uncomfortable silences and abbreviated presentations. With proper preparation time, using a note card with a brief outline should be all that is necessary for prompting. Clear organization enables speakers to speak extemporaneously. It is much easier to remember points when they follow in a logical progression, so try to put them in sequences that build your confidence. — **Do Not Memorize, And Organize Well**

Confidence increases when speakers are interested and involved with their topics. Topics should be so important and interesting to the speaker that he or she wants to get the ideas across. Involvement in the topic helps focus attention on what is being said rather than on who is saying it, which decreases nervousness. — **Get Involved With Your Topic**

Proper attitudes go along with topic involvement. Speakers have a responsibility to be sincerely interested in what they have to say. Speakers must also remind themselves that their physical responses are normal reactions. The audience is an important factor to consider. Audiences usually want speakers to succeed, especially in classroom situations. The classroom audience is generally the most sympathetic audience speakers will ever encounter. — **Develop A Proper Attitude**

PRINCIPLES

In order to make a successful presentation, a speaker should practice certain principles of good delivery. The first principle is to look natural. If you are stiff or artificial, you will look uncomfortable and awkward. The audience may see this as a lack of confidence, which might greatly affect its perception of the speaker's ethos. At the other extreme, if you seem theatrical or overly dramatic, you may be perceived as false and insincere. The good speaker strives for a natural, easygoing style of presentation. — **Look Natural**

> Talking and eloquence are not the same; to speak, and to speak well, are two things. A fool may talk, but a wise man speaks.
>
> Ben Jonson

Match Delivery and Content
The delivery should be carefully coordinated with the content of the speech. Body movement and vocal expression should add to the presentation, not detract from it. Superficial gestures and inappropriate facial expressions can distract the audience's attention. In a humorous episode of television's "All in the Family," Edith Bunker prepares for a Tupperware party. While practicing her welcoming speech, she tries to coordinate a gesture with her opening sentence, "I welcome you with open arms." Rehearsing time and time again, Edith tries to find the right moment to hold out her arms, palms up, facing the audience. Obviously uncomfortable with the gesture, Edith is not sure whether it should be made before, during, or after her spoken welcome. Although her awkwardness is humorous, it emphasizes the importance of using natural gestures that complement the verbal message and avoiding those gestures that detract from it.

Some personalities become associated with one particular gesture, but most speakers use a variety of gestures and vocal expressions. A sudden change in volume, a pause in delivery, or a firm shake of the head can all be effective in punctuating a particular idea or argument. However, the speaker must be sure that the various vocal expressions and body actions support the verbal message and do not contradict it.

Make It Appropriate
Another principle of good delivery concerns the choice of an appropriate style of presentation. The delivery of a speech must be considered in relation to the audience, the situation, and the speaker. Chapter 9 discusses audience analysis in terms of message selection and preparation. An awareness of audience characteristics is also important in terms of delivery. For example, the tone of voice used when speaking to an audience of children is quite different from the tone of voice used when speaking to adults. Regardless of the age of the audience, the speaker should never talk down to them. Talking down is most often projected more by the delivery than by content. For instance, teachers' attitudes toward their students can sometimes be inferred from their tone of voice. Students often resent teachers who give simple instructions with overenthusiastic energy, as if to say, "Now children, today we are going to. . . ." While you may speak differently to children than to adults, you must remember that no audience, regardless of age, wants to be patronized.

A good speaker also takes into account any special disabilities that members of the audience may have. For example, if some audience mem-

(Thomas Hopker, Woodfin Camp & Associates)

bers have hearing problems, the speaker should adjust his or her volume accordingly.

It is very important to make sure that the delivery is appropriate to the situation. To do this, you must first consider the occasion of the speech. For example, if you are delivering a eulogy at a funeral or memorial service, you should present your speech in a solemn manner. To do this, you should keep your volume low and the pace relatively slow. On the other hand, if you are delivering an after-dinner speech, you should seem enthusiastic and in good spirits. Lightness of tone, variation in pace, and free use of gestures, plus a happy expression on your face, are appropriate here.

You should also consider the setting for the speech. Your delivery will be influenced by whether the setting is a small conference room, an auditorium, or a large outdoor amphitheater. During important political debates, the candidates and their advisors usually visit the location of the debate beforehand. This helps them use each setting more effectively in terms of acoustics and space.

Obviously, your volume must vary according to the size and the acoustics of the setting. Size, acoustics, and seating arrangement also influence the basic mood or tone of your delivery. A casual, understated, and highly informal presentation may not come across well in a very large auditorium. On the other hand, a strict sense of formality can alienate the audience in a small and intimate setting. The effective speaker will choose

IMPROVING

Don't be afraid to be natural, to let yourself show through. Don't pontificate, or talk down to your audience. Talk up to them. Don't over-explain what you want to say, but, instead, assume that your listeners have the intelligence to understand your various points as you make them. And, if you suddenly realize that you have forgotten to make a certain point, don't be afraid to interrupt yourself and say, "Oh, by the way, I forgot to mention—." This merely shows your audience that you are fallible and human and makes your audience **like** you.

As you start to speak, look around your audience and pick out the friendly faces, and talk to them. In every group there are always a few that are all smiles and eagerness for what you have to say. They are your blessed allies, and you should make use of them as such. If the sheer physical fact of an audience unnerves you, play mental tricks on yourself. Imagine, for example, that these people are all your dear, close friends, and that you are talking to them in your own living room. Then, when you have familiarized yourself with your audience, be alert for the moment when the faces become less friendly, when the fannies begin to stir uncomfortably in the chairs, or when the audience appears to be looking at its collective wristwatch. That's the moment to start winding it up. There's nothing wrong with leaving a few of your listeners wishing you'd said a little more. They'll like you for that, too.

Learn to recognize—and avoid, any personal mannerisms, facial or vocal, that you may have—nervous throatclearing, for example, or vocalized ("Uh ... uh ... uh ...") pauses between sentences. Buy an inexpensive tape-recorder, talk into it, and then listen to and analyze yourself. Use a mirror and study yourself. Do you grin too much, or gesticulate with your hands too much? This is particularly important in front of a television camera, where hands flying up in front of the picture frame seriously distract the viewer from you and what you are trying to say or sell. President Kennedy discovered that he had a habit of standing in front of an audience with his hands thrust in his pockets, jangling the keys and coins therein. It was his mother, Rose, who first pointed this out to him, and got him to stand with his hands hanging loosely at the sides, or resting easily on the lectern. It's all right to move about casually as you talk, to scratch your chin occasionally, to shift position slightly, to cross your legs from time to time—anything that makes you seem at ease and natural.

From Stephen Birmingham, "How to Speak in Public without Butterflies," in Communication Vibrations, ed. Larry L. Barker (Englewood Cliffs, N.J.: Prentice-Hall, 1974), p. 66. Copyright 1973 by Stephen Birmingham. Reprinted by permission of the author and his agent, Brandt and Brandt.

the degree of formality according to the setting. A quiet and casual talk would be effective in a classroom, where the audience is close enough to perceive subtle gestures and expressions, but the same kind of presentation would be very inappropriate in a concert hall.

Delivery must always be appropriate to the speaker's personal style or manner. The key here is to know your own personality and behave naturally—remembering that being a speaker does not mean being an actor. For example, Jimmy Carter was noted for his natural, easygoing style during his election campaign. He was unpretentious in his manner, and his characteristic smile helped him to establish a warm relationship with his audiences. Throughout the campaign political observers watched him gain self-confidence and increase the effectiveness of his personal, informal style.

Regardless of the situation, when you are true to yourself you will project sincerity and honesty. Aim for a delivery that is consistent with your own personality.

> Speak the speech, I pray you, as I pronounced it to you, trippingly on the tongue; but if you mouth it, as many of your players do, I had as lief the town-crier spoke my lines. Nor do not saw the air too much with your hand, thus; but use all gently: for in the very torrent, tempest, and—as I may say—whirlwind of passion, you must acquire and beget a temperance, that may give it smoothness.
>
> William Shakespeare

If the speaker fails to develop and maintain a positive relationship with the audience throughout the presentation, the purpose of the speech will be lost. **Rapport** is almost entirely the result of delivery. For example, eye contact with the audience increases credibility and makes the audience more trusting of the speaker. A warm conversational manner can achieve the same effect. _{Establish Rapport}

Rapport is also important because a good speaker-audience relationship can overshadow weak spots in the message itself. Entertainers devote much energy and talent to projecting a feeling of warmth toward their audience. Tony Orlando, a contemporary singer who at one time had his own network television show, was particularly skillful at manipulating the audience in his favor. Following the opening of one show tour, a critic noted, "But he's after much more than our admiration; he wants us to genuinely like him. . . . He obviously wants us to know he's up there working—and sweating—for us. . . . [His] vocal talent is negligible at best, but the rapport still carries the day."[7]

PHYSICAL DELIVERY

The term **delivery** covers many different elements of a speaker's presentation, including physical delivery and vocal expression. The physical elements of delivery can be divided into various body movements, such as posture, gestures, and facial expressions (including eye contact). Also included in the physical aspect of the presentation is the way a speaker uses accessories, such as note cards or a lectern.

As a speaker, you must be aware of your body as an important source of communication. In fact, the body is so expressive in communicating ideas and feelings that many of our verbal expressions are based on descriptions of body movements. For example, a person who maintains a positive attitude in times of adversity is said to keep a "stiff upper lip." Someone in great suspense or suffering extreme anxiety is said to be "sitting on _{Posture and Body Movements}

[7]Glenn Lovell, "Orlando 'Works' His Audience," *The Sun Sentinel*, 5 April 1977.

the edge of his seat." These figures of speech accurately describe the body movements of people in these situations. Someone watching a Hitchcock film may very well be sitting on the edge of his or her seat. Similarly, the actress who did not get the part she hoped for may be keeping a "stiff upper lip" to stop it from trembling.

Our body movements, especially posture, are closely related to our physical and emotional states. On the physical level posture can reveal whether a person is tired, energetic, or in pain. On an emotional level posture can reveal whether a person is tense, relaxed, depressed, or excited. Posture also tells us something about a person's self-image. People with a healthy measure of self-confidence move about easily, stand up straight, and hold up their heads. Those individuals who are shy, ill at ease, or ashamed of themselves are more likely to slump, slouch, and keep their heads and eyes lowered.

An audience's perception of a speaker is influenced by body movement and posture. While there are few specific rules governing this aspect of delivery, there are some simple guidelines. In order to appear poised and confident, you should stand at ease. If you are too stiff, the audience may feel uncomfortable. At the other extreme, a very relaxed posture may be perceived as too casual. A skillful speaker should appear confident but comfortable.

As a speaker, your movements, like your posture, should be natural, not forced. Although you should stand relatively still and avoid pacing, natural movements can add to your delivery. You can use body movements to energize yourself and your audience. A speaker who does not move from one space seems dull and restrained. Appropriate body movements free the speaker from the confines of space and spark the audience's attention.[8] Body movements can also convey meanings. A speaker who leans forward when revealing something new suggests to the audience that they are being made privy to this information. A step toward the audience suggests that the speaker is embracing them and breaking the imaginary barrier between speaker and listeners.

Gestures In addition to movements of the whole body, you can use a variety of gestures. **Gestures** can convey many different meanings, depending upon the context. For example, the "V for victory" sign used by Churchill in World War II became the peace sign of the 1960s. Some gestures convey meanings in and of themselves, while others are used as a part of the verbal message.

Traditional gestures are those movements of the hands and arms that have been associated with particular meanings. The boxer who has won a fight might clasp his hands above his head in a gesture of victory. Similarly, the modest speaker might push the palm of his or her hand toward the audience to still listeners' applause.

[8] Morris R. Bogard, *The Manager's Stylebook* (Englewood Cliffs, N.J.: Prentice-Hall, 1979), pp. 95–96.

Other gestures are emphatic in nature and tend to punctuate the verbal message. When presenting a forceful argument, the speaker might pound a fist on the lectern to support the idea. Or a speaker may wave an index finger to focus the audience's attention on a particular thought. These gestures can serve to underscore the speaker's message, but should be used sparingly so that they don't lose their effectiveness.

Gestures can be descriptive in nature and work to enhance the verbal message. For example, try to describe a spiral staircase while keeping your hands behind your back. The feat is nearly impossible. Descriptive gestures are particularly effective when you ask the audience to visualize what you are saying. A simple gesture to illustrate size, quantity, shape, or distance can lend support to the speaker's description.

All gestures—traditional, emphatic, and descriptive—must be used purposefully if they are to add to your delivery. Here are a few things to keep in mind when using gestures:

1. Avoid gestures that make you feel uncomfortable. Awkward or self-conscious movements detract from your delivery.
2. Be careful to coordinate your gestures with what you are saying—timing is important here.
3. A gesture should not call attention to itself apart from the spoken message.
4. Use gestures only when they will really add to your presentation—when used to excess they lose their effectiveness. Can you imagine a speaker who pounded the lectern at each and every strong point in the speech? The result would probably be more humorous than forceful.

In public speaking, as in other interpersonal exchanges, facial expressions are important to communication. A look of disappointment, a smile of delight, or a frown of disapproval can all be more powerful than a spoken message. In fact, it has been found that facial expressions have greater impact than verbal messages when the two are inconsistent.[9] Facial expressions also play an important role during job interviews. In fact, applicants have a better chance of being hired if they smile and use eye contact.[10]

Facial expressions are important in establishing rapport with the audience, but the skillful speaker does not want to manipulate the audience by using them. An audience can usually sense when a smile is phony in much the same way a parent can often tell when a child is lying. Once again, as with all body movements, facial expressions should be natural extensions of the verbal message. If you are genuine about the content of your speech, then your facial expressions will be consistent with your words.

Facial Expressions

[9]A. Mehrabian, *Silent Messages,* 2d ed. (Belmont, Calif.: Wadsworth, 1981), p. 76.
[10]Paul V. Washburn and Milton D. Hakel, "Visual Cues and Verbal Content as Influences on Impressions After Simulated Employment Interviews," *Journal of Applied Psychology* 58 (1973): 137–40.

Gestures can convey a variety of meanings, depending on the context.
(United Press International)

(United Press International)

(United Press International)

(United Press International)

(United Press International)

Eye Contact Of all the different parts of the face, the eyes are the most important in establishing the speaker-audience relationship. Good eye contact helps to establish rapport and speaker credibility. A speaker who looks at the audience appears more straightforward and honest than one who does not. In a study of speaker training in the areas of eye contact, gestures, and initial/closing speaking behaviors, it was discovered that eye contact training produced the greatest effects on both improved audience ratings and speaker self-confidence.[11] A relationship between eye contact and speaker credibility has also been established.[12]

Although eye contact is important in delivery, it is impossible to look at the entire audience at one time. The effective speaker scans the audience and looks directly at individual members seated in various locations. An empty stare or unfocused, wandering eyes do not add to your

[11]E. L. Black and G. L. Martin, "A Component Analysis of Public Speaking Behaviors across Individuals and Behavioral Categories," *Communication Education* 29 (1980): 273–82.
[12]Steven Beebe, "Eye Contact, A Nonverbal Determinant of Speaker Credibility," *Speech Teacher* 23 (January 1974): 21–25.

delivery. To increase the effectiveness of eye contact, you should try to make all the members of the audience feel as if you are talking to them individually.

When speaking to an audience, it is usually more comfortable to stand behind a lectern. The key word here is stand, not *hide.* Since body movement is an essential aspect of delivery, you must be clearly visible to the audience. A speaker can use this spatial relationship by moving away from the lectern to develop rapport with the audience or by remaining behind it to preserve formality.

The Lectern and Note Cards

A lectern provides a space for your notes or outline. Of course, the use of written materials depends on the type of delivery. An impromptu speech, which by definition is without preparation, would not involve the use of notes. However, an extemporaneous speech, which is carefully prepared but not memorized, might require notes or an outline, especially if the speech is long or complicated. Of course, when a speech is to be read, the complete text must be available to the speaker.

When using note cards, you must be sure that they are written carefully; also, the number of cards should be limited to as few as possible. You should also be careful not to rustle cards or papers, especially when using a microphone.

VOCAL DELIVERY

The second major element of a speaker's presentation is the voice. *Vocal delivery* involves the mechanics of vocalization, vocal characteristics (including pitch, volume, rate, and quality), and pronunciation. Very often inexperienced speakers pay little attention to their vocal delivery, believing incorrectly that the voice cannot be altered in any way. Even though one's physical makeup influences vocal quality, much can be done to improve vocal delivery.

To understand how to improve vocal delivery, it is important first to be aware of the mechanics of vocalization.[13] Voice and speech depend on phonation. In simple terms, *phonation* is the process by which air is pushed through the vocal cords, which then vibrate to produce sound. The sounds or tones produced in this way are what we call *voice.* Since air is responsible for the vibration of the vocal cords, the breathing mechanism plays a basic part in phonation.

The Mechanics of Vocalization

When you exhale, air from the lungs travels up the bronchial tubes to the larynx. (See Figure 12–1.) The *larynx,* commonly known as the *voice box,* contains two thin membranes, or vocal cords, which vibrate as the air passes through them. The sound waves that result from this vibra-

[13]Virgil A. Anderson, *Training the Speaking Voice,* 3rd ed. (New York: Oxford University Press, 1977).

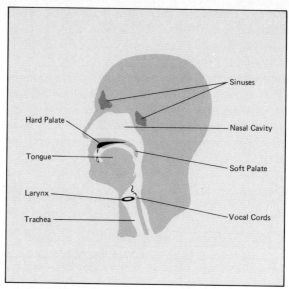

FIGURE 12-1 Elements of Vocal Delivery.

tion are the basic voice sound. Functioning like a valve, the vocal cords are controlled by muscles that regulate the amount of air passing through. In order to produce speech sounds, the cords move close enough together to partially block the escaping air and alter the tone produced.

The process of phonation is not complete until the sound produced in the larynx is resonated throughout the vocal chamber of the mouth, nose, and throat. **Resonance** is responsible for both the amplification and enrichment of the voice. Without these chambers or cavities to give the sounds support and resonance, vocal quality would be quite unpleasant.

To better understand this process, place your finger on the bone of your nose and feel the vibration as you hum. The sound is resonating in the nasal cavity. When you have a cold or a stuffy nose, your voice sounds different without this additional resonance.

Articulation is the process by which voice is altered into recognizable speech sounds. These speech sounds consist of vowels and consonants, the building blocks of our speech.

The consonants and vowels are formed when sounds are modified by the articulators. These include the lips, teeth, tongue, jaw, gum ridge, and palates, in addition to the nose, throat, and oral cavities. Consonants are produced as the articulators interfere with the passage of sound. Each consonant is produced by a different articulator as it interferes in some way with the flow of sound. For example, the "p" sound is made by joining the lips, which block the passage of air for a moment and are then quickly released. A "t" sound is produced when the tip of the tongue is placed along the gum ridge. The articulators in each case alter the sound produced by the vibrations of the vocal cords.

Vowels are produced by altering the size and shape of the nose, throat, and oral cavities. For example, contrast the shape of the mouth as you say "ah" and "oo." Unlike consonants, vowels do not require interference by the various articulators.

Poor articulation is usually the result of misuse of the articulators. For example, someone who has a lisp is not placing the tongue against the gum ridge to produce the "s" sound. Usually correction of this fault involves making a speaker aware of the error and having him or her practice the proper articulation of the sound.

Sometimes the problem is not one of carelessness or incorrect use. A person with a defective articulator will have problems producing proper speech sounds. For example, someone with an extreme overbite may have a lisp due to the improper meeting of the upper and lower teeth. With patience and practice most of these people can improve their articulation to the point where their speech fault is negligible.

Now that you have a basic idea of how speech is produced, we can discuss the various characteristics of the voice. Vocal delivery involves four vocal characteristics: pitch, volume, rate, and quality.

Vocal Characteristics

PITCH   The *pitch* of the voice refers to how high or low the voice sounds. A person's natural pitch is determined in part by the length and width of the vocal cords. Women's vocal cords are characteristically thinner and longer than men's, so women have higher-pitched voices. Each voice can produce sounds ranging in pitch from high to low. Tensing the vocal cords produces a higher pitch, while relaxing them lowers the sound. Skillful singers and speakers are able to widen their pitch range and develop pitch control by practicing appropriate voice exercises.

When you have developed control of your pitch, you can use this skill to advantage. A variation in pitch adds color and vitality to a delivery and can also be used as a means of emphasis or to identify a speaker's emotional states.[14] The most boring speakers have little pitch variety. They speak in monotones, without emphasizing important points with their voices. As you may know, it is easy to be lulled to sleep by a monotonous voice, even when the topic of discussion is interesting.

VOLUME   The second vocal characteristic is *volume,* which means intensity or loudness. Once again, as with pitch, each of us has a volume range that allows us to project various degrees of loudness, ranging from a whisper to a scream.

A person whose voice is perfectly audible in conversation may have difficulty projecting before a large audience. Therefore, in rehearsing the delivery of a speech, you must adjust your volume to the room in which you will be speaking. Obviously, the most brilliant oration is meaningless

---

[14]G. Fairbanks and W. Pronovost, "An Experimental Study of the Pitch Characteristics of the Voice During the Expression of Emotion," *Speech Monographs* 6 (1939): 87–104.

if you cannot be heard. You should also try to overcome any distracting noise that may interfere with the transmission of the message, such as fans or nearby traffic.

While the most important point is simply to be heard, you can also adjust volume to add to your overall presentation. Variation in volume makes you sound more dynamic; it can also emphasize your main ideas and underscore important arguments. If you build to a crescendo, you will add impact to the verbal message in the same way a musician does when playing a melody.

RATE   ***Rate*** of speech is another important vocal characteristic. If you talk too quickly, the audience may not be able to keep pace. At the other extreme, if your speaking rate is too slow, the audience may lose interest. The main concern is audience comprehension. The nature and degree of difficulty of message help to determine a suitable rate of speech. A new or complicated message may call for a slower delivery than a subject with which the audience is familiar. An effective speaker will vary the rate of speech, pausing and slowing down to give emphasis to some material and speeding up at other points.

(United Press International)

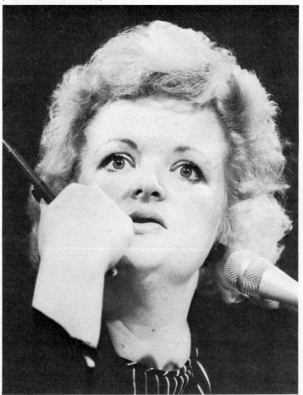

QUALITY One of the most difficult characteristics to control is vocal quality. ***Vocal quality*** refers to the timbre of the voice, the characteristic that distinguishes one voice from another. A resonant quality is desirable, so that the voice sounds deep and mellow. Voices that are too thin, strident, nasal, or breathy sound unpleasant and should be improved. Each of these qualities is the result of poor phonation. Understanding the vocal process and doing voice exercises can improve vocal quality, but it takes time to change something that feels natural to you.

Factors Influencing Your Voice

In addition to voice exercises, there are other factors that can influence the sound of your voice. The first of these is your physical makeup. This factor involves the various parts of the vocal mechanism described under phonation—namely, the lungs, vocal cords, larynx, and resonating chambers.

Psychological factors also influence a person's voice. When you are anxious or excited, the tension may localize in the vocal cords, creating a higher pitch than normal. If you are relaxed and at ease, your voice will sound much more pleasant.

A third factor that influences voice is environment. Members of the same family often seem to have similar voices. The similarity is partially genetic and partially environmental. You pick up inflections from the people around you, including family members, peers, and members of the same ethnic group.

In addition to the influence of your immediate circle of acquaintances, your voice is also affected by regional dialects. Different regions of a country have varying speech and voice patterns that make their use of voice and language unique. A person from the South may have a "drawl" that is quite distinct from the "twang" of a Midwesterner. However, regional differences usually affect pronunciation more than voice quality.

Improving Vocalization

The best way to improve your voice is through voice exercises. You must first be able to hear your own voice and decide which aspects need improvement. Thanks to modern technology, most speakers can hear themselves on a tape recorder. This enables you to analyze your voice and practice a variety of exercises. You must decide, perhaps with the aid of a speech therapist or vocal coach, whether the problem concerns phonation, articulation, or pronunciation.

If the area in need of improvement is phonation, or the production of sound, then the problem may be one of force, duration, or quality. You might find that your voice often trails off at the end of a sentence, or that the volume is so low that you cannot be heard. In either case the problem is one of force.

Many people breathe incorrectly, and improper breathing can impair phonation. Some individuals lack force because they are not using their resonating chambers as efficiently as possible. Exercises to increase the use of these cavities add to a speaker's amplification.

Some people cannot speak for a long period of time without losing their voices. This can pose a serious problem for a person with many speaking engagements. Imagine the distress of politicians on the campaign trail who find their voices giving out after speaking for an extended period of time. Voice fatigue usually comes from improper use of the different parts of the vocal mechanism.

Basically, vocal sound should be supported by the partition of muscles and tendons between the chest and abdomen known as the diaphragm. This muscle is responsible for involuntary breathing and is one of the strongest muscles in the body. The muscles of the throat and the vocal cords are easily strained, while the diaphragm is virtually tireless. Through prescribed exercises you can learn to "support" your voice correctly and avoid hoarseness and voice loss. However, it takes time and practice to overcome the bad habits of years. As mentioned previously, problems of articulation usually stem from careless speech habits. Unless a person must compensate for a physical defect such as a harelip, poor articulation can be improved by concentrated effort and practice. We can all be inspired by individuals who are born deaf and are never able to hear the sound of words; with a great deal of perseverance, many of them have learned to articulate well enough to be understood in conversation.

An understanding of how various sounds are made will help you to improve articulation. Practice drills are good reinforcement for correcting problems of articulation, but you must make a conscious effort to carry over the correct production of speech sounds into everyday conversation as well as public speaking situations. Faulty articulation is particularly bad for the public speaker, since an audience is easily distracted by poor speech. Mumbling and speaking carelessly affect the audience's perception of you. A speaker whose pronunciation is clear and distinct makes a more favorable impression than someone whose speech is sloppy.

Pronunciation

Pronunciation can be important to the improvement of both speech and voice. Standards of pronunciation are often determined by geographical area or imposed by occasion or education. Americans speak the same language, but pronunciation varies according to region. While geographic regions have changed in terms of speech patterns, one can still find a difference between Northern, Midwestern, and Southern speech. In addition to the three major regions, there are numerous subdivisions. For example, New Yorkers do not sound like Bostonians, even though they are both considered northern.

Certain speakers strive for what is called "standard American speech," the type of speech exemplified by Walter Cronkite and other national newscasters. Although still preferred in some circles, standard American pronunciation is not a prerequisite for success. Neither John Kennedy's New England speech nor Jimmy Carter's Southern style hurt their political aspirations. The key is not regional pronunciation but careful articulation.

In addition to regional background, your pronunciation is influenced by the occasion and by your education. Certain situations, such as job interviews or press conferences, require careful pronunciation. Any person speaking before a group should pay special attention to pronunciation. If a speaker makes an error, the audience's attention may be temporarily distracted. Poor pronunciation can create a bad impression.

Education affects pronunciation in the sense that exposure to language through reading, speaking, and listening results in increased vocabulary and knowledge of the way different words are pronounced. Education includes more than formal schooling. As you read, study, travel, and speak with educated people, your vocabulary and language skills, including those related to pronunciation, improve.

Sometimes an incorrect pronunciation of a word becomes acceptable due to its widespread misuse. Thomas Middleton, columnist for the *Saturday Review,* wrote,

> The truth about pronunciation, whether we like to admit it or not—and most of us don't—is that the correct pronunciation of a word is the way in which it is generally pronounced, and there are a great many words that are pronounced in more ways than one.[15]

There are several ways you, as a speaker, can improve pronunciation. If you are unsure of the way a word is pronounced, look it up in the dictionary. Be particularly careful to find out the proper pronunciation of the names of people and places mentioned in your speech. If you are quoting someone or acknowledging a particular person or organization, it is important to pronounce the name correctly.

Pronunciation, articulation, and phonation have always been concerns of the public speaker. Since we all rely on voice and speech for much of our communication, we should strive to improve our vocal delivery.

STYLE

We recognize that the Reverend Billy Graham has an effective style of oration, and those of us who remember or have heard recordings would agree that Martin Luther King, Jr., and John F. Kennedy each had a unique and powerful delivery. But what is style?

In simple terms, style is the way an individual speaker gives ideas meaning through his or her particular brand of verbal expression and delivery. Style deals with both the wording and the delivery of the message. It includes the speaker's choice of words, the use of language, sentence structure, and the characteristics of delivery. Since style is made up of so many variables, each speaker's style is somewhat different. Some speakers have pet phrases that they include in their speeches, some are very

[15]Thomas Middleton, "Light Refractions," *Saturday Review,* 3 April 1976, p. 58.

plain-spoken, and others rely heavily on the use of metaphor or flowery language.

Style also applies to syntax, or sentence structure. Sometimes a speaker may invert subject and verb to achieve a stylistic effect. For example, a disgusted sportscaster might say, "Never have I witnessed such a poor display of teamwork." Run-on or choppy sentences can also be used to achieve a stylistic effect. Although a good speaker should adhere to the rules of grammar, "poetic license" of sorts can be used to achieve a desired effect.

Our concern here is primarily with the element of style that applies to a speaker's physical and vocal delivery. Of course, while every speaker develops a personal style, you should be able to adapt your style to fit the audience, occasion, topic, and purpose of your speech. Basically, your style may be formal or informal, with varying degrees in between.

Quite logically, a formal style is best suited to a formal occasion. We would expect, for example, that both a president's State of the Union address and a college valedictory speech would be formal. A casual treatment of either of these speeches would demean their importance.

The characteristics of formal style include serious and impersonal tone, correct use of grammar, sophisticated stylistic devices, and avoidance of slang. The physical and vocal delivery should be dignified and serious.

A serious tone is projected by the manner in which you present yourself and your message. Although you need not be solemn, you should be dignified. There is no room for flippancy in a formal presentation. To emphasize the importance of the message, you should keep an impersonal tone by avoiding the use of personal pronouns.

More often than not, the speaking engagements in which we find ourselves tend to be more casual than formal and require a less formidable style. An informal style is characterized by a light and personal tone, use of fairly simple sentence structure and vocabulary, and a bending of grammatical rules, if necessary. An informal style allows the speaker to add warmth to the presentation with informal language and humor.

Very few speaking situations are either strictly formal or informal. Since most fall within the two extremes, you will have to adapt your style accordingly. For example, although we might think of an after-dinner speech as being informal, the appropriate presentation would depend on the nature of the occasion as well as the audience. You should evaluate each speaking situation individually to determine the right delivery.

Characteristics of Style
Although each speaker is different, there are certain desirable characteristics that help to make any speaker's style effective. The first of these is *accuracy,* which requires a precise use of words. Very often you know what you want to say but have trouble getting the idea across to the audience. If an audience walks away not knowing what was said or misinterpreting the message, then you have failed in your basic purpose. As a

(United Press International)

United Press International)

Style and context

speaker, you must choose the words that most accurately convey your message. Avoid words that are too abstract or general, as well as words that are open to many different interpretations. Words such as *good, bad,* and *nice* are really ambiguous and add little to a presentation.

Closely related to accuracy is **clarity.** The main consideration here is audience comprehension. A complicated description of a medical procedure that is perfectly clear to a surgeon may be totally confusing to an audience of laymen. Therefore, you must adapt your language and style to fit the needs of the audience.

Appropriateness is another characteristic of style. As mentioned previously, a speaker's style should fit the occasion, the audience, and the type and purpose of the speech. Each presentation should reflect consideration of all of these factors.

Another characteristic of effective style is **economy,** or the greatest efficiency of language. If you use the right words in the most efficient way, your message will be more meaningful. There is no need to use many words when a few will do. If you are concise, accuracy and clarity will be achieved as well. However, conciseness should not undermine comprehension, which sometimes makes it necessary to repeat ideas.

The final characteristic is a **lively quality** in the selection of words. Although economy is a virtue in terms of style, sometimes a speaker will use a phrase or expression that leaves a lasting impression on the audience. A poetic statement, a memorable expression, an unusual figure of speech, or a melodic phrase will jump out at the audience and capture its attention. The speaker must not overuse this quality, however, or the impact will be weakened.

Remember, we want it frank, but not too frank—hard-hitting, but not too hard-hitting—controversial, but not too controversial. Now do good, but not too good."
(© 1980 by S. Harris)

An impressive style is not, of course, achieved without careful preparation and practice. Style, like good public speaking skills in general, *can* be learned, but not without the interest and effort it takes to achieve any valuable goal. If you are determined, if you strive to understand and use the communication principles suggested in this book, then more than likely you will be rewarded with the attainment of your goal: satisfying communication, the sharing of yourself and your experiences with your fellow human beings.

SUMMARY

The importance of delivery in public speaking cannot be overestimated. A speaker's delivery is the vehicle for the communication of the message. Good delivery is essential in capturing and maintaining audience attention and also affects speaker credibility, audience comprehension, and persuasive impact.

There are several delivery approaches for the student of public speaking to consider. The imitative approach proposes a close study of models of public speaking, the mechanical approach follows strict rules of elocution and oration, and the adaptive approach relies on the speaker's evaluation of audience variables.

Principles of good delivery include a natural appearance, consistency of expression and content, rapport with the listeners, and a presentation that is appropriate to the audience, the situation, and the speaker. The physical aspects of delivery include body movements, posture, gestures, facial expressions, eye contact, and the use of the lectern and note cards. An awareness and natural use of these elements can greatly enhance the verbal message.

The good public speaker should understand the vocal aspects of public speaking. Good phonation, resonance, and articulation are essential to message audibility and comprehension. An awareness of pitch, volume, rate, and voice quality will enable the speaker to capture and hold the listener's ear. Vocal delivery is influenced by physical, psychological, and environmental factors. Serious students of public speaking may improve their powers of vocalization by practicing appropriate vocal exercises.

Pronunciation is another element of vocal delivery that must not be overlooked. Good pronunciation is essential to message comprehension and speaker credibility.

The style of delivery may be as important as the content of the message. The speaker may choose between varying degrees of formality. After a while, every speaker usually develops a unique personal style. Choice of words, use of language, and syntax are all effective stylistic elements. Basically, every speaker should aim for a style that is accurate, clear, appropriate to the occasion and setting, economical, and striking. Although this may seem a difficult task, the results will be worth the effort.

Exercises

GROUP EXPERIENCES

Coaching on the Sidelines

Description: Politicians have long been aware of the importance of public speaking. Today ghostwriters, communication consultants, and many other specialists work together to help "present" the politician to the public. This activity will give you the opportunity to act as coach or consultant to a politician.

Procedure: Divide into dyads. You and your partner have been hired to help Laura Martinez present herself to the public for the upcoming campaign. Laura is totally naive about public speaking. She does not know what to do with her hands, how fast to talk, what to say, or how to say it. Needless to say, you have a big job ahead of you. Write a plan for getting Laura ready for the public. You might want to incorporate some practice speaking sessions, the use of videotape, and so forth, to prepare Laura. Share your plan with the other groups and compare the strategy plans.

Discussion: Did you forget any important steps in your plan? Can you improve a person's speaking ability? Can you create "charisma" in a person? How can delivery affect the credibility of a person?

Timing

Description: A good delivery is absolutely essential for a successful presentation, along with voice, gestures, and body stance: They all play an important role in a public speaking situation. A good delivery should be carefully coordinated with the content of the speech. If the gestures and facial expressions do not come at the right time, they will distract from the speech itself. This activity gives you an opportunity to see the effects on an audience of the timing of facial expressions and gestures.

Procedure: If you have a theatrical flair or a dramatic side to your personality, then this is the activity for you. Write a 3-minute speech designed to sell a product of your choice. Practice the delivery of the speech several times until you have completely *uncoordinated* your gestures and facial expressions with your words. This will be difficult, because when your voice is excited, your face will have to look bored. If you state that there are three good reasons to buy your product, you may want to use a hand gesture *after* you finish saying this. In whatever way possible, by making the timing wrong, your "presentation" should look like a comedy routine. Try it out by presenting it before a class or a group of people.

Discussion: What were the reactions to your poorly timed talk? Did the audience remember what you had to say or the way you said it? Did you feel self-conscious or overdramatic? Whatever effect you created, chances are good that the lack of timing did hurt the impact of your speech. Next time you give a speech, be natural, and you will see that the facial expressions, gestures, and content of the speech will complement one another.

VOICE LESSONS

Description: A speaker's vocal delivery involves four things: pitch, volume, rate, and quality. By studying and practicing each quality, you can improve your speaking voice. The following voice drill is designed to help you identify specific characteristics of your voice.

Procedure: Divide into dyads. With the help of your partner, practice the following line: "A person whose voice is perfectly audible in conversation may have difficulty projecting before a large audience." Say the line six times for each characteristic, focusing first on pitch, then volume, then rate, then quality. For instance: With rate, the first time you should say the line very slowly, and gradually get faster, so that by the sixth time you are saying it very fast. Your partner should select the number of the repetition (1 to 6) that is the best rate for an audience, and then do the same for the other characteristics.

Pitch. Go from a very high pitch to a very low pitch.

Volume. Go from a very soft voice to a very loud voice.

Rate. Go from speaking very slowly to speaking very quickly.

Quality. Go from a very nasal quality to a deep and resonant quality.

Discussion: Are you surprised by any of the selections made by your partner? Feedback is important, particularly about the voice, since we cannot hear ourselves the way others hear us. A common problem in speaking is rate. Speakers tend to think they are speaking at a slower rate than they actually are. Try to remember and practice what your partner selected as the best rate, volume, pitch, and vocal quality for you.

PERSONAL EXPERIENCES

1. Listen to a live speaker or a televised speech. Listen carefully to the vocal characteristics of the speaker (pitch, volume, rate, and quality). Is the speaker using his or her voice for maximum effectiveness? What things, if any, would you change about the speaker's voice?
2. Observe the kind of gestures you use when talking to another person. Do you use a lot of gestures? Do you make gestures in close to your body, or are they expansive? Do you feel self-conscious when you use your hands? You use gestures as a natural part of your everyday conversations; there is no reason why your gestures cannot be just as natural in a speech. Watch them. Feel comfortable with the way your hands move. If you feel comfortable, so will others.
3. Imagine that you are going to give a speech before an audience of a hundred people. In addition, you will be talking about something that excites you. Since looking forward to giving a speech is very important, what could you do to "psyche" yourself up?

DISCUSSION QUESTIONS

1. What are the basic factors to consider in the presentation of a speech? Is any one factor more important than the others?
2. What physical aspects of a presentation are important for a speaker to consider?
3. What things make you "unique" as a speaker? (Consider style, vocal quality, delivery, and so on).
4. What methods can you use to improve your delivery?
5. What plan would you make for yourself in order to improve your public speaking skills?

COMMUNICATION THROUGH THE MASS MEDIA

Exploratory Questions

1. What are the characteristics of mass communication?
2. How would you describe delayed and limited feedback in mass communication?
3. What is gatekeeping, as practiced by industry, government, and sponsors?
4. What are some differences among the four electronic forms of mass communication?
5. What are the three functions of mass communication?
6. What are the differences between the persuasive purposes of advertising and public relations?
7. How does television violence and advertising influence children?
8. What are four areas affected by mass communication?
9. What are the three major divisions of radio and television station organization?
10. What is demassification, and what are some examples of demassified media?

> The medium is the message.
>
> Marshall McLuhan

It is now time to turn our attention to mass communication. To fully understand the scope of mass communication and the way in which it differs from other dimensions of communication, let us examine the following situation:

> Several months before primary elections, Marion Thompson, a virtual unknown in politics, declared her candidacy for the state senate. Yet in little less than three weeks, Marion Thompson's name became a household word. People saw her on television, heard her on radio, and read about her in newspapers and magazines. As they drove along the highway, they saw her name splashed over billboards. As they went shopping in town, they were bombarded with leaflets introducing the candidate and summarizing her position on key issues. Her name appeared on t-shirts, on bumper stickers, and on placards on buses and trash cans. After an intense campaign and a stunning victory, Marion Thompson attributed her success to mass communication and effective use of the media.

The different types of mass communication used in Marion's campaign—radio, TV, and various forms of print media—all share common characteristics. In his book *Broadcasting in America,* Sydney Head suggests that the term **mass communication** must imply at least five things:

1. Relatively large audiences.
2. Fairly undifferentiated audience composition.
3. Some form of message reproduction.
4. Rapid distribution and delivery.
5. Low unit cost to the consumer.[1]

In other words, mass communication is the spreading of a message to an extended audience through rapid means of reproduction and distribution at a relatively low cost to the consumer. In each case a message is trans-

[1]Sydney W. Head, *Broadcasting in America,* 3rd ed. (Boston: Houghton Mifflin, 1976), p. 81.

ported from its original source to a widespread audience through an intermediary channel such as radio, television, or newspapers.

Although all forms of mass communication affect our lives, the most widely used and influential forms are newspapers, radio, TV, and film. The importance of these media can best be expressed in numbers. There are approximately 10,000 different newspapers published in the United States, including shoppers' guides, entertainment listings, and "scandal sheets." The role of the newspaper keeps changing. At first it was entirely informative in nature; then, before the days of electronic media, it developed an important entertainment function, which disappeared after the advent of radio and TV. Yet today, due to keen competition among papers and other forms of media, newspapers once again include many features in addition to the daily news. For example, a recent *New York Times* slogan says, *"The New York Times* is a lot more than the news." To substantiate this claim, the *Times* now offers a weekly section devoted to the home, one to weekend entertainment, and another to lifestyles.

Although many of us are children of the TV age, statistics about radio broadcasting help us realize the importance of radio both as a news medium and as an entertainment medium. There are close to 7,000 radio stations in the United States alone. Such a demand for the use of the airwaves has made it necessary to regulate the air frequencies and to use AM/FM bands in the interests of fairness and efficiency.

Interestingly enough, there are considerably fewer TV stations, with approximately 700 commercial stations and 200 educational channels. Yet the impact of TV as a medium of entertainment, information, and education is truly unparalleled.

CHARACTERISTICS OF MASS COMMUNICATION

Both print and electronic media share certain unique characteristics. Mass communication overcomes the barriers of time and space. This time phenomenon can be illustrated by "Roots," Alex Haley's serialized drama, which traced his African ancestry through enslavement to freedom. In 1977 the story was condensed into eight installments, totaling twelve TV hours. One hundred and thirty million viewers witnessed part or all of 200 years of semifictionalized American history. Suddenly, events that had occurred many years ago became "real" once more as a result of mass communication.

The ability of mass communication to encompass vast boundaries of space is expressed by Marshall McLuhan's term **global village.** Global village suggests that the world is smaller than before due to advances in mass communication (especially the telephone, TV, and satellites). People in one part of the world can witness an event as it is taking place in another. People all over the world now share one another's joys and sorrows. For example, our enthusiasm in watching the Olympic games as they are transmitted live to various countries throughout the world is cer-

> I am entirely persuaded that the American public is more reasonable, restrained and mature than most of the broadcast industry's planners believe. Their fear of controversy is not warranted by the evidence.
>
> Edward R. Murrow

tainly a contrast to the horrors of war we experienced each night on TV during the years of the Vietnam war—the first fully televised war. Advances in mass communication have made the world smaller; the distance between people and the space between countries no longer seem as great a barrier to communication.

Delayed Feedback By definition, mass communication suggests a widespread audience separated from a source by a great distance. Therefore, a receiver's feedback or response to a message is most often limited and delayed. For example, a person watching a charity telethon may be moved to respond immediately by calling in a pledge. Yet the sheer mechanics of the situation create a certain delay in feedback. There are varying degrees of delayed feedback, ranging from a few minutes, as in the above situation, to several weeks or even months. A consumer responding to a TV commercial for a particular brand of deodorant may not purchase the product until his or her current supply runs out, which may be days or even weeks later. Consumers may not even realize that they are responding to a mass communication message. The fact that the source is inaccessible and that a medium is needed to transmit the response are major reasons for the delay in feedback. For example, if listeners are outraged by a remark heard on TV or radio, the best they can do is call the station. Yet even this action takes a certain amount of time and cannot represent total listener reaction, particularly in terms of nonverbal feedback.

Gatekeeping As one might expect, the enormous scope of mass communication requires some control in the selection and editing of the messages that are constantly transmitted to the mass audience. The term *gatekeeper,* originally used by Austrian psychologist Kurt Lewin to identify the people or organizations who control news items in the communications channel, has now come to mean any individual or organization that influences a mass communication message.[2] There are gatekeepers within the mass communication industry itself; within the government; and within big business. Each group sets certain standards and limitations that serve as guidelines for both content and delivery of a mass communication message.

[2]Kurt Lewin, "Frontiers in Group Dynamics," *Human Relations* 1 (1947): 5–41.

INDUSTRY GATEKEEPING   To understand the concept of gatekeeping, we need to examine the news media. Every major paper and station is flooded with news stories fed to them by the major wire services, organizations that send news stories and features by direct telegraph to subscribing newspapers and TV and radio stations. Obviously, the news media cannot relay all of this information. Since neither time nor space allows for the printing or broadcasting of each and every news event, media personnel at various levels must determine which items they consider the most newsworthy. In effect, the information that is fed to the various news media goes through a filtering process. Stories that appear on the front page in a Midwest daily may be put on the back page of a New York newpaper, if printed at all. Yet you need not make comparisons across state lines to see that news selection and editing are very subjective. Examine two papers published in the same city and compare headline stories and the location of various news items. Sometimes a story that appears in the first few pages of one paper is entirely omitted in another. Writers, editors, publishers, and other media personnel determine length and placement of the news copy. While some stories must be included, they are often condensed or distorted. For example, an involved story about suspected corruption at the state or local level may be published as fact by news services in a different state or locality because they don't have the time or space to devote to a story that does not directly influence their readers or viewers. This, then, is industry gatekeeping.

GOVERNMENT GATEKEEPING   In addition to a filtering system that controls message selection, agencies such as the Federal Communications Commission (FCC) and the courts also exert influence on media content. In their roles as gatekeepers, the FCC and the courts must protect the in-

The beginnings of a new medium of mass communication: a television set on display at the 1939 New York World's Fair.
(RCA)

> It is better to be making the news than taking it.
>
> *Winston Churchill*

terests of the public. To assure proper use of the public airwaves, the FCC issues a license before a station may broadcast. A license is granted for a period of three years, after which time the station's performance is evaluated. A review of the station must show that the station has abided by the rules and regulations set forth by the FCC and that it has offered a public service. You may have noticed that sometimes when a TV or radio station's license is up for renewal, the station will invite letters from the audience to comment on how it has served the public interest. A station that has not been granted a license or that has had its license taken away may no longer broadcast.

Two important FCC controls are the equal time rule and the fairness doctrine. The **equal time rule** applies to candidates for political office. It says that a station must give all candidates the same amount of time under the same terms. Thus, if one candidate is interviewed by a station, other candidates must be given the same coverage. If a candidate buys air time to advertise his or her candidacy, other candidates must be given the same option, even if it means that the station has to preempt regular programming.

When the Kennedy-Nixon debates were broadcast in 1960, Congress suspended the equal time rule so that stations would not be overwhelmed by requests to put many minor candidates on the air. Yet, in 1976 the FCC handled the Carter-Ford debates in a completely different way. Stations can bypass the equal time rule if coverage of a candidate is considered a newsworthy event. Therefore, the FCC concluded that the presidential debates sponsored by the League of Women Voters were a newsworthy event that should be reported, thereby getting around the equal time rule.

Unlike the equal time rule, which involves people, the fairness doctrine mainly involves issues. The **fairness doctrine** states that all stations must provide some time to discuss controversial issues and that each station must encourage opposing viewpoints. Therefore, if a station offers an editorial opposing school busing, it must ask for and air the views of a spokesperson in favor of the issue. Or, if in the course of a commentary a speaker denounces a particular person or organization, that individual or group must have the right to respond.

While all government attempts to control mass communication can be interpreted as infringements of constitutional rights, guidelines used to determine whether something is obscene or pornographic are particularly controversial. Although periodically revised, court rulings that define obscenity and pornography are characteristically vague. Decisions about obscenity are now left up to the individual community, which must decide if the material in question has any "redeeming social value," or—if taken as a whole—the material "appeals to prurient interest." As you can see, the guidelines are extremely vague and subjective. Yet, despite this, the conviction of actors in the X-rated movie "Deep Throat" on "conspiracy to corrupt morals" charges, and a controversial 1977 court case that banned the sale of *Hustler* magazine, reflect governmental gatekeeping in the area of pornograpy and obscenity.

ECONOMIC GATEKEEPING   Advertisers are the primary financial support for mass media and thus control media industries to some extent. The broadcast media sell time, while the print media sell space. Since media buying is expensive, advertisers want some control over the content of anything they sponsor.

To show the influence of a TV network sponsor, we can point out that during the McCarthy era in the early 1950s, a sponsor could dictate who could or could not work either on camera or behind the scenes of a program. Some sponsors were known to blacklist anyone suspected of being sympathetic to the Communist Party.

The influence of advertisers goes beyond politics and has sometimes been known to dictate taste. Since the sponsor wants to capture a large audience to assure the greatest exposure for the product, advertisers have sometimes been known to attempt to control content so that programming will appeal to the largest audience possible.

Sometimes a sponsor's influence can work to the audience's advantage. For example, a sponsor might pressure the network to curb the amount of sex or violence in a program it sponsors.

MASS COMMUNICATION MEDIA

Now, more than at any time in history, we are a media society. No day goes by without our feeling the effects of mass communication. That's not true, you say, "I don't watch TV every day!" Maybe not, but did you wake up to news on the radio, read a paper over breakfast, play an album, read a billboard, go to the movies, read a book, or get a magazine at the newsstand? We employ mass communication daily by using it to inform us of world events, to help escape into another realm, or to plan our weekends based on weather reports.

We have already examined the characteristics of mass communication. We will now look at four of the most important forms of mass communication: film, recording, radio, and television.

Film

From its beginning as a method of recording history, film has developed into a major form of recreation and entertainment. Film has been around longer than any other electronic medium, and it stays alive because it is the most creative and artistic of all media. The "film experience" (1) is of high technical quality (visually and aurally), (2) stimulates involvement,

(3) provides a comfortable environment (food, seating, no interruptions, and so on), and (4) is the most realistic of all mass media forms.[3] Trends have included the 1920s era of Charlie Chaplin silent films; the 1930s musicals with Fred Astaire and Ginger Rogers; the patriotic films featuring Humphrey Bogart in the 1940s; the 3-D and youth-oriented themes of the 1950s; the experience/involvement films such as *Psycho, The Sound of Music,* and the Beatles' movies of the 1960s; and, finally, the disaster films such as *The Poseidon Adventure, Jaws,* and *The Towering Inferno* of the 1970s. The seventies gave us films of social comment such as *One Flew Over the Cuckoo's Nest, All the President's Men,* and *Coming Home;* while the late seventies and early eighties often gave us movies focused on music, such as *Saturday Night Fever, The Buddy Holly Story, The Rose,* and *A Star Is Born.* Recent films have also revealed an enchantment and curiosity with space exploration and travel, particularly films such as *Star Wars* (nine sequences to be completed before the director is "done"), the *Star Trek* sequences, and *E.T.: The Extra-Terrestrial.* What's next? Although no one knows what next season will provide, we know there will be something for everyone, because film readily adapts to the events and needs of the time.

Recording Is there a special song that reminds you of the first time you fell in love? Do you play a certain album when you're lonely and want to think? Can some music make you wiggle your toes or hop in the car? Music is everywhere in our society, from Muzak in doctors' offices to country western or punk rock in the local nightclub. Just as we remember songs from different periods in our lives, we also remember different decades by the music that was popular at the time. The Big Band and swing era of the 1940s gave birth to the first recording hero, Frank Sinatra. The Comets arrived in 1955 with "Rock Around the Clock," and then the popular Elvis gave birth to rock 'n' roll in the late 1950s. The early 1960s was best known for the Beatles and later for songs of social discontent and alienation. The 1970s was a decade of no real trend, with gentler rock, hard rock, disco, punk rock, new wave music, and the rise of country and western music.

The recording industry has music for all ages and tastes. Since record buying is dominated by people under thirty, recorded music is thought of generally as a youth medium. Eight out of every ten singles are bought by people under twenty-five, and two-thirds of all albums are bought by people under thirty. Many try to make it big in recording, but hopes are often shattered. To break even, a single must sell 25,000 copies, and an album must sell 85,000.[4]

Radio Driving to class or to work, or driving out of town, many of us turn the radio dial, looking for a favorite station. It is usually fairly easy to find a station to meet our needs since there are 3,500 AM stations and 700 FM

[3]E. J. Whetmore, *Mediamerica,* 2d ed. (Belmont, Calif.: Wadsworth, 1982).
[4]Hiebert Bohn and Donald F. Unguvait, *Mass Media II,* 3d ed. (New York: Longman, 1982).

COMMUNICATION THROUGH THE MASS MEDIA

stations playing all types of music. It has not always been so convenient, yet radio has been popular for over forty years. During the 1930s and 1940s, radio was the television of today, with situation comedies, musicals, political addresses, and game shows. The late 1940s was a time of great change because of the development of television. Sponsors were quickly changing over to the visual medium. To save radio, a deejay format was introduced in 1951. With the deejay format, stations began to design programs for specific audiences—today we have everything from all-music to all-talk radio.

The success of radio is often attributed to its mobility. Portable transistors allow us to carry radios in our pockets and bring them anywhere from beaches to offices. Radio is also the most reliable form of communication because it can use batteries instead of electricity. Further, radio is beneficial to advertising. Many small organizations cannot afford the expense of TV and can still get publicity through radio inexpensively.

Television

You are a member of the television generation. Men, women, and children find it easier to identify television personalities such as Captain Kangaroo, "Hawkeye" Pierce, Charlie's Angels, or J. R. Ewing than members of the president's cabinet, former schoolteachers, or even some friends. Television is the most powerful and influential mass medium. In 1941 only 5,000 to 10,000 homes had television, but today 97 percent of all homes in America have at least one TV.

Unlike film, recording, and radio, which now cater to specialized audiences, television designs programs to please every viewer. Cartoons, documentaries, soap operas, variety shows, game shows, adventure series, sports spectaculars, movies, news, educational shows, and family shows try to meet the needs of all viewers. Some people watch TV to satisfy social needs by receiving information from news shows, fireside chats, or "Meet the Press." Others get vicarious experiences from programs such as "Wide World of Sports" and "Wild Kingdom." People escape into other worlds and live fantasies by loving and hating men and women on soap operas such as "Another World" or "One Life to Live." Still others reinforce their sense of values by watching shows such as "Barnaby Jones" and "Quincy," where good always wins over evil. The variety and flexibility of television make it America's most popular form of entertainment.

FUNCTIONS OF MASS COMMUNICATION

In Chapter 9 we identified the purposes of public speaking: to inform, to persuade, and to entertain. Basically, these three purposes also describe the primary functions of mass media.

To Inform

Although there is considerable overlap among these three areas, one can say that the dissemination of information belongs primarily to the news media, both electronic and print. Yet the news media have come a long way from just "telling it like it is." Throughout the country local news shows have expanded their format to include human interest stories as well as news features. Even the coverage of the news has changed dramatically. Instead of merely reporting events, reporters and broadcast journalists have become news analysts who discuss the implications of important news stories.

GOOD NEWS VS. BAD NEWS   Today the broadcasting of news events is so immediate that the impact of a story hot off the press (or hot off the wires) can have a jolting effect. On certain days we may turn on the radio news report and hear nothing but bad news. A war, an earthquake, a plane crash, a murder can all be news events on any given day. The immediate reporting of these unfortunate events is bound to have an effect on listeners.

In fact, several studies have been conducted to test the effects of good news versus bad news on people's feelings and interpersonal relationships. In one such study subjects exposed to good news were found to have more positive feelings than those exposed to bad news. Furthermore, the subject's feelings also influenced his or her interactions with others.[5]

Some individuals have a preference for receiving their news from newspapers, while others rely on TV or radio. Even within each medium, people most often select a particular newspaper or a particular channel for a report of the daily news. Surveys show that most Americans believe that TV journalists such as Walter Cronkite and David Brinkley are the most credible sources of news.

However, it has been found that the TV news program is less effective in influencing viewers on political issues than newspapers and paid TV advertising.[6] This can be explained by the format of the TV news program, which gives brief coverage of many stories each evening. Therefore, viewers are not exposed to in-depth coverage that might affect their voting habits. Since most stories are given limited coverage, a viewer may walk away from a TV news program not knowing which stories are most significant. Newspapers and other print media suggest the significance of various stories by the space allotted to each story, its location in the paper, its layout, and the boldness of its headline. However, a story of great visual appeal or catastrophic dimension will probably have greater effect when seen on television.

PUBLIC BROADCASTING SERVICE   We cannot talk about the information media without mentioning educational television or the Public Broadcasting Service, a nonprofit organization that attempts to emphasize the edu-

[5]Russell Veitch, "Good News—Bad News: Affective and Interpersonal Effects," *Journal of Applied Social Psychology* 6, no. 1 (1976): 69–75.
[6]R. D. McClure and T. E. Patterson, "Television News and Political Advertising: The Impact of Exposure on Voter Beliefs," *Communications Research* 1 (1974): 3–31.

"Put your shirt on. This is Masterpiece Theatre!"
© Ladies Home Journal and Joseph Farris

cational and enlightening aspects of television. Unlike commercial networks, which sell air time to sponsors, educational stations buy programs
from the PBS network with money obtained from donations, federal
funds, and commercial grants. You might notice that at the beginning or
end of a program on PBS, the source of funding for the program is announced: "This program was made possible by a grant from. . . ." This
type of sponsorship, which eliminates the need for advertisers, represents
one of the most striking differences between commercial and public
broadcasting.

Unlike commercial networks, PBS has attempted to realize the educational values of television. Many of its programs are instructional in nature, the most widely known being "Sesame Street," a program for pre-
school children.

PBS also provides a forum for many experimental and innovative
programs that would be too risky for commercial sponsors. PBS does not
aim its entire schedule of programs at a "mass audience"; instead, it offers
programs that appeal to a limited audience, a practice that would be im-

possible for a commercial network. Unfortunately, the artistic principles and practices that make PBS unique also create difficulties. Aside from obvious financial difficulties, PBS stations are sometimes uncertain as to just what their educational function should be.

DIFFUSION OF INFORMATION **Diffusion** of information refers to the way the public learns about new events, products, changes in policy, ideas, philosophies, and so forth. We might guess that most of our information comes from the mass media. However, studies have shown that although the mass media are particularly effective in informing the public of major news stories and events that have just occurred, they are much less effective when information has less news value or concerns something new about an event or idea that is already known. While many people learn about an assassination or an earthquake through the media, information concerning a change in library hours or a change in traffic regulations must be diffused in a different manner. A much-cited study by Bradley S. Greenberg showed that 50 percent of his sample said that they had learned about the Kennedy assassination from another person.[7]

The diffusion of information from one individual to another is based on the principle of **homophily,** which is the degree to which two interacting individuals are similar in characteristics such as beliefs, values, education, social level, and so on. Diffusion of information occurs most often when a source and a receiver are alike. A student is more likely to acquire information from another student, a construction worker from another construction worker, and so on.

The diffusion of information can be analyzed in terms of change agents and opinion leaders. A **change agent** is someone who is responsible for making policy and creating change. By the nature of their position, change agents are usually not homophilous with the people to whom they must disseminate information. The change agent generally interacts with an **opinion leader,** who is more homophilous with the general public and disseminates information to them. Opinion leaders are usually respected by their peers and have considerable influence in forming and changing attitudes within their spheres of influence.

Mass communication has certainly aided the diffusion of information. Opinion leaders rely on the mass media for reports of certain news events, which they in turn disseminate to the general public. For example, when the controversy regarding landing rights for the Concorde SST began, protest leaders relied heavily on the media for information. As new developments arose, protest leaders would report and analyze important events for their followers. Due to mass media as well as to telephones and telegraphs, the process through which information is diffused has been greatly speeded up.

[7]Bradley S. Greenberg, "Diffusion of News about the Kennedy Assassination," *Public Opinion Quarterly* 28 (Summer 1964): 225–32.

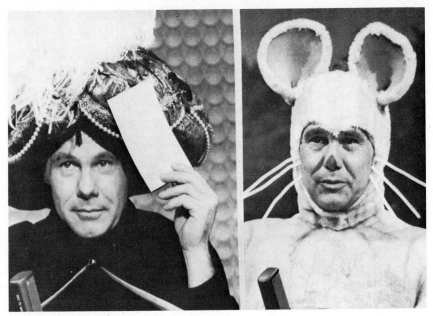

(United Press International)

The most common function of mass communication is entertainment. Although radio, TV, and films function as information media, entertainment provides the primary source of their revenues.

To Entertain

     Entertainment covers many different things. For example, entertainment sections in newspapers include comics, horoscopes, and advice columns, as well as crossword puzzles and other word games. In television entertainment includes game shows, situation comedies, soap operas, movies, drama, variety shows, and sports events. Radio entertainment today consists primarily of music, although radio plays, talk shows, and comedy routines make a major contribution. When we talk about film, we are talking mainly about an entertainment medium, with the possible exception of documentaries. What do all these forms have in common? By nature, an entertainment medium is one that provides the consumer with some sort of escape or diversion from the realities and anxieties of daily living.

Another function of the mass media is persuasion, as presented by advertising for products, political candidates, service organizations, charities, businesses, and so forth. Both electronic and print media have great persuasive potential, but, depending on the nature of the message, a full-page ad in a major newspaper can sometimes have greater impact than a minute of air time. There are media specialists who analyze where and how messages should be placed to have the greatest influence. One study found that 40 percent of the consumers in a sample population of 3,000 chose newspapers as the most reliable medium for advertising; 10 percent

To Persuade

chose radio; and 6 percent chose TV. Forty percent of the sample population felt that there was no difference.[8]

ADVERTISING

Each day our dreams, fears, desires, and concerns are analyzed by advertisers anxious to sell products.[9] *Advertising's* chief purpose is to persuade people to buy and to continue to buy certain products. Radio and TV advertisements are geared to the particular audiences that will be tuned in. During a weekday afternoon soap operas that attract millions of women are interrupted with commercials featuring laundry, cleansing, beauty, and feminine hygiene products. Through demographic analysis companies have found out about the types of people in viewing audiences and what products they would be most interested in buying.

Many of you can easily recall certain advertising slogans or commercials. These advertising messages must do more than keep attention to be successful. No matter how interesting a radio or TV spot may be, if it fails to influence consumer buying habits, it fails. Advertising has been widely accepted in the print media, but many people view broadcast advertising as an invasion of privacy. They resent their lack of control over the type and length of commercials. For this reason, many TV viewers are turning to cable television or remote-control devices to turn off advertising. Consumers can have a voice in methods of advertising. Because of consumer complaints about exaggerated claims, broadcast regulations now govern the content of advertisements.

One medium can be more successful than another for certain products. Radio is most effective in announcing items such as drycleaning specials, food discounts, and clothing sales, where the visual appeal is not as important as the information. TV is highly successful where both visual and verbal content is important. Seeing how a drop of super glue suspends a 500-pound weight is more effective than just hearing about it. Pet food campaigns have been particularly successful through TV advertising. For centuries pets were fed with table scraps, but during the last fifteen years, advertising has encouraged Americans to spend $2.5 billion each year on pet foods.[10]

In today's society advertisers and politicians depend heavily on mass media. How else would sponsors promote new products, or candidates introduce themselves to the general public? Very often, however, consumers are unaware of the widespread influence of the mass media. A consumer may buy a product without realizing that the seed for that purchase was planted by a TV commercial or newspaper ad.

[8]"Media Advertising Credibility," *Journalism Quarterly* 53 (Summer 1976): 216–22.
[9]Vance Packard, *The Hidden Persuaders* (New York: McKay, 1957).
[10]Thomas Whiteside, "Onward and Upward with the Arts (Pet Food)," *The New Yorker*, 1 November 1976, pp. 51–98.

While a fine line is drawn between advertising and public relations, advertising is generally concerned with selling a product; and public relations, with selling an image. ***Public relations*** is a more subtle form of advertising, which is designed to influence attitudes and beliefs. McDonald's is interested in selling its food products, but it also tries to gain recognition by giving contributions to charity, sponsoring restaurant tours for children, and writing articles about employee satisfaction.

Corporations are not the only organizations interested in public relations. Nonprofit groups, governmental agencies, churches, and universities are all involved with publicity campaigns. These organizations use public relations agents and agencies to get specific information to the public via the news media. One of the goals of public relations is to utilize space free of charge. Television news coverage of a political candidate participating in a national walk-a-thon is probably more influential in projecting a favorable image than a $50,000, thirty-second, prime-time TV spot.

Although many people resent the persuasive impact of advertising and public relations, we must also realize that this influence can sometimes be constructive. Self-help groups such as Alcoholics Anonymous and different social service agencies use the media to help make people aware of the groups' existence as well as to persuade those in need to seek out their help.

EFFECTS OF MASS MEDIA

There is considerable controversy about whether mass media serve to reinforce or change preexisting ideas. This question has been studied in the context of both political campaigns and commercial advertising. In the 1940s and 1950s, studies by Bernard Berelson and Paul Lazarsfeld contradicted the long-held theory that people's voting habits were easily swayed by persuasive messages in the media. According to their studies, voting behavior is most influenced by family and acquaintances, and voters select those political messages that reinforce preexisting beliefs. Yet additional studies in the 1960s and 1970s found that a voter may sometimes completely change his or her vote as a result of a political message. Thus far the results of studies dealing with advertising are inconclusive. The question remains as to whether people are capable of withstanding ad campaigns or are manipulated by media sponsors.

Children and TV

With the new forms of communications has come a new set of questions. One of the most compelling questions concerns the effect of television on children. TV is one of the most widespread influences on today's youth.

THE NATURE OF THE MEDIUM

In accepting an honorary degree from the University of Notre Dame a few years ago, General David Sarnoff made this statement: "We are too prone to make technological instruments the scapegoats for the sins of those who wield them. The products of modern science are not in themselves good or bad, it is the way they are used that determines their values." This is the voice of the current somnambulism. Suppose we were to say, "Apple pie is in itself neither good nor bad; it is the way it is used that determines its value." Or, "The smallpox virus is in itself neither good nor bad; it is the way it is used that determines its value." Again, "Firearms are in themselves neither good nor bad; it is the way they are used that determines their value." That is, if the slugs reach the right people firearms are good. If the TV tube fires the right ammunition at the right people it is good. I am not being perverse. There is simply nothing in the Sarnoff statement that will bear scrutiny, for it ignores the nature of the medium, of any and all media, in the true Narcissus style of one hypnotized by the amputation and extension of his own being in a new technical form. General Sarnoff went on to explain his attitude to the technology of print, saying that it was true that print caused much trash to circulate, but it had also disseminated the Bible and the thoughts of seers and philosophers. It has never occurred to General Sarnoff that any technology could do anything but add itself on to what we already are.

From Marshall McLuhan, Understanding Media: The Extension of Man (New York: McGraw-Hill, 1964).

The average youngster will have watched 15,000 hours of television by the time he or she is seventeen, second only to sleep in terms of time consumption.[11]

There has been considerable investigation of the effect of TV on children. Not all findings are consistent. Some theories suggest that television provides vicarious reinforcement; that is, imaginary participation in an activity that is rewarding for the characters on the screen will reinforce this same type of behavior in a real-life situation. This does not imply a negative or positive value. Yet, when the activity is violent, or when youngsters cannot separate themselves from fantasy, this effect can be harmful.

Another criticism of television is that television stifles a child's creativity. To prove this claim, a research team from the University of Southern California exposed 250 intellectually gifted elementary school students to three weeks of intensive television viewing. Based on pre-test and post-test evaluations, the study found that the children showed a "marked drop in all forms of creative abilities except verbal skills."[12] This experiment provided empirical data on an effect that many elementary school teachers have observed for some time.

Since children watch television for a number of reasons, ranging from entertainment to loneliness, they unknowingly become involved in a process of "observational learning"; that is, they learn certain things by

[11]"What TV Does to Kids," *Newsweek*, 21 February 1977, pp. 63–70.
[12]"What TV Does to Kids," p. 65.

simply watching the behavior of TV characters. The amount of observational learning that takes place depends upon several factors, which include:

1. The degree to which a child identifies with a television character.
2. The degree to which the child sees some usefulness for the particular behavior.
3. A belief that behaving in the way presented on TV will be successful.
4. The relative newness of the ideas or behavior presented on screen.
5. The reality of the TV portrayal and the situation.[13]

Children learn many different things through observation, including skills, values, norms, roles, and sex stereotypes. What a child learns can be either positive or negative, depending on content.

Another important effect of TV is that it often replaces parental influence and supplies role models for children and adolescents who have inadequate ones at home. The TV set can become a substitute parent, a baby sitter, and a replacement for family interaction. This effect goes against the welfare of the individual.

TV VIOLENCE We cannot discuss TV and children without emphasizing the effects of TV violence. Once again, not all findings agree. However, after reviewing twenty-five years worth of hard data, including the fifty most comprehensive studies dealing with 10,000 children from every possible background, Michael Rothenberg, a child psychologist at the University of Washington, concluded, "Viewing violence tends to produce aggressive behavior among the young."[14]

In addition to producing aggressive behavior, it is interesting to note how TV violence affects our reactions to violence in real life. Some people say that exposure to very violent scenes makes viewers more sensitive to the painful consequences of violent actions. Yet there seems to be more support for the notion that TV violence "desensitizes" its audience to violence in real-life situations. According to this view, the audience becomes apathetic or accepting of violent acts in society.

To test this theory, psychologists Ronald Drabman and Margaret Thomas designed several experiments in which they had some children watch violent segments from various TV shows. After the experimental group had viewed the segments, both groups (experimental and control) witnessed what the experimenters had set up as a violent real-life situation. They found that subjects who had witnessed the violent segments took considerably longer in seeking assistance than subjects in the control group. In fact, certain subjects in the experimental group did not go for

[13]Eisenhower Commission Report on Violence in TV, September 1969.
[14] "What TV Does to Kids," pp. 63–64.

help at all. The pscyhologists suggested two possible reasons to explain this apathetic reaction. TV violence shows either that aggression is part of life and should be taken casually or that what happens in real life is insignificant compared with the violence seen on TV.[15]

Of course, the movie industry has also been faced with pressure concerning violence in films. The rating system imposed by the movie industry in the late 1960s was an attempt to deal with this matter, although both sex and violence determine the rating. While the rating system does not alter the content of the film, it does serve to keep children from seeing certain films and warns other viewers what to expect. This same function is served by the disclaimers that precede certain TV programs.

TELEVISION COMMERCIALS   Recently there has been concern about the effects of television advertising on children. Especially on Saturday mornings, children are bombarded by enticing cereal, candy, toy, and game commercials. In a thirty-six minute time period, at least six minutes are devoted to advertising. Like the advertising designed for adults, children's advertising encourages youngsters to persuade their parents to buy and use certain products. The commercials often offer rewards and prizes such as iron-on decals and toys inside the box.

Parents display mixed emotions about children's television advertising. Investigations of parental attitudes suggest that the average level of concern is not as high as some consumer groups would have us believe. However, the majority of studies note that although parents verbalize concern, there is little relationship between parental dissatisfaction with commercials and parental monitoring of television viewing.[16]

Parents are faced with endless demands from their children. Yielding to and denying children's requests for products varies according to the product category and whether or not the item is for the child's consumption. Cereals are bought two-thirds of the time they are requested.[17] Toys and games are not as easy for children to get unless they are for Christmas. Notice the increase of prime-time commercials geared to children prior to Christmas. The results of one study indicate that parents yield to 43 percent of Christmas gift requests. The percentage would be higher, but some products that look superior on TV are often made of cheap plastic materials that parents hesitate to buy.[18]

By now you may be wondering what happens when a child's request for the latest Wonder Woman doll is denied. In young children the most obvious reactions are disappointment and anger. One survey sug-

[15]"TV Aggression Teaches Apathy," *Psychology Today* 10, no. 6 (November 1976): 36–37.

[16]A. Feldman, A. Wolfand, and D. Warmouth, "Parental Concern about Child-Directed Commercials," *Journal of Communication* 27 (Winter 1977): 125–37.

[17]T. S. Robertson, "Parental Mediation of Television Advertising Effects," *Journal of Communication* 29 (Winter 1979): 12–25.

[18]T. S. Robertson and J. R. Rossiter, "Children's Consumer Satisfaction," working paper, Center for Research on Media and Children (Philadelphia: University of Pennsylvania, 1976).

(United Press International)

gests that children get angry if they feel their parents cannot afford a product. Other children blame themselves for not being good enough to receive the latest honey-coated cereal that builds strong muscles. Even though parent-child relations are strained when requests are denied, the strain usually lasts for only a short period of time.[19]

Although we have already touched on mass communication and politics, we should review some of the research designed to test the effects of mass media on political campaigns. Some people believe that mass communication is the key to political victory. Certain political observers even suggest that Nixon lost the 1960 presidential debates and the election because he was not as "telegenic" as his opponent (that is, he did not come over on television as well as John F. Kennedy).

Political Campaigns

John Carey, a communications expert from the University of Pennsylvania, made a study of the news coverage of several 1974 congressional elections. He analyzed the reporting of three networks, three major news magazines, and the major newspapers. Carey found that the primary focus of most reports was on "campaign actions and their strategic value." Although the newspapers reported only what each candidate said, the magazines and news stations were more concerned with the effect of a candidate's statement or action. Issues and philosophy were secondary to strategy.[20]

[19]Robertson and Rossiter, 1976.
[20]John Carey, "How Media Shapes Campaigns," *Journal of Communication* 26, no. 2 (Spring 1976): 50–57.

Television, if used effectively, can aid a political campaign. As previously noted, the presentation of a political figure on a regular news show does little, if anything, for the candidate. In order to use the medium most effectively, candidates apparently have to purchase television spots to introduce themselves and their ideas. Although news coverage is free and spot commercials are expensive, the commercials have a much greater impact. Whether or not this exposure reinforces or changes viewers' voting habits is still inconclusive. However, in terms of exposure and information, the advertising spots have a much greater effect than news coverage.

Of all the different media, television is the most expensive and therefore must be used most efficiently. Advertising agencies sometimes plan a media campaign for a political candidate in much the same way that they promote a new product. In fact, books such as *The Selling of the President,* by Joe McGinniss, have explored this similarity.

Sex Stereotyping The mass media have usually reflected society's attitudes towards sex roles, and so, until recently, little effort was made to contradict sex stereotypes. Women were portrayed as passive, while men were by and large shown as aggressive and powerful. If you were to look at the TV programs of earlier decades, you might think that every woman in the country was a hard-working housewife who wanted only to stay home and care for husband and children. Occasionally, a spitfire like Lucy, Gale Storm, or Anne Southern would show that women could have spunk, although their exploits always involved scheming and inevitably backfired. During the early days of TV, there were proportionately fewer women on TV than men, and seldom did you see them on a news program. In the print media women's magazines catered to the housewife and mother, assuming that this was the only possible female audience.

(United Press International)

While things have certainly not changed entirely, we have begun to see a shift. We now have TV situation comedies about single women and widows. We see these women as the family breadwinners, sometimes competing professionally with men. A look at both local and network news shows reveals an increase in female newscasters, many of whom are in key spots.

The increasing number of women in today's work force has brought about changes in the mass media. For example, today there are magazines published just for the working woman; and more and more the various news and entertainment media are covering stories relevant to women as well as men.

The mass media are so important in our lives that they often have an effect on the shaping of the events they cover. Sometimes events are planned with an eye toward media coverage. The Superbowl is a perfect example of a spectacular event that grew out of the media. On a smaller scale, basketball and football games that are broadcast live allow time out for a word from the sponsor. **Shaping of Events**

There are numerous examples that show how media can shape events. A politician may delay a press conference until a broken TV camera is repaired, or a track star may be asked to repeat a final lap so that his or her action can be recorded on film.

Sometimes the media overstep their bounds in shaping events. A major network was once accused of contributing money to invasionary forces in Haiti in return for the right to film the takeover. Although the event never came off, the thought that it might have succeeded is rather frightening.[21]

Related to media influence in shaping events is the effect of mass media on government. In a society where there is free speech and free press, the media serve as watchdogs over the government. For instance, exposing the Watergate affair was the work of two reporters for the *Washington Post*. After the Watergate scandal was uncovered, TV aired the Congressional hearings, which affected public opinion and ultimately the Nixon administration, ending in the president's resignation. In addition to the watchdog effect, the media also serve the government by disseminating information to the public. **Effects on Government**

APPEARING ON RADIO AND TELEVISION

Let's now turn our attention behind the scenes and look at the organization of a broadcasting station. Since the broadcasting industry is dependent upon performers, we will conclude this section with some discussion about performing on radio and television.

[21]Don R. Pember, *Mass Media in America,* 3rd ed. (Chicago: Science Research Associates, 1983), p. 36.

Jobs at a broadcasting station range from artistic to financial positions. While the organization of each individual station may vary, certain similarities do exist. Basically, the organization of all stations can be broken down into three major areas: management, sales, and production.

Since broadcasting is a multimillion dollar industry, the management area is of great importance. Management must assume the financial functions of accounting and bookkeeping as well as major responsibilities related to keeping the station in operation. Depending on the size of the station, distinctions may be made between general administrative functions and business management.

Because commercial broadcasting depends on selling air time to sponsors, the sales department of any station serves as its financial life-support system. Again, depending on size and volume of sales, some stations separate this department into two sections: one to deal with local sales and one to deal with national sales.

The production end of the broadcasting industry includes a variety of functions, some operational, others creative. One of the most important aspects of production is the programming department, which deals with the selection of programs and the scheduling of air time. Large stations tend to divide this department into major areas such as sports, arts, community affairs, and so on. Other production responsibilities include coordinating all operations and overseeing artistic considerations.

When you think of how complex the broadcasting industry has become, with many stations providing programming twenty-four hours a day, you can see the need for a highly specialized pattern of organization to assure the smooth operation of the station.

Inside a
Television
Studio A look inside a television studio reveals an array of cameras, monitors, and lights. The amount of equipment and sophistication of the video system is determined by the size and productivity of the station. Local stations have modest setups in comparison to the large studios of network-affiliated stations.

The first visit to a TV studio can be both fascinating and disillusioning. While the activity in the studio is very exciting, the discovery that so much of television is illusion may be disappointing. For example, you may find that the backdrop for a TV talk show, which looks so glamorous on the air, is really very ordinary. Or a set that is supposed to be the large and luxurious living room of your favorite soap opera character may turn out to be a closet-sized piece of cardboard. Even the most basic television lighting and camera work can create many illusions, not to mention those created by the more sophisticated special effects equipment.

A studio is divided into two areas: the main studio, where the camera work is done, and the control room, where the master console is located. The technicians who work this console are able to control the picture that viewers see at home. The individuals who monitor the video console can produce a composite picture by mixing images from two or more dif-

(Prentice-Hall Photo Archives)

ferent cameras; they can dissolve from one shot to another; and, when the equipment is sophisticated enough, they can even create split-screen or superimposed images. For example, during a television debate the console may create a split-screen effect so that both opponents can be seen at the same time.

A study of the television studio is not complete without a look at the people who work in it. The producer organizes a show, coordinates schedules, and supervises the overall production. Among his or her other responsibilities are the overseeing of financial matters, promotion, and the technical aspects of the production. It is the producer's job to see that a production runs smoothly.

While the producer is concerned with the production as a whole, the director is in charge of the creative aspects of the production. A good theater director is not necessarily a good television director, or vice versa. A good television director must make the most of the creative elements of television—for instance, the director must realize the sensitivity of the camera in picking up nuances and be sure that the camera captures the intended effect.

The producer and the director are powerless without the aid of other people whose jobs are also behind the scenes. The floor manager is an intermediary between the director and the actors. It is he or she who cues the actors, tells them where to stand, where to sit, where to cross the floor, and so on.

Camera operators are a necessity, as is the technical director. The latter is in charge of the control console, at which he or she coordinates the video and audio mechanisms.

The next time you watch your favorite television show, think about all the people and equipment that make it possible. Even the simplest news show requires sophisticated equipment and highly trained personnel.

Of course, one of the most basic parts of the broadcasting industry is the "talent," the term used to describe the men and women who perform on radio and television. Usually thought of as having the glamorous jobs in the industry, the "talent" includes newscasters, sports announcers, actresses, actors, disc jockeys, and game show hosts, to name just a few.

Talent may also include amateurs who are invited to participate in local programs. In fact, you may one day be invited to discuss a school project or community event at a local broadcasting station. When you accept such an invitation, you should prepare for a communication environment that is different from any you have ever experienced. Understanding the conditions placed on professional performers will help you to be a better communicator.

Regardless of their particular roles, performers must adapt to the medium in which they are working. For example, when working on radio or television, a performer must get used to working without feedback, since most often there is no audience present. Therefore, an individual must develop a sixth sense to determine the effect his or her material or delivery is having on the audience at home.

Other adjustments that a radio or television performer must make concern the limitations imposed by the audio and video equipment. On the air a radio performer must speak into the microphone; the TV performer must not only be near enough to the microphone but must also be in camera view. Therefore, natural movements and expressions must sometimes be consciously curtailed.

In addition, both radio and television performers must contend with numerous technical cues as well as technical distractions. The smoothness of a performance is determined by how well a performer maintains his or her concentration. Of course, working on a tape that will be aired at a later time allows for retakes and editing, two luxuries that are not part of a live broadcast.

While there are certain similarities in performing on radio and television, there are also considerable differences. The most important tool of radio performers is their voice. Think about different radio personalities you have heard. What is it that you like or dislike about their voice quality or style? Many of the characteristics that we discussed in our chapter on delivery play an important part in radio performance. Rate, emphasis, vocal expression, pronunciation, and articulation are all areas that need much practice if you are interested in pursuing a career in broadcasting.

Performing on television adds many new dimensions to the list of "things to do" before going on the air. While a radio performer can hide behind a microphone, the television performer is under close scrutiny. Clothing, personal appearance, and body movements are extremely important. You may have noticed that when a station is breaking in a new sportscaster or newsperson, it takes a while before the person feels and looks comfortable before the camera. An unseasoned performer might very well feel self-conscious and uneasy when first appearing on television. Again, performers must learn to use the medium and make it work for them.

THE FUTURE OF MASS COMMUNICATION

Unlike other forms of communication, the development of mass communication has depended on advances in technology. The first major contribution to this development was the invention of the printing press, which led to the print media. For hundreds of years print was the only form of mass communication. Radio, television, and film did not become realities until the twentieth century. Since the electronic media have such a powerful impact on our daily lives, it is almost impossible to imagine what our lives would be like without them.

Yet many advances in mass communication have occurred in just the last few decades. Words such as "cassette," "satellite," and "transistor" are now part of almost everyone's vocabulary, although they were developed only recently. The development of mass communication has certainly not stopped; we can expect that as our technology becomes even more sophisticated, there will continue to be additions to the realm of mass communication.

One way to view recent advances such as the introduction of satellite communication is through the concept of **demassification.** This term, coined by futurist Alvin Toffler, is tied closely to the notion that the wave of the future will be the use of channels of communication targeted at highly specialized interest groups rather than at the overall masses. The Concept of Demassification

Indeed, we need only look around us to see that the age of demassification is already upon us. The present nature of the print media is only one example of the many changes which have been made in the process of transmitting information. No longer are the nation's major newspapers thriving as they did in earlier years. In the fast-paced world of high technology, particularly in the mass media, the oldest form of mass communication is losing readership every day to a virtual avalanche of highly specialized mini-circulation weeklies, biweeklies, and "shoppers" which serve specific communities and towns. Likewise, the deaths of major national magazines such as *Look, Life,* and the *Saturday Evening Post* (and their replacement by virtually thousands of mini-magazines targeted at small, special-interest markets!) seem to show that, indeed, demassified media are flexing their muscles. Pilots, housewives, camera nuts, teenagers, tennis players, and women in general may purchase any number of periodicals targeted specifically at their interests. Likewise, the growing popularity of regional magazines such as New England's *Yankee,* Dallas's *D,* or

Western Farmer seem to reflect the growing interests of an increasingly de-massified audience.[22]

The print medium, however, is not the only medium which is courting the demassified audience. Television and radio are becoming more highly specialized. In radio the late seventies and early eighties have witnessed the emergence of all-news radio stations aimed at the educated middle class; hard rock, soft rock, religious rock, and punk rock stations, each aimed at a different sector of the youth audience; classical music stations targeting upper-income adults; and foreign language stations targeting the many ethnic groups which are part of our society.

The nature of television viewing has also changed in this direction during the seventies and the eighties. Think for a moment of the variety of options that we have: sports networks; all-news networks; cable systems; news, weather, and sports information services; and the emergence of systems such as Columbus, Ohio's, QUBE—a two-way cable system

[22]Alvin Toffler, *The New Wave* (New York: Bantam Books, 1981), pp. 158–60.

which allows viewing audiences to send as well as receive information.[23]

Last, and perhaps one of the greatest contributors to the age of de-massified media, is the current information explosion and technological advances in the computer world. Not only do computers facilitate the flow of information in the fast-paced interactions of corporations; but the computer has made possible feats such as teleconferencing, the transmission of information through TELEX, as well as more recent advances in "computer conferencing." Computer conferencing allows two or more people to communicate through computer terminals in their offices or homes. An example of such a use of conferencing is the existence of the Electronic Information Exchange Service, which allows scientists, planners, and educators in several countries to conduct discussions concerning energy, economics, politics, or space satellites with one another through the use of teleprinters and video screens. Such a system also allows them to do so across varying time zones and at whatever time of the day or night they choose to work.[24]

As you can see, the shape of mass communication is rapidly changing. The possibilities are limitless, as the science fiction of today becomes the reality of tomorrow.

SUMMARY

Mass communication can be defined as the spreading of a message to an extended, mixed audience, using rapid means of reproduction and distribution, at a low unit cost to the consumer.

The most outstanding characteristic of mass communication is its dependence on an intermediary channel to transmit a message from the initial source to a diverse audience. In addition, the sender-receiver relationship of the mass communication process suggests an element of delayed and limited feedback.

The scope of mass communication is enormous, overcoming the barriers of time and space. Because of this, regulation and direction are necessary. This control, known as gatekeeping, comes from the different media, the government, and various economic interests.

Mass communication media have continued influences on their audiences. Four forms of electronic media are film, recording, radio, and television. Each has been developed to meet the changing needs of our society.

Mass communication serves a number of functions. It can be used to inform, to persuade, and to entertain. The informative function of mass communication is primarily concerned with the news media. Newspapers and radio are still important forms of news media, and under some circumstances they are even more effective than TV in fulfilling this function.

The entertainment function of mass com-

---

[23]Alvin Toffler, p. 163.
[24]Alvin Toffler, pp. 252–53.

munication is quite diversified. Comics in newspapers or a quiz show on TV both entertain an audience. TV and film are primarily entertainment media.

The persuasive influence of the media is recognized in advertising for political candidates, service organizations, charities, and manufacturers. The relative persuasiveness of one medium over another depends upon the nature of the message as well as the individual medium.

While there has been considerable research on the effects of the mass media, many of the findings are inconclusive. Edu-

cators, psychologists, and sociologists are among those interested in the effects of mass media. Some of the areas they have explored include the effects of the media in terms of violence, politics, and government.

We also looked at the operations that go on behind the scenes at a broadcasting station, including station organization and management. We then commented on performing on radio and television. We can only guess where the advances of the future will lead us, as our discussion of demassification made clear: Where we go from here is limited only by the boundaries of imagination.

Exercises

GROUP EXPERIENCES

Delayed Feedback

Description: Mass communication, by definition, suggests a widespread audience separated from a source by a considerable distance. As a result, a receiver's feedback or response to a message is most often limited and delayed. There are varying degrees of delayed feedback, ranging anywhere from a few minutes to several weeks or months. For example, a television commercial urging a customer to purchase a particular brand of detergent may have a delayed response of several weeks until the consumer runs out of his or her current brand of detergent. This activity will give you the opportunity to identify various degrees of delayed feedback.

Procedure: Television and radio both operate on the premise that a receiver's feedback or response to a message is both limited and delayed. For this activity you are to identify two examples from radio or television of (1) immediate, (2) delayed, and (3) long-term feedback. For the purpose of this activity, we will define immediate feedback as a response that occurs within a 30-minute period; delayed feedback includes responses up to two weeks; long-term feedback involves responses that require more than two weeks.

Discussion: What are the effects of the varying degrees of delayed feedback on the receiver? Have you ever considered writing to a television show for a specific purpose and later decided that it would take too long to get an answer? Do you think that the nature of television and radio feedback reduces the number of written responses from viewers? How do television and radio stations attempt to accurately assess the feedback of receivers? Are you aware of the various degrees of delayed feedback with which you respond to mass media?

Industry Gatekeeping

Description: Every major newspaper and television station receives numerous stories fed to them by the wire services. However, neither time nor space allows for the printing or broadcasting of each and every news event. Media personnel at various levels determine which items they consider the most newsworthy. This activity will give you the opportunity to select the stories you and a team of experts consider to be the most newsworthy.

Procedure: Divide into groups of four. You and your three group members will be industry gatekeepers. As a team, it is your responsibility to report the best news in the limited amount of air time available.

Each class member is responsible for bringing six news stories to class; two national stories, two state stories, and two local stories. From the pool of news items, each group should be given eight national, eight state, and eight local stories selected at random.

Each group is given 30 minutes to prepare a 5-minute television newscast. During this preparation period group members should select the stories they feel are newsworthy. All group members should be involved in the broadcast. All newscasts should be evaluated by class members on a scale of poor, fair, average, good, or very good.

Discussion: What variables contributed to a successful or unsuccessful newscast? What criteria did your group develop for the selection of news items? Do you consider the task of gatekeeping a difficult one? After listening to other newscasts, what criteria would you develop now for selecting items that are newsworthy?

The Big Debate

Description: One of the most compelling questions with regard to television is the effect of television on children and adolescents. Although there has been considerable research on the effects of television, findings are inconsistent. Some of the criticisms of television are that it stifles creativity, promotes violence, and has a negative effect on social morality. This activity will give you a chance to view both sides of the controversy.

Procedure: All class members should research the effects of television on children and adolescents. Half the class should be instructed to find evidence to support the continuation of television programs, while the remaining half should find evidence of the negative effects of television. After the research has been collected, four class members should be selected to participate in a debate. One team (two members) will represent the position that television produces negative effects on children and adolescents (the negative position). The second team, also consisting of two members, will represent a major network (the affirmative position). The following format should be used for the debate:

Affirmative Speaker 1: 5 minutes
Negative Speaker 1: 5 minutes
Affirmative Speaker 2: 5 minutes
Negative Speaker 2: 5 minutes
Negative Speaker 1: 2 minutes
Affirmative Speaker 1: 2 minutes
Negative Speaker 2: 2 minutes
Affirmative Speaker 2: 2 minutes

Following the debate the class members should reevaluate their positions on the topic.

Discussion: What is your opinion on the effects of television on children and adolescents? Can you support your position with research findings? Can you identify any of the effects television has had on you? Can the effects of television be controlled or directed? How?

PERSONAL EXPERIENCES

1. For a period of one week, watch a late-night movie every night. Try to watch a combination of romantic, humorous, violent, and horror shows. Then keep a TV dream diary in which you record in detail all the dreams that you have. It would be best to record your dreams first thing in the morning, before you do anything else. What relationship, if any, do your dreams have to the television shows that you viewed?

2. How are you influenced during presidential campaigns? List the various ways in which you receive information about the candidates. How many of those sources involve some form of mass communication, such as televised debates, radio, or newspapers? How has mass media changed national elections?

3. How does television reinforce or alter sex stereotypes? Select six different television serials and identify whether or not they reinforce sex stereotypes. Identify the methods in which programs characterize males and females according to sex stereotypes. Are there programs that attempt to change or even revise sex stereotypes?

DISCUSSION QUESTIONS

1. How do mass media differ from other communication systems (intrapersonal, interpersonal, and group communication)?

2. What are the positive and negative effects of television on its viewers?
3. What do you envision for the future of mass media? Describe the advances in technology that you feel will take place in the next thirty years. For instance, do you anticipate three-dimensional television in every home?
4. How does mass communication overcome the barriers of time and space?
5. Identify the television shows that are used primarily to (a) inform, (b) persuade, and (c) entertain. Are the most successful shows a combination of all three purposes?

APPENDIX A
Children's Television Viewing, The Parent's Role

ELTON H RULE
President American Broadcasting Companies, Inc.

INTRODUCTION

getting attention

establishing ethos

stated purpose

I am here today in three capacities. The first is as a native Californian—this has been my home for most of my life, and I only regret that my job requires me to be away from the Golden State most of the time. I have been here, though, for most of the last month, enjoying the sun and the ocean, my friends and my family—including the newest addition, my four-year-old grandson.

I mention him—his name is Patrick Elton Dunne—because being here in California and seeing him has reminded me again of what a wonderful place this is to raise children, and also because my second capacity today is that of a parent—a person who has children, and now a grandchild as well, and who thinks often of the many large and small influences that shape our children into adults.

My third capacity today is that of a broadcaster, which I have been most of my adult life—a person who has some responsibility for one of those influences, the television set in the living room. It is only in the last few years that most of us, parents and broadcasters alike, have realized just how sizable a role television plays in the lives of our children. The realization has been a sobering one. We have spent a great deal of effort trying to discover just what it is that our children get from their television watching—and when we haven't liked the answers, trying to improve the situation. We have asked what the proper role of television ought to be in the growth of our children, and where the responsibility for it lies. In the next few minutes, I would like to offer a few of my own conclusions on this subject.

BODY

ethos, ethics

Let me begin by admitting one of my own personal prejudices. We have all heard a great deal about what's wrong with the younger generation: that they are alienated, apathetic, illiterate, promiscuous—and so forth. No doubt there are a good many children who do have those and other problems. But my own feeling is that, by and large, today's youngsters are turning out very well. At six and at 16, they are often surprisingly mature and interesting people—people who know more about their world, and themselves, than I would have expected.

If there's any truth to this impression, I also believe that the presence of television may have been one positive contributor. Television is, after all, a window on world wider than any previous generation has ever known—one that offers an incredible exposure to people, places, and events that were once only topics in textbooks. And television is an effective communicator—from one recent study at Michigan State University, we know that there is a distinct correlation between how much television young children watch, and how much they know about current events and discuss these events with their parents. More than that, television can aid personal, emotional development; in entertainment as well as informational programs, children can gain insights into how other people live, how they relate to each other and especially how they deal with problems common to us all.

assertion

support

That's not to say television cannot cause problems for children. It can. This has been brought home to us very forcefully by parents of all descriptions since television began to assume a greater role in their home lives. Beginning about five years ago, our industry—and ABC in particular—embarked on an intense and still-continuing search for ways to improve its programs as they relate to younger viewers.

problem/counterargument

support: vague testimony

goal

This effort has involved not only those in the industry, but a broad spectrum of educators and child psychiatrists, not to mention a great many parents and children. It has brought to the screen programs altogether new to the medium—from Saturday morning news programs for children to original weekday afternoon dramatic specials both for and about children. It has brought a new policy, called "family viewing," to evening television; it provides for early-evening programs which are suitable for viewing by the entire family. And it has completely changed the face of the weekend programs made specifically for children.

examples

One major area of concern has been the portrayal of violence (or the threat of violence) in these programs. Early on, we at ABC pledged ourselves to eliminate gratuitous acts of violence from our programs, and as a result of similar actions throughout the industry, the overall amount of violence has been declining on television. To eliminate all acts of violence would be to deny reality, however, so we needed also to learn to ensure that what violence remained had constructive value. We knew relatively little about how to do this at the beginning, so we spent $1 million on two five-year research projects by three distinguished experts in the area.

problem

assertion

goal

That phase of their work is now completed, and from their findings we have been able to develop some workable guidelines for the producers of our programs and for our own editors. Let me cite some examples: The presentation of violence should exclude details which could be imitated by a viewer; it should be used clearly as a dramatic example of what should not be done; and the negative consequences of such violence should be demonstrated. There is much more to be done in this area, and our research is continuing, but I think we are definitely moving in the right direction.

examples
solutions

In addition to the question of violence, we were concerned about the ideas young viewers were getting from the programs they watched. Recently, one of our consultants, Dr. William Hooks of the Bank Street College of Education, made a list of some

problem

testimony

of the qualities we would like to shine through our programs. It is keyed to the word "respect," and I would like to repeat it here:

respect for the individual;
respect for differences;
respect for religious beliefs and ethnic qualities;
respect for all animal life and for the environment;
respect for private and public property;
respect for moral values;
respect for the feelings and sensitivities of others;
and, not least, repect for oneself.

We hope all the programs our young viewers see can live up to this principle of respect. We take very seriously our responsibility for our younger viewers.

But let me emphasize that ours is only a part of the overall responsibility for the effect that television has on our children. We in the television industry can control our programs and what happens to them right up to the point where they enter the home. But in the living room or the family room, control can be exercised only by parents. The most constructive use of television for children can come about only through the sharing of responsibility by broadcaster and parent.

Recently, the Roper Organization asked a national sample of parents with children under the age of 16 what sorts of rules they had for their children. As you'd expect, a sizable majority had strict rules about what their children ate, what time they went to bed on weeknights, when they did their homework (if they had homework), and knowing where they went when they left the house.

But the Roper people also asked parents what sorts of rules they had about television viewing. And they found that only about two-fifths had rules about what programs their children were allowed to watch. Less than a third of those with children under the age of 12 have rules about letting children watch television after 9 p.m. in the evening. And those who do have such rules based them on the lateness of the hour, not on the kinds of programs which are on at that hour. We know, too, from other research, that most parents are not present when their chidren do the greatest part of their viewing.

What this appears to mean is that parents who take active charge of most of the elements of their children's upbringing allow a kind of anarchy to prevail where television viewing is concerned. To me, this is a cause for real concern. Children are unique creatures, with their own personal areas of knowledge and ignorance, their own needs and fears and insecurities. No television program, no matter how sensitively it is designed, can be guaranteed to affect all children in the same way.

A given television program may inform a child—or it may confuse him. It may delight a child—or it may disturb him. The difference is the degree of his parent's involvement. Eda LeShan, a noted expert in the field of child psychology, tells the story of a mother whose marriage was collapsing. She thought she and her husband had shielded their problems from their 11-year-old son, until the day she and her son watched an ABC Afterschool Special dealing with divorce.

The mother reported that "as the program went on, Andy kept inching closer and closer to me. I put my arm around him and suddenly realized his whole body was trembling. It was a terrible shock. I realized that he had known all along what was going on, was terrified, and that my husband and I should have discussed it with him a long time before. That program kicked off the most honest and important conversation I'd ever had with my child." We can all wonder what effect the program would have had on the child if his mother hadn't been there.

That's an extreme example, but a revealing one. Let me offer a different one, from a study conducted at the University of Texas not long ago. An episode of a television program was shown in which playing hooky was involved. With one group of preschoolers, a teacher commented during the show that "that boy is in trouble. He did not go to school when he was supposed to. He was playing hooky, and that is bad." The other group didn't get that comment. Before and after the show, both groups were asked whether they thought playing hooky was all right. For the boys, the percentage of those who thought playing hooky was a bad idea increased 75 percent among those who heard the teacher's comment; it decreased among those who didn't. For the girls, the number improved 120 percent among those who heard the comment, and 80 percent among those who didn't.

Based on observations of this sort, the Texas study concluded that "parents are the single most important contributor to a child's development. Furthermore, while most parents believe they are in hopeless conflict with the ever-present television, the project's results indicate parents can directly and easily moderate the influence of television. The results indicate that parents should not let the television become a surrogate parent. Instead, parents should watch television with their child and talk about the programs."

Eda LeShan put the same thought very succinctly: "No (television) program can seriously damage a child in any way if a concerned and loving adult shares the experience and uses it as an opportunity to talk about feelings."

So much for the problem. How is it to be solved? To begin with, I do not believe that parents are thoughtless, selfish creatures who have abandoned their children to the television set—any more than I believe that television is a vicious electronic monster programmed to corrupt the youth of America. I do think, though, that there are a good many parents who are still learning how to cope with the presence of the television set in their home, who— not knowing quite what to do about it—do nothing at all about it.

For that reason, we have tried to draw together from our outside consultants—people like Dr. Melvin Heller, an eminent child psychiatrist at Temple University, and the people at the Bank Street College of Education—a few suggestions for parents to help them deal with their children and their television set. They may sound a little obvious, but they can make a difference.

note transition
support

statistics

assertion

assertion/testimony
PROBLEM

SOLUTION
ethos

testimony

solutions/
assertions

clarification

clarification

clarification

clarification

ethos

First suggestion: Know what your children watch. See the programs for yourself, and read about them as well. Not every program is suitable for every child of every age, especially late at night when we offer programs designed for more mature audiences. All the television networks provide advisory notices when the subject matter of a program may be unsuitable for younger viewers, but the final decision must rest with the parents, who know their children best. It is imperative that parents make those decisions actively, not by default. And it's useful, too, if children know the standards by which their parents select programs for viewing.

Second suggestion: Watch television with your children. No, this does not mean watch every program with your children; there's absolutely no harm in their watching television while you snatch an extra hour's sleep on Saturday morning. But do try to watch some of the things your children watch, in the morning and the afternoon as well as the evening. That is the only way to know how they react, as well as what they are reacting to.

Third suggestion: Comment on the things you see with your children. When you read stories to your children at bedtime, you probably comment on the things you are reading. Even the smallest remarks, such as "gee, that was scary, wasn't it?" can make a difference in the effect an episode has on your children.

Fourth suggestion: Use your family television viewing as a basis for conversations. Many families find serious discussions difficult during their children's growing-up years; communication about personal feelings and experiences is sometimes almost nonexistent. But those feelings can often be unlocked, and those experiences shared, if parents will use similar situations seen on television to initiate dialogue with their children. And there are also a number of educators who have devised games and other techniques by which parents can use television to further their children's education.

And, finally, a fifth suggestion which does not come from our consultants, but from me: Let us know what you think of the programs you watch with your children. It is an unfortunate truth that exceptional programs, for children as well as for adults, cost more than routine programs. We do not begrudge the cost of exceptional programs for children, any more than we begrudge the cost of covering a presidential election or the Olympic Games, but we need to know when our efforts succeed.

CONCLUSION

repetition of
main points

problem

Whether a child watches five hours of television a week, or 25, his viewing is an important part of his life. Knowing that imposes an awesome responsibility on all of us in the television industry, and we have committed ourselves in the strongest possible terms to live up to that responsibility. But the quality of our efforts can only be as good as the use to which they are put in the home. For parents who pay little or no attention to their children's television viewing, television is no more than an electronic babysitter, an informative and entertaining gadget whose value will vary from child to child in unpredictable—and sometimes undesirable—fashion. This we must try to avoid.

On the other hand, for parents who grasp firmly their share of the responsibility, who actively involve themselves in their children's viewing experience, television can be—and will be—a significant and constructive contributor to the growth of the generation of young people that will take over where we, their parents, leave off. That is the goal all of us should work toward. At ABC, we are doing everything we can to reach that goal, and we hope all of you will share this responsibility with us.

solution

From *Vital Speeches* 43, 1 (October 15, 1976), pp. 24–26. Speech was delivered before the Rotary Club of Los Angeles, Los Angeles, California, September 3, 1976.

Appendix B
Sample Student Outlines*

I. Introduction
   A. "Outside, the London nightlife is just beginning. Trafalgar Square is crammed with curious tourists, St. Martin's Lane bustling with anxious theatregoers. Inside, a lone woman makes a fateful decision. Is this what I've become? A thief? A scavenger? Heaven help me, I'm reduced to stealing food to live. Is this my curse for becoming the Spiderwoman?"
   B. Comic books are a part of every kid's and many adults' lives.
   C. Comic books are a part of the media in the United States.
      1. As a medium, comic books reflect some of society's attitudes and values.
      2. Three comic books, Red Sonja, Ms. Marvel, and Spiderwoman, reflect our notions about women.
II. Body
   A. The three comics are published by Marvel Comics, but each has its own history.
      1. Red Sonja first appeared in 1975.
         a. The origin of Red Sonja is unclear.
         b. Red Sonja lives in the "Hyporian Age" in the distant past.
      2. Ms. Marvel was presented in January 1977.
         a. Ms. Marvel has amnesia and does not know her origins.
         b. Ms. Marvel is a superhero in the tradition of Superman.
      3. Spiderwoman is the newest of the female superheroes, with her first issue appearing in April 1978.
         a. Jessica Drew (Spiderwoman) is half-spider, half-woman from another world.
         b. Spiderwoman is attempting to learn to live on Earth.
   B. Violence is an aspect of all three comics, but each deals with violence in a different way.
      1. Red Sonja is a graphically violent comic book.
         a. The only weapons Red Sonja uses are her blade and sword.
         b. Red Sonja kills for self-preservation and pay.
      2. Ms. Marvel fights violence in true superhero tradition.
         a. The violence in the comic is beyond the comprehension of mortal man.
         b. Ms. Marvel involves fantasy violence where no one is killed or seriously injured since they are super villains.

*These outlines were prepared by Debbie Smith of Southwest Texas State University and are reproduced with her permission.

3. Spiderwoman uses violence only for justifiable reasons.
    a. Spiderwoman fights for the good of society.
    b. In the first issue, she does not use her full power even against a criminal.
C. Each of the three comics makes a statement about women.
    1. Red Sonja is considered the "she-devil with a sword."
        a. The comic does not deal with women's rights specifically since it is set in the distant past.
        b. Red Sonja fights her battles alone.
    2. It is obvious from the title Ms. Marvel that this comic has been influenced by the women's movement.
        a. Ms. Marvel's slogan is, "This female fights back."
        b. Carol Danvers (Ms. Marvel's alter identity) is the editor of a feminist magazine.
    3. Spiderwoman is learning how to deal with her identity while living on Earth.
        a. The comic says, "To know her is to fear her."
        b. Spiderwoman is searching for her own identity.

III. Conclusion
A. The comics present strong, independent women.
B. Solo female superheroes, while not very real, do suggest a growing awareness of women.
C. But perhaps the comics say it best: "Like the Valkyre guards of Valhalla, she sweeps across the face of the earth, arms as widespread as an eagle's wings, eyes burning, jaw set, every sinew throbbing with battle anticipation . . . her name is her own, but for want of something better we may call her Marvel, MS. MARVEL, and because of her the world may never be the same."

I. Introduction
A. A New York couple—Hans Kabel, seventy-eight, and his wife Emma, seventy-six—were assaulted twice in less than two months.
B. The older people in our cities are viewed as victims or potential victims of criminals.
    1. Most are poor and unable to move.
    2. The elderly are living in fear in the cities.

II. Body
A. Fear of a criminal attack is now the major concern of the elderly.
    1. New York City officials believe that there are thirty victims for every crime reported.
    2. Chicago demonstrates the plight of the elderly.
        a. On the South Side the elderly are faced with gangs of potential assailants on the first of the month, when Social Security checks arrive.
        b. On the West Side no one goes out after dark.
    3. Statistically, the elderly are not victimized more than any other age group, but the impact is more severe.
        a. Physical injury is greater for the elderly in an assault.
        b. Emotionally, elderly persons' lives are governed by fear of an attack.
B. The assailants of the elderly are young juvenile criminals.
    1. The crimes are called "crib jobs" because it is like taking candy from a baby.
        a. The youngsters usually operate in teams.
        b. The elderly are young criminals' ideal victims.
    2. The rights of juveniles are so well protected that it is almost impossible for there to be repercussions.
        a. About 75 percent of the juveniles apprehended have been arrested before.
        b. Prosecutors are prevented from revealing a juvenile's arrest record.

3. Judges do not know if they are dealing with a first offender or a longtime criminal.
4. A juvenile who had beaten and robbed an eighty-two-year-old woman was released on a $500 bond even though he had sixty-seven previous arrests, one for murder.
5. Violent crime against the elderly is increasing.
   a. In Seattle violent street crime has increased 18 percent.
   b. In New York two sixteen-year-olds raped a seventy-five-year-old woman.
   c. In Detroit an eighty-year-old woman was killed because she clung to her purse.
C. Cities have started several programs to help solve the problem.
   1. Seattle engages policemen to serve as decoys.
   2. Chicago, Los Angeles, and New York have received federal funds to start self-help and victim assistance programs.
   3. San Francisco provides an escort service for the elderly.
   4. In Charleston, W. Va., elderly residents call in to the police department each day.
   5. In some cities high school students serve as escorts for the elderly.
D. The best solution is to have more policemen patrolling the streets.
   1. New York City has done this in a few areas, and it has been very successful.
   2. It is the solution most often recommended by the elderly.

III. Conclusion
A. Crimes against the elderly are significant and increasing.
B. Solutions exist that can help solve the problem.
C. Unfortunately there are also counterproductive solutions. The Kabels, the elderly couple mentioned at the beginning of the speech, used a counterproductive solution—dual suicide—saying they did not want to live in fear anymore.

I. Introduction
A. In 1960 chains and conglomerates controlled 30 percent of the nation's newspapers and 46 percent of the readership.
B. In 1977 chains and conglomerates controlled 59 percent of the newspapers and 71 percent of the readership.
C. There has been a growing concern about the increasing group ownership of American newspapers.

II. Body
A. Increasing chain ownership is not viewed as threatening by some people.
   1. Chain ownership saves newspapers.
      a. Small newspapers that are going under are bought by large chains.
      b. The chains have more money to invest in the newspapers to keep them in business.
   2. The chains are improving the quality of the newspapers they buy.
      a. The chains hire more staff for the newspapers.
      b. The chains add additional news services.
   3. Some of the leading newspapers in the country, such as the Washington Post and Los Angeles Times, are owned by conglomerates.
B. Chain ownership is perceived as destructive to the press in the United States.
   1. Chains are concerned with profits.
      a. Profits take precedence over quality.
      b. Concern with profits conflicts with serving the public interest.
   2. Competition is necessary for a good press.
      a. Without competition an inferior product can be produced without challenge.
      b. With chain ownership there is no competition.

3. Chains do not improve the quality of the newspapers.
   a. Papers tend to stay mediocre if bought by a chain.
   b. Outstanding newspapers have never been created by chains.
C. Chain ownership threatens the free press.
   1. Chain ownership violates the intent of a strong, free press.
   2. Newspapers play a special role as sources of opinion and information that should not be controlled by a limited number of owners.

III. Conclusion
   A. Chain ownership has reached epidemic proportions.
   B. The trend is continuing at a fast rate.
   C. Something should be done to prevent domination of such an important source of public information as newspapers.

GLOSSARY

ABSTRACT: Words used to represent feelings or thoughts that cannot be sensed directly.

ACCENTING: Use of gestures such as nods, blinks, squints, and shrugs to help emphasize or punctuate spoken words.

ACCEPTANCE SPEECH: A speech designed for the acceptance of an honor or award.

ACCURACY: Precise use of words.

ACHIEVED ROLE: Position in society which is earned by individual accomplishment.

ACTION STATEMENT: Describes what has been done, what is happening currently, or plans for the future.

ADVERTISING: Method of persuasion concerned with influencing people to buy or to continue to buy a product.

AFFECT DISPLAY: Body change that conveys internal emotional states.

AFTER-DINNER SPEECH: In general, a form of entertainment speech intended to make the audience feel relaxed and comfortable.

ALL-CHANNEL NETWORK: Communication network in which all positions send and recieve messages to and from all other positions.

ALLIANCE: A helping relationship established with someone else in an organization.

ALTERNATING MONOLOGUE: Unproductive communication in which each person knows the other is speaking but does not listen openly to what is being said.

AMBIGUITY: Language difficulty caused when one symbol (word) has several different meanings.

AMBIGUOUS FEEDBACK: Response which gives no indication that the message has been received positively or negatively.

ANALYTIC STAGE: Time when child learns that word symbols may consist of separate units and begins to experiment with their order.

ANECDOTE: Brief story that relates to an important idea in a speech.

APPRAISAL INTERVIEW: Designed to get and evaluate information about a worker's past performance and future potential.

APPROPRIATENESS: Use of language style that is adapted to the occasion, audience, type, and purpose of the speech.

ARBITRATION: Method of creating compromise solutions for intra-group conflict through an intermediary.

ARTICULATION: Process by which the voice is altered into recognizable speech sounds.

ASCRIBED ROLE: Postion in society based primarily on sex, age, kinship, and other factors which are out of a person's control.

ASSIMILATION: Process of incorporating some aspect of the environment into the whole set of mental functionings in order to make sense out of what goes on around us. Also, the transformation of messages to fit personal attitudes and expectations.

ATTENTION: Screening of stimuli so that only a select few come into focus.

ATTITUDE: Learned tendency to react positively or negatively to an object or situation.

ATTRACTION: Positive attitude, movement toward, or liking between two people.

AUTHORITARIAN LEADER: Individual who directs the group with goal-oriented behaviors and firm opinions about how to achieve group goals.

AVOIDING: Relationship disintegration stage in which one or both parties act as though the other person does not exist.

AWARD PRESENTATION: A speech designed for the presentation of an honor or award.

BABBLING STAGE: Language development stage in which a baby makes all the sounds found in all languages of the world.

BALANCE THEORY: Tendency for individuals to strive for symmetry in attitudes, values, and beliefs.

BARGAINING: The give-and-take process among two or more groups in an attempt to form a compromise solution.

BARRIER: Factor that causes incorrect meanings or no meanings to be communicated.

BELIEF: Anything a person accepts as true.

BIOFEEDBACK: A form of external self-feedback used to control physiological processing.

BODY MANIPULATION: Movement originally associated with body functioning, but that has come to be used unconsciously and independently of bodily needs.

BODY OF SPEECH: Portion of the speech which elaborates and clarifies the main points for an audience.

BONDING: Final stage of relationship development; usually signifies commitment through a formal contract.

BUSINESS CONFERENCE: Small group within an organization which meets to disseminate information or develop solutions to current organizational problems.

BUSINESS ORGANIZATION: Designed to give the greatest benefits or profits to the owners.

BYPASSING: Situation in which people argue or reach an impasse when they are actually in agreement.

CASUAL AUDIENCE: Small, heterogeneous group of people who gather at the same place for a short period of time.

CAUSE-AND-EFFECT PATTERN: In a speech, a persuasive structure of organization which establishes a relationship between two events.

CENTRALITY: Degree to which group communication revolves around one person.

CHAIN NETWORK: Similar to the circle communication network except that the members at each end of the chain send messages to and receive messages from only one position.

CHAIN-OF-EVENTS PATTERN: Informative organizational structure based on the development of a series of steps, with each step dependent upon the previous one.

CHANGE AGENT: One who is responsible for making policy and creating change.

CHANNEL: Means by which a message is communicated.

CHRONOLOGICAL PATTERN: Informative pattern of organization which follows a subject through time.

CIRCLE NETWORK: Communication network in which messages are sent to the left and right of a position, but not to other members in the group.

CIRCULAR RESPONSE: Mutual feedback between speaker and audience which increases participation and strengthens the bonds between them.

CIRCUMSCRIBING: Controlled disintegration stage with less total communication and expression of commitment.

CLARITY: The art of saying exactly what is meant, thus increasing audience comprehension.

CLIQUE: Habitual relationship that develops between employees.

COERCIVE ORGANIZATION: Uses force over members as a major means of control.

COGNITIVE DISSONANCE: State of imbalance between pieces of knowledge and/or feelings that individuals try to resolve.

COGNITIVE PROCESSING: Storage, retrieval, sorting, and assimilation of information.

COHESION: Degree to which group members identify themselves as a team.

COMMERCIAL (COMMONWEALTH) ORGANIZATION: Designed to serve public interests.

COMMUNICATION: Process that involves interdependent and interrelated elements working together to achieve a desired goal or outcome.

COMPARISON-CONTRAST: Defining a word, idea, or concept by pointing out similarities and/or differences between it and something with which the audience is already familiar.

COMPLEMENTARY MESSAGES: Nonverbal messages that complete or accent explanations and/or descriptions.

CONCERTED AUDIENCE: Collected group of individuals with an active purpose and mutual interest without separation of labor or strict organization of authority.

CONCLUSION OF SPEECH: Final portion of speech, which summarizes and reinforces the speaker's point of view.

CONCRETE: Symbolizing objects or events that can be pointed to, touched, experienced, or felt.

CONFORMITY: Acceptance of a group's norms.

CONNOTATION: Meanings beyond the objective reference of a word (abstract meaning).

CONTEXT: Circumstances that surround and give meaning to words and statements.

COORDINATION: Principle that all points within a subdivision of a speech outline must be related.

COVERT STIMULI: External changes or actions received at the subconscious level.

CREDIBILITY: Determination of whether or not a person is worthy of belief or trust.

DECEPTION: Nonverbal clues which suggest falsehood but do not reveal what information is being withheld or falsified.

DECODE: Act of interpreting a message.

DEDUCTIVE PATTERN: Persuasive structure which applies a previously accepted generalization to a specific case.

DEDUCTIVE REASONING: Moves from the general to the specific.

DEFENSE MECHANISM: Method of resolving anxiety produced by intrapersonal conflict.

DELIVERY: Physical and vocal elements of a speaker's presentation.

DEMASSIFICATION: Using channels of communication to reach highly specialized interest groups.

DEMOCRATIC LEADER: Individual who guides rather than directs the group, leaving most decision making to the group itself.

DEMOGRAPHY: Statistical study of populations (age, sex, educational levels, etc.).

DENOTATION: Objective reference of a word (its factual, concrete meaning).

DESCRIPTION: Method of defining a word, idea, or concept.

DIFFERENTIATING: Relationship state characterized by increased interpersonal distance.

DIFFUSION OF INFORMATION: Manner in which the public learns about new events, products, and changes in policy, ideas, philosophies, and so forth.

DIRECTIVE INTERVIEW: Structured and planned interaction situation which is generally conducted by using a step-by-step outline or format of questions.

DISCUSSION GROUP: Group of three or more persons characterized by cooperation among members, face-to-face interaction, shared perceptions, and verbal and nonverbal communication.

DOGMATISM: Personality trait characterized by a closed mind and a reluctance to accept new ideas and opinions.

DOWNWARD COMMUNICATION: Information messages directed to subordinates within an organization.

DYAD: Two people in close physical contact.

ECONOMY: Use of the right words in the most efficient manner.

EMBLEM: Commonly recognized sign (usually a gesture) which communicates a message usually unrelated to an ongoing conversation.

EMOTIONAL PROCESSING: Nonlogical response of an organism to a stimulus.

EMPLOYMENT INTERVIEW: Situation in which employers and applicants attempt to get pertinent information before making hiring decisions.

ENCODE: Process of generating and creating a message to be sent to a receiver.

ENVIRONMENTAL SETTING: A physical condition, such as noise or crowding, that affects listening behavior.

EQUAL TIME RULE: Stations must give all political candidates the same amount of time under the same terms.

ETHOS: Perception of the speaker by the audience (source credibility).

EULOGY: Farewell speech which marks someone's death.

EVALUATING: Weighing evidence, sorting fact from opinion, and determining the presence of absence of bias or prejudice in a message.

EVALUATION GROUP: Uses information from the fact-finding group to determine the scope of a problem and the priorities in finding a solution.

EXIT INTERVIEW: Situation designed to find out how an employee feels about the company, work environment, and job conditions after he/she has decided to leave the position.

EXPERIMENTING: The "do you know" period of interaction development.

EXPLOITER: Individual whose goal is personal gain or profit.

EXTENDED EXAMPLE: Illustration or story carried out to considerable length in order to clarify or emphasize a very important idea.

EXTERNAL SELF-FEEDBACK: Part of a person's own message that is heard by the person.

FACT-FINDING GROUP: Type of problem-solving group which gathers as much information as possible about a particular issue or problem.

FAIRNESS DOCTRINE: All stations must provide time to discuss controversial issues and must encourage opposing viewpoints.

FAREWELL SPEECH: Expresses regret about leaving and thanks those left behind.

FEAR-AROUSING APPEAL: Threat or scare tactic designed to persuade.

FEEDBACK: Response to a verbal or nonverbal message by a receiver.

FEEDFORWARD: Anticipation of feedback from others.

FEELING STATEMENTS: Statements that reveal people's emotions to themselves and others.

FOREWARNING: Information of the speaker's intent given prior to the speech.

FORMAL COMMUNICATION: Structured communication situation in which more attention is paid to both verbal and nonverbal messages.

FORMAL COMMUNICATION STRUCTURE: Company rules, divisions of labor, and power control within an organization.

FORMAL PRESENTATION: The most structured form of organizational communication, in which responsibility is placed on one person to create interest and motivation to listen.

FORUM: Type of public discussion in which the audience actively participates in the discussion.

FUNCTIONAL ROLE: Role that aids the group in accomplishing its objectives by keeping the discussion on course.

GATEKEEPER: Individual or organization that controls or influences a mass communication message.

GESTALT: Viewing an object or event as "a whole" rather than looking at its individual components.

GESTURE: Movement of the body that communicates messages to others.

GLOBAL VILLAGE: Theory that the world is smaller than before due to advances in mass communication.

GROUP: Any number of people with a common goal who interact with one another to accomplish the goal, recognize each other's existence, and see themselves as part of a group.

GROUP REVENGE: Systematic venting of anger or jealousy by a group.

HABIT: Repetitive behavior so automatic that a person is unaware of it.

HEARING: Physical act of receiving sounds.

HEIRARCHY OF HUMAN NEEDS: Five basic human drives, as described by Maslow. They include physiological, safety, live, esteem, and self-actualization needs.

HOLOPHRASTIC STAGE: Language development stage in which children use one word to mean a number of things or run together several words to signify one thought.

HOMOPHILY: Degree to which two interacting individuals are similar in characteristics such as beliefs, values, education, social level, and so on.

HUSTLER: Individual who is gifted at compromise and influences others through cleverness, wit, and charm.

HYPOTHETICAL EXAMPLE: An event or incident that could possibly occur but that did not really happen.

IDENTIFICATION: An attempt to find security by forming a psychological bond with other persons or groups.

ILLUSTRATION: Use of verbal examples or visual aids to help clarify information.

ILLUSTRATOR: Body expression that accents or adds emphasis to a word or phrase, shows the direction of thought, points to an object or place, depicts spatial relationships, rhythms, or bodily actions, or demonstrates shape.

IMITATIVE (LEARNED) BEHAVIOR: The belief that interaction with other human beings is necessary for language development.

IMMEDIACY: Degree of liking or disliking for a person or task.

IMPROMPTU SPEECH: Presentation made on the spot without any preparation.

INCREASING LEVELS OF DIFFICULTY PATTERN: Informative organizational structure used to present complex topics clearly and logically.

INDUCTIVE PATTERN: Persuasive structure which presents several specific cases that serve as a basis for a generalization.

INDUCTIVE REASONING: Moves from the specific to the general.

INFORMAL COMMUNICATION: Relaxed communication situations in which speakers are free to be themselves.

INFORMAL COMMUNICATION STRUCTURE: Interpersonal relations that develop among employees in addition to the formal communication structure.

INFORMAL NETWORK: Messages sent haphazardly within an organization (grapevine, rumor, etc.).

INITIATING: Relationship development stage in which conscious and unconscious judgments are made about others.

INNATENESS THEORY: Belief that evolution is responsible for the ability to produce and use language.

INSULATION: Isolation of contradictory feelings and/or information.

INTEGRATING: Relationship stage when two persons agree to meet each other's expectations.

INTENSIFYING: Relationship stage when steps are taken to strengthen the bond between two persons by asking for and reciprocating favors.

INTENSITY: Determines which stimuli individuals will attend to when bombarded by many different ones.

INTENTION STATEMENT: Statement that lets others know the purposes and motives behind one's statements and actions.

INTENTIONAL COMMUNICATION: Occurs when messages are sent with specific goals in mind.

INTERACTION: The sharing and communication of ideas and emotions with oneself or others.

INTERACTION WITH EMPATHY: Communication that involves deep understanding between the participants, feeling their pain and sharing their joy.

INTERACTION WITH FEEDBACK: Communication situation in which there is give-and-take by both participants.

INTERFERENCE: Any factor or barrier that negatively affects communication.

INTEGRATION: Proposal of new alternatives and new methods of organization to resolve intragroup conflict.

INTERGROUP CONFLICT: Interaction which often benefits a group by increasing goal-oriented activity and causing members to value their work more highly.

INTERMEDIARY: Messenger between the source and receiver.

INTERNAL SELF-FEEDBACK: Messages picked up through bone conduction, nerve endings, or muscular movement.

INTERPERSONAL COMMUNICATION: Shared interactions that take place between two people.

INTERPRETIVE STATEMENTS: Statements that indicate a person's understanding of a situation.

INTERVIEW: Dyadic communication situation designed to get information for employers and applicants by asking and answering questions.

INTIMATE COMMUNICATION: Occurs between people who understand each other and are willing to share trust and take risks.

INTIMATE DISTANCE: Spatial zone of interaction stretching from actual contact (touching) to 18 inches.

INTRAGROUP CONFLICT: Interaction which often destroys a group by reducing cohesion, decreasing productivity, and causing members to discredit their achievements.

INTRAPERSONAL COMMUNICATION: The sending and receiving of messages within an individual.

INTRODUCTION OF SPEECH: First portion of speech, which captures the audience's attention and prepares them for the rest of the speech.

KINESICS: Study of body movement.

KORZYBSKI'S LAW OF NON-IDENTITY: A word is not the thing it represents.

KORZYBSKI'S LAW OF NON-ALLNESS: A word cannot symbolize all of a thing.

KORZYBSKI'S LAW OF SELF-REFLEXIVENESS: A word can refer both to something in the real world and to itself.

LABELING: Identifying an object, act, or person by name so that it may be referred to in communication.

LAISSEZ-FAIRE LEADER: Individual who offers the group no direction and gives advice only when the group asks for it.

LANGUAGE: Communication of thoughts and emotions by means of a structured system of symbols (words).

LARYNX (VOICE BOX): Transforms vibrations of air to produce basic voice sounds.

LATERAL (HORIZONTAL) COMMUNICATION: Information messages between peers at the same hierarchical level.

LEADER: Any person who helps the group reach its goals.

LEADERSHIP: Behavior which helps the group reach its goals.

LEAKAGE: Nonverbal behavior which implies that information is being given inadvertently.

LEVELING: Minimizing or omitting information from a message.

LISTENER: The person receiving the message.

LISTENER FEEDBACK: Involves verbal and nonverbal responses to a message.

LISTENING: A process that involves hearing, attention, understanding, and remembering.

LIVELY QUALITY: Selection of words that leave a lasting impression.

LOGOS: Rational approach to persuasion based on logic and reasoning.

LONG-TERM MEMORY: Permanent storage of information for future reference.

MAINTENANCE ROLE: Functional role which is concerned with the feelings and emotional behavior of the group.

MANAGER: Individual who leads, conducts, and oversees procedures on behalf of the company or organization.

MANIPULATION: Method of dominating and controlling others, frequently through skillful use of vebal and nonverbal communications.

MANIPULATOR: Individual who seeks control over people and events.

MASS COMMUNICATION: Process by which messages are transmitted rapidly and inexpensively through some mechanical device to a large, diverse audience.

MATURITY: Differential stages of personal growth and behavior patterns.

MEMORY STORAGE: Storage of information that a person chooses to remember.

MENTOR: Individual who takes a special interest in new employees and acts as a model for those who are younger and/or less experienced.

MESSAGE: A sign or symbol which has meaning for both the sender and the receiver. The information to be communicated.

MESSAGE SOURCE: Person communicating the message.

MUTUAL BENEFIT ORGANIZATION: Designed to give members the greatest benefits from participation.

NEGATIVE FEEDBACK: Response which indicates that a receiver has misunderstood a message.

NETWORK: Interconnected channels or lines of communication used in organizations to pass information from one person to another.

NONDIRECTIVE INTERVIEW: Planned interaction situation in which freedom is given to participants in terms of how they ask questions and give responses.

NON SEQUITUR: Argument which involves an illogical order of thoughts.

NONVERBAL SYMBOL. Symbol other than spoken or written words used in the communication process.

NORMATIVE ORGANIZATION: Controls actions of members through compliance with social norms.

ONE-SIDED PRESENTATION: Persuasive speech approach in which the speaker presents only the side of the issue he or she supports.

OPEN (PUBLIC) DISCUSSION: Group meeting conducted before an audience who listens and/or participates.

OPEN LISTENING: Ability to forget personal concerns and biases so that responses are intelligent and sympathetic.

OPERATIONAL DEFINITION: Clarification used only for the duration of the speech.

OPINION: Positive or negative reaction to or statement of an attitude.

OPINION LEADER: Receiver of information from a change agent, who then disseminates it to the general public.

ORAL COMMUNICATION: Messages that are transmitted out loud from one person to another.

ORGANIZATION: Collected group of individuals constructed and reconstructed to work for goals that could not be met by individuals acting alone.

ORGANIZATIONAL COMMUNICATION: Focuses on ways to analyze and improve managerial styles, work environments, leadership, the flow of information, job satisfaction, and productivity in formal organizations.

ORGANIZED AUDIENCE: Group of listeners who are directed totally toward the speaker with strict labor and authority lines.

OVERT STIMULI: Internal or external changes or actions received at the conscious level.

PANEL: Type of open discussion in which a group of well-informed people exchange ideas before an audience.

PARALANGUAGE: Variations in the voice which give clues about emotional states, sex, age, status, etc.

PASSIVE (PARTIALLY ORIENTED) AUDIENCE: Captive listeners who have no choice but to listen to the speaker.

PATHOS: Approach to persuasion which appeals to the emotions.

PERSONAL DISTANCE: Spatial zone of interaction from $1\frac{1}{2}$ to 4 feet, used for casual interactions.

PERSONAL INTERVIEW: Interaction conducted on a one-to-one basis with a person who has information or knowledge about the topic of your speech.

PERSONALITY CLASH: Interaction and relationship styles that fail to work well together in organizations.

PERSUASION: A deliberate attempt by one person to modify the attitudes, beliefs, or behavior of another person or group of people by transmitting a message.

PHILEME: Smallest unit of behavior which indicates a person's level of intimacy.

PHILEME FAMILY: Set of related philemes associated with specific levels of intimacy.

PHONATION: Process by which air is pushed through the vocal cords, which then vibrate to produce sound.

PHYSICAL DELIVERY: Various body movements that a speaker uses during a speech (gestures, eye contact, posture, etc.).

PHYSIOLOGICAL PROCESSING: Subconscious and conscious physiological responses to internal stimuli.

PITCH: Highness or lowness of vocal tones.

PLATFORM: Situation in which the audience participates in the exchange of information.

POLARIZATION: Point at which the audience members recognize their role as listeners and accept someone else as a speaker.

POLICYMAKING GROUP: Makes changes or takes actions after the evaluation group offers its recommendations.

POSITIVE FEEDBACK: Response which indicates that the receiver has understood a message.

POST HOC, ERGO PROPTER HOC: Argument which suggests a cause-effect relationship based on sequences of events.

POSTURAL ADJUSTMENTS: Unconscious arrangement of the body to make it easier to receive stimuli.

PRIMACY EFFECT: Arguments presented first in a speech tend to have persuasive effect.

PRIMARY GROUP (PSYCHE GROUP): Collected group of individuals who function as a support system for its members.

PRIVATE (CLOSED) DISCUSSION: Group meeting held without an audience to listen or participate.

PROBLEM-SOLVING GROUP: Most often a private group which follows a logical, step-by-step procedure to find solutions to problems.

PROBLEM-SOLVING PATTERN PROBLEM-SOLUTION METHOD: Persuasive structure of organization based on a logical, step-by-step analysis of a particular problem.

PROFESSIONAL: Individual whose goal is to help others reach their fullest potential while being committed to his or her own job.

PROGRESSION: Arrangement of ideas in a logical order in a speech outline.

PROJECTION: Attributing personal traits, motives, or behaviors to others.

PROXEMICS: Study of how people react to the space about them, how they use it, and how their use of space communicates information.

PUBLIC COMMUNICATION: Usually a one-way process in which one person addresses a group in a lecture or public speech.

PUBLIC DISTANCE: Spatial zone of interaction from 12 to over 25 feet, used in formal addresses or lectures.

PUBLIC RELATIONS: Method of persuasion concerned with promoting an image.

PUBLIC SPEAKING: Communication situation in which one speaker directs a message to an audience.

QUALITY: Vocal variations such as harshness, breathiness, stridency, and smoothness of delivery.

RAPPORT: Development and maintenance of a positive relationship with an audience throughout a speech.

RATE: Speed at which words are spoken.

RATIONALIZATION: Attempt to justify personal failures or inadequacies.

REACTION FORMATION: Denial of what the person or the society considers unacceptable feelings or behaviors while advocating an opposite position.

REAL EXAMPLE: An event or incident that actually happened.

RECALL: Reconstruction of information that has been stored.

RECEIVER: Person (or persons) who attends to the message of the communication process.

RECENCY EFFECT: Arguments presented near the end of a speech tend to have persuasive effect.

RECEPTION: Process by which the body receives stimuli.

RECEPTOR ADJUSTMENTS: Physical changes in sensory receptor organs to make it easier to receive stimuli.

RECOGNITION: Awareness of familiar information based on previous experience.

RED HERRING: Argument intended to cloud an issue or distract attention from the main point.

REFERENCE GROUP: Group that gives a person a sense of identity and help in establishing personal attitudes and a value system.

REFERENT: Actual object as it exists in reality.

REGULATORS: Body movements or expressions that control verbal communication.

REMEMBERING: Receiving and interpreting a message, and adding it to the mind's storage bank.

REPEATING: Nonverbal behavior that conveys the same message as the verbal message.

REPETITIVE INTERACTION: Organizational situation in which members interact with established roles, responsibilities, and relationships.

REPRESSION: Keeping thoughts and feelings beneath the conscious level.

RESONANCE: Variations in voice from a thin and quiet voice to a loud and booming voice. Also, movement of air through the mouth, nose, and throat which gives amplification and richness to the voice.

RESPONDING: The completion of the communication process by the receiver through verbal and/or nonverbal feedback.

RÉSUMÉ: Written summary of an individual's educational background, work experience, job objectives, interests, etc.

RETRIEVAL: Bringing back into conscious awareness information which previously has been stored in the brain.

REWARD APPEAL: Persuasion that promises listeners personal gain or profit if they believe or behave in a desired manner.

ROLE: Behavior a person performs to meet the expectations of others in different social settings.

ROLE SHIFTING: Understanding one's own style of communication in order to adapt to the styles of others.

SATURATED: Point at which a person is overloaded with information.

SELECTED AUDIENCE: Group of people collected together for a specific purpose.

SELECTIVE PERCEPTION: Screening out a large number of stimuli to permit an individual to attend to just a few.

SELF-ACTUALIZATION: Development of a person to his or her fullest potential.

SELF-ASSERTION: Skill of speaking out for oneself by stating desires, feelings. and perceptions.

SELF-CONCEPT: A person's attitude about and view of the self.

SELF-DISCLOSURE: Process of revealing significant aspects of the self to others.

SELF-ESTEEM: Enduring evaluation of oneself.

SELF-FEEDBACK: Perception of a person's own nervous system via muscular movements as the person hears himself/herself speak.

SELF-FULFILLING PROPHECY: Positive or negative experiences which color the self-concept and create expectations which influence later behavior.

SELF-SERVING ROLE: Counterproductive role which has a negative effect on a group's emotional climate as well as on its ability to reach its goal.

SEMANTIC (LINGUISTIC) STEREOTYPING: Assuming automatic relationships between linguistic styles and personal traits.

SEMANTICS: Study of relationships between word symbols and their meanings.

SENSE: Subjective feelings about a symbol (word).

SENSE STATEMENTS: Messages that describe one's perceptions of sight, sound, taste, smell, and touch.

SENSORY STORAGE: Ability to hold some information for a fraction of a second after the stimulus disappears.

SERIAL TRANSMISSION: Communication through a number of individuals who act first as receivers and then as transmitters of messages.

SERVICE ORGANIZATION: Designed to give the greatest benefits to clients.

SEX ROLE: Position that is ascribed, defined, and encouraged by each society's culture for males and females.

SHARPENING: Magnifying some details of a message.

SHORT-TERM MEMORY: Process by which data are analyzed, identified, and simplified to be conveniently stored and handled.

SIMPLICITY: Principle that a speaker should keep the outline of a speech simple, with each line representing a single piece of information.

SMALL GROUP COMMUNICATION: Process involving three or more persons with a common goal and potential for interaction between members.

SOCIAL DISTANCE: Spatial zone of interaction from 4 to 12 feet, used by people meeting for the first time or by people conducting business.

SOCIAL FACILITATION: Influence of one audience member on another.

SOCIAL ROLES: A person's duties, skills, and norms defined by ascribed and achieved roles.

SORT: Selection of the most relevant information from the brain's storehouse of knowledge.

SOURCE: Initiator of the communication process.

SPATIAL PATTERN: Informative organizational structure based on the relation of one part to others or to geographical progressions.

SPEECH OF ACCEPTANCE (AWARD PRESENTATION): Presentation that focuses on the many ways a recipient qualifies for an award, or a method of saying thank-you.

SPEECH TO ENTERTAIN: Informal speech designed to bring the audience pleasure.

SPEECH TO INFORM: Designed to increase audience learning and comprehension.

SPEECH TO WELCOME: Presentation to a group, or to an individual about to join an organization or attending a meeting.

STAGNATING: Relationship disintegration stage in which all efforts to communicate are abandoned.

STIMULI: Elements which cause a reaction in one or more of a person's senses.

STIMULUS-RESPONSE INTERACTION: Communication situation in which the speaker proceeds in a set manner, independent of responses made by the listener.

STYLE: Individual selection, organization, and use of language.

SUBSTITUTES: Nonverbal messages that take the place of words.

SUBORDINATION: In a speech outline, subdivision of a main idea into subordinate points, each of which must be related to the preceding category.

SURVEY: Detailed gathering of information by questionnaire, observation, interview, etc.

SYMBOL: Word or nonverbal sign used to represent objects, ideas, and feelings to others.

SYMBOLIC PROCESS: Use of words as symbols to represent objects or concepts.

SYMBOLIZATION: Visual form of coordination, subordination, and progression of a speech outline.

SYMPOSIUM: Form of public discussion in which a group of experts presents its views, one speaker at a time.

TASK-ORIENTED ROLE: Functional role that is directly related to a group's goal.

TEMPO: Rate of speech in a given amount of time.

TERMINATING: Final relationship disintegration stage, which may be either quick or delayed.

TERRITORIALITY: Possessive desire or ownership reaction to the space and objects around us.

TESTIMONY: Information derived from a direct witness to an event or from an expert in a particular field.

THESIS STATEMENT: Sentence that presents the specific purpose of the speech.

THINKING-SPEAKING TIME DIFFERENTIAL: Listener's time to summarize and evaluate what has been said; people think several times faster than others can talk.

THRESHOLD OF CONSCIOUSNESS: Boundary between conscious and unconscious awareness of stimuli.

TOLERANCE OF AMBIGUITY: Ability to accept poorly defined and unclear situations.

TOPICAL PATTERN: Informative organizational structure in which information is presented according to specific category or classification.

TRAIT: Quality that distinguishes one person from another.

TRANSACTIONAL ANALYSIS: Method used to improve interpersonal relationships by identifying how people use Parent, Adult, and Child ego states.

TRANSITION: Statement which smoothly connects one idea to the next.

TRANSMISSION: Process by which messages are sent from a source to a receiver.

TWO-SIDED PRESENTATION: Persuasive speech approach in which the speaker presents both sides of an issue.

UNDERSTANDING: Analyzing the meaning of percevied stimuli so that they make sense.

UNINTENTIONAL COMMUNICATION: Messages (usually nonverbal) which are given without communicators being aware of them.

UPWARD COMMUNICATION: Information messages directed to superiors or those of higher status within an organization.

UTILITARIAN ORGANIZATION: Controls members through wages, promotions, tenure, and rewards.

VAGUENESS: Caused by the relative meaning of words which need more precision in usage.

VALUE: Moral or ethical judgment of things that are important to an individual.

VERBAL COMMUNICATON: Symbols which have universal meanings for all involved in the communication process.

VISUAL AID: Anything (other than the speaker) that is used to get a message across to an audience.

VOCAL DELIVERY: Mechanics of vocalization, vocal characteristics, and pronunciation.

VOCAL QUALITY: Timbre of voice, which distinguishes one voice from another.

VOICE: Sounds or tones produced through phonation.

VOLUME: Intensity or loudness of speech sounds.

WELCOMING SPEECH: A speech presented to an individual or group about to join an organization or attend a particular meeting or seminar.

WHEEL NETWORK: Two-way communication network with all communication directed to and from a centralized position.

WORD: Structured system of symbols which when joined with other words creates language.

WRITTEN COMMUNICATION: Primarily verbal messages conveyed in writing.

Y NETWORK: Communication network in which the central position does not communicate with one of the members.

INDEX

Abstract words, 28
Abstraction, 28
Accenting, 69
Acceptance speech, 311
Achieved roles, 111
Action statements, 135
Active listening, 48
Addington, D.W., 89n
Advertising, 392
Affect displays, 72
After-dinner speech, 311
Age, 260–61
All-channel network, 221
Allen, R.K., 210n, 220n
Alliances, 223
Alternating monologue, 145
Ambiguity, and vagueness, 28
Ambiguous feedback, 12
Amiable style, 30
Analogy, reasoning from, 295–96
Analytic stage, of language development, 26
Analytic style, 30
Anatol, K.W., 212–13n, 298n, 302n, 310n
Anderson, E., 36n
Anderson, V.A., 365n
Anecdotes, 343
Animal communication, 9
Anxiety, 353–55
Appeals, emotional, 298–301
Applbaum, R.L., 212–13n, 298n, 302n, 310n
Appraisal interview, 225
Appropriateness, 373
Arbitration, 192
Architecture, 85
Ardrey, R., 141
Aristotle, 253, 301
Articulation, 366
Ascribed roles, 110–11
Assimilation, 116–17, 216
Athos, A.G., 108n

Atkinson, D., 140n
Attention, 48
Attitudes, 120, 265
    change theories, 306
    speaker, 355
Attraction, 139, 141
Audiences, 259–78
    analysis, 259–68
    analysis as an art, 277
    casual, 270
    concerted, 272–73
    demographics, 260–64
    effects of environment on, 274–75
    increasing learning of, 286–91
    interaction with speaker, 275–77
    methods of investigating, 268–70
    organized, 273–74
    partially orientated, 270–71
    participation, 291
    passive, 270–71
    selected, 272
    style of delivery and, 356–58
    types of, 270–74
Authoritarian leader, 179
Avoiding, 144
Award presentation, 311

Babbling stage, of languge development, 26, 56
Baird, J.E., 209n, 216n
Balance theory, 306
Bales, R.F., 195n
Barbara, D., 48
Barbour, A., 158n
Bargaining, 192
Barker, L.L., 6n, 50n, 119n, 278n
Barnlund, D.C., 221n
Barriers, in communication, 12–13
Bassett, R.E., 288, 334n
Baxter, L.A., 87n

Beebe, S., 364n
Behavior, language and, 34–37
Beighley, K.C., 353n
Belief, 121, 264
Berelson, B., 393
Biofeedback, 118
Birdwhistell, R., 70–71
Birmingham, S., 358n
Black, E.L., 364n
Black, J., 229
Blake, R., 85n
Bledsoe, J., 32n
Bodaken, E.M., 195n
Body, of a speech, 330–31
Body image, 105
Body manipulators, 73
Body movement, 70–71, 359–60
    and posture, 73–78
Bogard, M.R., 360n
Bohn, H., 386n
Bolles, R., 238
Bolton, R., 208n
Bonding, 143
Bradley, B.E., 254–57, 268–69, 354n
Brady, J., 223n
Brady, S., 140n
"Brainstorming," 188
Brilhart, J.K., 169n, 184–85
Brooks, W.D., 224n, 244n, 354n
Buchli, V., 52n
Business conference, 227–28
Business organizations, 211
Bypassing, 173

Carey, J., 397
Carter, J., 358
Casas, J.M., 140n
Cash, W.B., 225n
Casual audiences, 270
Cause, reasoning from, 294–95
Cause-and-effect pattern, 338
Centrality, 220
Chain, 221
Chain-of-events pattern, 336
Champagne, M., 195n
Change agent, 390
Channels of communication, 10–11, 214–16
Chase, J., 76
Chelune, G., 132n
Chomsky, N., 25
Chronological pattern, 334–35
Circle network, 221
Circular response, 277
Circumscribing, 144
Clarification, 342
Clarity, 136, 373
Clark, A.J., 306n
Cliques, 223
Closed discussion group, 169
Clothing, 84–85

Coercive organizations, 211
Cognitive dissonance, 309
Cognitive processing, 116–17
Cohen, A.R., 301n
Cohesion, group, 190–91
Colors, 85–86
Commercial organizations, 211
Commonwealth organizations, 211
Communication:
    animal, 9
    apprehension, 353–55
    barriers in, 12–13
    basic elements of, 9–13
    channels of, 10–11
    context of, 13
    defined, 5–6
    dimensions of, 6–9
    downward, 216–18
    effective group member, 171
    feedback, 11–12
    formal, 7
    goals, 286–319
    horizontal, 219
    informal, 7
    informative, 292
    intentional, 7–8
    interpersonal, 14, 15, 130–63
    intrapersonal, 14–15, 104–27
    lateral, 219
    levels of, 13–16
    man-machine, 8
    mass, 14, 16, 380–409
    message in, 10
    nonverbal, 6, 66–101
    oral, 6
    organizational, 15–16, 208–49
    personal assessment of, 45
    persuasive, 292
    public, 15, 252–83
    receiver/decoder, 11
    small group, 15, 166–205
    source/encoder, 10
    unintentional, 7–8
    upward, 216–19
    verbal, 6
    written, 7
Communication goals, 286–319
    information exchange, 286–91
    persuasion, 291–309
    special occasion communication, 311–14
Communicator style, 29–32
    characteristics of, 30
Comparison, 344
Complementing, 67
Comprehension, vocal skill and, 353
Concerted audiences, 272–73
Conclusions, 304–5
    of a speech, 331–33
Concrete words, 28
Concreteness, 28
Conflict resolution, 157–59

Conformity, groups, 193
Conklin, F., 94n
Connotation, 28
Consonants, 366
Content, delivery and, 355
Context, 13, 136
  nonverbal communication, 92
Contrast, 344
Conversational listening, 48
Coordination, 341
Courteous listening, 48
Covert stimuli, 114
Credibility, 140–41, 265
Critical listening, 48–49
Crowell, L., 172
Crystal, J., 238
Cummings, H.W., 192n

Darwin, C., 74–75
Davis, M., 155
Deception, 68
Decision-making, standard agenda for, 186–89
Decoding, 11
Deductive pattern, 337–38
Deductive reasoning, 293–94
Defense mechanisms, 123–24
Definitions, 343–44
De Fleur, M., 299n
Delivery, speech, 351–77
  apprehension, 353–55
  style, 371–74
  vocal delivery, 365–71
Demassification, 403
Democratic leader, 179
Demography, 260
Description, 343–44
Deutsch, M., 157
Dewey, J., 186, 338
Differentiating, 143
Diffusion of information, 390
Directive interview, 226
Discriminative listening, 49
Discussion group, 168–69
Dogmatism, 122
Downward communication, 216–18
Drabman, R., 395
Driver style, 30
Dyad, 130–31
Dyadic relationships, development of, 141–44

Eakins, B.W., 263n
Eakins, R.G., 263n
Economic gatekeeping, 385
Economy, 373
Educational level, 261–62
Edwards, R., 119n
Ekman, P., 71, 73n, 75n
El Assal, E., 229n

Electronic media, 326
Elrod, E., 58
Emblems, 71
Emotional processing, 117
Emotional self, 105
Employee styles, 222–23
Employment interview, 225
Encode, a message, 10
Entertainment, 259
Environmental factors:
  and audiences, 274–75
  nonverbal messages, 85
Environmental setting, 49–50
Epstein, S., 106n
Equal time rule, 384
Esteem needs, 112–13
Ethics, of public speaker, 253–57
  ends justify means approach, 255–56
  ethos-centered approach, 256–57
  situation ethics approach, 256
  social utility approach, 256
Ethos, 301–2
  audience, 353
Etzioni, A., 211n
Eulogy, 313
Evaluating, 47
Evaluation groups, 170
Evidence, use of, 303–4
Example, reasoning from, 294
Examples, 342–45
Exit interview, 225
Experimenting, 142
Exploiters, 222
Expressive style, 30
Extended example, 343
External self-feedback, 118
External stimuli, 114–15
Extrinsic motivation, 286–87
Eye behavior, 77–78
Eye contact, 364

Facial expressions, 75–77, 361
Fact-finding groups, 169
Fairbanks, G., 367n
Fairness doctrine, 384
Family communication, 153
Farewell speech, 312
Fear, 354
Fear-arousing appeal, 298–99
Federal Communications Commission (FCC), 383–84
Feedback, 11–12, 55–61, 136–38
  delayed, 382
  effective, 59–60
  effects of, 58–59
  functions of, 57–58
  of group member, 172
  interaction with, 148
  self, 118–19
  types of, 56–57

Feedforward, 138
Feeling, 298–301
Feeling statements, 134–35
Feldman, A., 396n
Festinger, L., 309
Field, H.S., 236n, 238
Film, 385–86
Fisher, B.A., 5n
Forewarning, 304
Formal communication, 7
Formal communication structure, 213
Formal presentation, 228–29
Forum, 169
Frank, T., 211n, 222n
Friesen, W., 71
Functional roles, 173
Funk, F., 214n

Gabarro, J.J., 108n
Gaebelein, J., 50n
Gallup Opinion Index, 269
Gardiner, J., 59n
Gatekeeper, 382
Gatekeeping, 382–85
  economic, 385
  government, 383–85
  industry, 383
General Semantics, 33
Gestalt tasks, 118
Gestures, 360–61
Giammatteo, D., 176–77, 181
Giammatteo, M., 176–77, 181
Glass, G.V., 83
Global village, 381
Goetzinger, C., 219n
Goldberg, A.A., 158n
Government gatekeeping, 385
Greenberg, B.S., 390
Griffin, E.A., 275
Group, 167
Group membership, 263–64
Group pressure, 194
Group revenge, 223
Groups:
  cohesive, 191
  conflict, 191–93
  discussion, 168–69, 183–84
  evaluation, 170
  fact-finding, 169
  policy making, 170
  primary, 168
  problem-solving, 169
  psyche, 168
  research for discussion, 184–86
Gruber, K.J., 50n
Gumperz, J., 35

Habits, 106
Hakel, M.D., 361

Haley, A., 381
Hall, E.T., 79
Hamilton, M.L., 76n
Harte, T.B., 344n
Hass, G., 303n
Hazen, M.D., 266
Head, S.W., 380
Hearing, 44–45
Heider, F., 306–9
Heisel, D.M., 118n, 149n
Hess, E.H., 77n
Hierarchy of human needs, 112–13
Hirsh, R.O., 49n
Holley, W.H., 236n, 238
Hollingworth, H.L., 270
Holophrastic speech, 26
Homophily, 390
Horizontal communication, 219
How To Find A Job (D. Larson), 238
Humor, 305
Hurt, H.T., 82n
Hustler, 222
Hypothetical example, 343

Idea development, 288–89
Identification process, 124
Illustrations, 343
Illustrators, 72
Imitation, of language, 25
Immediacy, 215
Impromptu speech, 313
Increasing levels of difficulty, 335–36
Inductive pattern, 336
Inductive reasoning, 293–94
Industry gatekeeping, 383
Informal communication, 7
Informal communication structure, 213
Informal networks, 219
Information:
  exchange, 258, 286–91
  transmission of, 23
Informative communication, 292
Informative speech:
  conclusion, 331
  patterns of organization, 334–36
Ingham, H., 107
Initiating, 142
Innateness theory, of language development, 24
Insufficient evidence, 296
Insulation, 124
Integrating and integration, 142–43, 192
Intellectual self, 106
Intensifying, 142
Intensity, 115
Intention statements, 135
Intentional communication, 7–8
Interaction, 23
  with empathy and feedback, 148
Interference, 119
Intergroup conflict, 191–93

Intermediary, 215
Internal locus of control, 121
Internal self-feedback, 119
Internal stimuli, 114
Interpersonal attraction, 139–41
Interpersonal communication, 14–15, 130–63
  analyzing, 145–51
  clarity, 136
  context and timing, 136
  development of dyadic relationships, 141–44
  dyadic versus small group, 130–32
  effective, 132–35
  feedback and, 58
  feedback and feedforward, 136–38
  and interpersonal attraction, 139–41
  model, 130
  nonverbal behavior, 138–39
  open listening, 136
  situations, 152–59
Interpersonal conflicts, resolution of, 158
Interpersonal listening, 48
Interpretive statements, 134
Interviews, 225–27
  as source material, 324–25
Intimate communication, 154–57
Intimate distance, 79
Intragroup conflict, 198
Intrapersonal communication, 14–15, 104–27
  feedback and, 58
  hierarchy of human needs and, 112–13
  process of, 113–19
  and the self, 104–8
  and self-concept, 108–11
  variables effecting, 119–24
Intrinsic motivation, 286–87
Introduction, of a speech, 328–30
Invitation committees, 269

Jacobson, L., 153n
Janis, I.L., 193n
Job Hunting Secrets and Tactics (K.W. Stanat), 238
Job searches, 229–45
  after the interview, 244–45
  finding job possibilities, 238–41
  the interview, 241–44
  preparing for the interview, 229–31
  researching the company, 241
  responsibilities of the interviewee, 231, 233, 235–41
  the resume, 235–38
Jobs '77 (W.N. Yeomans), 233
Johari Window, 107–8

Katz, M., 154n
Kazickas, J., 191n
Kibler, R.J., 6n
Kiesler, C.A., 304
Kiesler, S.B., 266, 304
Kinesics, 70–71
Kipnis, D., 180n

Kleinke, C.L., 138n
Knapp, M., 141, 142n
Kochler, J.W., 212n
Korzybski, A., 33–34
Kraus, S., 299
Kulgren, J.A., 287n

Labeling, 23
Laissez-faire leader, 179
Language, 6, 22–41
  and behavior, 34–37
  development of, 23–27
  effective, 37
  functions of, 22–23
  and meaning, 27–34
"Language acquisition devices," (LAD), 25
Larson, D., 238
Larynx, 365
Lashbrook, W.B., 195n
Lateral communication, 219
Lazarsfeld, P., 393
Leaders, 178–82
  characteristics of, 178–79
  emergence of, 180–81
  skills of, 181
  types of, 179
Leadership, 177–82
  styles of, 179–80
Leakage, 68
Learned behavior, language as, 25
Learning, audience, 286–91
Lecturn, 365
Lekkowite, M., 85n
Lenneberg, E., 24
Leveling, 216
Levenson, H., 122n
Lewin, K., 382
Lewis, M., 192n
Linder, D., 303n
Linguistic stereotyping, 35–36
Listener:
  attitude and needs of, 49–50
  feedback, 56
Listening:
  barriers and aids to, 49–55
  developing skills for, 53–55
  of group member, 172
  habits, 51–52
  process, 44–49
  types of, 48–49
Lively quality, 373
Logical fallacies, 295–98
Logos, 292–98
Long, L., 192n
Long-term memory, 116
Love needs, 112
Lovell, G., 359n
Lowenthal, H., 299
Luft, J., 107
Lull, P., 214n

Mahler, W., 225n
Maintenance roles, 173–75
Man-machine communication, 8
Managers, 222
"Managing Interpersonal Relations," (MIR), 30, 32
Manipulation, 122
Manipulators, 222
Markiewicz, D., 305
Marriage, 145
Martin, G.L., 364n
Maslow, A.H., 85n, 112, 223n
Mass communication, 14, 16, 380–409
   advertising, 392
   Broadcasting in America (S. Head), 380
   characteristics, 381–85
   functions of, 387–92
   future of, 403–5
   media, 385–87
   public relations, 393
Mass media, 385–87
   appearing on radio and television, 399–403
   effects of, 393–99
   film, 385–86
   radio, 386–87
   recording, 386
   sources, 269
   television, 387
Maturity, 123
McClung, T., 302
McClure, R.D., 388
McCroskey, J.C., 82–83n, 353, 344n
McGinniss, J., 398
McLuhan, M., 381, 394
McVetta, R.W., 83n
Meaning, 27–34
Mehrabian, A., 215n, 353, 361n
Memorization, 355
Memory storage, 116
Mentoring, 223–24
Messages, 10, 49–50
   nonverbal, 6–7
   organizational, 213
   source, 49–50
   verbal, 6
Middleton, T., 371
Millard, R.J., 83n
Miller, G.R., 13
Miller, S., 132n
Mills, G.E., 340n
Minnick, W.C., 300n
Mintz, N.L., 85n
Montgomery, B., 29n
Motivation, 286–87
Mouton, J., 85n
Music, 87–88
Mutual benefit organizations, 211

Negative feedback, 12
Networks, 216–20
   structures, 220–21

News, good versus bad, 388
Nitt, T., 75n
Non-allness, 33
Non-identity, 33
Non sequitur, 297
Nondirective interview, 226
Nonverbal behavior, interpersonal communication
   and, 138–39
Nonverbal communication, 6, 66–101
   awareness of, 92–94
   functions of, 66–69
   types of, 70–92
Nonverbal symbols, 6
Normative organizations, 211–12
Norton, R., 29–30
Note cards, 365
Nunnally, E.W., 132n

Objects, 85
Occupation, 262–63
Office politics, 223
One-sided presentation, 303
Open listening, 136
Operational definitions, 344
Opinion, 121
Opinion leader, 390
Oral communication, 6
Organization, 273
   definition, 208
   service, 211
   types of, 211–12
   utilitarian, 211
Organizational communication, 15–16, 208–49
   business, 211
   characteristics of, 209–11
   coercive, 211
   commercial, 211
   commonwealth, 211
   communication in, 221–24
   dimensions of, 212–16
   and job searches, 229–45
   means of control, 211
   mutual benefit, 211
   networks, 216–20
   normative, 211–12
   situations, 224–29
   structures, 213–14, 220–21
Organized audiences, 273–74
Outlining, 339–42
Overt stimuli, 114

Packard, V., 392n
Panel, 169
Paralanguage, 88–90
Partially orientated audiences, 270–71
Passive audiences, 270–71
Passive listening, 48
Past experience, 109–10

Pathos, 298–301
Patterson, T.E., 388
Pearce, W.B., 52n, 94n
Pember, D.R., 399
Performance, feedback and, 58–59
Person perception, 140
Personal appearance, 83–85, 224
Personal distance, 79
Personal interviews, 269–70, 324–25
Personal orientation, 119–21
Personality:
    clashes, 223
    group interaction and, 189–90
    language and, 29
    traits, 121–22
Persuasion, 258, 291–309
    attitude theories, 306–9
    techniques, 292–306
    types of, 291
Persuasive communication, 292
Persuasive speech:
    conclusion, 331–32
    patterns of organization, 336–39
Phileme family, 155
Philemes, 155
Phonation, 365
Physical delivery, 355, 359–65
Physical self, 105
Physiological processing, 117–18
Piersol, D., 214n
Pitch, 88, 367
Platform, 291
Platz, S.M., 354n
Polarization, 275
Policymaking groups, 170
Political campaigns, 397–98
Porter, R.E., 86n
Positive feedback, 12
Post hoc, ergo propter hoc, 297–98
Postural adjustments, 48
Powell, L.S., 289n
Prejudices, 121
Price, K., 180n
Price, W., 260
Primacy, 305
Primary group, 168
Printed material, 326
Private discussion group, 169
Problem-solution method, 338
Problem-solving:
    group, 169–70
    process of, 186–89
Processing, 115–18
Professional, 222
Professionalism, 221–24
Progression, 342
Projection, 123–24
Pronovost, W., 367n
Pronunciation, 370–71
Proxemics, 78–83
Psyche group, 168
Psychological needs, 112

Psychological variables, audiences, 264–65
Public Broadcasting Service, 388–90
Public communication, 15, 252–83
    audiences, 259–78
    ethical responsibility of speaker, 253–57
    purposes of, 258–59
    See also Mass communication
Public distance, 79
Public Opinion Polls, 269
Public opinion polls and surveys, 269
Public relations, 393
Public speaking, 252
    purpose of speech, 267–68

Quality, 88

Radio, 386–87
Rapport, 359
Rate, 368
Rationalization, 123
Ray, D., 211n, 222n
Reaction formation, 124
Real example, 343
Reardon, P., 238n
Reasoning, 292–98
Receiver/decoder, 11
Recency, 305
Reception, 115
Receptor adjustments, 48
Recognition, 116
Recording, 386
"Red herrings," 296
Redcall, 116
Reference groups, 110
Referent, 27
Reflective thinking process, 186
Regulating, 69
Regulators, 72
Relationships, development and disintegration,
    141–44
Remembering, 47
Repeating, 66
Repetition, 289
Repetitive interaction, 210
Repression, 124
Resonance, 88, 366
Responding, 47
Resume preparation, 235–38
Retrieval, 116
Reward appeal, 298
Robertson, T.S., 396–97n
Role shifting, 31
Roles, 110–11
    functional, 173
    maintenance, 173–75
    self-serving, 176
    in small group communication, 173–76
    task-oriented, 173–74
Rosenfeld, L., 88n, 192

Rosenthal, R., 153n
Ross, R.G., 264n, 354n
Rossiter, J.R., 396–97n
Rothenberg, M., 395
Rule, E.H., 410

Safety needs, 112
Saturated, 220
Scheidel, T., 172
Schmidt, S., 180n
Schramm, W., 13n
Scott, M.D., 82n
Seating arrangements, 81
Selected audiences, 272
Selective perception, 115
Self, the, 104–8
Self-actualization, 113
Self-assertion, 133
Self-concept, 108–11
Self-disclosure, 132
Self-esteem, 123
Self-feedback, 56
Self-fulfilling prophesy, 110
Self-monitors, 138
Self-reflectiveness, 34
Self-serving roles, 176
Selling of the President, The (J. McGinnis), 398
Semantic stereotyping, 35
Semantics, 27
Sense, 27
Sense statements, 133–34
Sensory storage, 116
Serial transmissions, 216
Serious listening, 48
Service organizations, 211
Sex, of audience, 263
Sex role stereotypes, 74, 111, 398–99
Sharp, H., 302
Sharpening, 216
Short-term memory, 116
Signs, reasoning from, 294
Simons, H.W., 301n
Simplicity, 340–41
Situation, 13
Situational feedback, 138
Small group, 167–68
Small group communication, 15, 131, 166–205
  analysis, 194–96
  definitions, 167–68
  development of, 176–77
  factors affecting, 189–94
  functions, 168–70
  leaders and leadership, 177–82
  participation, 170–73
  problem solving, 182–89
  role structure and status, 173–76
Smell, 90–92
Smith, A.P., 235
Smith, D., 416
Smith, M.L., 83n
Smith, Mrs. W.J., 76

Smitherman, G., 35n
Social distance, 79
Social facilitation, 275–76
Social feedback, 138
Social interaction, 145–48
Social Inter-Course (M. Knapp), 141
Social listening, 48
Social roles, 111
Socioeconomic status, 262
Sort, 116
Source credibility, 301–2
Source/encoder, 10
Source materials, 324–26
Spatial patterns, 335
Speech anxiety, 353–55
Speeches:
  acceptance, 311
  after-dinner, 311–12
  arranging the body of, 334–39
  audience learning and, 286–91
  entertaining, 259
  eulogies, 313
  farewell, 312
  gathering source materials, 324–26
  impromptu, 313
  informative, 258
  narrowing the topic, 323–24
  outlining principles, 339–42
  parts of, 326–34
  persuasive, 258–59
  platform format, 291
  principles of effectiveness, 313–14
  purpose of, 267–68
  selecting the topic, 322–23
  supporting material for, 342–46
  welcoming, 311
  See also Delivery, speech
Spicer, C., 288, 334n
Stage fright, 353–54
Stagnating, 144
Stanat, K.W., 238
"Standard American Speech," 370
Statements, 133–35
  action, 135
  feeling, 134–35
  intention, 135
  interpretive, 134
  sense, 133–34
Statistics, 345–46
Steenbock, S., 305
Steil, L.K., 50n
Steinmetz, S., 158n
Stereotypes, nonverbal communication, 93–94
Stewart, C.J., 225n
Stimpson, D.V., 83n
Stimuli, 113–15
Stimulus-response interaction, 148
Stitt, C., 180n
Stotland, E., 301n
Student-teacher communication, 152–53
Style, 365–68, 371–74
  of language, 29–32

Subordination, 341
Substitutes and substituting, 67
Sultan, F.E., 132n
Support, 344–45
Survey, 326
Symbol, 10, 22, 27
Symbolic process, 27
Symbolization, 342
Symposium, 169

Task-oriented roles, 173–74
Taste, 90–92
Television, 387, 393–97
  appearances on, 399–403
  children and, 393–95
  commercials, 396–97
  and gatekeeping, 385
  parents role in children's viewing, 410–15
  and sex stereotyping, 398–99
  violence, 395–96
Tempo, 88
Terminating, 144
Territoriality, 80–83
Testimony, 346
The Social Contract (R. Ardrey), 141
Thesis statement, 328–29
Thinking-speaking time differential, 54
Thomas, M., 395
Thompson, E., 287n
Thourlby, W., 84
Threshold of consciousness, 115
Time, 86–87
Timing, 136
Toffler, A., 404–5n
Tolerance of ambiguity, 122
Topical pattern, 334
Topics:
  narrowing, 323–24
  selecting, 322–23
  speakers, 355
Touching, 90, 138
Traits, 121
Transactional analysis (TA), 148–51
Transitions, 333–34
Transmission, 23, 118
Two-sided presentation, 303

Understanding, 46–47
Unguvait, D.F., 386n
Unintentional communication, 7–8
Unity principle, 106–7
Unreasonable extrapolation, 296–97

Upward communication, 218–19
Utilitarian organizations, 211

Vagueness, 28
Valentine, M., 219n
Valsiner, J., 75n
Values, 120, 264
  of Americans, 300
Van Riper, C., 56n
Veitch, R., 388
Verbal communication, 6
Verderber, R.F., 174–76n, 257n
Violence, 158
Visual aids, 289–91
Vocal characteristics, 367–69
Vocal delivery, 365–71
Vocal quality, 369
Vocalization, 365–70
  improvement of, 369–70
  mechanics of, 365–67
Vogel, R.A., 224n, 244n
Voice box, 365
Volume, 367–68
Vowels, 366–67

Wackman, D.B., 132n
Ward, J.M., 87n
Washburn, P.V., 361
Watson, K.W., 50
Weiss, W., 305
Welcoming speech, 311
What Color Is Your Parachute? (R. Bolles), 238
Wheel, 221
Where Do I Go From Here With My Life (J. Crystal and
      R. Bolles), 238
Whetmore, E.J., 386n
Whiteside, T., 392n
Widgery, R.N., 265n
Williams, C.L., 132n
Williams, M., 353n
Wilson Learning Corporation, 30
Wiseman, G., 278n
Wolfe, D.M., 301n
Words, 22
  person's response to, 33–34
Written communication, 7

Y network, 221
Yeomans, W.N., 233–41
You Are What You Wear: The Key to Business Success (W.
      Thourlby), 84